STEAL THIS CLASSROOM

Teaching and Learning Unbound

Jody Cohen and Anne Dalke

Before you start to read this book, take this moment to think about making a donation to punctum books, an independent non-profit press

@ https://punctumbooks.com/support

If you're reading the e-book, you can click on the image below to go directly to our donations site. Any amount, no matter the size, is appreciated and will help us to keep our ship of fools afloat. Contributions from dedicated readers will also help us to keep our commons open and to cultivate new work that can't find a welcoming port elsewhere. Our adventure is not possible without your support.

Viva la Open Access.

Fig. 1. Hieronymus Bosch, *Ship of Fools* (1490–1500)

STEAL THIS CLASSROOM. Copyright © 2019 by the authors and editor. This work carries a Creative Commons BY-NC-SA 4.0 International license, which means that you are free to copy and redistribute the material in any medium or format, and you may also remix, transform and build upon the material, as long as you clearly attribute the work to the authors (but not in a way that suggests the authors or punctum books endorses you and your work), you do not use this work for commercial gain in any form whatsoever, and that for any remixing and transformation, you distribute your rebuild under the same license. http://creativecommons.org/licenses/by-nc-sa/4.0/

First published in 2019 by punctum books, Earth, Milky Way.
https://punctumbooks.com

ISBN-13: 978-1-950192-37-3 (print)
ISBN-13: 978-1-950192-38-0 (ePDF)

DOI: 10.21983/P3.0261.1.00
LCCN: 2019945942
Library of Congress Cataloging Data is available from the Library of Congress

Copyediting: Molly Johnson
Interior design: Alli Crandell
Cover design: Vincent W.J. van Gerven Oei

STEAL THIS CLASSROOM

Teaching and Learning Unbound

Jody Cohen and Anne Dalke

We dedicate this work and play to one other, and to all the people in our lives who have made our connections so engaging. We write with profound acknowledgment of deep time and the greater whole, of which we are such a small part, on which we have such an impact, which we threaten daily. We write out of love, and into struggle.

CONTENTS

PROLOGUE
1 WELCOME TO THE ECOTONE

INTRODUCTION
6 WHAT TO DO WITH THIS, PEDAGOGICALLY?
…in which we advocate for a form of sustainable pedagogy that flourishes amid diversity and disequilibrium, in hopes of expanding current notions of teaching inside and outside of classrooms.

SPACES

ONE
36 BEING HERE
…in which we teach in jail, with an emerging awareness of both power relations and interactional possibilities.

TWO
78 PLAYING
…in which we leave the college classroom to explore city, countryside and what is "proper" on campus.

THREE
118 HAUNTING
…in which we reflect on how social class shapes educational opportunities and outcomes.

INTERMISSION
160 WHEREFROM, WHO TO?

TIMES

FOUR
172 SILENCING
…in which we acknowledge the ways in which conferences and classes might be less oriented to knowing, more to being with the unknown.

FIVE
206 UNBECOMING
…in which we attend to the disabling costs of achievement, and imagine alternatives to the conventional time frames of academia.

SIX
236 LEAKING
…in which we ask how to teach to, for and in varying positions of vulnerability and trauma.

INTERMISSION
272 WHY WRITE AS WE DO

RELATIONS

SEVEN
280 BEFRIENDING
…in which we consider the origins of our stories, and the ways in which critical friendships can interrupt and renew institutional life.

EIGHT
316 SLIPPING
…in which we trace a racial history of exclusion and attempted inclusion, seeking out an active politics of difference.

NINE
346 REASSEMBLING
…in which we query the notion of accessibility, re-orienting ourselves to accommodation as ever-shifting interdependency.

EPILOGUE
388 UNEXPECTED RULES

390 BIBLIOGRAPHY

ACKNOWLEDGMENTS

So many people to acknowledge and appreciate! We begin with the amazing speed, acumen, persistence, and generosity of the "super-readers" of several drafts of the whole book: many thanks to our friends and colleagues Alice Lesnick, Joel Schlosser, and Michael Tratner. Deep appreciation as well to many others who generously gave time, energy, and valuable insight into portions of this project: Sophia Abbot, Sukey Blanc, Sue Castagnetto, Elizabeth Catanese, Carol Cohen, Alison Cook-Sather, Giovanna DiChiro, Barbara Dixson, Wil Franklin, Kevin Gotkin, Kristin Lindgren, Carolyn Long, Mark Lord, Clare Mullaney, Rachel Martin, Judie McCoyd, Joshua Moses, Rebecca Reumann-Moore, David Ross, Jomaira Salas, Corey Shdaimah. And to our students, many of whom offered helpful responses to particular chapters in which their courses are featured: "InClass/Outclassed" in 2011, "Play in the City" in 2013, "Identity Matters" and "Eco-Literacy" in 2014, "Arts of Resistance" in 2015, "Changing Our Story" in 2015 and 2016.

We thank Bryn Mawr College for the opportunities we've had for continued teaching and learning, and also for two Faculty Research Awards, which supported our publication costs. We thank the College, too, for bringing us Edward Dimendberg, who guided the move of our nascent idea into a proposal, gave us a title, and helped us negotiate a contract. Compelled and intrigued by the "spontaneous acts of scholarly combustion" that are punctum books, we also thank the press; in particular, its founding director, Eileen Joy, for her quick, enthusiastic response and the crucial encouragement we needed to bring this project to fruition; and co-director Vincent W.J. van Gerven Oei, for so ably coordinating the final phase of production.

We owe tremendous thanks to Ann Dixon, whose multi-valenced, steady and invaluable support included hosting on Serendip first all our classes, then our developing manuscript, as she advised us on many matters of content and technology. Alli Crandell's tremendous creativity, unfailing patience and good humor has made working on the on-line version a constant discovery. We are glad, too, for the crucial assistance of Molly Johnson and Bryn Thompson in the final stages of copyediting and permission-gathering.

We are deeply appreciative of our husbands, Jeff Dalke and David Dan, for their steady company-keeping, listening, and insightful reading of many iterations of chapters, titles, photos. And grateful beyond measure—for responses, encouragement, and moving forth with their own lives in ways that both inspire and impel us—to our children, Jessye, Lucas, Lena, Lily, Sam and Marian, and to their families, including Naima and Julia, that next-yet generation coming after.

Gabriele Diwald, *Coldgrunge* (2012). CC-BY https://flic.kr/p/dfkuTL

PROLOGUE
WELCOME TO THE ECOTONE

It's an April afternoon, cold and rainy, two years after we start this project. One of us takes a break from writing to visit her mother, who asks, "What are you working on, exactly?"

"It's a book about teaching. Called *Steal This Classroom*."

"Seal? Why would you seal it?"

"No. *Steal*."

"Steel? Like bracing yourself?"

"No. *Steal*."

"What are you stealing it from?"

A friend answers:

> "Stealing the classroom" away from the current power-structures.... Stealing away the current capitalistic value system for an ecological based system...like Robin Hood and Little John...stealing from the rich to give to the poor.

Another friend rejects that legend, says the title doesn't really work for him:

> Your book uncovers what is hidden behind the ways classes normally interact, attends to the unexpected results of various educational activities. You're calling up all sorts of things that folks don't generally notice, revealing the underside of teaching and learning—but you're not pulling down the system. Your relation to the college is not a criminal one....

This refrain of questions, and their answers, haunt the stories we tell here, which are sometimes ambiguous, less explanations than holding places,

> where impasses can be kept and opened for examination, questions can be guarded and not forced into a premature validation of the available paradigms…the work of giving-to-read those impossible contradictions that cannot yet be spoken.
> —Barbara Johnson, *The Feminist Difference*

We share scenes—in classrooms on our campus, also in an urban high school, a public library, a playground, a prison—where what happens takes us by surprise; then dig into such moments, looking for what else might be going on: institutional pressures, socioeconomic differences, tangles with individuals and ideas, diversities not acknowledged but operating. We explore how such moments of uncertainty, often constructed as failure, might be breakthroughs that produce powerful learning for educators and students—how failure itself might not be what it seems. And while our focus returns always to pedagogy, we move back and forth between micro and macro, enacting a continual interplay across individuals, groups, and institutions: past, present, and future.

> We arrive with twenty-some of our first-year students at a small "special admit" high school in the city; in a large corner classroom, twenty-some high school students sit interspersed amid desks and chairs they've left open for us. We welcome everyone and explain our activity, the game of "Barometer," in which we will read statements aloud, asking participants to respond by locating themselves on a continuum from "agree" to "disagree." We ask for five volunteers from each school. The high schoolers put themselves forward quickly, the college students more tentatively. I read out the first statement: People need to go to college to be successful. The high school students move quickly to "agree," college students to "disagree." The division is absolute. There is an intake of breath as I ask, "Why are you standing where you are?"
>
> Another class is structured around a series of enactments, in which students find themselves "playing" characters from their

lives with whom they don't share aspects of their identities…or whose perspectives or values might disturb or even horrify them. A white student's story of her friend group spurs her group's enactment, and she takes up the role of a character mocking Asian students. Afterwards, she talks about…how she hasn't been able to shake off "speaking as." In an enactment cutting between quick sketches of a Chinese student's experiences in college and… phone calls with her mother, we witness what she doesn't share with her mom: a cacophonous cultural remix at the college, then a humiliating body search at the international airport.

On Halloween, each of the students comes to my class dressed as another. When I walk in, to peals of laughter, they ask if I can identify their costumes. I realize that they've been paying much closer attention than I have to how each of them performs and presents self. I'm thinking, what an appropriate ritual for a cluster of courses focused on "Identity Matters!"…when one of the students reports having "such a different experience of this day—one of deep discomfort and fear…seeing myself reflected by another…was really disconcerting,…classroom identity is not a whole understanding of my self, and I've spent my entire life working to keep it that way…"

This is story-telling as a form of theorizing,

> in the play with language, since dynamic rather than fixed ideas seem more to our liking.
> —Barbara Christian, "The Race for Theory"

We teach at a liberal arts college, the kind of place that has small numbers, considerable resources, and other structures that encourage close working relationships among students and their faculty, who share a commitment to teaching for critical understanding. Our experiences suggest that colleges like the one where we teach might act as a political-and-spiritual cell culture, a hive of resistance groups with the capacity to challenge the leading paradigms in American education. Although this may not be the dominant ethos on campus (and our college certainly isn't marketed this way), we construct an alternative tale, exploring a pedagogical orientation that is ecological in the largest sense, engaging teachers and students in re-thinking classroom practices, and our larger lives, as complex, enmeshed, volatile, ever-expanding eco-systems.

We also call on theories to tell stories; not solving the contradictions but abstracting from the immediate, allowing us to see differently what is happening. We weave through our own voices—stories, images, and propositions—those of students and colleagues with whom we have taught and learned. We offer a dialogue, working across verbal and visual forms, telling some hard stories, inviting others in response, demonstrating the complex playfulness of collaborative and transdisciplinary forms of teaching and learning, incorporating concrete suggestions about how academic and other structures might work to open this up. Our intent is porous and interactive, inviting reader-participants into pedagogical spaces where they might attend to the shifting borderlands between what we're more familiar with and what feels edgy, new—with the goal of transfiguring what spaces of teaching and learning are and can be-and-do.

We think that, if the liberal arts behaved more like ecology, and less like our human endeavors to control the environment, small U.S. colleges could function more as border ecologies, where we refuse to inherit both the ruins of classical education, and the industrial rigidity of No Child Left Behind and Race to the Top. Asking what might be possible in the intensity and instability of borderlands, we track the chaotic and unpredictable, both unconscious and environmental, as deeply educative, creative, stretching our zone of the possible. These are ecotones, transitional spaces that are testing grounds, places of danger and opportunity. We trace new shapes our teaching and learning take, as liminal spaces and excursions, arising in the midst of separations between school and not-school, self and other, inside and out. Traversing the edges of promise, desire, nervousness, and threat, surprising conjoinings that are neither this nor that, contained yet uncontainable, inviting always the unexpected.

Seeing where else this kind of work-and-play might be happening, how broadly we can construe "classrooms" as testing grounds, paradoxically boxed-in spaces that cannot keep their promise to enclose, categorize, or name. And thus can become productive of conditions ripe for breaking through, where real and abstract reverse, melt, the distinction between them disappearing:

> The trouble is that when you take an evolutionary view of Earth, an astonishing reversal takes place. Suddenly, things that you think of as real—this cat over here, my cat, whose fur I can stroke—become the abstraction, an approximation of flowing, metamorphic processes, processes that are in some sense far more real than the entity I am stroking…our immediate experience is a workable approximation that makes sense only on a very limited island of meaningfulness.…What disappears is the commonsensical idea that what appears to be immediate is also real.…I propose that in order to accommodate…all that Darwinism entails…ecological criticism…must embrace nonessentialism…a platform for recognizing each life-form as…a temporary manifestation of an indivisible whole.
> —Timothy Morton, "The Mesh"

This, then, is what follows. All manifestations are temporary.

INTRODUCTION
WHAT TO DO WITH THIS, PEDAGOGICALLY?

Piercing the Skin of the Classroom

We write collaboratively as two experienced teachers. Drawing on stories from our own classrooms, advocating for a form of pedagogy that flourishes amid diversity and disequilibrium, we bring together analytical frameworks from Environmental Studies with those that attend to the irreducibility and unknowability of the unconscious. The alteration in educational practice that we describe recognizes and responds to the uncontrollable, yet resource-rich, complexities of classroom life, particularly for teaching and learning as social and environmental justice work.

Our commitments to radical teaching rely on long-standing pedagogical traditions with a strong concern for social justice; they also require a readiness to let go of agendas, to pierce the skin of the classroom, recognizing (for instance) the gaps between subjects and objects, goals and outcomes. (That such a prospect can be scarily unsettling may account, in part, for why so much schooling is organized to assess what is already known, rather than to explore what has not yet been recognized.) In this companion website and book, we tell stories of learning in multiple contexts, hoping to constitute an on- and off-line community that will expand current notions of teaching inside and outside of classrooms.

We philosophize and enact pedagogies that call forth, explore, and propagate those uncertain moments when teachers and students lose hold of what they think they know. Looking for a way to refresh and renew education, at a time when it is derided and defunded, we begin with "the ecological thought" of profound connectedness, and move across the permeable membrane of self and environment, organism and medium, seeking the sorts of spaces many of us both resist and long to explore, where our histories, nightmares, and desires "blow our covers" as rational subjects. We identify these spaces as ecological events, interconnected and unbounded, ultimately unpredictable and unknowable. Drawing on the language of John Dewey and Walker Percy, we name these as sites of "the live creature," where we find what we have not sought.[1]

1. John Dewey, "The Live Creature," in *Art as Experience* (1934; reprint, New York: Perigee, 1980), 3–34; Walker Percy, "The Loss of the Creature," in *The Message in the Bottle: How Queer Man Is, How Queer Language Is, and What One Has to Do with the Other* (New York: Farrar, Straus and Giroux, 1975), 46–63.

> Two students in a first-semester writing seminar elect to work together to investigate the college as a "contact zone" where Muslims and non-Muslims interact. When one wants to explore Muslim students' views on sexuality, the other withdraws from their collaborative project.
>
> In the midst of a fast-moving discussion of identities and schooling, a white student talks about people who lack resources in their neighborhoods and school systems as "they" and "them." That quick, tight feeling hits the stomach; don't heed it, succumb to the flow of conversation, until after class when a Black student approaches: "This makes me so tired," she says.
>
> Towards the end of a semester exploring the rich intersections of identity and environment, we are prodded by a strange short story, in which plants are sentient, into painful recognition of a dual (dueling?) set of anxieties: we want not to be separated from the world; we also very much want boundaries to protect ourselves from it. "How can we simultaneously be part of such a long history, have such an important influence," a student asks, "and yet be so late in realizing what has happened and so utterly impotent in our attempts to fix it?"

It is important for teachers to acknowledge the huge range of what's happening in their classes, some of which we might become aware of, some not: a spectrum that includes not just the audible and visible (how students speak, or remain silent, how they gesture with voice and body), but also all the undergrowth, the desires, fears, and "ghosts" that accompany the classroom "presence" of each one of us. Such acknowledging prompts questions, sometimes requires interventions: to speak to this student after class; to offer another kind of feedback on that student's writing; to offer in-class writing time, an activity structured in pairs, a conversation burrowing into some aspect of text designed to surface some of what lies beneath, or, alternatively, to allow it, for now, to recede.

We may experience such moments in the classroom as a stomach ache, a twinge, an alert, signaling the necessity to slow down and listen to painful dissonances. Each of these stories—and many others we have to tell—uncovers a self that does not at first recognize itself, accessing the unconscious wherefrom we often surprise ourselves, a process within the medium of the larger world that is unresponsive to methods of "command and control,"[2] overflowing instead with what we cannot predict.

Eve Sedgwick opens her wonderful essay on "Pedagogy of Buddhism" with an image of these sorts of movements, an example of "near-miss pedagogy" in which the teacher's intention fails in reaching the learner: "Cats may be assuming the role of educator when they bring prey indoors to their human owner...perhaps cats who release living prey in our houses are trying to give us some practice, to hone our hunting skills."[3] Having attended for years to such "near-misses," we foreground these slippages in the dialogue of teaching and learning, as instances in which teachers and learners, in our entanglement with each other and with the emergent complexity of our world, are more, less, or *other* than we think we are.

Rejecting the lure of a unified, closed, and stabilized system, we evoke "ecologies" on both the smallest scale (we teach environmental studies), and the largest, following Timothy Morton's description of ecological thought as "picaresque—wandering from place to place, open to random encounters"; "surrounded by an otherness, something that is not the self, in an infinite web of mutual interdependence where there is no boundary or center."[4]

This "outside" space of uncertainty, incompleteness, and conditionality is also located inside each of us. Where the intermeshing of everything stretches deep into the varieties of the human

2. C.S. Holling and Gary Meffe, "Command and Control and the Resource Management," *Conservation Biology* 10, no. 2 (April 1996): 328–37.

3. Eve Sedgwick, "Pedagogy of Buddhism," in *Touching Feeling: Affect, Pedagogy, Performativity* (Durham: Duke University Press, 2003), 153–54.

4. Timothy Morton, *The Ecological Thought* (Cambridge: Harvard University Press, 2010), 48.

unconscious, we follow Elizabeth Ellsworth in evoking a palpable sense of this realm of human experience as diverse, unruly, and fertile.[5] We conceptualize the unconscious as broad, almost metaphorical, and use it to reference all that lies beneath, beyond, and peripheral to our cognizant awareness; all that we hope and fear, know and don't, as individuals who are always also part of personal and cultural histories, presents, vicissitudes.

The question, to which we invariably return, is what to do with this, pedagogically. Educational texts often draw on a literature of cognition to illuminate the nature of learning. We call on such resources, along with much of the current work in Environmental Studies and psychoanalytic feminism, but side-step the specific targeting of each of these genres to attend carefully to the more ambiguous spaces of learning and teaching. We acknowledge the authority we carry as teachers: selecting texts and assignments, designing experiences inside the classroom and out, assessing our students. But we also look to re-direct that authority: pedagogy as we understand and practice it is less about "leading the student out" (as in the conventional meaning of the word) than about complex people being in relation in a shared space. We work the paradox, acknowledging both that we occupy an authoritative position *and* that we cannot forecast or control what happens in the richly complex and multifarious exchange that is teaching and learning. In the midst of this, we look to distribute authority more widely: to make the terms of such decision-making part of ongoing meta-conversations, both in our classes and in this book.

We have organized this project so that form and content inform and interrogate one another. We conceptualize a shifting relationship of subject and object, foreground and background, organism and environment, as cued visually by the "all over" work of Jackson Pollack, verbally by Paula Gunn Allen's refusal of the figure-ground distinction.[6] "Self" and "environment," "classroom" and "world," "teacher" and "student" are all transactional, malleable categories, imbricated in one another. Conceptualizing the boundaries of the

---

5. Elizabeth Ellsworth, *Teaching Positions: Difference, Pedagogy, and the Power of Address* (New York: Teachers College Press, 1997).

6. Paula Gunn Allen, "Kochinnenako in Academe: Three Approaches to Interpreting a Keres Indian Tale," in *The Sacred Hoop: Recovering the Feminine in American Indian Traditions* (Boston: Beacon Press, 1986), 222–44.

classroom as permeable, we look to bring the complexity and unknowability of selves, and the complexity and unpredictability of the medium in which they live and learn, into the classroom and out again.

We present spaces, times, and relations as "temporary manifestations,"[7] categories through which we engage in and with the world, three areas where we locate elements often covered over by the effort to control teaching, learning, living. "Spaces" signify classrooms and other learning places as arbitrarily bounded containers that overflow, short-circuit, re-ignite: buildings and landscapes, institutions and ideologies, wildscapes and cities. "Times" evoke themes of temporal transit and passage, problematizing the conventions of "class time" as measured and unquantifiable, conjuring instead the multi-layered histories of individuals and institutions: the traces of the past, of experiences, thoughts, feelings that find their way often unacknowledged into the learning space. "Relations" conjure embodied forms of identity, including gender, race, and ability, colliding with each other and other matter in emergent, unpredictable, yet patterned ways that re-charge learning. As counterpoints to the linearity of language, we include photographs we have taken, punctuating and eliding the written narratives—which are interrupted, too, by dreams, stories, and the voices of others than ourselves.

The web site is interactive, offering points of entry for readers to contribute to the project. Current work that attends to the ecology of the event, such as Patti Lather's reach toward a social science that features a politics of complexity,[8] models the way in which we envision our readers as co-creators who both extend and challenge our project. Students who have engaged with us in the pedagogical work we explore here, along with colleagues with whom we have worked in transdisciplinary settings, already speak in these pages. Inspired by the interviews at Figure/Ground Communication,[9] we also hope for links to locations distinct from our own: those occupied by high schoolers, incarcerated students, urban gardeners, and others with differently hopeful stories to tell about teaching and learning.

7. Timothy Morton, "The Mesh," in *Environmental Criticism for the Twenty-First Century*, ed. Stephanie LeMenager, Teresa Shewry, and Ken Hiltner (New York: Routledge, 2011), 29.

8. Patti Lather, *Getting Smart: Feminist Research and Pedagogy With/In the Postmodern* (New York: Routledge, 1991).

9. Laureano Ralon, *Figure/Ground: An Open-Source, Para-Academic, Inter-disciplinary Collaboration*.

Reconceiving Sustainability

This project has its origins in a very real question, which we have been feeling in our guts for the past few years: whether, at this stage in our lives, our own teaching practices are sustainable ones. In early summer 2011—as we each enter our fourth decade of teaching, and seventh decade of living—we begin co-designing a new freshman writing seminar on the complex relationship between social class, being "in class," and being "outclassed."[10] We make a commitment to one another to restrain ourselves, to find space for rest and renewal, to help each other manage what we see as the coming overload. But it is clear, long before the fall semester begins, that we are *terrible* at setting limits as individuals, and even worse at doing so for one another. In fact, working together seems to make things much worse.

We have chosen for our course a rich, complex topic, with tendrils that reach both deep, into the life of the campus community, and wide, 'round about the world. We bring to our collaborative work on this subject decades of social justice activism, as well as our own fertile academic minds, filled with years of pedagogical experiments that have worked—not to mention lots of new ideas we want to try out for the first time. Talking together of course only stirs that pool, generating more thoughts and possible actions for the class. We also have the help of, and make the commitment to mentor, two seniors at the college who are working as our student partners in a collaborative, reciprocal process sponsored by the college's Teaching and Learning Initiative.[11] Their thoughts further complexify our own. Then we are each assigned fourteen first-semester students, which means adding twenty-eight additional hearts and minds to the mix. We agree, as well, to work in partnership with a high school classroom in the city, thereby extending even further the range of the territory, physical and metaphysical, through which we are to travel.

The unpredictable feeds fear. Of course.

---

10. "In Class/OutClassed: On the Uses of a Liberal Education," Emily Balch Seminar, Bryn Mawr College (Fall 2011).

11. Alison Cook-Sather, Catherine Bovill and Peter Felten, *Engaging Students as Partners in Learning and Teaching: A Guide for Faculty* (San Francisco: Jossey-Bass, 2014), 6–7.

"When we try to pick out anything by itself," said John Muir, "we find it hitched to everything else in the universe."

—*Coming into Contact: Explorations in Ecocritical Theory and Practice*

…opening, always, to infinite possibility is the foundation of stable practice.

—Shunryo Suzuki, in Mary Rose O'Reilley, *The Garden at Night: Burnout and Breakdown in the Teaching Life*

And multiplying the parts multiplies the unpredictability.

> I love to teach with someone else. It augments the process of diffusion, the spreading out not just of authority and power but of focus that makes the classroom a more equitable and more permeable space.
>
> —Jane Tompkins, *A Life in School*

More equitable. More permeable. Also more uncontrollable.

In teaching that class, and reflecting afterwards on what happened in it, we uncover a paradox.

We begin by acknowledging the limits—of time, of human energy, of space, money and new ideas: the very real material-and-mental constraints which often make it seem that we are working within a system that is running down. Our initial plan, in sketching out a design for "sustainable teaching," is to "take" more time, and "create" more space: we will search for naps, practice meditation, swim, do yoga, remind one another to slow down, breathe deeply....

In the process of teaching our course, however, presenting several conference workshops about it, writing several essays, then designing and creating this website and book, we find a complement to our (understandable!) desire to set limits, in the counterintuitive realization that the world in which we operate as teachers and as human beings is an infinitely capacious one. We have the experience of relying on that which we do not know, on the unending supply of the surprising,[12] which lies hidden in the complexities of our students' unconscious, and in our own. Limitlessness, we come to understand, is a richer way to think about sustainable pedagogy than is seeking new and better boundaries.

JODY: In the early 1990s I spend a year as a researcher in the classroom of my colleague and friend, Marsha Pincus, an excellent teacher in an urban school. One form our work together takes, partly

---

12. Anne Dalke and Alice Lesnick, "Teaching Intersection, Not Assessment: Celebrating the Surprise of Gift Giving and Gift Getting in the Cultural Common," *Journal of Curriculum and Pedagogy* 8 (2011): 75–96.

because our days in the same space are so full of other demands, is an exchange of letters. In one of these, I describe a dream:

> I am in a strange land, perhaps foreign, and you are there as a kind of presence, maybe a guide, someone who lives there. Two incidents/images stand out....
>
> We are standing together in a large institution not unlike [the high school where you teach]. You are white, all the teenagers there are Black, but then too you have a Black daughter. Many of the kids have been rounded up and penned in a huge enclosure, and you ask me to go check on your daughter, who is there. I want to do as you ask, and I go to the top floor. A white woman, a substitute, agrees without emotion to open the entryway to me, but it is too small, I can't go through, I can only look down on a huge auditorium filled with Black teens. There are thousands of them…calmly milling around, and in a while a bell rings and they are no longer detained. I haven't been able to find your daughter.
>
> When I go outside I am again somehow guided by you, although you are not there. I come to a wide river crossed at the top by another river, so that the two form a large "T." The water is crystal clear, and in the distance there are waterfalls. Closer, people with their shirts off are wading. Through this remarkably clear water I see on the bottom a rich tile mosaic of many shades of blue, green, aqua. The sun is bright and this mosaic is dazzling. I realize that I am allowed or invited to enter the water, to wade, and to study (and here this word has an almost spiritual significance) the mosaic.[13]

I'm drawn into this mosaic of human beings immersed bodily in an ineffable geometry of color and form: bodies, design, and environment mingle and meld, evoking something of the rich possibilities and vulnerabilities of learning and teaching.

ANNE AND JODY: When Environmental Studies first begins to emerge as a field of study, it positions itself primarily as a critique of the cornucopia of conventional thinking, in which scarcity is

13. Jody Cohen, "Restructuring Instruction in an Urban High School: An Inquiry into Texts, Identities, and Power," Unpublished dissertation, University of Pennsylvania, 1993.

thought of as an economic phenomenon, remediable by entrepreneurs. Environmental scholars and activists replace linear thinking about "disposal" with circular conceptions of recycling resource use; "exploration" and "expansion" are superseded by goals thought to be both more "stable" and "sustainable."[14] We are all encouraged, thereby, to recognize the limits of our various practices.

With the more recent emergence of post equilibrium ecology, which highlights the flux of ecosystems—never in balance, always in recalibration—the ecological vision has become a much more unstable one. It is in that world that we position ourselves, as advocates of a paradox that joins the "cornucopia of diversity" that is the natural world[15] to an awareness of the unboundedness of everything that binds us together. We are all interconnected, and those interconnections are inexhaustible.

We think that we can actually learn to rely on the capaciousness and strangeness of the universe—which emphatically includes the unpredictability of our own and our students' minds. We evoke such strangeness in the dreams that emerge in this chapter. As ecocritic Patrick Murphy observes,

> We are continuing to live in a world filled with many strange and unforeseeable things, and an increasing number of them are of our own creation...they contain the nature from which we and they arose. While we cannot exactly trust the wild variability...to provide predetermined answers for every unanticipated occasion....we can trust that...spontaneity and unpredictability...will open numerous avenues down which to walk into the future.[16]

This paradox—that we teach, learn, and live in an interrelated world, one that is both limited and unbounded—has emerged for us, over the course of thinking through this project, as our central pedagogical hinge. We follow here the thinking of a range of ecological critics, as well as that of educational theorist Elizabeth Ellsworth, whose response to the unpredictable "uptake" of the teaching

14. Greg Garrard, ed., *Teaching Ecocriticism and Green Cultural Studies* (New York: Palgrave Macmillan, 2012); Eugene Odum and Gary Barrett, *Fundamentals of Ecology*, 5th edn. (Belmont, CA: Brooks and Cole, 2004).

15. Joan Roughgarden, *Evolution's Rainbow: Diversity, Gender, and Sexuality in Nature and People* (Berkeley: University of California Press, 2004).

16. Patrick Murphy, *Ecocritical Explorations in Literary and Cultural Studies: Fences, Boundaries and Fields* (Lanham, MD: Lexington Books, 2009), 117.

position is not to try and control students' responses, but rather to celebrate, activate and explore the multiple subject positions that are called into play in pedagogical exchange. We join Ellsworth in her understanding of the unconscious as offering a conditional space in the classroom that can become palpable in its diversity, unruliness, and fertility; where the "unspeakable" can enter in the guise of hunger, desire, fear, "ignore-ance."[17]

The unconscious, in our own understanding, encompasses a diversionary "playground,"[18] including exhibits of the unimaginable and the bizarre. For us, this is a broad, almost metaphorical term, which we use to reference all that lies beneath, beyond, and peripheral to our cognizant awareness; all that we as human beings are and bring; all that we hope, fear, know, and desire, as individuals who are always also part of personal and cultural presents and histories. We re-orient ourselves from the field of performance, where Ellsworth locates herself, to that of the ecological imagination, the linked-to-it-ness of everything, which stretches deep into the varieties of the human unconscious.

ANNE: Friends Association of Higher Education, a group of Quaker college educators, has long served as a deep source of nurture for me; I have a number of good friends whose company I eagerly seek out at the yearly conferences hosted by the organization. As I began planning to teach my first Environmental Studies course, I am heartened to learn that the topic of the 2012 conference is "Building Sustainable Academic Communities," and I invite Jody, my good friend and colleague in the Bryn Mawr College Education Program, to lead a session with me about "Crafting Sustainable Teaching Practices." Early in the morning before we are scheduled to fly to Ohio for the conference, I have a powerful dream, one that figures much of both the hope and fear that ecological activism evokes for me.

17. Ellsworth, *Teaching Positions*, 95, 38.

18. Anne Dalke and Paul Grobstein, "Story-telling In (At Least) Three Dimensions: An Exploration of Teaching Reading, Writing, and Beyond," *Journal of Teaching Writing* 23, no. 1 (2007): 91–114.

> I find myself in a camp-like setting with many friends, coming to the end of a joyful shared time. We all link arms, and are gaily marching together, when a loud voice announces that the end of the world is coming. We look up to see huge, rolling ocean waves approaching us.
>
> The sight is awesome, and exhilarating. I begin to sing, "Roll on, thou great blue ocean, roll!" as the group moves forward, leaping together into the water. Looking up, we see that the waves are now topped by huge ocean liners, and I begin to worry that they will slam into us; I brace myself for the assault. As I dive underwater, I realize that I cannot breathe, that this dying will not be glorious, but a gasping struggle for breath.... I wake, relieved (as one always is in such situations) that the dream isn't "real," that I do not have to struggle, that I am not dying. And yet (as is often also the case) the after-effects of the dream linger through the day, casting an emotional shadow that makes me uneasy about boarding the plane.

Years later, this dream, and the contrary emotions it evokes, are still very present to me: compounding an astounding sense of the power of the world in which I live, with an overwhelming fear that I and my companions cannot re-direct these dynamics and will be destroyed by them. Attending to the environment exhilarates and terrifies me in equal measure; I fear that it may also terrify my students.

ANNE AND JODY: The next morning, we co-lead the session we have planned, about the importance of attending to the unconscious in the classroom.[19] A keynote in our discussion is Elizabeth Ellsworth's claim that the best teaching practices are not just "unrepeatable," but "impossible"—because both we and our students bring to our classroom encounters all of our unconscious intentions, hopes, desires, fears. The classroom is full of these "Other" presences, which cannot easily—not ever, really, in Ellsworth's formulation—be knit into productive dialogue.[20]

That same afternoon, we hear Stephen Potthoff, who teaches Religious Studies at Wilmington College, describe the work he does

19. Anne Dalke and Jody Cohen, "Crafting Sustainable Teaching Practices," workshop presented at the annual conference of Friends Association of Higher Education, Wilmington, OH, June 22, 2012.

20. Ellsworth, *Teaching Positions*, 17, 18, 64.

as the "dream keeper" for a group of tropical ecology students in Costa Rica. Stephen invites his fellow travelers to investigate how their dreams might mediate their encounters with the beauty, complexity, and mystery of exotic tropical ecosystems. What shape do the students' journeys assume, on the inner stage of their dreams? What effect does the outer world have on their inner life?

Inspired by Stephen's claim that dream experience mediates a process for confronting and working through the natural fears of going to a new environment, we begin to explore together the possibility of reconceptualizing our shared work in terms of dreams and other clues to the usually unacknowledged presence of the unconscious in the classroom.

Thinking ecologically, we acknowledge that everything we do is hitched to everything else; there is no escaping the larger world in which we operate. Timothy Morton makes this graphic: "something leaks from the dump back into the town, because boundaries are never rigid and thin. Inside the thinking process, inside the meaning process, are the traces of exteriority that these processes struggle to exclude…'There is no outside'…there is no 'away.'"[21]

That there is no "outside," no "away"—that the "outside" is always "inside," and vice-versa—also means that we never lack the resources we need to keep the engine going. The image that Merton uses is that of the garbage dump; another that we find useful is that of Maxwell's demon,[22] canonical, if challenged, in emergence studies as the model for a perpetual motion machine. Opening the door, allowing slower molecules to cross into the second chamber, the demon enables the heat of the system to equilibrate. So too do we, as teachers, guide and nudge, listen and alter the shape of the conversational ebb and flow.

Although the system Maxwell imagines is a closed one, what most interests us is the structure of the open classroom, always re-generated, periodically and temporarily pushed over into a chaotic state by the unruly unconscious of those interacting within it. Sustainability,

21. Timothy Morton, "Practising Deconstruction in the Age of Ecological Emergency," in *Teaching Ecocriticism and Green Cultural Studies*, 159.

22. James Clerk Maxwell, *Theory of Heat* (1871; reprint, New York: Dover, 2001).

as we now understand the term, involves repeated acts of energy exchange that are non-depleting, life-giving, capable even of reversing entropy by drawing on, and thereby paradoxically renewing, the resources from which they arise. As David Orr has observed,

> all education is already environmental.... The point of ecocritical pedagogy is to make its existing environmentality explicit and, above all, sustainable.
> —*Teaching Ecocriticism and Green Cultural Studies*

We see Orr and here raise him one, with the claim that "making environmentality explicit" involves not only making the content of our courses more ecological, but also making our pedagogical practices expressive of ecological thinking. This can happen at the level of language: imagine here the "surplus of cognitive linkage" revealed when a literary critic analyzes the sort of wordplay that "exposes buried links and structures."[23] It can happen in social science research: consider Bruno Latour's explanation that every thing is "also an assembly," every "indisputable fact...the result of a meticulous discussion at the very heart of the collective," dragging "behind it a long train of unexpected consequences that come to haunt the collective by obliging it to reshape itself."[24] And it most assuredly happens in the world of quantum physics, as Karen Barad makes clear: "To be entangled is...to lack an independent, self-contained existence. Existence is not an individual affair...individuals emerge through and as part of their entangled intra-relating."[25] As we hope to demonstrate here, deep ecology is also at work in every classroom exchange. The conceptual intersection among all these nodes is an acknowledgement of the interrelatedness of the whole system, from which no part is extractable, and which thereby perpetually renews itself.

And so we step into the realm of the complex, playful, wild, *irreducible* nature of our natures, both interior and exterior; call on literatures that explore the role of the unconscious in teaching and

---

23. Mary Thomas Crane, *Shakespeare's Brain: Reading with Cognitive Theory* (Princeton: Princeton University Press, 2000), 33.

24. Bruno Latour, *Politics of Nature: How to Bring the Sciences into Democracy*, trans. Catherine Porter (Cambridge: Harvard University Press, 2004), 193.

25. Karen Barad, *Meeting the Universe Halfway: Quantum Physics and the Entanglement of Matter and Meaning* (Durham: Duke University Press, 2007), ix.

learning, as well as on the emerging field of eco-criticism; and look to our own classroom experiences as spaces for opening up the implications of ecological thinking for the project of teaching and learning. We evoke a resilient ecosystem, where the playful and the fearful together fertilize unexpected, ungainly, and eloquent responses.

> …the universe in its emergence is neither determined nor random, but…an intuitive, non-rational process… If our daytime experience is needed for awakening to the phenomenal world, our nighttime experience is needed for communion with those numinous powers from which the daylight forms themselves come into being.
> —Thomas Berry, "The Dream of the Earth"

> …the unconscious, the most subversive element in psychic life, seems to be catching up with us.
> —Jane Gallop and Carolyn Burke, "Psychoanalysis and Feminism in France"

Teaching to the Unconscious

The presumed linkage between time spent and measurable outcomes, which guides so much schooling assessment and evaluation,[26] rests on the singular assumption that teaching is directly "taken up" as learning. But if teaching is a "perfect fit" with learning, why are schools filled with issues of discipline, lack of motivation, and failure?[27] Why is there always so much going on "outside the lines"?

It is our argument that the heavy drivers of time, measurement, and a narrowly productive status quo, which define so much of U.S. schooling today, not only fail to match the complex world in which we learn and live, but also sacrifice the diversity necessary for creative responses to the inevitability of change. We are inviting here

---

26. Raymond Callahan, *Education and the Cult of Efficiency: A Study of the Social Forces that have Shaped the Administration of the Public Schools* (Chicago: The University of Chicago Press, 1962); Jeannie Oakes, et al., "Schooling: Wrestling with History and Tradition," in *Teaching to Change the World*, 2nd Edition (Columbus, OH: McGraw-Hill Higher Education, 2006), 2–39; Diane Ravitch, *The Death and Life of the Great American School System: How Testing and Choice are Undermining Education* (New York: Basic Books, 2010).

27. Ellsworth, *Teaching Positions*, 44.

a look "outside," to the fertile, unpredictable, immeasurable, and even unruly dimensions of human experience, for an enlarged site of teaching and learning in, for, and about change. We explore the notion that what's outside the lines constitutes a rich soil, fertile with the shit, so to speak, of our unconscious as well as our conscious lives. What lies "outside" is available for teaching and learning of another, richer ilk, akin to the nested, overlapping, and often unpredictable ecosystems of the natural world.

As Anne's dream, with its wild swings between exaltation and terror, reminds us, "the 'between' of perception and conscious is there—even if we can't see or control it."[28] This "between" might be conceived as the negative space in a picture of teaching and learning, the space that is not pointed to, for example, by looking at student products or outcomes; it is a space we find highly enticing. While

> the unruly and unresolved dynamics of self and society that reign in that space between perception and cognition cannot be directly observed or regulated, those dynamics can be accessed indirectly. They can be engaged with and responded to indirectly, metaphorically, through literary allusion, through the difference between address and response…through attention to the absences which structure what is present, through attention to that which does not fit.[29]

As Gallup and Burke observe, the unconscious is always at our heels whether or not we are aware of it, "catching up with us" in the classroom as elsewhere, threatening the stability of pedagogy as definable intent that does—or in fact could with any reliability—result in predictable, measurable learning.[30] This is made visceral in the Noblet Marseilles version of the Tarot deck:

> The card representing The Fool pictures a figure striding to the right while beneath and slightly behind him to the left an unidentifiable creature extends its claws toward his bared genitals. The figure is unaware of this creature, and his stance is poised, open, and in motion, precariously available as he sets out to learn the world. The fool, standing for the unconscious, might be de-

28. Elizabeth Ellsworth, *Places of Learning: Media, Architecture, Pedagogy* (New York: Routledge Taylor and Francis, 2005), 50.

29. Ellsworth, *Teaching Positions*, 51.

30. Eric Toshalis, "The Identity-Perception Gap: Teachers Confronting the Difference Between Who They (Think They) Are and How They Are Perceived by Students," in *Culture, Curriculum, and Identity in Education*, ed. H. Richard Milner (New York: Macmillan, 2010), 15–36.

"Tarots Marseille de Jean Noblet," 1650, refreshed by Jean-Claude Flornoy, 2001. By permission of Letarot editions and the J-C Flornoy estate.

scribed as an early form of the perpetual motion machine: he can turn up anywhere, and always brings element of surprise. This seventeenth-century representation anticipates our contemporary understanding of the complex relationship between human beings and the world, between "inside" and "outside" as a crux of learning.[31]

31. Ellsworth, *Teaching Positions*, 48.

Other educators have looked to the unconscious for clues to larger, deeper ways of understanding human drives, propensities, resistances, and capacities as learners. Confronting the challenges of addressing their own and their students' deep assumptions about human difference, researchers have looked to psychodynamic theory to explore what lies beneath people's conscious beliefs about "self" and "other." Grasping these elements of the unconscious has helped educators address "the contradictory nature of stereotypes" in ourselves and our students.[32] Ann Berlak, for instance, offers us ways to teach about and to students' adaptive unconscious, by generating role-plays that call up old scripts with new responses, in order to inscribe alternative patterns.[33] In these frameworks the unconscious is a somewhat mappable terrain; by inferring something of these aspects of ourselves and others, we can teach "to" the unconscious and in this sense provoke different kinds of learning.

32. Rachel Martin, *Listening Up: Reinventing Ourselves as Teachers and Students* (Portsmouth, NH: Heinemann Boynton/Cook, 2001), 62.

33. Ann Berlak, "Challenging the Hegemony of Whiteness by Addressing the Adaptive Unconscious," in *Undoing Whiteness in the Classroom* (New York: Peter Lang, 2008), 47–66.

Here we attend to those aspects of the unconscious that remain more elusive and wild, even uncontrollable, the playful or disturbing dimensions of ourselves that cannot be directly harnessed in teaching. For Ellsworth, the "self" capable of the kind of rational performance most often sought in classrooms is itself illusory: "The fact of the unconscious then, 'explodes the very idea of a complete or achieved identity'—with oneself through consciousness, or with others through understanding." Using the film studies notion of "mode of address" to talk about who the teacher and the curriculum "think students are," Ellsworth describes the "eruptive, unruly space between a curriculum's address and a student's response [as] populated by the difference between conscious and unconscious knowledge, conscious and unconscious desires." Rather than suggesting ways to bridge this gap, Ellsworth argues that it is to be preserved as the space of agency and of learning; she claims that it is actually this "resistance to the banalities of normalization that makes agency possible." If such a thing as a "perfect fit" were possible, it would in fact guarantee that no learning would happen here.[34]

34. Ellsworth, *Teaching Positions*, 41, 43–44.

Here's another story, where hopefulness and the fear of crisis intersect uncertainly. In May 2013, Bryn Mawr, Haverford, and Swarthmore host a two-day workshop for faculty members teaching in the Tri-College Environmental Studies Program. The first day is full of doom-and-gloom, and we are feeling very discouraged about this new venture of ours. We find ourselves wondering how, amid so many pressing concerns, we will possibly be able to motivate our students. How can we teach ecologically, without leading us all into despair?

But then Mark Wallace, a Religion professor at Swarthmore, opens the second day of presentations with what he identifies as the "delicate, special, strange flute-like sound" of a wood thrush:

> I wake up every morning to this spectacular sound, although I haven't ever seen one. Its population has been cut in half since the 1960s; and it doesn't come to feeders; it lives off of grubs and insects on the ground.... This is my approach to Environmental Studies. I know, from teaching religion, that stories of destruction don't motivate students. I try instead to do advocacy scholarship: not just sharing data, facts, and information, but inculcating a deep sense of spiritual kinship, love, and passion for the natural world, a family connection that will make them care about preserving it. We won't try to save the planet if we don't fall back in love with it.[35]

35. Mark Wallace, "The Introductory Environmental Studies Course," panel discussion at the Tri-College Environmental Studies Workshop, Swarthmore College, May 16, 2012.

At the end of Mark's presentation, however, a colleague confesses that, as a late riser, "those birds in the morning bother me tremendously!" He elaborates on his various stratagems: purchasing an air gun to drive them off, and—when this does not work—switching his bedroom to distance himself from the morning song that disturbs his sleep.… And so, he asks, how do we judge a song such as this one? Do we assess it as beauty? Or as a crisis, needing intervention? One man's inspiration, it turns out, is another's murderous rage. How to accommodate such diversity? How to teach ecologically?

The classroom is almost by definition contained by four walls, and when we think of going "outside" it, we're usually talking about going to some other place, on a field trip (as we describe repeatedly in Chapter Two of this project).[36] We are suggesting, however, that recognizing the aversions, dreams, fears, and longings located beneath and beyond the conscious, cognitive work we do in the classroom, as well as in faculty workshops, gives us access to yet another "outside," poses another way of creating unexpected intersections among the individual, the classroom, and what lies beyond: "a pivot point between our inner and outer worlds."[37] This "outside," a space of uncertainty, incompletion, conditionality, and learning, is in fact a quality of experience: it is an outside that is paradoxically located inside each of us.

We bring passionate curiosity to the question of how best to acknowledge those "unruly and unresolved dynamics of self and society,"[38] because we see them as clues to classroom life as part of a larger ecosystem. We know the exhaustion—also the fear, frustration, anger, disaffection, sense of futility—that can arise, both in our own work and that of our students, when we teach and learn without clear limits. On the other hand, we also recognize the exhaustion of the drive toward the "perfect fit," the curriculum and pedagogy that engender full (and presumably measurable) understanding. This kind of education, in which the classroom acts as bounded container, leads to unsustainable teaching practices, marked generally

36. See Chapter Two, "Playing."

37. Ellsworth, *Places of Learning*, 47.

38. Ellsworth, *Teaching Positions*, 51.

as "teacher burnout"—or as boredom. Recognizing such exhaustion as part of the system, a signal to its shifting nature, leads us to turn, now, to locate the resource of the unbounded unconscious in the context of ecological thinking.

Theorizing Ecology

For a number of years, progressive educators such as Victor Nolet, Stephen Sterling, and David Orr have been calling for "a fundamental change in educational culture," "a new paradigm for the preparation of teachers"[39] that is not just "*about* sustainability" or "*for* particular sustainable development outcomes," but rather re-conceptualizes education *as* teaching sustainability: "nurturing critical, systemic and reflective thinking; creativity; self organization; and adaptive management."[40] This powerful agenda for educational change, incorporating sustainability not just in terms of content, but also context and process, aims to prepare us all "for lives and livelihoods suited to a planet with a biosphere that operates by the laws of ecology and thermodynamics."[41]

We here take the ideas of these and other environmental critics as catalysts for looking closely at what "thinking ecologically" might mean for our pedagogical practice. For both of us, teaching practice has always been centrally about social justice; race, class, and gender have been key markers describing the ground we traverse repeatedly with our students. More recently immersed in Environmental Studies, we have come with surprised awareness to understand ecology as a formative way of thinking-and-doing justice in school. The human categories that have so long marked our way are becoming differently inflected, as our awareness of the eco-system expands: the interior world of the human psyche, the exterior world of identities and relationships, the world of what is not-human are intersecting, colliding, and overlapping in unsettling ways. Post equilibrium ecology and resilience thinking, among

[39]. Victor Nolet, "Preparing Sustainability-Literate Teachers," *Teachers College Record* 111, no. 2 (February 2009): 409, 416.

[40]. Stephen Sterling, "An Analysis of Sustainability Education Internationally: Evolution, Interpretation, and Transformative Potential," in *The Sustainability Curriculum: The Challenge for Higher Education*, ed. John Blewitt and Cedric Cullingford (London: Earthscan, 2004), 43–62, 56–57.

[41]. David Orr, *Earth in Mind: On Education, Environment, and the Human Prospect* (Washington, DC: Earth Island Press, 2004), 27.

ANNE: I never answer my cell phone when I'm in the midst of a conversation; this is my way of being present where I am.

JODY (who always answers her phone, which rings frequently): This is my way of being available to "the larger present."

…reality is open, unspeakable, beyond concept.
—Timothy Morton, "Practicing Deconstruction
in the Age of Ecological Emergency"

other concepts central to Environmental Studies, are helping us re-think our social justice pedagogy.

Over the past few years, as we have undertaken our belated education into the field of Environmental Studies, and expanded our activism into matters ecological, we have begun to see the ways in which the dominant paradigms in education, like classic views of ecology, have been based on a view of human nature as stable, predictable—and so trainable. This view of children as malleable lends itself to a "command-and-control" approach to education that is remarkably similar to outmoded understandings of the "management" of natural resources.[42] Such an approach seeks optimization of certain narrow kinds of productivity to meet a narrow set of needs, and a concomitant destruction of the resources—like trust, affection, and an enlarged set of possibilities and commitments—that could make other versions of the future possible.

A clear contemporary example is the testing paradigm in education. Current cheating scandals in Pennsylvania and elsewhere are readable, on one level, as the decisions of particular adults and students to "scam" the tests to improve their individual and schools' performances. Expressed ecologically, the widespread nature of cheating suggests that these practices are the predictable consequence of an ecosystem fixed on maximizing a certain kind of productive outcome, despite the dynamic complexity of human beings who (like the natural world of which we are a part) are astonishingly diverse in our perceptions, desires, and inclinations as learners. As Brian Walker, David Salt, and Walter Reid explain, ecologists now understand that "the ruling paradigm—that we can optimize components of a system in isolation from the rest of the system—is proving inadequate to deal with the dynamic complexity of the real world."[43]

We see contemporary ecological theory as offering an alternative model for thinking about education, one based on the understanding that ecosystems are always changing—*and that such changes cannot be entirely controlled*. Classrooms populated with

---

42. Holling and Meffe, "Command and Control," 328–37.

43. Brian Walker, David Salt and Walter Reid, *Resilience Thinking: Sustaining People and Ecosystems in a Changing World* (Washington, DC: Island Press, 2006), 8.

"the third participant," "the ghostly traces of what we manage to ignore,"[44] exemplify this "new ecology," which apprehends that "stable structures like equilibrium or homeostasis do not accurately reflect natural systems…wherever we seek to find constancy we discover change."[45]

We find current narratives of post equilibrium aptly descriptive of the nested ecosystems of the classroom, and the varieties of conscious and unconscious processes that are so unpredictably there at play. Timothy Morton's work, in particular, which urges us to query our presumptions about the "nature" of "nature," comes quite close to the bone in its description of the rich unruliness of the environment as "the strange stranger…any entity whose arrival we can't predict, whose being is fundamentally uncanny and unfathomable.… There is a strange strangeness in every life form on Earth, quite literally: we share their DNA…yet we aren't them."[46] Although the role of the teacher in such unpredictable systems follows no recipe, it is critical: demanding an ongoing awareness of risk and opportunity, a willingness to support students in learning that stretches, that may well unbalance and dis-comfort them; asking that we listen and make—sometimes unmake or remake—decisions in the face of uncertainty, stay present with students and ourselves.

We are not even "quite" ourselves. Anne's dream about the "great blue ocean" suggests that the mysterious unconscious both dwells within and encompasses us all. Multiple other ecological metaphors have been evoked to represent this mystery. As Ursula LeGuin puts it, "We all have forests in our minds. Forests unexplored, unending. Each of us gets lost in the forest, every night, alone."[47] Virginia Woolf notes that we sometimes prefer that loneliness to accompaniment: "Human beings do not go hand in hand the whole stretch of the way. There is a virgin forest in each; a snowfield where even the print of birds' feet is unknown. Here we must go alone and like it better so."[48]

---

44. Ellsworth, *Teaching Positions*, 64–65.

45. Steve Mentz, "Tongues in the Storm: Shakespeare, Ecological Crisis, and the Resources of Genre," in *Ecocritical Shakespeare*, ed. Lynne Bruckner and Dan Brayton (Farnham, Surrey: Ashgate, 2001), 156–57.

46. Morton, "Practicing Deconstruction," 160–61.

47. Ursula K. LeGuin, "Vaster than Empires and More Slow," in *The Wind's Twelve Quarters* (New York: Harper and Row, 1975), 148.

48. Virginia Woolf, *On Being Ill* (1926; reprint, Ashfield, MA: Paris, 2002), 11–12.

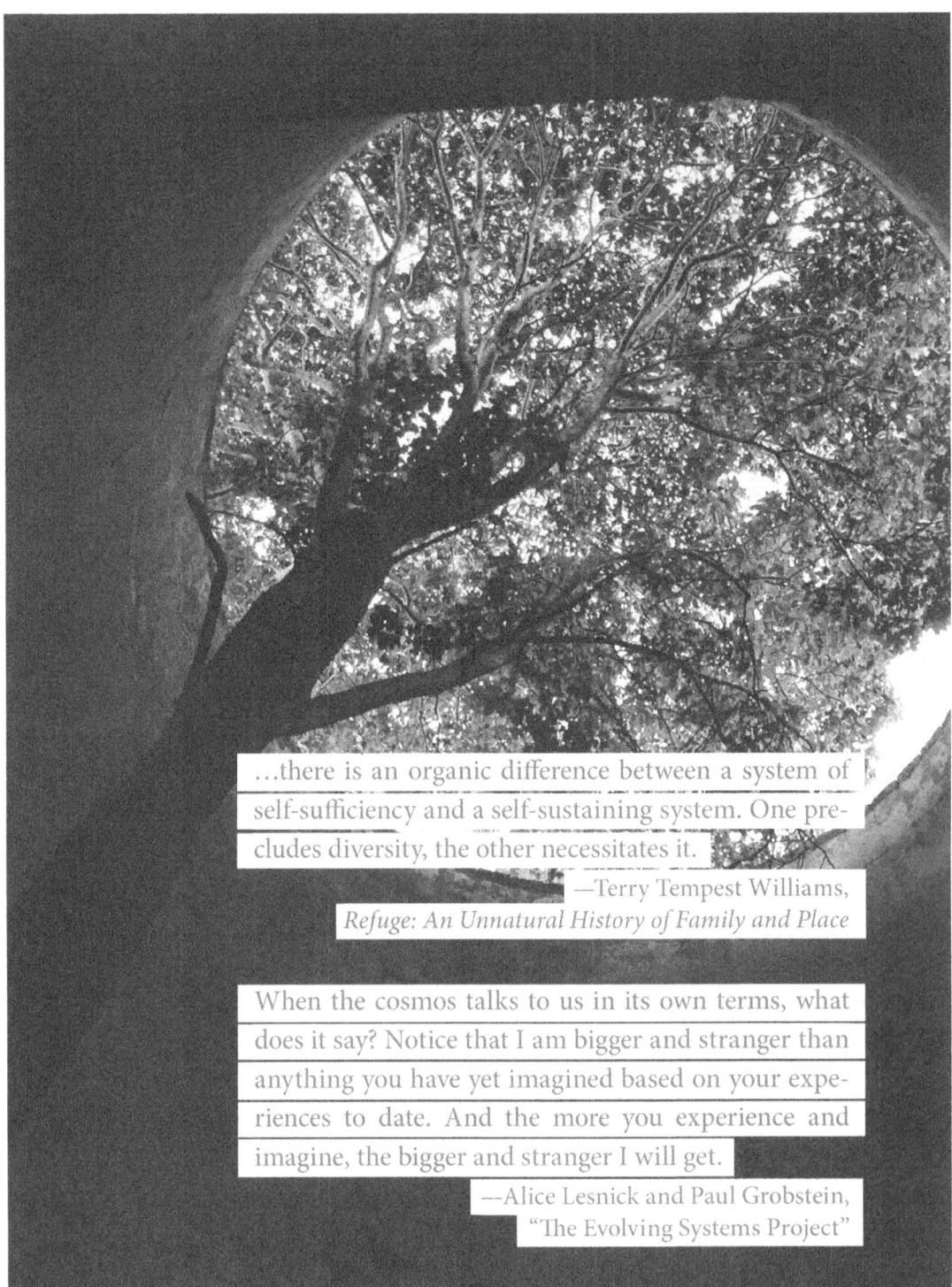

> ...there is an organic difference between a system of self-sufficiency and a self-sustaining system. One precludes diversity, the other necessitates it.
>
> —Terry Tempest Williams, *Refuge: An Unnatural History of Family and Place*

> When the cosmos talks to us in its own terms, what does it say? Notice that I am bigger and stranger than anything you have yet imagined based on your experiences to date. And the more you experience and imagine, the bigger and stranger I will get.
>
> —Alice Lesnick and Paul Grobstein, "The Evolving Systems Project"

We believe that ecological narratives, such as those by Morton, LeGuin, and Woolf, illuminate our thinking about classrooms filled with these "strange strangers"—the unfathomable dimensions of ourselves and others—and lead us as well into some insight regarding the possibility of sustainable teaching practices in such spaces. All ecosystems, including both natural and built environments, thrive not on optimizing productivity, but on diversity and redundancy.

Ecologists argue that any attempt to manage an ecosystem "should facilitate existing processes and variability rather than changing or controlling them.… Prescriptions and cookbook approaches generally should be avoided…the systems with which we work are idiosyncratic and endlessly varied. No single, detailed prescription can be of much use."[49]

We understand classroom ecosystems in this way: filled with abundance, excess, fecundity, and redundancy, "idiosyncratic and endlessly varied." C.S. Holling underscores the "dynamic, inherently uncertain" nature of ecosystems, which have "multiple potential futures."[50] In such an unbounded context, acting to create resilient, sustainable systems does not entail seeking "prescriptions and cookbook approaches," but rather paying attention to what's going on in multiple layers.

We think that attending to a larger range of experience than is often expressed in college courses may enable a more resilient means of teaching than other educational modes currently being advocated. Much "teaching to the test" and outcome-based educational work has short-term optimization as its goal.[51] We explore here an alternative in more flexible, open-ended teaching practices that thrive on diversity, even though—or precisely because—they may include frightening, often unrecognized aspects of ourselves, others, and our histories.

Thinking about what makes it hard for us and our students to rely on this abundance, the huge resource of the universe and the unpredictable interactions of our own unruly selves within it, we

49. Holling and Meffe, "Command and Control," 334.

50. C.S. Holling, "Surprise for Science, Resilience for Ecosystems, and Incentives for People," *Ecological Applications* 6, no. 3 (1996): 734.

51. Callahan, *Education and the Cult of Efficiency*; Oakes, "Schooling"; Ravitch, *The Death and Life of the Great American School System*.

continue to work on finding and developing the wherewithal to let down into that struggle, to take on the fears of various kinds that limit our reliance: war, trauma, hunger, political and self-oppression, the very particular pressure, when being schooled, to get it right…

In doing so, we are seeking the resilience of systems, in particular the systems of schooling, but this work also entails the emotional resilience of individuals, and we recognize the necessity of creating a foundation of safety for the kind of pedagogy we describe, a space for open learning in the context of schooling. We look to the notion of a pedagogy like D.W. Winnicott's "holding environment"[52] that is grounded on the dialectic of trust and risk as a container for play and exploration, a dialectic that is unlikely to emerge in a more controlled situation.

We offer here an alternative way of thinking about "unbounded" teaching, of recognizing our classrooms as part of larger ecosystems characterized by limited time, space, and resources, and by an unlimited, often "unruly" fecundity and diversity that do not submit to the limitations of injunction, testing, command, or control. The dimensions of minds and feelings that lurk below the surface of our usual classroom selves are essential to the running of that whole system. We believe that acknowledging their role in teaching and learning is crucial to encouraging the expression of difference and variability, from which our mutual responsibility for sustainable systems will continue to emerge.

52. D.W. Winnicott, *The Family and Individual Development* (London: Tavistock, 1965).

SECTION I
SPACES

CHAPTER ONE
BEING HERE

Entry

When you ride the train in, especially when you are by yourself, you feel an almost physical body-pull backward. This creates a weird sense of simultaneous forward and backward movement, like the body parts of a snake rearing back to strike or a cartoon with strong lines moving through your body in both directions, criss-crossing, canceling out. Even as the train hurtles past the landscape of backyards on tracks on old factory shells, and closer to the cluster of prisons strung out under the highway. What are you doing here? This question is in your marrow, fortunately hidden from view as you hop in the van with your students and are waved through by guards, then stow belongings in a metal locker, except your state-issued ID which you hand to representatives of the state as you wade through one machine and hand-stamp, two human pat-downs, three heavy-duty gates.

Now you realize you are smiling. Smiling? Polite rage.

Bringing ridiculous idealism based on knowing the people incarcerated here are human beings, just like all of us, bringing fear: what if this isn't true? And you hear from people working in this system: These women will con you if you let them, you can't believe what they tell you, and, sometimes from the women: Everyone is here for a reason. You don't ask the reason.

In a class held elsewhere for incarcerated women, a theater teacher "challenges these women to think about what words mean, to ask and begin to answer, *'Why are we here?'*"[1] You want to grab the edges of this question and stretch it into a tent or a trampoline: why are we all here? Some of us here in this prison? Some of us in college? All of us in this shared classroom space on Friday afternoons? Why here on this earth, and what to do about it?

And what about the COs? You practice what a colleague calls "professional flirtation" with the correctional officer at the front desk: maybe she'll let in the transparent bags you've purchased especially for bringing in materials; your student in spiked loafers, and the one who's only brought her student ID; forgive the pocketknife another forgot about in his jeans. You smile to make contact. The CO is a middle-aged woman with a round brown face and friendly smile, uniform pockets wide across her chest. Under the ultraviolet your hand turns palest blue. Up on the third floor the CO is late, doesn't have the call sheet, just back from hip surgery, and so ready to retire. Her replacement has a sudden, loud, and lovely laugh. The ex of another is on staff at your college.

You wait. They announce your program or don't, call the units or not, you wait. Your colleague and your college students—three or five or eight, some who've been coming in with you for years, some new and sitting forward, leaning back, crossing legs as: Slowly you are joined by one or two "inside women," and another, another—and sometimes you hear: they didn't make the call, the officer wouldn't let me out last week, she's in the hole, she's having her baby, (and occasionally) she left. Which could mean home, with that range of possibilities, or gone to a long-term facility. Framed by spiky black hair, the officer on late shift coaches you in how to make the procedures work a little better for you.

How about a class with COs *and* incarcerated women? suggests your colleague. The social worker raises her shapely brows.

Waiting.

---

1. Rena Fraden. *Imagining Medea: Rhodessa Jones and Theater for Incarcerated Women* (Chapel Hill: The University of North Carolina, 2001), 84, italics added.

Interlude: Speaking as, for, of, with

At a conference, a poet—a white woman, living 18 years in the deep South but not from there—opens by sharing her sorrow about the killings this past week in Charleston. Then she reads a series of poems she's written in the voices of people she's invented, composites of folks from her area.[2] You find her voice speaking these other voices evocative, the sense of persons and place almost mythical. Later your student—a Southerner, African American, and Latina—objects to the ethics of speaking for others, making up characters based not on research but on—what? Hearing how Southerners treat their dogs, for example? Five of us in a lively exchange at dinner, you're snagged between your own response and a strong respect for your student's perspective, probing connections between evoking, mythologizing, colonizing. One of us, an anthropologist with a literary bent, claims, I don't really see poetry and novel writing as "speaking for others" in the same way that anthropologists engage in the dubious task of "giving voice." Poets have license to invent; that's what they do. Your student is unconvinced: what gives them license?

Rena Fraden says,

> I took time to figure out how to write in my own voice about the voices of others. There is a delicate balance between critical distance and passionate advocacy, as there is between writing of and about without wanting to write for or instead of someone else...[3]

Writing now, you worry about this: how to speak in your own voice *and* call up the voices of others—the women who are incarcerated, your college students, the COs, your colleague with whom you've been in this every step; know the presence of other voices reverberating in your head could paralyze you. And if you write only *as* yourself, do you risk taking up too much space? (You remember Teju Cole's description of the self-absorption of "white saviors.")[4]

2. Ann Fisher-Wirth, "Extractive & Underground Poetics: Readings and Conversation," plenary session at the biennial conference of the Association for the Study of Literature and the Environment, Moscow, ID, June 25, 2015.

3. Fraden, *Imagining Medea*, 23.

4. Teju Cole, "The White Savior Industrial Complex," *The Atlantic*, March 21, 2012.

Edgily moving in and out of the classroom, trying to exhibit patience as you press the CO to announce your program on the loudspeaker, you reenter into the soliloquy of the sole woman in blue in class so far today, offering a message for the college students: They should "stand on the wall," observing everything from that position and enacting the Biblical story in which God instructs his people to defend the city: "Enemies will come with battering rams, trying to tear down the wall you've built." The "enemies"—"the critics, the cautious, the committed"—will try to distract them from that work. The students listen raptly, write furiously. And when one of you asks where she came by this lesson, wanting to read the text, she tells you she received it as a prophecy.

Begin Again, with Power Differentials

You cross this threshold with colleagues, students; travel in trains and vans together, sharing your news of family, school, weekend plans; forget to know you're free. Enter with new books and those marbled, soft-bound composition pads, with pencils, nametags, lesson plans, once with microscopes, enter inured to procedures because after all you are free. Though you too have committed crimes of intention and accident, you all will walk out after shift change on Friday afternoon, on your way to campus, farm, gym, home, party, knowing that "many compassionate, dedicated, and decent people walk into prison education settings and try to build an illusion that the 'inside' of their classrooms are 'outside' of the racism, White supremacy, and White privilege realities" that incarcerated people will encounter when they reenter their communities; knowing that the huge percentage of formerly incarcerated people, even those who are newly educated, "will not be the next-door neighbors or work colleagues of their prison educators."[5]

Still, you, your colleague, your students are also not all neighbors. Some of you know well the crimes committed against you, if

5. Tony Gaskew, "Developing a Prison Education Pedagogy," in *Bringing College Education into Prisons*, ed. Rob Scott (San Francisco: Jossey-Bass, 2015), 76.

not those you commit; long to share your own mistakes with the women inside; have relatives inside and feel somehow responsible; send *A Thousand Splendid Suns* to your friend from high school now in prison. And tonight friends will ask about the jail, what it's like, what you do there, and you'll shrug, tell but not tell. You'll think of the good you mean to bring and receive, worry about the harm you might also cause as "actors in the system" who "contribute to and benefit from oppression,"[6] and then you'll try not to think of it at all because, after all, it's your Friday night too.

And still, you and your students must carve out work in the world, as one of you, en route to graduate school in social work, heads to an internship investigating prisons overseas, another to a fellowship where she'll continue teaching inside; you present with colleagues at conferences, gain cache in the social justice arm of the academy. An article on "educational and penal realism" cautions that desires "to serve in activist roles have limits, through convergence with personal economic interests."[7] Who is working for social justice on behalf of whom, in this circumstance of profound power differentials? And what could *working with* look like?

In imagining a "pedagogy of solidarity," Gaztambide-Fernández argues that

> educators are called upon to play a central role in constructing the conditions for a different kind of encounter, an encounter that both opposes ongoing colonization and seeks to heal the social, cultural, and spiritual ravages of colonial history.... This requires moving beyond tired conceptions of individual autonomy and rational consciousness...[and] recasting our day-to-day relations and encounters with difference. "What is at stake," to quote Judith Butler, "is really rethinking the human as a site of interdependency."[8]

Rethinking the human, you perceive networks of connection, how one human being's imprisonment creates another's paycheck, how someone's white is another's Black, how I am not free until you are.

---

6. Kenneth J. Fasching-Varner, et al., "Beyond School-to-Prison Pipeline and Toward an Educational and Penal Realism," *Excellence in Education* 47, no. 4 (2014): 423.

7. Fasching-Varner, et al., "Beyond School," 423.

8. Rubén A. Gaztambide-Fernández, "Decolonization and the Pedagogy of Solidarity," *Decolonization: Indigeneity, Education & Society* 1, no. 1 (2012): 42.

Being in Class (1)

Since photos are not allowed, see this: a dim squarish, windowless room of indeterminate color lit by ceiling fluorescents, long tables pushed to the edges to make room for a circle of those curved plastic chairs, not curved to any body you know. Shot from above, this resembles a ritual clearing.

This is how you teach: An introductory go-round with names and a question, either connected to the book or not, serious or playful or both. If you could have a superpower, what would it be? I'd fly right out of here. If you were a marine creature? And then you're in the book: sometimes all or most of the participants have done the reading, and some have gone on and finished and can't wait to talk about the ending, but often some have gotten the book and others not, some have read and others not. This goes for the college students too. So often you start by asking those who've read to share their responses and questions, and this might take us in. Or read a passage together, go from there. You mean to write to a prompt and then share, though often don't get there, and end around the circle with a sentence or word as you drop nametags into the bag.

All or most are reading *Bodega Dreams*, so your first go-round, this time, is about characters: a lot of you pick Sapo, Chino's best buddy who's making it on the street, because he's real; and a number choose Blanca, Chino's wife and a good girl; one goes for Negra, Blanca's edgier, darker sister, and you've been thinking about her too. No one chooses Vera because she's really evil which means you don't care about anyone but yourself.

Then the conversation gets going on whether Chino—who's struggling with the dual identities of schoolboy and streetguy—is ratting when he goes to the cops. What's the difference between ratting and telling? This is a nuanced and spirited conversation, with some saying it's about motivation (Is it just to save yourself? Is it spiteful, or for some greater good?), and about whether and how

From our reading list, 2012–2015:

Audre Lorde, "Silence into Action"
Alice Walker, "Beauty"
Jennifer Gonnerman, *Life on the Outside: The Prison Odyssey of Jane Bartlett*
Elaine Brown, *A Taste of Power: A Black Woman's Story*
Ernesto Quinonez, *Bodega Dreams*
Octavia Butler, *Kindred*
Karen Russell, "St. Lucy's Home for Girls Raised by Wolves"
Maya Angelou, "Phenomenal Woman"
Sapphire, *Push: A Novel*
Chimichanda Ngozi Adichie, *Americanah*
Jeanette Walls, *The Glass Castle: A Memoir*
Khaled Hosseini, *A Thousand Splendid Suns*
Marjane Satrapi, *Persepolis: The Story of a Childhood*
Susan Nussbaum, *Good Kings, Bad Kings: A Novel*
Janet Mock, *Redefining Realness: My Path to Womanhood, Identity, Love & So Much More*

you are implicated in the wrongdoing. Last week there was a fight at the jail: not going to anyone as it was coming on but then telling later, trying to make your own deal a little sweeter—that's ratting.

Kindred opens with an arm in a wall—physical and symbolic manifestation of a Black woman time-traveling to save a white ancestor. "St. Lucy's Home for Girls" schools young females raised by wolves, now in the throes of cultural assimilation. A graphic in *Persepolis* parallels the explosions of partying and bombing in Tehran. In these texts you explore the inexorability of the past; the tension of accommodation and resistance; the relationship between celebration and violence.

You know why you're here. These are exhilarating, nuanced classroom conversations in which you draw on connections between the texts and your lives to sharpen and deepen your analyses. Megan Sweeney claims that reading "enables some women prisoners to gain self-knowledge, contextualize their experiences in relation to larger frameworks, mediate their histories of victimization and violence, and develop an understanding of the limits and possibilities of individual agency."[9] Yes, and too, you feel language as alive, ideas as agents in our classroom.

Longtime prison educator Rob Scott warns that while teaching in prison can be exhilarating and inspiring for teachers, this doesn't mean that you are doing radical work inside. Scott suggests that one "of the roles of radical teaching is to expose the silence on power relations as a phenomenon of choice."[10] You want to do this, try to figure out what he means, what it might actually look and feel like to teach toward this. During planning sessions at the college you explore the implications of power relations in the classroom—tongue probing sore tooth—but inside again you shy away: want neither to flaunt nor to deny power, and thus too readily comply with silence.

See now a short, silent clip, black and white: women of various shapes and sizes, skin tones and hair color, wearing boxy shirts and pants or college casual, leaning in to invest, leaning away and

---

9. Megan Sweeney, *Reading Is My Window: Books and The Art of Reading in Women's Prisons* (Durham: University of North Carolina Press, 2010), 6.

10. Rob Scott, "Distinguishing Radical Teaching from Merely Having Intense Experiences While Teaching in Prison," *Radical Teacher* 95 (Spring 2013): 22–32.

withdrawing into themselves, as words meander and then shoot like spit across our circle.

You read a passage from *Bodega Dreams* about school as utterly alienated from the lives of these characters, then veer into a discussion of parents' roles in their children's education. She says she tried to be there to check her children's homework but often couldn't be; she jumps in, says, You *have* to be!; but I was working three jobs to put food on the table!; and: my father always checked that homework anyway, no matter what! You got to have priorities! Bodies shifting, voices high, hard, pleading.

And of course in this moment, everyone is here, no one home checking children's homework.

And yet, Avery Gordon describes our lives in terms of "hauntings":[11] we are in more than one place, time, material reality, both here and there, now and then, sitting in this circle and at home, where you might be checking your children's homework.

And yet, you are in this room in this moment: your splintering voices creating a cacophony of guilt and accusation, longing and regret. What choices do people make, do people have, in light of poverty, race, history, stacked decks, necessary priorities? And time is up. Your colleague starts to close class, you interrupt to say something, anything, about listening/respecting/learning from and with each other; you feel this to be misguided, inadequate; realize later that it misses the underlying stream of desire. Could a politics of desire help us interrogate this "shadow discourse of personal responsibility,"[12] the larger picture that embraces social context? Is there an opportunity here to interrogate ways that dominant ideals inflect individual guilt, divisions, and judgments among the people in this room? And even this "near-miss" teaching moment[13] begins to lift a curtain on the web of power relations in which you are all enmeshed.

You have dinner with three friends, all social workers, and they take you to task: You're raising all these trauma-triggering subjects,

11. Avery Gordon, *Ghostly Matters: Haunting and the Sociological Imagination* (Minneapolis: University of Minnesota Press, 1997).

12. Michelle Fine and Jessica Ruglis, "Circuits and Consequences of Dispossession: the Racialized Realignment of the Public Sphere for U.S. Youth," *Transforming Anthropology* 17, no. 1 (2009): 20.

13. Eve Sedgwick, "Pedagogy of Buddhism," in *Touching Feeling: Affect, Pedagogy, Performativity* (Durham: Duke University Press, 2003), 154.

and then just leaving—?! They ask questions about where the women might go during the week when we are not there. You know they're trying to support you, feel caught nevertheless.

At your planning session you talk with your colleague and students, share worries about reactivating trauma, consider ways to mitigate: Should you be telling the social worker more? You fear compromising confidentiality. Checking in more explicitly at beginning and end of sessions? You are not therapists.

Fraden notes, "In theory, the disciplines of education, therapy, and art can be clearly separated, but in the jails, in practice," it may be difficult "to separate drama's ability to educate from its ability to provide therapy." Theater director Rhodessa Jones "deliberately mixes them up, the education and therapy folded together into what she has called 'creative survival.'"[14]

You wonder about the relationship between recognizing the enormity of trauma and acknowledging what Avery Gordon calls "complex personhood,"

> the second dimension of the theoretical statement that life is complicated. Complex personhood means that people suffer graciously and selfishly too, get stuck in the symptoms of their troubles, and also transform themselves. Complex personhood means that the stories people tell about themselves, about their troubles, about their social worlds, and about their society's problems are entangled and weave between what is immediately available as a story and what their imaginations are reaching toward.[15]

You talk with your husband, who works as a therapist. He says that just as trauma reorganizes the brain to shield the self, other experiences can reorganize the brain to open up. He tries to help people move from identifying as victims toward a larger sense of complex personhood, to claim a sense of self that is more than their trauma. Activating this "adaptive resilience" engages a sense of agency, of competence, of a dense, available network of connections. Your role is different, he acknowledges, but brains are porous: what

14. Fraden, *Imagining Medea*, 76.

15. Gordon, *Ghostly Matters*, 4.

is happening outside is also inside; what happens in book group is part of how people are processing identities: the self is intellectual, people take what you say seriously.

Though you never ask the women why they are here, sometimes stories get told. You hear Fraden's caution: "Storytelling can be a con game, a trick used against one's foes. It can also be the beginning of a different drama—a way to imagine, if not live out, a new life."[16] Stories can weave new narratives, skeins of connection. Tuesday morning your team meets, works through the nitty gritty of the upcoming class: which passages, who will do the intro, how about the copying? Also, teaching questions: what kinds of gaps are we leaving that might summon stories "reaching toward" new imaginings, toward each other?

16. Fraden, *Imagining Medea*, 48.

Interlude: Dreams and Transitions

We are in a medium-security facility built to house females who are awaiting trial and/or have a short sentence. So technically, it's a transitional space. Though transitional does not necessarily feel transitory, even for those of us who arrive at 1 pm and leave at 3:30. And the jail itself feels like a kind of limbo, a state of in-between, as during shift change when everyone freezes in place. You wonder how the birds skittering at the edges of hallways enter and exit these windowless spaces.

And you are learning/discerning the language of incarceration: security, facility, inmates, females, corrections, prisoners, offending, offenders, convicts, inside women, incarcerated women, ex-offenders, ex-cons, parolees, re-entry, recidivists, victims. Words like glue-paper.

The language of higher education is not so sticky, more abstract: college and university, students, scholars, professors, academe, also rigor, assessment, achievement.

"The Inside-Out Prison Exchange Program is a creative link between two of the largest and most highly-funded institutional and social structures in our country: academia and prisons."[17]

At a higher education in prison conference, summer 2014:

> FACULTY #1: A big limitation in college programs is lack of internet access.
>
> FACULTY #2: The internet is the modern modality for exploring the world.
>
> CO #1: We don't want to re-victimize someone. Inmates can use the internet to get in touch with their victims. Unless you can guarantee me 100% that the internet won't be used to hurt, I won't grant access.
>
> CO #2: This is what criminals do on the internet. They will abuse it. Criminal minds will use it for their advantage.
>
> ALUM: I want to problematize the language being used here. I am highly offended by what you said. Let's check how we are having this conversation. How do you balance security and self-actualization?

Caught in the conundrum of other and self, inside and out, you follow your colleague's direction toward porosity: a refusal or at least a reconsideration of the existence of self and other, inside and out. And you grope toward a conception of "self" and "other" as both distinct and not, or every body

> a "multiplicity of multiplicities." Every body is a heterogeneous and complex network of entities that is itself an entity or unit. ... Far from being impenetrable castles with well defined boundaries defining what is inside and what is outside, bodies are permeable down to their most intimate recesses. Bodies are more like sponges than marbles. Even marbles are a sort of sponge..."[18]

A college student entitles her posting "Fear the fear":

> I had a terrible nightmare after I came back from [my first day at] the prison that I dreamt about myself being a prisoner with death penalty, spending the last day of my life with my parents.

17. "The Inside-Out Prison Exchange Program," Temple University, 2016.

18. Levi R. Bryant, "Stacy Alaimo: Porous Bodies and Trans-Corporeality," May 24, 2012.

> The nightmare was not as scary as some of my other nightmares that I was chased by killers or my life was in danger yet it still scared me more than any other dreams.
>
> I did not actually feel the difference between the class in prison and the class here in Bryn Mawr because both classes are engaging and thought-provoking. I was surprised by how women in the prison recognized their status and paralleled their experiences with class reading. However, I was shocked by my own dream that I suddenly realized deep in my consciousness, I was scared by the difference between them and us. I was further scared by how subtle our fear could be hidden and how much did our fear change us unconsciously. And I think that is exactly how culture works in our everyday life.[19]

19. "Fear the fear," February 8, 2015 (1:49 p.m.).

Back at the prison: After you put your papers, pencils, books through the electronic scanner (all inside the transparent plastic bag, until they disallow this, before they again allow it, sometimes), you wade through the body scanner, then hands out to the sides, step closer for a pat down, shoulders arms torso legs, oddly gentle, get your hand stamped, and are buzzed inside along with your compatriots and others in uniform—an officer, black-robed chaplain, heavily veiled woman who runs Muslim services—through the first heavy-duty metal door and before the second, and you can still see back to the waiting room and glimpse the outside door beyond that. You are situated between these two, the outside and the inside, visible to other shadowy uniformed figures in a glassed-in techni-tower above and before you. You might get buzzed through again quickly, then move through the second heavy-duty door into the hallway and the next pat down and ultraviolet before the elevator takes you up. Or you could wait in this linoleumed square, maybe 5' × 5', for some immeasurable time, smelling a lunch of fish and something starchy mixing with ammonia and, faintly, hygiene products, and it is during this time that you lose your capacity to speak lightly to your colleagues and to think of anything really except confinement.

Being in Class (2)

We discuss Janet Mock's memoir, *Redefining Realness*. Only two people had the book and did the reading, so we read together a passage about Mock seeing her dad *as* her dad, then her discovery that people on the block see him as "that crackhead."[20] Two women talk about themselves as a "crackhead" or "dope fiend." I'm not this anymore, says one, and, People have all these different sides of themselves: although I'm wearing blue now, this isn't who I am. And another, slowly enunciating:

> I need to acknowledge this as a reality I've lived in order to challenge and change it. I'm wearing blue and this is who I am, at least for now, and knowing that is an important part of my being able to "redefine [my] realness." I am not a mom right now because I'm here, not with my children. And my oldest, my daughter won't talk to me, she hasn't forgiven me for those years when I cared more about getting high than about being a mom.

You stop listening; think of your oldest, your daughter. You are moms here together, sitting in this bare box with college students who might be but are not your birth children. Jane Maher writes about using autobiographical essays to teach writing to women in prison:

> Try pointing out a run-on sentence or ask for clarifying details in an essay that described a scene in the prison visiting room during which an 11-year-old daughter asked her mother, who has a life sentence, what would become of her body when she died in prison.[21]

You lean forward to insist (but is this intrusive/too certain/wrong?). You *are* a mom. Your daughter wouldn't be *not* talking to you if she didn't know you are her mom. She shifts in her seat.

At the conference on higher education in prison, a CO sitting on a panel with her deputy commissioner in the room: Corrections is like another planet. Here a spoon is a spoon is a spoon. There, a spoon is a weapon. You need to think about things you would have no reason to think about anywhere else.

---

20. Janet Mock, *Redefining Realness: My Path to Womanhood, Identity, Love & So Much More* (New York: Atria Books, 2014), 56.

21. Jane Maher, "Teaching Academic Writing in a Maximum Security Women's Prison," *New Directions for Community Colleges* 170 (Summer 2015): 82–83.

You struggle to acknowledge these intersections: the yearning mom, the spoon. Look to the words of the colleague who brought you into this work:

> Restorative justice principles suggest that crime...breaks relationships...restorative values include respect, care, self-determination, participation, interconnectedness, and humility... responding to crime requires responding to the unjust social context in which it occurs.... Restorative Justice Pedagogy aims to use restorative justice knowledge as a way to empower people to build relationships, communities, and leaders and to prevent future harm.... The RJP experience speaks to the importance of creating community in the classroom to facilitate the openness and sharing necessary for personal transformation.[22]

What earlier mother-daughter relationship might be "restored" here? In your own parenting, there is much that you suspect neither you nor your daughter would want to return to. And too the difficult question of who will rebuild this relationship, "prevent future harm." "Transformation" makes you uneasy, with its resonances of conversion, of change on some cellular level, suggesting a mythical skid-free future, "a hall pass through history."[23]

LESSON PLAN FOR FRI., 3/20/15

1. Two weeks ago, we asked for some writing: Pick one scene from your life, and tell that story. Then comment on the ways in which you have made it real (or decided not to...) We were asking about representation...anyone want to read these...?

You play "2 truths and a lie" in small groups. All the lies have a ring of truth: plausibility lies with the listener.

This week many have read the book, so you plunge in via the title: *Redefining Realness* is about the question of what is "real" for Janet Mock, a trans woman of color who grew up working class and poor in Hawaii and Los Angeles; who is she "really"? What is the truth here? You probe: What makes someone really a woman? How much does this have to do with genetics, how much with choices,

---

22. Barb Toews, "Toward a Restorative Justice Pedagogy: Reflections on Teaching Restorative Justice in Correctional Facilities," *Contemporary Justice Review: Issues in Criminal, Social, and Restorative Justice* 16, no. 2 (2013): 2–3.

23. Ta-Nehisi Coates, *Between the World and Me* (New York: Spiegel & Grau, 2015), 33.

with presenting yourself, with products of presentation; is that hyper-feminine woman in the peach gown on the book's cover *really* her? Clearly, she's female! But: she has to go further in showing she's a woman, because she isn't *really* a woman. Janet Mock isn't and never will be truly female, because of her "equipment." Though she had "the surgery." But: what part of all this does genitalia play in "realness"?

11. Two main ideas to work with: passing/not being read:

Dorian Corey…describes "realness" for trans women (known in ball culture as femme queens) as being "undetectable" to the "untrained" or "trained." Simply, "realness" is the ability to be seen as heteronormative, to assimilate, to not be read as other or deviate from the norm. "Realness" means you are extraordinary in your embodiment of what society deems normative.[24]

These thoughts surrounding identity, gender, bodies, and how we view, judge, and objectify all women brings me to the subject of "passing," a term based on an assumption that trans people are passing as something that we are not.… This pervasive thinking frames trans people as illegitimate and unnatural. If a trans woman who knows herself and operates in the world as woman is seen perceived, treated, and viewed as a woman, isn't she just being herself? She isn't passing; she is merely being.[25]

On co-constructing ourselves, in relationship with others: "When I think of this time with Wendi, I'm reminded of a line from Toni Morrison's Sula: 'Nobody was minding us, so we minded ourselves.' I was her sister, and she didn't want to leave me behind. We needed each other to create who we were supposed to be."[26]

You talk about "heteronormativity"—parse for meaning at the college, the prison, get into a spirited discussion of the heavy presence of masculine clothing and body products in the women's jail. Why is this, and what does it mean? They don't want us to look and feel attractive, female. Don't want us to *be* attractive or attracted to each other. Even the deodorant is male, everything. Easier and cheaper to buy massive quantities of what the men use. Still: I know

---

24. Mock, *Redefining Realness*, 116.

25. Mock, *Redefining Realness*, 155.

26. Mock, *Redefining Realness*, 135.

I'm attractive. And it's not really about my equipment.

This is a space where women sit with each other, think and laugh and listen, shoot out sharp words (and once, waiting for the first class of the semester, someone punches someone in the nose), push and cajole and appreciate each other, and sometimes there is touch. Touch is forbidden: sitting by so the thighs touch, maybe tops of arms, holding hands, any kind of little stroking of skin, of course hugs. This desire for touch, for skin to skin somehow so dangerous that the late-shift CO —usually so calm and clear—goes off on the cuddling, threatens that if she sees this again someone won't be allowed back to class. Love, lust, contact, caring, connection; desire desire desire. Even the flat blue squared out clothes elastic waistband no hugging of the body can't diminish all that flesh of many shades and textures. In closing circle she says that now there's this woman here, describes her strong body and her attitude. Connection and power lurk here, the power to touch, to prohibit touch, to desire.

> v. Write a story about when you were a different version of yourself. Go 'round and share something of what you wrote.

In the end, you don't (re)define "realness."

"The purpose of art," James Baldwin wrote, "is to lay bare the questions hidden by the answers." He might have been channeling Dostoyevsky's statement that "we have all the answers, it's the questions we do not know."[27]

The discussion of what's "real" seems to you like this: Circling answers together (biological "equipment," clothing and other accoutrements, how you see yourself, how others see you) takes you all behind the curtain, to a place of questions, impolitic questions about commerce, desire, power.

You visit with your mom and her friend—88 and 93 respectively—at her friend's "home," a cell-like room in the basement of a facility where the upper floors are swanky, the lower floors not. Your mom's friend, now in a wheelchair, has a worn hardback copy of *Finnegan's*

[27]. Claudia Rankine, *Citizen: An American Lyric* (Minneapolis: Graywolf Press, 2014), 115.

Wake lying open on her bed. Her ankle is bruised and swollen from yet another fall, still she is elegant. She is the mom of an eminent queer theorist, was also your high school English teacher, and when she asks questions about your class at the prison, you don't evade these as you so often find yourself doing; instead you describe our discussions of *Redefining Realness*. Later, you go buy her a copy, knowing that she will read you reading.

Interlude: Inside and Out

All this time one participant, an effervescent trans woman of color, is not in class, since she's at trial. Which several of you read about compulsively online in "most viewed stories." You are angry that the media uses over and over a single photograph, somber and frightening: full frontal, rounded forehead, heavy jaw, eyes flat. A mug shot?

Then you hear she's back but staying apart, gathering herself, and then she returns to your group, post-trial with her hair in a natural and quieted bow, dealing with the looming threat of a sentence so long you are shocked. At issue in the courtroom, says the media, has been her "not showing remorse." Back on the block, post-trial and pre-sentencing, she asks you to submit petitions attesting to her character. You are happy to see her, note her muted demeanor, and feel that desire to do whatever you can to help. Simple as that. Though of course it's not at all simple. Your crew checking in afterwards split and conflicted, and then as you check with others, only more so: The most experienced prison educator you know warns that she never does this kind of thing, since it smacks of favoritism, and can endanger the program; your colleague's husband, a lawyer, warns that judges resent letters from people who know little of the case or the defendant, and this could well backfire. Your son says to step back, you're charmed by her. You all discuss, vacillate, finally lie by omission.

Your colleague reports a heavy early morning dream: in prison, on an elaborate staircase—you were going up, as the women were going down. You were bringing in Easter baskets, but not getting them delivered. You were in a train station and had missed the train.

At the end of an early semester inside, your college students realize that you might be compounding an already distressing power imbalance. Weigh your inside arts-based curriculum, focused on reflection and tailored to squeak through the narrow window of institutional approval, against the college curriculum of shared political analysis. You get a knot in your belly. Remember that the women inside expressed great appreciation for this opportunity to work with fewer words, with images. How to balance needs, imagine new ways in? That night you email your mentor, Michelle Fine, who writes back quickly, notes the delicacy of working with a CO in the space, and suggests asking the college students to write about "conversations you wish you could've had" with the women in the jail:

> A conversation about racism and sexism in America, especially sexism. I wanted them to explore how their crime is related to concrete, named circumstances greater than the individual's wrong-doing.
>
> I wish I was brave enough to share experiences I had in common and to admit some of my own faults to make the conversation more equal.
>
> Do you like us? Why? Do you think we're better (cooler, smarter…) than you? * can be directed either way.
>
> I wish we could've talked about the tension of bryn mawr students being able to leave at the end of the day. Or the broad topic of power relations between us.
>
> A conversation about ways the prison/justice system could improve. A conversation about fighting the system.
>
> I think I really wanted to talk about the social forces/institutions/environments surrounding these women's experience and choices…it just made me feel so trapped and sad to hear the internalized self-blame rhetoric…[I wanted] to lighten the weight I felt in their hearts and voices.

Your students balk at the women blaming themselves, making sense of their troubles in religious terms rather than via political analysis:

> I think about these frustrations I have and I am torn. I want to condemn religion for encouraging self-responsibility, but I also want to celebrate its ability to help these women cope.[28]

28. HSBurke, "After last class…," November 9, 2013 (2:32 p.m.).

Religious language suggests the possibility of redemption—a sense of future return on investment, spiritual and otherwise. There's a longing here, a capacity to imagine another version of your life, your self. What's the relationship between this willingness to step into desire and a political analysis that slices into history to lay bare present-day injustices?

Michelle Fine and her university-based colleagues design and implement a collaborative research project with incarcerated women. When outside researchers are disturbed by

> the resonances between the "discourses of redemption" used by inside researchers and other discourses blaming poor women for their troubles, inside researchers remind them that most of the women here have committed crimes. The discourse of redemption serves as a "powerful coping strategy for women desperate to understand themselves as separate from the often destructive behavior that led them to prison." This recognition paves the way to rereading the data in search of "connective tissue" between past and present selves, bringing social context, community, and history into the "present, ever-changing self."[29]

29. Michelle Fine et. al, "Participatory Action Research: From Within and Beyond Prison Bars," in *Working Method: Research and Social Justice*, ed. Lois Weis and Michelle Fine (New York: Routledge, 2004), 106–7.

In his powerful writings on racial history and the argument for reparations, Ta-Nehisi Coates slams the seductive turn toward redemption as a false salve, bringing instead an unrelentingly realistic analysis of race and class politics in this country that won't let you hold onto anything redemptive.

A student in her first semester with the program says she feels "relaxed" in prison, much more so than at the college, where she feels she's losing a power struggle with a professor. A friend with decades of experience teaching inside says that she "loves being in

jail," where the expectations are lower than in the academy. Another student recommits to her college career because of her engagement at the prison; talks about how "real" prison seems to her, mostly because it is so "raw," less filtered, restrained, anxious than college classrooms. How much of your being here is because of this sense of emotional access, its feeling more porous, more open, more surprising than the "rigor" touted in institutions of higher education? And who is seeking redemption—even if of another sort?

Being in Class (3)

We are reading aloud a passage from *Push*, and the women can barely do this. They're hating it, and what they're hating most is the language of Precious, the young narrator who opens with "I was left back when I was twelve because I had a baby for my fahver.... I got suspended from school 'cause I'm pregnant which I don't think is fair. I ain' did nothin'!"[30]

In our reading there's stumbling and laughter, embarrassment and rage: this is not proper English, how people talk not write, some people talk this way. If someone comes up to me talking this way, I don't even talk with them. Talk about why Sapphire chooses this language, why she couldn't tell it in "proper English," why the grammar gets better in the course of the book as Precious learns. But it makes me feel stupid to read it! This is supposedly how black people talk. I don't talk like this, I mean I might with some people. *What's Black English?* I'm not Black, I'm American. I teach my daughter proper English!

You don't talk about how Precious, who is sexually abused by her father, can also feel sexual in those scenes; how he is portrayed as vicious and uncaring, the mother as also abusive, deceitful, a "welfare queen"; how learning to read *looks* like the answer, though surely doesn't create jobs or equitable policies. Later you wonder whether your focus on language masked discomfort with other

30. Sapphire, *Push: A Novel* (New York; Vintage, 1997), 3.

traumas, with charged representations of character and naïve presumptions about education.

You've never felt whiter; are full of heat now—not about *Push*, which you could take or leave, but about language, real varied beautiful and nonstandard English, this language in the mouths of people disowned a second later, whispered in ears, breaths. You try to intercede on behalf of some "other" whose language you feel compelled to defend: you raise questions about who "owns" English, who gets to say what's "proper," what's acceptable to put in a book. These questions ring false since they are not real questions, but rather your attempt to testify on behalf of this language that is not yours.

> I teach my daughter proper English. But last time she got on the phone with me she's all "I be this, that"—I'm like, what?! Let me talk to your father!
>
> Let's just agree: we're not talking about this book next week!

Franz Fanon's concept of the "epidermalization of inferiority" traces "the metaphorical absorption of racial inferiority through the skin and into the mind."[31] Listening to urban students, Fine and Ruglis hear how external conditions "crossed membranes from what was outside the child, in the school building, to what *was* the child."[32]

Prison educators take this on:

In his "Humiliation to Humility Pedagogy," Gaskew draws on incarcerated Black men's life experiences to investigate the "three dimensional elephant…racism, White supremacy, and White privilege."[33] In the Medea project, Rhodessa Jones and Shawn Reynolds aim to uncover "the connections between an individual and the system of power," believing that "understanding social context, moving with others and not alone—will transform the oppressed and apathetic into people who believe they can think and thus act for themselves and also for others…."[34] These are educators of color. Teaching while white, you speak the language of interviews,

---

31. Jason G. Izarrary and John Raible, "'A Hidden Part of Me': Latino/a Students, Silencing, and the Epidermalization of Inferiority," *Equity & Excellence in Education* 47, no. 4 (2014): 441.

32. Fine and Ruglis, "Circuits and Consequences," 24.

33. Gaskew, "Developing," 71.

34. Fraden, *Imagining Medea*, 70.

of commercial exchange, of the courts. You always see race—see colorfeatureshairtextures, see how racial difference animates a world of difference, see the daily risks of mothers, fathers, uncles of Black children. Except when you don't.

In a recent essay in *The New York Times*, Nell Painter offers a chilling description of whiteness as a binary with a choice between bland culturelessness and venal racism, a "toggle between nothing and awfulness."[35] A third option eschews a visceral involvement, acknowledging race privilege and racism, trying to "comply with the new rules of diversity" as though this is someone else's problem.[36] Absent still: an unnamed option swimming insistently at the edge of your peripheral vision, an opportunity to bring into focus a whiteness that contends with what is real and what is possible, necessary.

What of the white women in prison and in this classroom, strangely invisible in both the media and the literature? So much of what's being written is about men, African American and Latino, sometimes African American women and Latinas. These white women aren't Piper Kerman. One woman, has to be from Northeast Philly, telling us about how she's never been like that but now so in love with a woman in here. Another whose age is masked by her wispy hair around gone mouth folding in on itself, mumbling long stories about Catholic girlhood, ferociously grateful at the end of class. The woman with tangled white-hair dreads, from a years-ago class, headed back out with no home, no idea where her son—labeled schizophrenic—is, last she knew on the streets, and who says out loud with almost a sense of just speaking her interior: you know, we all have one more crime in us.

35. Nell Irvin Painter, "What Is Whiteness?" *New York Times*, June 20, 2015.

36. Jennifer Delton, "Escaping Whiteness," *HuffPost Media*, July 12, 2015.

Interlude: The "Criminal Mind"

Your colleague tells this story at a conference. It is quickly queried by a co-presenter who was incarcerated for thirty years, now out and in school. She asks instead, what crime might we be forced to commit, unable *not* to commit, given our circumstances? The problem isn't internal, is not about "criminal mind."

This idea of "criminal mind" is a persistent fascination among some students who hear about our classes at the jail. Calling up individual pathology rather than systemic scrutiny, it invites delectation and a respite from responsibility. You question a psych major, pushing back on her desire to learn more about the criminal mind, and she doesn't join the project after all; a missed opportunity for contact?

In gestalt, contact is desirable, a better state than alienation. Through a continual shifting of the "contact boundary" between self and other, environments, feelings, and ideas, we can come to "experience in awareness," and from this develop a capacity for change.[37] Like Fanon's epidermalization, contact can become a metabolic process that travels beneath the skin, making possible an encounter that reformulates. Contact is also neutral, since anything can happen here, and there is no recognition of power differentials.

In classrooms as "contact zones,"[38] power relations become part of the equation. People are "transformed in and through the encounter as subjects" in a pedagogy of "unpredictability."[39] What can be frightening and also beautiful here is this element of surprise in discovery—not just of the other, but also of a self you haven't known or been: the econ major whose hungry inquisitiveness resurfaces as a gentler desire for connection.

This process of re-encountering one another and our selves astonishes: we all have one more crime in us, and likewise one more possibility, and another; in this process we mean and matter, and without guarantees of any kind. Maybe this is its own redemption.

---

37. lechatdargent (Simon Stafford-Townsend), "Gestalt Essentials: Contact, the Contact Boundary, and Awareness," *Le Chat D'Argent*, December 27, 2011.

38. Mary Louise Pratt, "Arts of the Contact Zone," *Profession* (1991): 34.

39. Gaztambide-Fernandez, "Decolonization," 51.

All entities or bodies are characterized by a porosity that allows the outer world to flow through them.…Entities flow through each other, influencing and modifying each other in all sorts of ways.…In interfacing with other entities, these entities are transformed as they pass through the body becoming something else and taking on a new organization.…Yet that is not all. The material that passes through a body also transforms that body.

—larval subjects, "Porous Bodies"

Being in Class (3, again)

Later, you see layers: our different perspectives on language and power. Beginning with your own history as an early devotee of James Baldwin, later a conflicted teacher of "Adult Basic Education" and then student of Literacy at the institution where white linguist William Labov claimed African American Vernacular English as a legitimate language—and also the histories of others here. And since teaching is a practice of do-overs, you will share your own history, commitments, admirations more freely; admit resistance to their resistance; attend to what's happening in our remaking of each other.

> LESSON PLAN FOR 11/7/14
>
> I. Introductions
>
> II. We promised not to go back to *Push*—but to continue our conversation about language, & when-and-why we use different forms of it. Describe June Jordan's essay, "Nobody Mean More to Me Than You and the Future Life of Willie Jordan," which opens with a story like what happened here last week: she had assigned *The Color Purple,* and her mostly urban Black students said it didn't sound right, didn't look right, that they could hardly read it…and didn't like it but once they started analyzing the language, they realized that it was perfect for portraying the characters and their location (as we discussed about *Push*) and also that they'd never learned to read and write their own system of verbal communication: Black English (Jordan's term).… so Jordan designed and taught a new class on "The Art of Black English," in which the students excitedly figured out the rules and the values that it expressed (person centered, present tense, clear communication…) but then the brother of another student @ the college was killed by the police, and they tried to write a letter of protest in Black English because.…
>
> Read excerpt: How best to serve the memory of Reggie Jordan? Should we use the language of the killer—Standard English—in order to make our ideas acceptable to those controlling the kill-

ers? But wouldn't what we had to say be rejected, summarily, if we said it in our own language, the language of the victim, Reggie Jordan? But if we sought to express ourselves by abandoning our language wouldn't that mean our suicide on top of Reggie's murder? But if we expressed ourselves in our own language wouldn't that be suicidal to the wish to communicate with those who, evidently, did not give a damn about us/Reggie/police violence in the Black community? At the end of one of the longest, most difficult hours of my own life, the students voted, unanimously, to preface their individual messages with a paragraph composed in the language of Reggie Jordan.... With the completion of this introduction, nobody said anything.[40]

What would you say…?

III. Other sources to refer to/distribute if/as needed: NPR blog, "Five Reasons People Code Switch"[41] and blog entry from Adichie's novel *Americanah*: "To My Fellow Non-American Blacks: In America, You Are Black, Baby"

IV. Write for 10 minutes about a time when you code switched: tell that story by focusing on what you were trying to accomplish. Think about your audience: who are you telling this story to? What kind of language would best reach them? (You could imagine that you are writing a blog!)

V. Two visitors are going to teach us about another kind of code-switching: using the language of developmental biology

VI. Handouts: essays from next week's visitors writing to return, & "Willie Jordan," if wanted.

We read from the June Jordan piece, talk more explicitly now about language and power—about code-switching in jobs people have had and for jobs they desire, in home and stores and streets, here and in college, with different individuals. Again we are here and not-here. The range of experience and knowledge in the room coming into greater focus, and with this an acknowledgment that those of us sitting here are in quite different relations to all this, not just by "inside" and "out" but also by gradations of race, class, education, family that signal whether you're making, following,

---

40. JUNE Jordan, "Nobody Mean More to Me Than You and the Future Life of Willie Jordan," *Harvard Educational Review* 58, no. 3 (September 1988): 398.

41. Matt Thompson, "Five Reasons People Code Switch," Code Switch, National Public Radio, April 13, 2013.

discerning the rules. And the woman who describes herself as American not Black: A man from Walmart came into our work readiness class, I ask if he'd hire me given what he knows about me, he says yes; I say, Everyone coming to the cash register will speak you know, ghetto, what if I do that too, I mean that's who I'll be talking to, would I keep the job? No, he says.

Still: proper English is necessary to communicate with more people, such as someone from Germany who speaks English; and for success in society. Still, you hear the whisper that someone's better, smarter, something if using "proper English."

So it's easy and hard: we're all teachers and all learners, yes, and structural racism and classism in the context of 21st century-style mass incarceration keeps us in our discrete places. But is there some way this contact among human beings sitting together in hard plastic chairs in a room lit only from within can ripple out to disturb the very conditions of its existence? (And what to do with the individual acts you don't want to hear, acts of carelessness, selfishness, impulsivity, cruelty, all the more shadowy because you know that, if not protected by birth and material reality, you might be inside for half-forgotten crimes: DUI, drugs, harboring....)

If contact isn't just epidermal but can go deeper, become our metabolizing of difference, of the external into our organs, then can teaching make this metabolic process visible and available as a working method? There's this indeterminacy:

> How do we ever really know whether and how our actions lead to any kind of reconfiguration of ideas or restructuring of inequality? What kinds of new mythologies of the self are lurking behind what we decide to do and how we decide to proceed in the world?[42]

Although "the differential resides in the place where meaning escapes any final anchor point, slipping away to surprise or snuggle inside power's mobile contours,"[43] still: try to teach *into* the space of indeterminacy, neither refusing nor owning outcomes, opening up to what might occur.

42. Gaztambide-Fernandez, "Decolonization," 55–56.

43. Chela Sandoval, *Methodology of the Oppressed* (Minneapolis: University of Minnesota Press, 2000), 179.

Interlude: Poetry and Porosity

We cannot trust the boundaries distinguishing inside from out.

You and your colleague acknowledge to each other those drifting dream-thoughts just before sleep: yes, you are here on your own soft sheets with your bathroom down the hall and your sleep meds to take if needed, and yet just as you fall asleep you imagine yourself there, in that bunk, risking a flush in the night that might wake your cellee. What are these walls separating in from out, you from me, so real and yet are they?

> Suddenly, things that you think of as real—this cat over here, my cat, whose fur I can stroke—become the abstraction, an approximation of flowing, metamorphic processes, processes that are in some sense far more real than the entity I am stroking…[44]

In your dream you are a trans-prisoner: inside but allowed to leave at night, though this evening no, the guard on duty doesn't know you, doesn't care about your story…

You wake in your own bed with the light streaming in through the portal window and the door to the roof. "The state of emergency is also always a state of emergence," writes Rankine.[45] In emerging, you resist the instinct to brush away the mesh of co-habitation, look to recognize instead "the vital porosity that exists among all human groups in the twenty-first century."[46]

Being in Class (4)

On Good Friday yours is the only program to show up, and after some checking, they let you in. You have forgotten to come up with an intro question, and when you invite one, a woman suggests "what Easter means to me." You say you're Jewish and Easter is just quiet, and a college student who's also Jewish loved the chocolate bunnies that are chocolate straight through, felt betrayed by the hollow ones. A Chinese student learned about Easter in school, part of learning English. Then

---

44. Timothy Morton, "The Mesh," in *Environmental Criticism for the Twenty-First Century*, ed. Stephanie LeMenager, Teresa Shewry, and Ken Hiltner (New York: Routledge, 2011): 19–21.

45. Rankine, *Citizen: An American Lyric*, 126.

46. Goli M. McCarthy, Rezai-Rashti and Cathryn Teasley, "Race, Diversity, and Curriculum in the Era of Globilization," *Curriculum Inquiry* 39, no. 1 (January 2009): 93.

a woman you've known for the longest, a warm-faced woman who is writing a children's book, says she'll be the first to talk about religion—"Thank you, Jesus!, who continues to die for my sins, which are many and continuing." Rush of laughter. And this seems to you part of the constant claim, from the women, the officers, the court, that people are here for a reason; and the laughter a valve momentarily releasing the pressure to take individual responsibility. For your colleague, the holiday marks a brother's death at 24: driving drunk on Saturday night, dying on Easter morning. Whose responsibility?

You invite in a colleague, a poet and teacher. She asks, If the sky were the color of your heart, what color would it be? You make "masks" with your fingers over your faces, a way of getting new perspectives, until someone peels away her fingers, says I'm still in jail. You read aloud a poem, in which the window speaks, and the "still in jail" woman says, If these walls could talk.... The poet talks about being able to travel in your imagination, not to run away from your current reality, but also not to believe that it is the only reality. At the end of your session, she asks you all to write a second time, but not to share it.

Interlude: Credit/No Credit

You tussle with the credit/no credit question. Your "program" is really just a class, now two, and your college has committed to supply books and writing materials for the year, but this is temporary and credit isn't even on the table. You're trying to connect with a community college program that maybe could count your classes...

But there's the one woman who struggles to read, wow can she sing, and a woman who looks so tired she can't hold her head up; lost her glasses, can't see the print; speaks in Spanish to your student; is always on page one; and wants to be in this classroom space. What about access for those who can't jump the hoops for the for-credit program: disqualified by debt, too young too old, didn't graduate high school, didn't pass the entrance exam...?

You listen in on an online conversation going on among folks doing education in prisons, in response to the news that Pell Grants might be reinstated "on an experimental basis" for some incarcerated students. There is hope, also questions about how governmental support might impact program quality. And the issue of who deserves free education is a hot one—among prison employees, whose own families might not be able to afford college, and also among your students.

A corrections officer at the higher education in prison conference:

> I still have mixed feelings about education in prison. My daughter and I paid for our own education, and she is still paying off her loans. They are receiving a gift that they haven't earned, through their behavior, and they need to pay that forward; there needs to be a citizenship component.

And back in our college classroom, a student speaks passionately about her family: her immigrant mom (husband in prison), her brothers and sisters, aunts, cousins—who will pay for their education? Others argue that this is a false opposition: none of these people are winners, only global capitalism winning here.

You have a disturbing exchange of emails with the person who runs the community college for-credit prison education program, which is understaffed, in its last year of funding, and frustratingly stymied by issues of disqualification on the way in and rising debt and other challenges on reentry. Their completion stats are dismal. These difficulties stem from a snarl of obstacles seemingly disconnected from the intent of the program and its funders, and contradictory to wider claims about the value of education:

> Statistical evidence overwhelmingly confirms that a college education reduces recidivism, increases employment opportunities, and strengthens communities. The Justice-In-Education Initiative seeks to provide greater educational opportunities to those who are or have been incarcerated, as well as to enrich the academic life of faculty and students wishing to engage in issues of contemporary justice.[47]

47. "$1 Million Grant Awarded from Andrew W. Mellon Foundation for New Justice-in-Education Initiative," The Heyman Center for the Humanities at Columbia University, May 12, 2015.

Being in Class (5)

You are reading *Good Kings, Bad Kings*, a novel told from the perspectives of teenagers and staff in an institution for juveniles with disabilities. A woman who has worked for decades in rehab proposes the intro question: If you were disabled, would you want to be institutionalized or cared for by family? Most of you choose an institution—for fear of burdening our families—although later, digging into the novel, you also acknowledge the dangers and problems of "the system" in such a place.

Women arrive slowly, one tells you she "ratted out" the CO who tried to prevent her from coming to class; sent a note to the major, as he had told her to. Another who enters always with a long, lilting "heyyyy," is in-and-out today three times, and in between socializes loudly in the hallway. The repeated interruptions aggravate you.

You name the "bad kings," people who run systems and make money from them, yet they too are pieces in a larger game. Would your judgment of them change if you heard their stories? Your student says, the story doesn't justify the actions. You take it to the penal system, note that it's not random who's inside. Not the COs either, you think.

The writing prompt is a passage about being in solitary confinement inside the institution, and you hear about spending two and a half years in solitary, learning to be closer to God, to know herself better, to feel free when she's "just in jail," to love. And: We are not taught to be by ourselves, what does it matter if your movement is restricted? You'll get out later…now, read a book. Now when I close my eyes I can identify sounds, I know which guard it is by their walk.

In your planning session you debate what to do with the in-and-out woman: feel she's disrupting, using you to get off the unit, but hate to further constrain freedom of movement. When on Friday she enters and announces she's just here to get the new book, your colleague follows her into the hallway and says (as you've agreed) that you're offering a book group, value her contributions but not the interruptions; she nods, understands, says she's researching her case. Your colleague feels like a CO calling her out.

In search of your own connections with disability, you begin with head-shaking—no, you don't have these experiences—and then one by one uncover forgotten connections: the way she compensated for a loss of hearing at age 10, the fear in her family that the new baby could inherit schizophrenia. Disability, especially disability that comes with aging, creates a kind of porosity among you.

Interlude: Dining Out

You drink wine and consume pan-Asian with a group that includes your colleagues and students along with a visiting speaker: a luminary, an older African American scholar whose work on race, class, and incarceration reveals deep historical fault lines, cavernous in the present. By you sits a student who has found a location—found herself really—in our prison work. Over sesame noodles and tofu you talk about an article you read for class on the corporatization of schooling in New Orleans,[48] then segue into conversation about your feelings toward the correctional officers. Joining you, the luminary speaks eloquently about the necessity to critique these "guardians of the state," despite their raced and classed resemblances to the women they guard. You are quiet but your student speaks up passionately for the complex positions and lives of the COs. Our visitor listens carefully, accedes.

As you draft this chapter, President Obama announces the experimental Second Chance Pell Pilot Program, to be made available to a "limited number of prisoners." Education Secretary Arne Duncan argues for this on the grounds that "America is a nation of second chances" and that "it can also be a cost-saver for taxpayers."[49] This appeal to national pride on behalf of a humanitarianism embedded in individualism, sharpened by capitalism, seems

48. Kristen Buras, "Race, Charter Schools, and Conscious Capitalism: On the Spatial Politics of Whiteness as Property (and the Unconscionable Assault on Black New Orleans)," *Harvard Educational Review* (Summer, 2011): 296–330.

49. Nick Anderson, "Feds Announce New Experiment: Pell Grants for Prisoners," *Washington Post*, July 31, 2015.

formulated to cut across divisions in the populace.

Tyrone Werts' sentence was commuted after 37 years in a maximum security men's prison in your state. While inside, he played an active role in the Inside-Out Program, and on the outside he works with a reentry program. Tyrone talks about the impact of education on men inside, noting that "those guys who went to college in prison and those guys who didn't go to school…think totally different."[50]

"Thinking totally differently" might well line up well with reduced recidivism and expenditures, but begins from a different pivot point, opens up to a radically wider view. The difference in orientation is striking.

There's excitement on the higher education in prison websites. You hope, maybe, a fissure in the walls…

50. Gabrielle Emanuel, "Pell Grants For Prisoners: An Old Argument Revisited," *NPREd*, July 30, 2015.

Being in Class (6)

You enter with cardboard boxes, cupcakes with crazy colored icing and Philly pretzels with mustard, soda: a celebration for your last day of this school year. You are in the gym—displacing the much larger Muslim religious group, and you hear complaints about this in the waiting area—because this is the only place you can bring food.

A large echo-y room where you converge under basketball hoops. The loudspeaker periodically statics out your conversation, a kind of blackout poetry in motion. Is the guard who tilts back on his chair outside the glass enclosure close enough to hear?

Your book is *Orange is the New Black*, you're ready with questions and critique. When the first response is "this is prison lite," many nod. Then she offers in a feathery voice, dazzling smile: I identified with this book, I feel just like Piper!

What?! You're not like her, she has this, we don't have *any* of that! (Not to mention that she's white, comes from wealth, goes back to wealth and safety of a kind that seems just a fantasy from here.) Maybe because her prison is federal, they do say that's different.

I wish I was on as much Prozac as you must be!

No, she says, living here—in jail—it's *living*, for now, living where I am and experiencing what's here, being here.

(Yes, and 17–30 years, depending.)

A woman in a black headscarf calls out: Oh no, I'm not doing *that*, they've got you institutionalized.

Oh no, do not say that to me!

And later, your colleague: In what ways are we also becoming (or how are we already) institutionalized?

> Even those with genuine interest in change operate within the landscape of educational and correctional racism and classism… all players within the free market, creating a contradiction that is not often discussed: the interests in fighting "the system" are tempered by the fact that those actors are themselves "the system" and operate within the rabbit hole of the free market.[51]

51. Fasching-Varner, et. al, "Beyond School," 423.

Down this rabbit hole, the conversation winds deeper: Some women talk about what they've done to get here—answering the question you don't ask—and a college student, passionately: College students are doing a lot of this same stuff on our campuses, the drugs at least, and they're there, not here! You talk about who is here and who is not, who is living here and who refuses, the many names of refusal tattooed on arms, bellies, breasts.

A woman, animatedly: Mostly I just sleep, that's the only way I can get through the time. (Just last week you learned from your students that this woman—mostly absent from our class this semester, or sitting silent and disengaged, or walking out—was an energized, highly involved participant in the other class last semester.)

Side-stepping the split between abolitionists and prison educators, Angela Davis maintains that you should work to "create more humane, habitable environments for people in prison without bolstering the permanence of the prison system."[52] And your colleague: But making this environment "more habitable" can indeed help to make it more permanent.

52. Angela Davis, *Are Prisons Obsolete?* (New York: Seven Stories Press, 2003), 103.

Again: the problem of your being here.

You have pulled in tight to hear each other over the crabby PA, sweet and salty melding on your tongues as you struggle with your lives and beyond your lives, with what you can do here and how to change this system in which you're all—with increasing clarity—interconnected. And you're feeling that not unfamiliar sense that even as you all reach hard, the questions too are hard, so gnarled and knotty, until finally she breaks in, the continuing sinner who you've known since coming here, who's been here years longer than anyone is supposed to stay: No wait, and you've never heard her talking urgent like this: Can I just say something? What I do, what we try to do is connect with each other, I try to be there for you… All are listening now. Like I'll say your name for something good, I'll let you know about an opportunity, I'll stick with you…we got more power together.

> *Weaving between what is immediately available as a story— and what your imaginations are reaching toward.*[53]

[53. Gordon, *Ghostly Matters*, 4.]

The end of class is rushed: the officer is off shift but his replacement is not here, so he's on you to leave. You go around, say a word about where you are: troubled, angry, complicated, upset…not the litany of inspired, content, thankful from other classes. A lanky and regal woman who often brings a sharp social analysis gives you this feedback for next semester: You've brought us books that really delve into the questions, now we need some solutions!

And then they are gone and you are emerging through gates and into the balmy brightness of a May afternoon. It is the Friday before graduation, and one of your students, a senior whose focus and ebullience has helped to carry your group, is crying, hard.

Begin Again, with Power, Relationship, and Transitivity
One of your students tells this story:

> In our small group there were two college students and one incarcerated woman. When it came time to present our work, that woman said, well I'm the only one in this group so I'll have to present! I said what do you mean, we're here, and she said, yeah but you'll be walking outtahere, we won't be partying with you tonight.

You develop relationships that occupy the space in between, that holding space of interactional possibility. Inside, one of the women has written a children's book and seeks your advice, another shares the graphic novel she's working on, inspired by *Persepolis*; on the outside, women's lives take them into nearby neighborhoods, and you catch sight of a familiar shoulder in the Italian market, your student is sure she glimpses someone on the train, meets another in her social work placement. There is joy and connection here, longing, questions.

> During the lesson planning class [in the jail] when someone stood up to be the teacher, watching her move around the classroom animatedly made me realize that movement is something we actually may not want to worry about restricting. I get the sense movement/closeness of bodies is so heavily policed already, by specifically shying away from activities involving more free movement, we are perpetuating this body policing.[54]

You make decisions about your class sessions—to include more movement, to bring in poetry or biology, to question the system you are part of—and yet you hit walls.

> In our last week of the book club, we talked more explicitly about the system of mass incarceration than ever before.... It was heartening to hear women speak about the system, and exciting to hear a woman ask how we fight the system. However, that question also upset me because I do not know the answer.[55]

54. sara.gladwin, "more on the subject of the barometer," February 25, 2014 (6:11 p.m.).

55. HCRL, "Final Field Paper," May 9, 2015 (2:58 p.m.).

As you "attempt to walk [and live] on the rickety bridge between self and other,"[56] sometimes it feels impossible to grasp both awareness of power relations and interactional possibility, and yet knowing this contradiction intimately, again and again, is what you are doing here.

And just as you come to see how power must shape the curriculum, you stop short: don't join "the church of 'everything is fucked up, so throw up your hands,' another form of "anesthesia."[57] Ongoing effort that insists on neither abjuration nor absolution is hard to come by. And perhaps requires a different grammar:

> More common in romance languages than in English, the verb form of solidarity—to solidarize with—is a transitive verb.... The questions that transitivity suggests have to do with our willingness to act in the world, to use Stuart Hall's (1986) famous words, "without guarantees." What unimagined and unimaginable outcomes might become available if we were willing to risk the possibility that we simply do not know where we are going?[58]

56. Peggy Phelan, qted. in Sweeney, 250–51.

57. Ta-Nehisi Coates, "How I Met Your Mother," *The Atlantic In Paris*: Dispatch #12, August 19, 2013.

58. Gaztambide-Fernandez, "Decolonization," 54–55.

Exit

At the end of our session, the poet asks us to write a second time, but not to share. We all have to plan our exits, she says.

"The true leap consists in introducing invention into existence."[59]

You stand at Holmesburg Station, and it is cold and windy, hot and still; empty because you've just missed the train back into the city. Again. This is a haunted station, the roofs of old factory buildings just visible over the barren rise of gravel and weeds and iron tracks, and you think, the trains don't run here anymore. There is no way back. You think this as the express goes by at a speed so fast and frightening it's like a cartoon of energy moving through a sound barrier.

59. Frantz Fanon, qted. in Gaztambide-Fernandez, "Decolonization," 61.

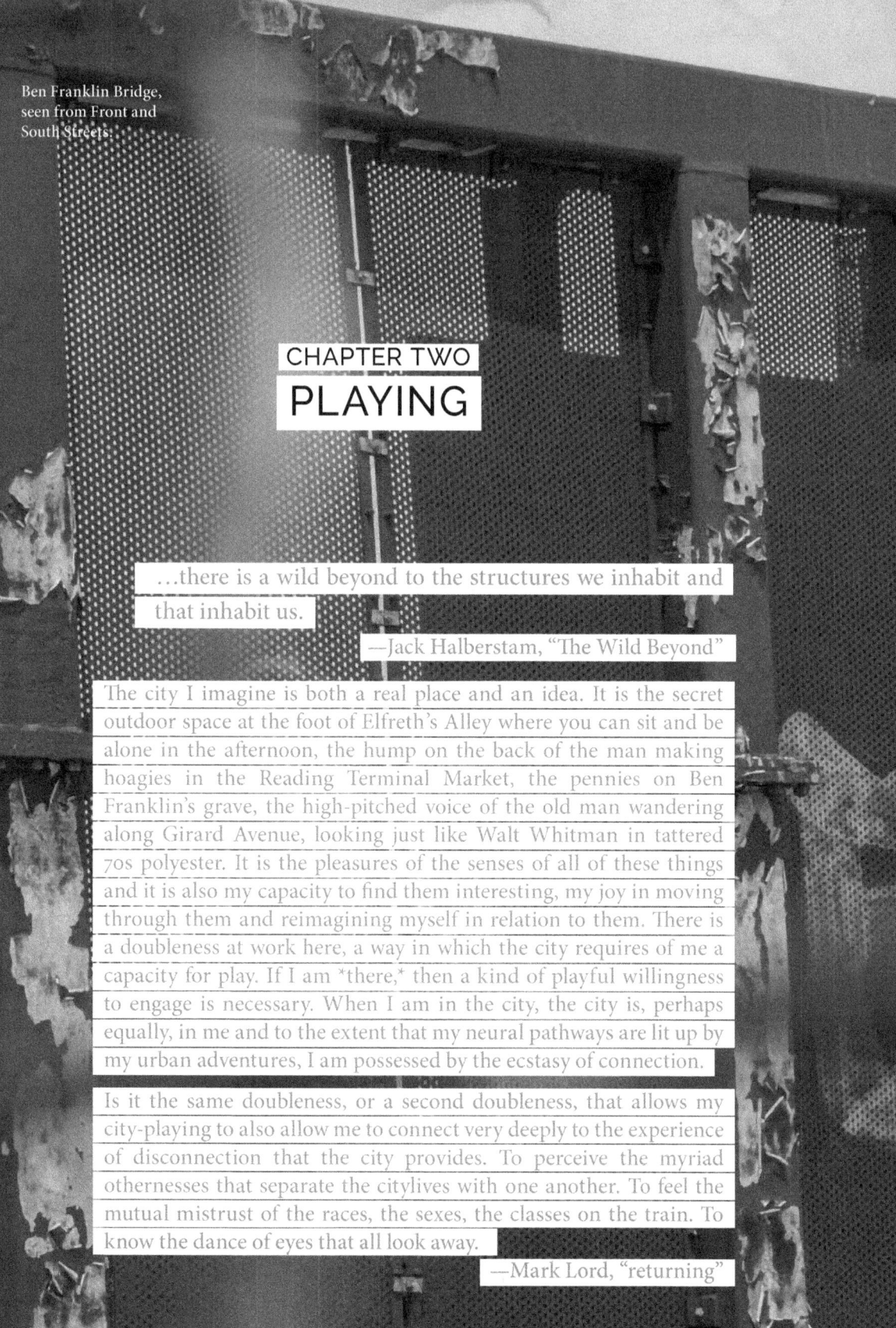

Ben Franklin Bridge, seen from Front and South Streets.

CHAPTER TWO
PLAYING

> …there is a wild beyond to the structures we inhabit and that inhabit us.
>
> —Jack Halberstam, "The Wild Beyond"

The city I imagine is both a real place and an idea. It is the secret outdoor space at the foot of Elfreth's Alley where you can sit and be alone in the afternoon, the hump on the back of the man making hoagies in the Reading Terminal Market, the pennies on Ben Franklin's grave, the high-pitched voice of the old man wandering along Girard Avenue, looking just like Walt Whitman in tattered 70s polyester. It is the pleasures of the senses of all of these things and it is also my capacity to find them interesting, my joy in moving through them and reimagining myself in relation to them. There is a doubleness at work here, a way in which the city requires of me a capacity for play. If I am *there,* then a kind of playful willingness to engage is necessary. When I am in the city, the city is, perhaps equally, in me and to the extent that my neural pathways are lit up by my urban adventures, I am possessed by the ecstasy of connection.

Is it the same doubleness, or a second doubleness, that allows my city-playing to also allow me to connect very deeply to the experience of disconnection that the city provides. To perceive the myriad othernesses that separate the citylives with one another. To feel the mutual mistrust of the races, the sexes, the classes on the train. To know the dance of eyes that all look away.

—Mark Lord, "returning"

Being T/here: The Doubleness of Play

When Mark Lord and I, who have been friends for many years, decide that we want to spend more time together, working and playing with the sorts of experiences and questions that matter most to us both—and that we hope might matter a lot to our students, beginning their first semester at Bryn Mawr—our new course on "Play in the City"[1] gets its start. We know we can have fun co-designing a course around questions of how we construct, experience, and learn in the act of play; that we can use that concept to unsettle some of our students' notions of what constitutes work, and education, and the work of education; and that it will bring us a particular pleasure to make the city of Philadelphia, eleven miles to the east of the College, our primary playground.

Our course will highlight play as a "way of knowing," of being both present and distant, simultaneously connected and disconnected from what we might encounter. We intend to use play as "an instrument for staging various kinds of open-ended exploratory interactions…producing, questioning, and overturning different forms of life."[2] We hope that our students will discover, thereby, how intellectual work can be a form of play, play a form of intellectual work—and so unsettle conventional understandings of education as a process of completing tasks with known outcomes. We're hoping, too, that they'll grab on to the pleasures of working this-a-way, begin to shift their sense of how stakes can shift in such a game: perhaps in some ways lower, in others higher, than in assigned tasks?

Play is structured by the environment in which it occurs; we also believe that it has the potential for re-structuring that space, re-drawing the frame in which it is performed. Using Philadelphia as our primary "text," a complex site open to observation, interpretation, and reinterpretation, gives us a space where we and our students can shape and re-shape their own identities, the way education is done, and perhaps what happens in the city as well.

1. "Play in the City," Emily Balch Seminar, Bryn Mawr College, Fall 2013.

2. Paul B. Armstrong, "The Politics of Play: The Social Implications of Iser's Aesthetic Theory," *New Literary History* 31 (2000): 211–23.

So, from the get-go: this project is political. As Adeline Koh explains,

> the ability to imagine, create, and live alternative realities…[is] the most political of acts…*play reimagines the world*…create[s] the potential to change it…"break[s] down our conventional, habit-dulled certainties about what the world is and has to be."³

For both Mark and me, the city has long functioned as such a site of intertwined personal and intellectual exploration, even (dare I say?) liberation. As he (re)tells the story, I first found my way to Philadelphia from the rural South, "looking to lose something, a set of familiar associations and ties, to gain anonymity and a capacity to play," while he came in from closer by, "was feeling the vapidity of my suburban life without associations or meaningful connections and came seeking events/scenes to tie myself to." Our points of departure differ, but each of us finds an alternative in Philadelphia, "the sense of excitement that comes from having been excused from the unitary identity you are cast into in your town/family/landscape of origin."⁴

Excused, by the complexities of the city, from our unitary identities.

In arranging for our students to spend time exploring Philadelphia, we are also seeking ways for them to expand their own sense of identity. We think that, through their connections to us, to one another, and to the city, they might learn ways of nourishing themselves, socially, emotionally, intellectually, culturally, spiritually, politically. Some of them will already be intrepid social and intellectual adventurers. We're hoping that—if we can extend the web upholding them beyond our suburban campus, if they can come to recognize that their resources encompass the larger metropolitan area—all of them might become more resilient in facing the pleasures and challenges of life in college and thereafter.

In "Urban Friction," an essay we will use in the course, Jonah Lehrer shows us some ways in which the city can exacerbate the sort

3. Adeline Koh, "The Political Power of Play," *Digital Pedagogy Lab*, April 3, 2014.

4. mlord, "poor b.b. (plus)," May 6, 2013 (11:21 a.m.).

of creative tensions we are seeking to pose for our students. Lehrer notes that "knowledge spillovers" happen in densely populated spaces, where the "sheer disorder of the metropolis" forces mingling across "social distances" and a "range of worldviews." Otherwise, he observes, everyone will "naturally self-segregate, choosing to spend time with people who are just like ourselves. (Sociologists refer to this failing as the self-similarity principle)."[5]

5. Jonah Lehrer, "Urban Friction," in *Imagine: How Creativity Works* (Boston: Houghton Mifflin, 2012), 182–83.

Lehrer vividly describes the entry of suburbanites into an expansive, diverse urban space, where they experience "'informational entropy' (the presence of disorder—think of a crowded sidewalk)." The "us" and "we" for whom he speaks here are clearly not urban dwellers, but those newly encountering the city: "the metropolis…constantly introduces us to the unexpected and curious….knowledge leaks from everywhere…we must engage with strangers and strange ideas…"[6]

6. Lehrer, "Urban Friction," 202.

Authorizing our students to attend to "leakage" and encounter "strangeness" indicates our plan to *use* play pedagogically. This is not exactly the same as *playing*, and hints at ways that the outcomes of our pedagogy may exceed our intentions.…

Lehrer celebrates such "spontaneous mixing, all those unpredictable encounters," as keeping the city "alive."[7] A similar interruption of design is also well demonstrated in Philadelphia's city plan, which Mark glosses this way:

7. Lehrer, "Urban Friction," 211.

> City Hall itself is a 19th century "play" on the Original Grid, covering over the Center Square. (That a part of this square is currently excavated delights me btw.) Even the grid is a slightly playful attempt to insert civic meaning between the two rivers, which are themselves an ecocentric "grid" of an irregular system. All the civic attempts to organize and regulate meaning in the city are subverted daily by the needs/desires/habits of actual people. And part of the majesty of the cityspace is its absolute resistance to efforts to fix its meaning—but also its reluctance to turn into complete chaos.[8]

8. mlord, "not changing mine," May 8, 2013 (6:19 a.m.).

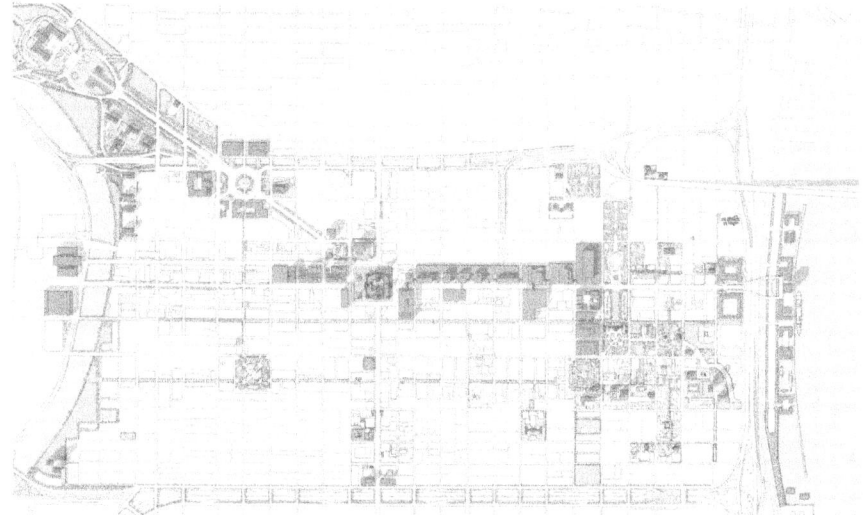

"The Site Plan," illustration from the Philadelphia City Planning Commission, 1963, in *Imagining Philadelphia: Edmund Bacon and the Future of the City*, ed. Scott Gabriel Knowles (Philadelphia: University of Pennsylvania, 2009). By permission of the Philadelphia City Planning Commission.

The multiple ways in which Philadelphia resists all "efforts to fix its meaning" makes designing a course in the city itself an endless exercise in meaningful play. Mark and I trade articles, books, websites, films. He dares me to make our conversations—and all the planning they entail—public. I do. He supplements this linear on-line record of our thinking-in-tandem[9] with a more tactile, spatialized process, using variously colored post-it notes to make visual the different dimensions of our emerging class. We take jaunts, together and apart, to various sites, meet up in city parks to brainstorm next steps, plot multiple trips for our students. Some of them will enter already savvy about how to take the commuter train, the high-speed line, the trolley; others will need to be guided by us into increased independence, as they travel first in small groups, then pairs, finally alone…

We design a course demonstrating our belief that classrooms and other conventional learning places are arbitrarily bounded containers that can overflow, short-circuit—and be re-ignited by playing and learning "outside." We select Serendip Studio, "a digital ecosystem, fueled by serendipity," as our "public playground,"[10] an

9. "Planning to Play," Bryn Mawr College, May 10, 2013–August 28, 2013.

10. *Serendip Studio*, Bryn Mawr College, 1994–2017.

on-line site where students will post, and we will respond to, all their writing. We order tickets to 17 *Border Crossings*, a series of short plays by Thaddeus Phillips, each examining the complicated process of stepping from one country to another.[11] We will also draw our students' attention to the Jewish *eruv*, intentional spaces now demarcated by clear, nylon fishing wire, strung between existing landmarks in Philadelphia.[12]

In making such choices, we are refusing the boundedness of campus and city, "inside" and "out." That refusal is a playful political intervention in the conventional maintenance of borders. We will repeatedly cross such boundaries with our students, together tracing out possible trajectories of play and threat, risk and refusal, as we "test the possibilities of contact" in "an emergent field of uncertainties."[13] Recognizing the boundaries of inside and out, acknowledging ways that play is often discouraged in classrooms, we look not only to go out but also to bring play into our classrooms.

Even before our students arrive, multiple cracks appear in our plan. (How could they not, given the unpredictable outcomes of playful exchange?) Throughout the summer, we negotiate with various administrators, trying to cobble together enough money to pay for each of our students to take the train into the city seven times, and to pay, as well, for their explorations there. Although Bryn Mawr has long advertised its proximity to the "expansive, global, civic community" of Philadelphia, it has not yet put many resources into funding access to Center City. We understand something about the economic challenges of running a small liberal arts college, but also find ourselves provoked by this particular instantiation: more attention is given to marketing our access to the city than to making it easy for our students to get there.

When our good friend and colleague Alice Lesnick explicitly re-frames that tension, we see how much she's raised the stakes of our game. During our summer of planning, Alice suggests that we think more carefully about whether our focus on "play" in the city

11. Thaddeus Phillips, 17 *Border Crossings*, FringeArts, November 13–17, 2013.

12. Joseph Brin, "Borders And Boundaries, Invisible To Most," *Hidden City Philadelphia*, October 23, 2013.

13. Deborah Bird Rose et al., "Ravens at Play," *Cultural Studies Review* 17, no. 2 (September 2011): 340.

might run the danger of exoticizing the space, making it seem as though we're framing it as a playground for those of us who will be coming in from our suburban college.[14] Alice asks, "Who is the 'We'?":

> This question seems to be flickering around a good deal of this thread. When your classes go "into" the city—what "we" will be so constituted? Whose city? When extrinsic and when intrinsic? What "we" pees on trees? How much of being within a "we" is about policing, or defining, boundaries? I've been remembering the old Take Back the Night times when I was in high school. Was that play? I remember feeling loose of some fear I knew when a girl in Philadelphia. Are today's Slut Walks play? Or, like Occupy, are they leveraging play as discourse?[15]

14. alesnick, "play/ground," May 6, 2013 (5:56 a.m.).

15. alesnick, "Who Is the We?" May 10, 2013 (10:50 a.m.).

Coming to college may require our students to take up the complexities of its location.

The politics of difference are now in play.

The Problematics of Practice

In early September, we welcome twenty-seven first-semester students, and so begin to enlarge the scope of our game. The arc of the semester plays out largely in the way we imagine—which means that, like all courses (but perhaps more so?) it is full of the unexpected. The students are (mostly) engaged, (mostly) delighted by our frequent jaunts into the city, (mostly) willing to explore both the experiential and theoretical dimensions of our work. They are simultaneously resistant to all of the above, especially as they begin to discover how political it can be to "play."

Early on, we ask them to use Robin Henig's "Taking Play Seriously" to reflect on their own childhood experiences of play, and then to consider the relationship between such experiences and their current intellectual life. In response to Henig's argument that "imaginative play…creates a person…who believes in possibilities… in acting out one's own capacity for the future," some of our students offer poignant accounts of being denied this "more diverse and responsive behavioral repertory."[16] Cathy Zhou, who has come to Bryn Mawr from Chengdu, China, writes:

> The essay of Henig totally recalled my memory of family times, when my father always complains how technologies have been ruining my childhood: I have never climbed trees or catched an insect in my childhood....But there was little time for playing since I was attending preschool classes and take piano, drawing, handwriting, taekwondo at the same time. [My parents] don't want me to be left behind by other kids, and arranged a busy schedule for me.[17]

Our students are even more tightly scheduled now, as they figure out how to juggle their new obligations at Bryn Mawr; our invitation to embrace play as a version of intellectual work provokes some grumbling about giving "carefully hoarded time for trips… between working on Saturdays, rehearsing for a play, and finishing homework."[18] The students' reticence is a reminder of the pressures at an academic institution where playful exploration is elusive and seems pitted against the call to accomplish, to own, to earn one's way through, to support others.

Acknowledging these constraints, we still insist that our students "unbind" from the classroom, go out from the line of seats or the circle of chairs that have (mostly) circumscribed their learning, and begin to engage the world more directly, with less teacherly mediation—and then reflect on what happens. Like Deborah Bird Rose and her co-authors in "Ravens at Play" (a lovely, deep piece on multispecies possibilities for social interaction), we have only inklings, setting out, of the diverse opportunities that may be "both opened up and foreclosed by any kind of play we might choose or be able to engage in with others."[19] We saunter out for adventure, planning to make ourselves "at home" in the city. The hard questions of cultural crossing—of access and belonging, appropriation and trespass, the politics of "playing"—are yet to come.

On our first trip, we participate in one of the productions of the

16. Robin Henig, "Taking Play Seriously," *New York Times*, February 17, 2008.

17. Cathy Zhou, "Personal Reflections," September 11, 2013 (1:20 p.m.).

18. Claire Romaine, "Stubborn Writer," December 19, 2013 (9:24 p.m.).

19. Rose et al., "Ravens at Play," 341.

Fringe Arts Festival. Headphones on, we sit side-by-side at tables in the reading room of The Free Library of Philadelphia, following cues—some written, some whispered—that guide us through a pile of books in front of us. We are each performer and spectator in *The Quiet Volume*, a self-generated performance that engages us in a "drama of turning pages, pointing fingers and eerily drifting thoughts," and so invites us to "listen to what's going on in our heads when we read."[20]

Quickly noticing that a number of our companions at the library tables are not listening to instructions through headphones, our students realize that they are participating in much larger, explicitly inequitable theater, both in the library and on the streets. They began to notice some "cracks" in the classic urban studies texts we've assigned them; the theories of Lewis Mumford, George Simmel, Sharon Zukin[21] seem distant from their own experiences, romantic versions of what they are encountering. Another student from China, writing under the name "Everglade," reports feeling

> dumbfounded…by so many homeless people in the brightest and most fancy part of the city…here they have the freedom to sleep in the perfect Logan Square or under the statue of a war hero, skateboard in Love Square, and look so vibrant under the warm Saturday sun. Just a few steps away, in the small streets straying from the broad and gorgeous Benjamin Franklin Pkwy, their scrawls are everywhere, and when they are merely standing there talking I can sense their movement like dancing. This is what Sharon Zukin says, "a kind of low-down but truer sense of where the self can develop".
>
> After wandering for a while, I went in the Free Library—also the territory of the homeless. I sat among them and started to enjoy the Quiet Volume…they were talking and smiling. They seemed warm, too, in their hoodies and caps.
>
> It seemed that I was so interested in the homeless people and considered them artistic hermits in the city. But then I came face to face to one. It was a total shock, when I was sitting on the terrace looking for my water kettle in my bag and a straggly old

20. "The Quiet Volume," FringeArts, August 2, 2013.

21. Lewis Mumford, "What Is a City?" *Architectural Record* (1937); George Simmel, "The Metropolis and Mental Life" (1950); "Sharon Zukin, The Cultures of Cities (1995)", urban-culturalstudies, May 21, 2012.

> man just walked towards me and started murmuring. Startled, I said I don't understand English and left. Well I wasn't lying, because I didn't understand a single word he said. But as I walked away I heard a sentence that I could catch, "I just wanna give you a compliment!" This should be a great example of the "serendipity" that I've long craved, but what did I do? I ran away in panic, maybe because the stereotypical fear of the homeless people. I felt regretful afterward—I should've chatted with him and explored lots of things that'd surprise me....
>
> So I'm not as open-minded as I thought. I should, and I will, open up more to different people and ideas, to surprise and excitement, to serendipity.[22]

22. Everglade, "Open to Serendipity," September 16, 2013 (12:01 p.m.).

Throughout this book, we celebrate the serendipity of surprise, advocate for openness to unexpected possibility. We also spend some time on the possible downside of such experiences: something unwelcome could happen, the students may not feel able to say "no" to what they encounter. We don't attend much, however, to the jolt of awareness of our own limitations, the disappointment in ourselves for not being able to seize a new opportunity. Everglade names such experiences here: how her trip begins playfully, becomes threatening; the value and also the risk of her coming to the city, the sense of exposure this entails.

Everglade reports panic, fear, and disappointment; a classmate describes another unsettling encounter in Philadelphia that leaves her feeling hopeless. Agatha Basia, who has lived in a number of different cities in Africa, Europe, and the U.S., begins her account by challenging Mumford's observation that "The city…is art; the city…is the theater":

> Is that the responsible thing to do? Make art and poetry of human struggle?
>
> I walk downstairs to the washroom in the Free Library in Philadelphia, because I still have a few minutes before the fringe festival performance begins…
>
> I go into the third stall. There is no latch on the door; instead,

> the hole where the latch should have been is stuffed with a thick wad of toilet paper. It holds the door closed so I don't mind.
>
> There is a woman in the stall to my left. She is sobbing. I don't know if she is standing or sitting, but she is shuffling her feet nervously. And she is sobbing, mumbling in a panicky voice. I can't understand everything she says because it doesn't seem to all be in English. But I can hear her words —between sharp, ragged breaths—that nobody knows, don't nobody know. Nobody.
>
> And her voice sounds like pain and fear. Airy, high and small. Choking and weary and trembling. Small.
>
> And I can't say anything. I can't ask her what is wrong or if there is any way I can help. There is much more than just the wall of a bathroom stall between us. I leave my stall, walk to the sinks and wash my hands. The woman is still in the stall, crying, speaking to herself as I dry my hands and walk outside. And that is that. I remain simply with the voice and tearful, frightened words of a faceless woman in a stall next to mine....[23]

Like Everglade, unable to make contact with someone who is unsheltered, Agatha places her sense of individual hopelessness in a larger context, believing that multiple social structures—"much more than just the wall of a bathroom stall"—keep her from speaking to her neighbor. On our first trip to the city, "play" has quickly become unsteady, destabilizing, bringing students face to face with social inequities, leaving some of them worried and troubled. We have moved rapidly from the celebration of undirected play, with which our course began, into a range of more complex and subversive forms, both experiential and theoretical. Henig's claims that "the aim is play itself"—with "unproductivity" its essential aspect, "open actions," "occasions of pure waste"[24]—are replaced now by challenging encounters with other people.

We begin to ask if we might use play to unsettle such situations, "to defy orthodoxy and top-down power, and envision a new society."[25] We read Mary Flanagan's assertion that "play is never

23. Agatha Basia, "Spectacle," September 16, 2013 (12:13 a.m.).

24. Henig, "Taking Play Seriously."

25. Pat Kane, "Protean Activism: The Constitutive Politics of Play," *The Play Ethic*, July 12, 2009.

innocent," follow her accounts of various forms of "critical play," challenges to the status quo that are intended to shift paradigms, the boundaries of what is permissible.[26] Slowly, as the students research a wide range of artists who "play critically," spend some time themselves alone in silence—first in a cell in Eastern State Penitentiary, next with a work of art they choose at The Barnes Foundation—then map their own trips into the city, exploring it in accord with their own desires and designs, they begin to recognize ways in which being playful in undirected but curious and thoughtful ways might guide them into larger questions, and also into larger meanings.

We now hear named some of the risks of what we are up to. We learn about Jeremy Betham's concept of "deep play," reprised first by Clifford Geertz,[27] then Diane Ackerman: "any activity in which 'the stakes are so high that…it is irrational for anyone to engage in it at all, since the marginal utility of what you stand to win is grossly outweighed by the disutility of what you stand to lose.'"[28]

As we begin sharing examples, comparing stories about when we each might have experienced deep play, some students struggle with understanding the role of such "irrational" activity, how appropriate high risk might be in the classroom. I describe teaching as my own preferred form of deep play. A student realizes that she has had the experience of playing deeply at another academic task: Yancy, who has also come to Bryn Mawr from China, and who finds it difficult to speak in class, articulates her own experiences

26. Mary Flanagan, *Critical Play: Radical Game Design* (Cambridge: MIT Press, 2009), 1–15.

27. Clifford Geertz, "Deep Play: Notes on the Balinese Cockfight," in *The Interpretation of Cultures* (New York: Basic Books, 1973).

28. Diane Ackerman, "Chapter One," *Deep Play* (New York: Random House, 1999).

> in the library on Friday night, with my computer. Silence is everywhere, and there is no one else in my eyes. Friday night, the wonderful night, because others take part in parties or play in their room, the library seems so spacious for me. I sip some hot milk and stare at my screen, there are massive codes here…my spirit is concentrated in those codes…I do not care how much time I will spend in this work, and how difficult the work is. Time is passing, the milk is cooler. I just sit here silently, tapping on the keyboard…. Those codes are…regular, beautiful and creative. The code is a new language used by people to express

> the beauty of the world and I just need to use a simple media to turn the codes into pictures to understand the writers' ideas. Isn't it amazing and fantastic?
>
> I know when I am writing codes, I experience the deep play… based on mental happiness…special because of its meaning and privacy…. I write the codes like the pilgrim looks for Mekka. We both need something to find the meaning of our lives.[29]

Slowly, other students begin to engage in writing that is deeply playful. Their work becomes more experimental. Mark and I create "text renderings" of their essays (noting words, phrases, sentences that have "heat," or "energy"); then they do this for one another. These risky attempts put them into new relation with one another. They make (mostly verbal) mosaics out of Terry Tempest Williams' fragmented text, *Finding Beauty in a Broken World*;[30] then mosaics—(mostly) visual, though one takes the form of a sound track[31]—to represent their spirited excursions to Philadelphia's Magic Gardens, then tracking down the street mosaics of Isaiah Zagar.

The students come to understand mosaic as a critical practice, a mode of playing with different juxtapositions of both visual and verbal material.

They learn to play with point of view, sharpening and shifting their "lenses," making them "distinctive," then "collective."

They take more risks in their writing, finding doorways and openings into play. One student says that

> this course gave me…the decision to write essays about questions that I don't have the answer to. This is terrifying…. But, more recently…I feel quite fearless…No reservations. No worrying about what Anne will say or what my classmates will say or (oh my!) what my future employers might say…. After I take away the intimidation and the roadblocks, I just go. And it feels like joy. Really, I feel quite joyous writing this right now…[32]

Another student, Paola Bernal, finds that writing "without filters"[33] leads her into sharp political critique, an awareness of how

29. Yancy, "Deep Play," November 18, 2013 (12:04 a.m.).

30. Terry Tempest Williams, *Finding Beauty in a Broken World* (New York: Vintage, 2009).

31. Agatha Slobada, "Julia of Eyes," Soundcloud.

32. tomahawk, "Ruminations on the Class," December 20, 2013 (2:38 a.m.).

33. pbernal, "Learning to Write Without Filters," December 18, 2013 (3:20 p.m.).

92 | STEAL THIS CLASSROOM

Phoenix, *A Mosaic With Pomegranate*, Photography Mosaic, Submitted for Play in the City, Sept. 22, 2013.

cultural boundaries are policed. Paola appreciates

> that museums ultimately mean well and all they want is to preserve these collections for more and more people to have a chance to enjoy as well. But, for my mother and many other underprivileged people who didn't have the opportunity of receiving an education or the chance to pursue higher education, art museums have become an unwelcoming place…. Art Museums are…feared.[34]

In Paola's experience, The Barnes Foundation

> is quiet and rigid; I'm walking in an architect's wet dream. This isn't a place for the people to learn about art, it's a showcase for the pompous and wealthy to wander and critique at their leisure. I feel like I'm invading someone's space, someone's dream. It doesn't feel right, I don't feel welcomed….[35]

Paola and her classmates begin to ask hard questions about intellectual property: should art belong to particular individuals, or be accessible to all? What about forgery, understood as admiration and celebration? What about re-mixing?[36] On their last foray into Philadelphia, when each student is traveling alone (as it turns out, in the midst of a snowstorm), they are not just playing in but with the city, tracing musical clefs in the snow, making their marks on a landscape where, as Tim Edensor and his colleagues observe, "play may best be conceptualized as always potentially emergent, with the potential to shift the actuality of the moment in unforeseen ways, generating encounters which could always have been otherwise."[37]

Still emerging for our students, as this semester ends, are the problematics our friend Alice named the summer before: "Who is the 'We'?" "Whose" is the city? Sited differently, Alice's questions echo those Lisa Delpit asked twenty years ago, in *Other People's Children: Cultural Conflict in the Classroom*. Delpit argued that process writing approaches fail to provide low-income students with access to the "codes of power" of "Standard" English:

> There is a political power game that is…being played, and if they

34. pbernal, "Art Museums: Do they enlighten or isolate people?" December 10, 2013 (2:48 a.m.).

35. pbernal, "Garden of Eden," November 25, 2013 (12:19 a.m.).

36. tomahawk, "The Barnes Foundation and Intellectual Property," December 1, 2013 (10:33 p.m).

37. Tim Edensor et al., "Playing in Industrial Ruins: Interrogating Teleological Understandings of Play in Spaces of Material Alterity and Low Surveillance," in *Urban Wildscapes*, eds. Anna Jorgensen and Richard Keenan (New York: Routledge, 2011), 65–79.

want to be in on that game there are certain games that they too must play.... Only after acknowledging the inequity of the system can the teacher's stance then be "Let me show you how to cheat!"³⁸

> 38. Lisa Delpit, *Other People's Children: Cultural Conflict in the Classroom* (1995; rpt. The New Press, New York: 2006), 39–40, 165.

In Delpit's formulation, play is very serious, its possibilities circumscribed by variable access to power. Our course has been highlighting similar questions: What enables play, we ask again and again—and what prevents it? Who gets to name the stakes at play? Who gets to play in the city, as in the classroom? How much security do "we" need to have, before we are "free" to take the risks of playing freely? Is this never possible? Does play always take place within restraints? And also always entail unpredictable consequences?

Like the unexpected interactions that Deborah Bird Rose, Stuart Cooke, and Thom Van Dooren trace with coyotes, then ravens, our own pedagogical play enters into and sets in motion a precarious, shifting landscape in which we encounter not only others but also ourselves as "strange strangers," whose gestures puzzle and elude us, eliciting responses we didn't know we had, restraints we weren't aware of, hadn't recognized as necessary. Rose, Cooke, and Van Dooren say they are "willing to test the possibilities of contact, but...at the same time suspicious of where our attention might lead." Reflecting on the consequences, for other species, of playing with humans, Rose and her colleagues ask,

> Was the best gift we could offer actually a restraint—that we would withhold ourselves...our play? We couldn't play in good faith, because while the game was a transient moment for us, it was a trajectory toward death for [them].... What we might become in the contact zone was thus constrained....³⁹

> 39. Rose et al., "Ravens at Play," 341.

We end our semester with many related questions about our own attempts to "play in the city": Has our concept of a playground been based on a presumption of naïve users? How transient have our interactions really been? What have been the consequences of our play for those who live in Philadelphia, or for others who may visit there? Should we have played more expansively—tried harder to make contact—or been more constrained? How might we have acted differently, more thoughtfully, more responsibly?

Agatha reprises the time we have spent together by saying that she still feels uncomfortable "about the concept of 'playing in the city,' as if the city were a playground. It's not easy for me to ignore all the hardships and political issues and absurd human drama that is played out in a city…."[40]

The experiences of other students lead them, like Agatha, to develop critical perspectives on play, identity, education, the city-suburban divide, social inequities…for these students, now, the "usual conventions of property, commodity and value" no longer pertain. Recognizing play in the city as a space of "productive, generative practices," "potentially transformative" and "subversive of power," they offer a strong articulation of what going "outside the classroom" might mean.[41] They query the sort of education offered on campus, and invite larger questions about what is "proper" both here and elsewhere.

Mark and I are left, too, with questions about the relationship between risk, privilege, and play. How might locating play outside classrooms mitigate or invite play inside them? At what times and in what places might play be destructive rather than beneficial?

"Stepping Off the Magic Ladder"

As humans we are (by nature or design) stakeholders: we act with intention and become invested in what we have made. Play is (by nature) impermanent: sometimes attached to outcomes, sometimes only loosely so, or to outcomes that are negotiable. "Learning to play" is a contradiction in terms, if we understand it to be about the orderly acquisition of knowledge. But if learning is moving amid grid and chaos, if learners are permeable to the knowledge that exists both within and outside us, then learning is play—and

40. Agatha Basia, "Decided. Dreams Collection." December 17, 2013 (8:57 p.m.).

41. Edensor et al., "Industrial Ruins," 65–79.

it entails risk and transformation: the risk of harm, of loss, of being lost; the transformation of ourselves in the universe—as happens to Max, when he goes off with the wild things.[42]

Such encounters can happen anywhere someone is open, although Lauren Berlant and Michael Warner observe that they are more likely to occur in an urban site, "always a host space," full of variety:

> One of the most disturbing fantasies in the zoning scheme...is the idea that an urban locale is a community of shared interest based on residence and property.... But...the local character of the neighborhood depends on the daily presence of thousands of nonresidents.... 'The right to the city' (Henri Lefebvre) extends to those who use the city.[43]

Wanting to continue this line of exploration, the following semester Jody and I join a co-teacher in economics in requiring our students to make bi-weekly jaunts into Philadelphia. This time they do so under the aegis of an interdisciplinary course cluster called a 360°.[44] Twelve students enroll together in three classes co-designed around the topic of ecological education. Experiencing and theorizing what it means to live and learn in the overlapping spatial zones of built and natural environments, including the diversity and disequilibrium of the natural world, again raises questions about the binaries of "inside" and "outside," owned and stolen, permanent and "just passing through." Rather than explicit instructions to "play," however, this time 'round, we offer a much more directed social and environmental justice agenda, with the specific goal of addressing inequity head-on.

Our group visits complex and highly compromised urban spaces of retreat and reflection—Wissahickon Valley Park, the John Heinz National Wildlife Refuge, Laurel Hill Cemetery—and once (when an ice storm prevents our planned travel to an arboretum) a special (and especially vivid) exhibit about colonialism at the Barnes Foundation, Yinka Shonibare's "Magic Ladders."[45]

When our transportation arrangements fail a second time, we

---

42. Jack Halberstam, "The Wild Beyond: With and For the Undercommons," in Stefano Harney and Fred Moten, *The Undercommons: Fugitive Planning and Black Study* (Brooklyn: Autonomedia, 2013), 7, 8, 10, 11.

43. Laurent Berlant and Michael Warner, "Sex in Public," *Critical Inquiry* 24, no. 2 (Winter 1998): 547–66.

44. "360° Course Clusters," Bryn Mawr College, 2016.

45. The Barnes Foundation, "Yinka Shonibare MBE: Magic Ladders," January 24–April 21, 2014.

PLAYING | 97

Trash at John Heinz
National Wildlife
Refuge, "America's First
Urban Refuge"

spend a morning at Harriton House, a former plantation, once farmed by enslaved people, from whose grounds the College had been created (we discover that there is a graveyard on campus, where some of the house servants are buried). Across the river from Philadelphia, in Camden, which Rolling Stone magazine termed "America's Most Desperate Town: Apocalypse, New Jersey,"[46] we make three visits to The Center for Environmental Transformation, where we spend half-days working on a community-based gardening project with a class of neighborhood fifth graders.

We are joined in these pursuits by an artist, who works with us to design a range of activities, guiding students on field trips and in responding to them by working with the material "stuff" of textiles and sculptures, paintings, photographs, and songs. All of this rather expansively suggests how creating in and from the outside can disrupt settled habits of classroom learning, providing alternative ways of perceiving, doing, and being.

Some of the students embrace this dimension of the cluster, report that it offers ways other than the usual academic modes of understanding and expressing, and helps them confront fears about doing creative work. At the same time—since this rich additional dimension is a demanding one—there is a looming sense of overwhelm. Several of the college students are unwell, and the winter weather is harsh, so we frequently find ourselves low in number, occasionally not meeting at all, or meeting against all odds. One Friday afternoon, our planned trip to Mill Grove, the home of John James Audubon, an early naturalist and artist, has to be scuttled because the roads to the west of the city are ice-covered. We head downtown instead, to see the exhibit of Yinka Shonibare's "Magic Ladders" at the Barnes Foundation.

I admit that I am seriously dragging my feet this morning—it seems as if there are TOO MANY OBSTACLES, and I am convinced that the universe is telling us to GIVE UP. I feel that we are trying too hard to *make something happen…*

But what happens is something of a revelation.

46. Matt Taibbi, "Apocalypse, New Jersey: A Dispatch from America's Most Desperate Town," *Rolling Stone*, December 22, 2013.

When we finally arrive, I am surprised and delighted by the Shonibare exhibit: grabbed first by the whimsy, by the color, and also as immediately by the complex representation of colonializing educational practices. Like others in our group, I am particularly struck by the "crossbred cultural background" of the Dutch wax textiles Shonibare showcases here, and later do a little reading to learn the history of how the Dutch came to peddle Indonesian-inspired designs to West Africa.[47] What strikes me in this account is how "ecological" it is—how demonstrative that "everything is connected," not just biologically, but culturally and commercially (the web site for Vlisco, for example, offers free delivery to Africa and elsewhere). Like the students (including some in this class), who attended the Black History Month dinner the night before, and found these fabrics on the tables, I am implicated in this chain: during a recent craft fair at the College, I and some colleagues sold Shakoshi bags, to raise money for the book group we offer in prison.

Shonibare's work is nothing if not playful—a very serious kind of play that showcases it as tantalizingly dangerous, political, and personal: in the form of the artist, his patron Barnes, and the figures that seem to illustrate and mock both the integrity of identity and identity politics. The exhibit gets me thinking about the sorts of appropriations and re-appropriations that have been enabled by colonialism; it gets me to apply some of my understanding of eco-systems, particularly the imbrication of everything in everything else, to social, political, historical dimensions. I begin to think differently about the assumption underlying "Play in the City": that we could leave the suburbs for a place apart, a place where we could be other than and separate from what we have been.

One of our students goes much further. In "Colonizing the Museum Exhibit" (alternatively titled "What's at the top of a magic ladder?"), Sara Gladwin develops a critique of conventional standards of educational value:

47. Julia Felsenthal, "The Curious History of 'Tribal' Prints: How the Dutch Peddle Indonesian-Inspired Designs to West Africa," *Slate* (March 1, 2012).

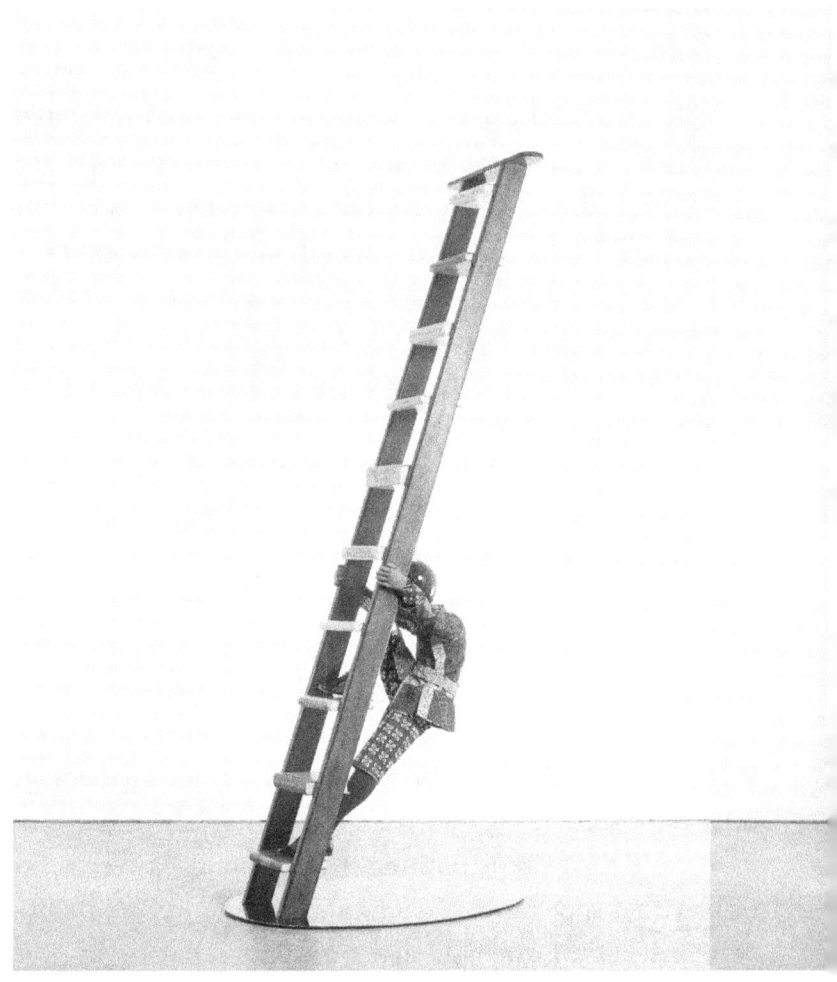

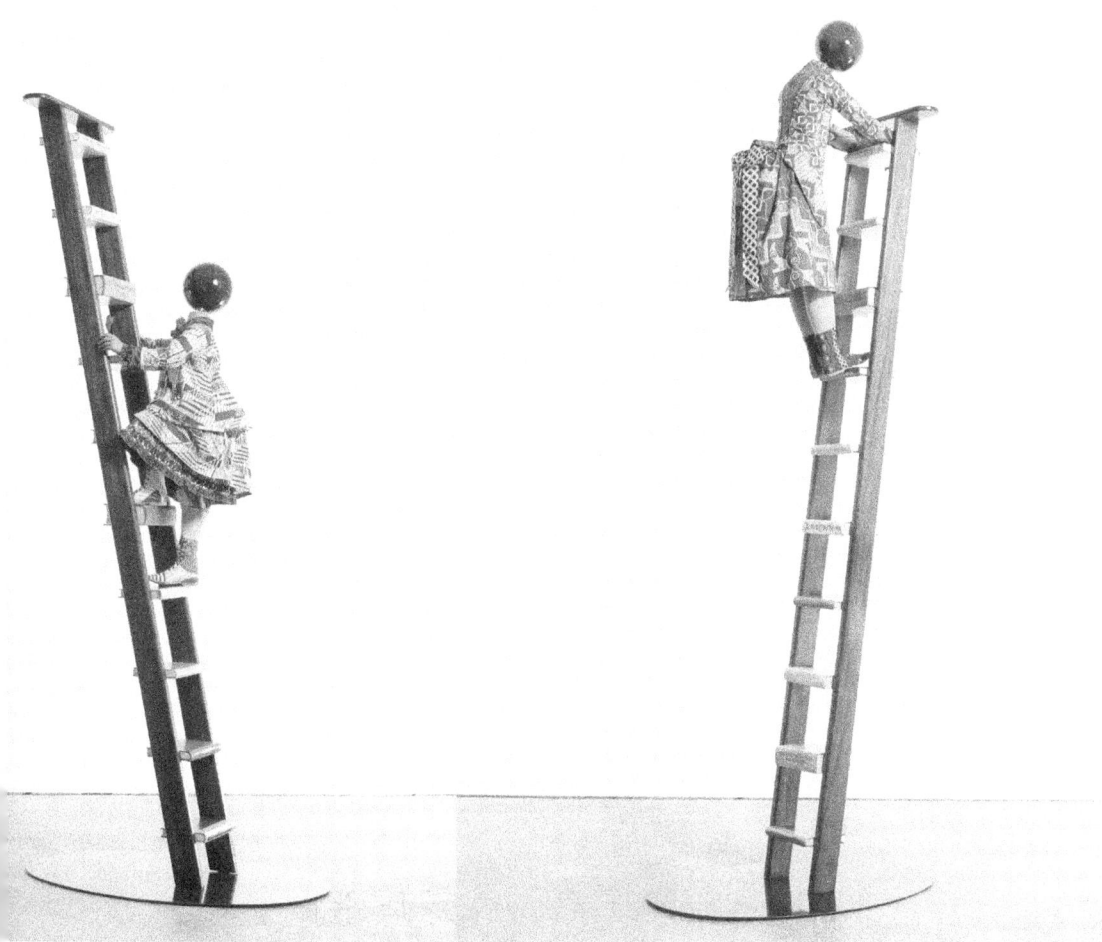

Shonibare Rahman Yinka, *Magic Ladder Kid I*, 2013. Copyright Yinka Shinbare MBE. All Rights Reserved, DACS 2017. Image Courtesy James Cohan Gallery. Photo: Stephen White.

I really did like the exhibit. It was thought provoking, and each piece was beautifully intricate. I especially appreciated the absence of subtlety in the allusions depicted; Shonibare unabashedly allowed the influences that shaped the artwork to be present and visible on the work…

As I was walking around the exhibit though, I felt distracted. I had come into the museum with a question already on my mind, planted there during our obstacle-filled journey to begin our field trip. I couldn't stop asking myself whether or not we were truly being ecologically literate if we weren't reading the signs from our environment that were telling us to stay home. What would it mean if we had made the choice to stop fighting the signs? Would we all have gone back and written posts reflecting on our environment that had obstructed our endeavor to become more ecologically literate, conscious and/or responsive through a field trip? Would we have opted for a different kind of trip, one that didn't rely on a phone call or vans or train schedules? Might we have found ourselves talking a walk through the Morris Woods, listening to our environment, waiting for more signs from it?

As I circled the room, I realized that debating about what could have happened didn't seem entirely ecological anymore either. We had arrived to Barnes now, and I needed to listen to my current surroundings. I began looking for answers in the art, though I only uncovered more questions. I wondered about the placement of the mirror on the parlor wall, and whether or not there was anything intentional about what you could see in the reflection. Did I become a part of the room? What about the artwork in the background of the reflection?….I wondered about the boy, in the center of the left side of the room, casually lounging on his stomach and reading, and how I didn't know anyone seemingly that young who would willingly read Plato. I bent down and read along with him, although I can't recall any of the two pages that were on display, other then something about a "theory of ideas." I left the side room almost immediately upon entering it, seeing that there were only men sitting at the table.

I examined every line of each description, and wondered who had written them, and whether Shonibare approved of the interpretations. Then I read the titles of every book on the magic ladders. There was something unsettling about the metaphor of the ladder. I started to feel consumed with a new question: what's at the top of a magic ladder?

I found myself walking out of the exhibit, and wandering around Barnes. I felt directionless but somehow not without purpose. I was searching for something, an answer; but I wasn't even sure what the question I was asking meant. As I walked, I was reminded of a piece titled Walking, by Henry David Thoreau, in which he writes:

> *…the art of Walking, that is…so to speak…sauntering; which word is beautifully derived "from idle people who roved about the country, in the middle ages, and asked charity, under pretence of going à la sainte terre"—to the holy land, till the children exclaimed, "There goes a sainte-terrer", a saunterer—a holy-lander… Some, however, would derive*

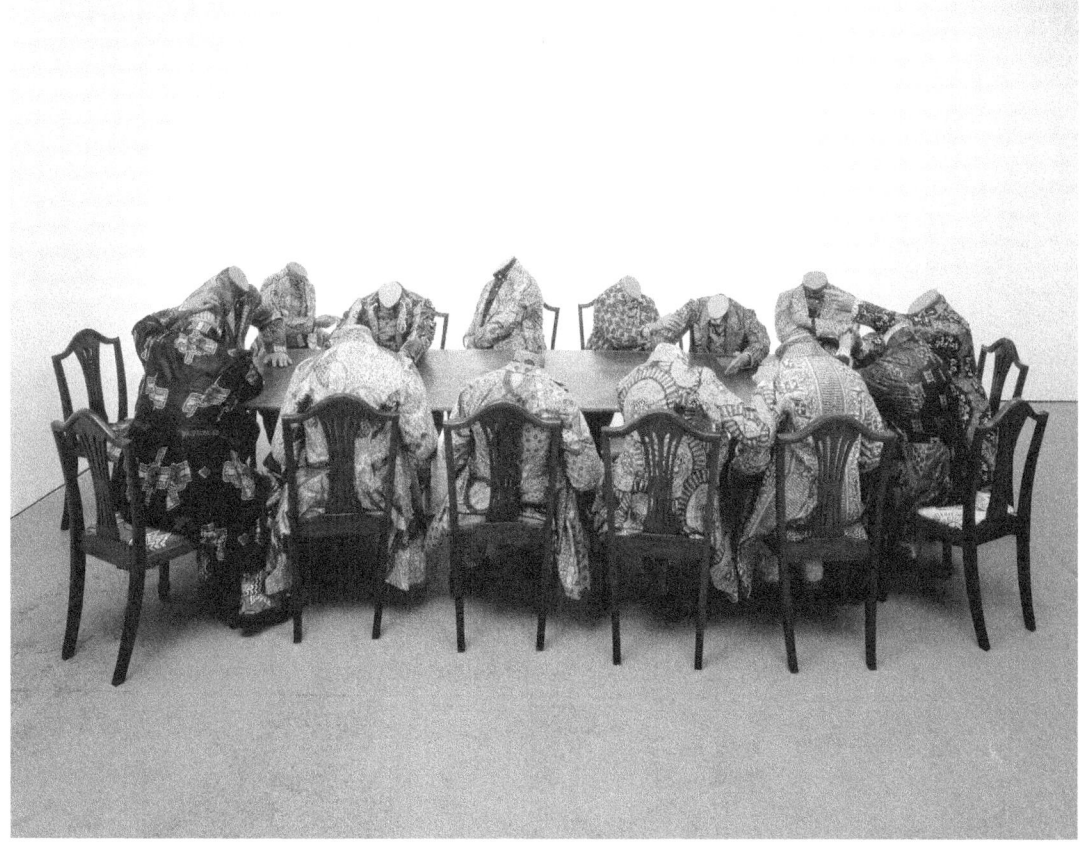

Shonibare Rahman Yinka, *Scramble for Africa* (2003). Copyright Yinka Shinbare MCE. All Rights Reserved, DACS 2017. Image Courtesy The Pinnell Collection, Dallas. Commissioned by the Museum for African Art, NY.

> *the word from sans terre, without land or a home, which, therefore, in the good sense, will mean, having no particular home, but equally at home everywhere. For this is the secret of successful sauntering... the Saunterer, in the good sense, is no more vagrant than the meandering river, which is all the while sedulously seeking the shortest course to the sea.... For every walk is a sort of crusade...*
>
> I felt the different textures along the walls and sought out the corners of each room; experiencing the physical boundaries of the space as tactilely as possible.... I ventured downstairs. I paid close attention to the feeling of my hand sliding down the stair railing, and heaviness in the feet as they collide with the floor and the floor pushes back. I think what I really wanted to touch and feel were those magic ladders; to put my weight on the cover of each book. I continued this kind of sensory exploration, until I felt that I had found another piece of the puzzle. It was a single sentence about the "Magic Ladder" exhibit, explaining that the books that Shonibare used for the ladder steps had come from the personal library of Albert C. Barnes. These books, which metaphorically provided the necessary knowledge to ascend the ladder, came from the creator of the museum. I started to further distrust the implication of the ladder, which seemingly dictates a hierarchy of knowledge. I became uncomfortable with the limited possibility of movement offered by a ladder, in which you could only go up or down.... The ladder, when applied to my life, becomes a metaphor for feeling trapped.
>
> What is so important at the top of a magic ladder?
>
> And if we get to the top, will we be too far removed from ground to actually perceive the environment we live in?[48]

48. sara. gladwin, "Colonizing the Museum Exhibit," paper written for 360°, Bryn Mawr College, February 17, 2014.

Sara raises a host of questions about what it means to be alive to the present in all of its ecological complexity—and then her physical and imaginative "sauntering" moves into direct confrontation with the ways in which different positions mark all encounters, distress all play:

> ...I walk down the stairs of the Barnes and...now I am worried about Henry and me, and what we think it means to walk.

I am picturing a scene, narrated by Virginia Woolf. The figure of a woman as she is walking, attempts to enter the library of a famous university:

> —but here I was actually at the door which leads into the library itself...instantly there issued, like a guardian angel barring the way with a flutter of black gown instead of white wings, a deprecating, silvery, kindly gentleman, who regretted in a low voice as he waved me back that ladies are only admitted to the library if accompanied by a Fellow of the College or furnished with a letter of introduction.

Not everyone is permitted to feel equally at home everywhere.

I think of the women I work with at [the] correctional facility. I think of their hunger for books. I think of the doors that shut as I walk out and leave them behind.

Sauntering, or the ability to be equally at home everywhere, is a beautiful but not always accessible art. For as much privilege as it takes to climb the magic ladder, and ascend to the top, it seems as though a certain amount of privilege is required to get off the ladder, to be a saunterer in the Thoreauvian sense. "If you are ready to leave father and mother, and brother and sister, and wife and child and friends, and never see them again—if you have paid your debts, and made your will, and settled all your affairs, and are a free man—then you are ready for a walk."[49]

49. sara.gladwin, "What's at the top of a Magic Ladder?", paper written for 360°, Bryn Mawr College, March 17, 2014.

As last semester, playing "outside" this time 'round leads to an interrogation of what happens—and can fail to happen—in classrooms. Sara articulates here some of the far-reaching implications of our decision to leave the college and encounter the world of play and art, of woods, fabrics, and ladders. What might it mean, she probes, not just to leave the classroom on a field trip, but to use that trip to step off the "magic ladder" of the educational system, and learn to saunter on one's own? Who is free to do this, and who is prevented from doing so? What are the risks? Who and what is threatened when we jump the grid?

The Impropriety of Property

Over the course of the next two months, "playing ecologically" in this way begins to stir up a range of further questions: from how we are being educated, to how we might live in the world, to what might happen after we die. The students have queries about permanence: how transient are we? How transient might (or should) our productions be? They ask about property: how might we think (think differently?) about ownership? When we visit the expansive, historic Laurel Hill Cemetery, for instance—rambling independently, then sitting and talking together among the tombstones—they are puzzled to see how much the wealthy people of Philadelphia have invested in creating permanent monuments of their having once been alive. Why haven't they been able to accept their "transience"? Might we ourselves learn to hold our lives—and the record of our living—more lightly?

These questions get carried back to campus, where our consulting artist invites us to an open studio to witness her process for creating an on-campus installation. When we gather for the demonstration, she acknowledges that, in her representation of the natural world, she uses material that is not ecological, and manipulates color and size to make the real appear unnatural, even bizarre.

Fresh from all those permanent gravestones in Laurel Hill, some students express concern about the materials for the project. Having researched a range of more transitory projects created by eco-artists, they are uncomfortable with the plan for an installation that uses a heavy, permanent material to remake the landscape.

When advertisements for our final celebratory event go up around campus, we worry that some of the students may resist an installation they see as not aligned with their evolving ecological understanding, by commenting on or even defacing it.

But actually? Something much more interesting—more playful, ecological, and transgressive—transpires.

We host the installation in an open space in the center of campus,

William Warner Memorial, Laurel Hill Cemetery

where the students put on an interactive performance, in which they use pieces of the installation as props for "playing house."

We picnic, and invite others to also move, enjoy, play.

Many do so, with gusto.

As various members of the campus community stop by in the days thereafter, the artist captures images of them playing with the installation.

The signage invites play at the site. Over the weekend, however, these activities extend beyond that space.

On Monday morning, we hear that every piece of the installation has disappeared. The artist is—of course!—upset, worried about possible loss and damage to the art. With the help of public safety officers, the campus is scoured, turning up pieces scattered behind dorms, on branches, beneath a hanging willow; the artist arranges for them to be promptly picked up and delivered home.

As we help to track down the missing pieces—asking our students, the deans, the housekeeping staff and security team to keep an eye out—our own reactions are mixed. After such an intense academic semester, all those months of hard work, hard weather, and ill health, we actually find ourselves smiling, to see students now taking up the invitation to "play," even redefining the terms of the game. Their hands-on engagement with the public installation suggests, to us, that it has been a success.

As Anne's husband observes,

> students are like squirrels—they take what they like and ignore what they don't…creativity is…a collective enterprise…like unscripted performance art, and here the movers and users were performers.… It's a story that evolved in a way that was not imagined (at least by me)…this is a happy story…impermanence is ecological; "permanence," like "forever," doesn't exist.…

Sara Gladwin, who has seen in Shonibare's "magic ladders" an image of her own entrapment in the educational structures of progressive education, sees an alternative in the dispersal of the installation. She muses on how, when art is placed in public spaces, the unpredictable public may become part of the material, altering what is made, how it is understood and used. She writes to the artist to explain that, when she first received her requests to help find what was missing,

> I immediately responded…that I would attempt to recover the lost piece, hoping to soothe some of your sense of distress. Upon further reflection about this issue, I had some additional thoughts about the missing piece.
>
> As I passed by the installation throughout the week, I would count the pieces, always checking to see if there were still thirteen. I was tickled to see students tentatively venture playing with the pieces, rearranging and reassessing their placement, stepping into the role of "artist," if only for that moment. It was not until the end of the week that the entire display was dispersed and scattered around campus. I wanted to express my strong belief that this was not evidence of a prank or intended with malice. My understanding is that moving the art from its original site was a continuation of the same playful and interactive spirit that was extended to the student body regarding the installation; placing them around the campus was another way of "rearranging" the installation so that it becomes part of the environment itself. By spacing out the pieces, the art display encompasses all of campus, rather than remaining isolated. Furthermore, the act of scattering, of spreading the art pieces out further and increasing their visibility, seems reflective of patterns of nature. Like bees carrying pollen from one flower to the next, the pieces were spread throughout the campus. Even the piece that was missing for a short time is a reflection of these same qualities.
>
> I was sad to see the installation leave the campus. Throughout the weekend, various students including myself had interacted with the biggest piece in its new area. Saturday evening, two other friends and I sat back to back on it, while one friend played the Ukulele and the rest of us sang. It could be argued that the installation piece was not crucial in creating this moment—and yet, there was something about sitting back to back on this piece of art that lent to a sense of connectedness and joy between the three of us.

> I felt like it was important for me to tell you that I believe the installation was a success because it prompted students to engage critically with their environment.
>
> This instance has led me to reflect on whether ownership and permanence are ecologically constructive concepts.... I am speaking not only about ownership over art but about ideas and education more broadly....[50]

50. Sara Gladwin, e-mail message to authors, May 19, 2014.

In asking that we attend to the "varying channels" from which art arises, as well as to how it may best be distributed, Sara is again an intellectual saunterer, both taking up our invitation to free herself for play and finding the space to critique that opportunity structure. Making her questions manifest in metaphors, in unexpected winter storms and books stacked to create ladders, in installations that disperse and reappear, Sara's reflections seem to us exemplary of how the politics of play may be made material. But as she herself points out, others may feel more snagged than freed by options such as those she's selected, which don't recognize other legitimate claims.

The Work of Play

Differences in teaching objectives and strategies are bound to emerge in the close quarters of a 360°. While we are inviting our students to play with the unexpected, and to do so en route to developing a political critique of "things as they are," our creative consultant is eager to engage them very differently, in the kind of exploration and extended labor involved in the practice of making art. Some of the students push back on the expectation that they create "refined tight work," preferring instead to experiment with projects they are unsure of. Trying to model for them each of the levels of hard work—inspiration, commitment, creation, edition, revision, presentation—that goes into art making, frustrated that they aren't pressing harder to fine-tune their projects, the artist identifies their location in a nested structure—a larger culture that does not value art, a college without an art program, a 360° with no art course—that she feels discourages many of them from fully taking up the challenges and possibilities of the work she is asking them to do.

Structural obstacles also bedevil our shared project from the get-go. Although all of us co-teachers expect our students to do the creative work, we have not scheduled a fourth course that would grant both time and credit for this labor. Some students feel that the cluster isn't organized to allow them to focus on their art projects. Jody and I listen carefully to students' concerns, respond by shifting expectations. And now we wonder: did our responsiveness discourage them from focusing on their creative work, rather than help them develop the discipline fundamental to making art? By allowing the students not to prioritize their own artistic endeavors, did we foster a light-hearted attitude toward the artist's work, even a disrespect for her installation?

The dispersal of the installation pieces, and our own mixed responses to this story, bring the implications and consequences of "the politics of play" to a particularly fine point. As Deborah Rose and her colleagues ask of their own encounters among coyotes and ravens: Who is positioned to play, and what risks do different players encounter? When and how does the play of some risk the well-being of others? In our 360° in particular, what does it mean to play with things that are not our own? A friend and colleague, Michael Tratner, observes,

> Moving the installation symbolizes moving the boundaries of what is presented to us—and yet seems a violation of what someone else has done. What kinds of violations of the rules we live by are playful, what kinds are hurtful to others, what kinds are liberating, what kinds are illusions of freedom?[51]

51. Michael Tratner, e-mail message to authors, June 4, 2016.

The students who "played" with the installation knew little of the extended negotiations involved in arranging the artistic consultancy, or of the costs of placing the materials.... Is it unfathomable that an artist, trying to make her living by creating works of art, should be

Seger Park Playground,
10th and Lombard,
Philadelphia.

asked to countenance the risk of losing those creations? Yet this too is complicated: who actually owns ("should" own?) the installation, if its construction and placement are paid for by the college?

Questions about what enables playing, pointed queries about who is excluded from play, what the limits of play should be, can be and *are,* animated the planning for "Play in the City," and lingered after that course ended. During explorations of environmental art in the following semester, we begin to see that the answers to those questions might be curiously "flipped," that the sort of playful attitude we are seeking might not necessarily be enabled by material privilege. Precisely the reverse could happen, if an investment in property, possession, and permanence entail attachment to outcomes and control.

Our friend Joel Schlosser, who is a political scientist, nudges us to acknowledge more frankly the limits of our claims:

> Play is a "political project," but how does it move from playing with politics—i.e. coming up against politics through play in ways that conventional academic approaches would miss—to playing politically—i.e. playing in ways that create power and use this power to disturb or disrupt regnant political orders? If it's always only the former then I think you may be promising too much when you talk about the politics.
>
> …Are the "politics of play" doing anything more than showing how the neoliberal world most of us inhabit prevents play? Does this provide any basis for challenging the political orders of dispossession and exclusion themselves?[52]

In other words: is our argument for dispossession one that can only come from privilege? (We think here of artist Vincent Desiderio's joyful celebration, when Kanye West appropriated his painting for a new music video: "A work of art goes out there, and there's a stream that activates and widens the communal imagination.…There was no money involved at all."[53] Isn't such a claim unlikely to be made by those who lack the public acclaim and wealth shared by Desiderio and West?) Asking this question, we recall Lisa

52. Joel Schlosser, e-mail message to authors, June 6, 2016.

53. Joe Coscarelli, "Artist Who Inspired Kanye West's 'Famous' Video: 'I Was Really Speechless,'" *The New York Times*, June 26, 2016.

Delpit's caution against embracing creative grammar for students who are disenfranchised.[54]

54. Delpit, *Other People's Children*.

In a system where we're in a tussle about the "public" in "public space"—where art always runs the risk of becoming commodified, with no guarantees of who will gain or lose in this transaction; where space, art, and ideas are always subject to re-appropriation—the moving of the installation pieces simultaneously signifies loss and a taste of new possibilities. Like the woman crying in the bathroom stall at the public library, like the headless batik-clothed figures seated around the table of global politics, the circulating installation figures a form of collective interaction that, as Edensor and his co-writers say about play, is "potentially transformative or subversive of power."[55]

55. Edensor, et al., "Industrial Ruins," 65–79.

From the moment that Mark and I first escort our students into city play, it is clear to us that "open-ended exploratory interactions" can have consequences in the real world. Our invitation to recognize such playful imagining as political is even more fully realized the following semester, when the 360° students re-arrange the installation. In doing so, they are threatening the artist's work, and her concerns about damage—eventually mitigated by the return of each of her pieces—are real ones, needing acknowledgment.

In the earliest Tarot decks, The Fool is often shown as a beggar, a risk-taker with little to lose; unlike other figures in the Major Arcana (the trump cards which form the foundation of the deck), The Fool doesn't even have a number, just the placeholder of zero. We now see our students as enacting the roles of archetypal fools, tricksters who take risks and transgress boundaries in service of their own impulses, their capacities to tap into unknown possibilities. The zone of play offers them a delicious, even purposive opportunity to experiment with such transgressions.

But what zone do we occupy, when we leave our classrooms to go "outside"? When we visit various urban spaces, encountering those who live there? When we return to our suburban campus, rearranging the pieces of art that have been installed there?

While we are urging our students to locate themselves in a zone of play, the artist occupies a different zone, one which encompasses both her aspirations and her livelihood. When our students put her installation pieces into circulation across campus, these two circles of work and play overlap, intersect, criss-cross in a border area where play gets serious, has very real consequences. Like the unpredictable, creative and consequential encounters of Deborah Rose and her colleagues with coyotes and ravens, our story describes an unsettled space of learning, where our students experiment with playing the trickster, and in so doing, carve a zig-zag path into a territory where art is taken seriously.

Taking our pedagogical direction from the politics of play means getting outside the classroom and questioning some of its primary presumptions, then bringing what we discover back in; it means continuing to grapple with nuances that sometimes feel like gaping divisions, sometimes like entering that "area of unrest" known as an ecotone.[56]

Bringing the concepts of political and ecological play into our understanding of the complexities of our interactions means that we are still wrestling with hard pedagogical questions: what can come of our going outside with our students to learn from the aftermath of what is unpredictable? We take up the startle of such encounters as openings into a world larger, more diverse and complicated than any of us can encompass. How to play in a way that helps students meet this world freshly, inventively, and respectfully; that recognizes and takes on some urgent injustices without ignoring other perspectives, without ceding to overwhelm? How to hover in a border ecology, where play, power, and property are always subject to question and revision?

Giving voice to such complexities are the sorts of activities we trace here: those of refusing institutional boundaries, the property they demarcate, the sort of "arrogant perception"[57] that knows

56. Rachel Carson, "The Marginal World," in *The Edge of the Sea*, 1955, posted 2016.

57. Maria Lugones, "Playfulness, 'World'-Traveling and Loving Perception," *Hypatia* 2, no. 2 (Summer 1987): 3–19.

where to draw such lines, and (eventually) the distinction between inside and out altogether. In his introduction to *The Undercommons: Fugitive Planning and Black Study,* Jack Halberstam refuses the "call to order" that occurs when the teacher picks up the book, and also quite wonderfully refuses "the academy of misery" that this order perpetuates. In the book that follows, Stefano Harney and Fred Moten describe at length an alternative to the "deadening labor" of the university, and ask, "What would be outside this act of the conquest circle, what kind of ghostly labored world escapes in the circling act…?"[58]

Our encounters in the Free Library mark some of this "ghostly labored world," as do Yinka Shonibare's "magic ladders." The dispersal of the installation marks some more.

Playing "outside" the classroom leads us beyond "the circling act," then invites us in once again.

58. Stefano Harney and Fred Moten, *The Undercommons: Fugitive Planning and Black Study* (Brooklyn: Autonomedia, 2013), 30–31, 34.

CHAPTER THREE
HAUNTING

Family Hauntings

We call our first-semester seminar "In Class/OutClassed," and pitch it this way:

> You have been in school for a number of years now, and you bring questions about the methods, means, and ends of education. Wherever you may be positioned in this process, however settled into or skeptical of it you may be, this course is an invitation to reflect on the assumptions that shape education in the U.S., as well as on the habits of thought and action it encourages. Schooling in the U.S. has been subject to two competing claims: that it "levels the playing field," giving all children an equal chance to succeed, and that—like our homes, neighborhoods, and employment—it remains deeply segregated by social class, characterized by "savage inequalities."
>
> In this course we examine the complex relationship between social class, being "in class," and being "outclassed." How does class shape educational opportunities and outcomes? What kinds of changes does each of us expect education to bring about in our own social position? To help us address such queries, we will read a wide range of educational autobiographies and theoretical analyses, focus on the case study that is Bryn Mawr, visit with students from a West Philadelphia school, and conduct workshops and interviews on campus.... Throughout, we will use a range of compositional (and de-compositional) forms to help us explore, analyze, and reinvent education—as we ask what kinds of alternative scenarios we might discover, imagine, and create together.[1]

[1] "In Class/OutClassed: On the Uses of a Liberal Education," Emily Balch Seminar, Bryn Mawr College, Fall 2011.

Along with Anne and two seniors, Jomaira and Sarah (Posse Scholars from working-class Boston, who are serving as our student consultants through the Teaching and Learning Initiative[2]) I am planning linked sections of this seminar. We all worry that it could become an exercise in shame and guilt, paralysis powered by intellect that hits at the gut. Can we find language to class and de-classify, act and re-enact our complex relations with each other and with others? How to teach toward "response-ability," carrying the etymological call for students to develop capacities for responding to others, so that "people with different kinds of precarious lives can begin to recognize each other and to recombine their efforts in order to produce a new vision, a new autonomy, creating something together"?[3]

As I begin to outline the story of this class, other tales begin to haunt me, seeping through the cracks of my understanding, tugging, taking me into foggier landscapes…

Avery Gordon describes haunting as "an animated state in which a repressed or unresolved social violence is making itself known.… The ghost demands your attention. The present wavers."[4]

---

[2]. "Teaching and Learning Institute at Bryn Mawr and Haverford Colleges," Bryn Mawr College, 2017.

[3]. Valerie Walkerdine, "Using the Work of Felix Guattari to Understand Space, Place, Social Justice, and Education," *Qualitative Inquiry* 19 (2013): 763.

[4]. Avery Gordon, "Some Thoughts on Haunting and Futurity," *Borderlands* 10 (2011): 2.

My mother's father Joseph was a Jewish intellectual, a communist who killed himself because (or so the story goes) of his anguish at not being able to provide enough for his family: my mother and her younger sister and brother. Their mother went on to raise her family on wages earned as a ticket-taker at the movie theater. This meant we got into the movies for free when we visited her in that neighborhood in Brooklyn that now seems to me a made-up place, a movie itself. I never knew my grandfather, who died when my mother was 14. And we could afford to pay for the movies, though my parents never finished compensating: my mother by scrupulous attention to what things cost, my father the opposite—choosing law instead of teaching, honing his palate, buying a home in a neighborhood known for its schools…

I feel as if I somehow witnessed my grandfather's death: mangled body on the sidewalk thrown from the second story apartment on top of the candy store that was, perhaps, to blame.

Observing that "the available critical vocabularies were failing… to communicate the depth, density, and intricacies of the dialectic of subjection and subjectivity…of domination and freedom, of critique and utopian longing," Gordon offers hauntings as a source of sociological insight: It's the "inert furniture" that does the trick, she says.[5]

5. Avery Gordon, *Ghostly Matters: Haunting and the Sociological Imagination* (Minneapolis: University of Minnesota Press, 1997), 5.

What lies in the space between body and fabric? Between the stuff of classed experience: where each of us went to school, whether we had health care, what we ate and drank? How might such detail help us creep into the cracks within and between, into what Gordon calls the "complex personhood" where people "remember and forget, are beset by contradiction, and recognize and misrecognize themselves and others…suffer graciously and selfishly too, get stuck in the symptoms of their troubles, and also transform themselves"?[6]

6. Gordon, *Ghostly Matters*, 4.

This chapter attends to such hauntings textured by class; juxtaposes analyses of personal and institutional histories "in which you touch the…ghostly matter of things: the ambiguities, the complexities of power and personhood… the shadows of ourselves and our society."[7] How do such shadows haunt the teaching of class in class? Although I never knew Joseph, his ghost has wended its way into my personal, political, pedagogical yearnings and commitments, pushing me to reach toward a different world. Reminding me how shadows where we live and learn might offer glimpses into other worlds.

7. Gordon, *Ghostly Matters*, 134.

Or, in another version, the family found him in the morning hanging from a rafter in that candy store. I don't know how I'd know these details, or how I might've come to make up these images, or which if either is true…since this story is never talked about in my family. Never.

Before the suicide (there's always a before), Joseph left Orange, New Jersey, where he'd been beaten for being Jewish, for being poor, and for being a socialist. He moved his family to Brooklyn, took them into Manhattan to hear music and eat in restaurants and visit the museums; found a giveaway piano and, somehow, money for lessons for my mom when her teacher said she had an ear for music. But he also berated her for not working harder in school and favored her sister, my Aunt Rita, who read ferociously while one-handedly scrubbing out clothes in the washtub Saturday mornings, and yearned for another social order….

Breathing shallowly now, I can feel the narrow hallways, even smell the permeating odors of Greek cooking next door to the apartment I was small in. I see the front steps in the tract housing of my elementary school years; the luxuriant athletic fields in high school, the courtyard where we got high and protested—chanting "fuck you" to the powers-that-be—and, in an interdisciplinary program in my senior year, calling teachers by their first names and analyzing familial dysfunction in *A Long Day's Journey into Night*. This was my trajectory into the middle class. Where my parents could choose babysitters and vacations, and where I learned to buck those choices by some of my own: dropping out of college to work at the Woolworth's lunch counter, saving my money for travelling around Europe with no end date in sight. Class mobility, choices…and college waiting for me when I got back. Later, graduate school and then, via some side-stepping, a job in the academy. A rowhouse first in the formerly glorious Germantown, and then, as the cracks in that social network became increasingly deep and troubling, a twin in a middle-income suburb. Two children whose friends often sported a display of considerable wealth. In contrast to my husband, though, who grew up in a factory town, I still always had a sense of having enough and more. Or access to that.

Nevertheless, as I sit here thinking—where to begin writing about class?—it is the ghost of my grandfather Joseph who joins me: Joseph who never had that sense of enough—for his family and for all those others,

Joseph:

after whom I'm named.

Institutional Hauntings

The first woman president of Harvard University, Drew Faust, was raised among very different ghosts, the landed gentry in Virginia. Counseled by her mother that "It's a man's world, sweetie," Faust reports arriving at Bryn Mawr in 1964:

> I will never forget Miss McBride up on the stage telling us to be humble in the face of Our Work. I had not before realized that I had Work....But Miss McBride's address instilled in me a newfound reverence for learning and scholarship.[8]

8. Claire Potter, "The Unfinished Agenda: Women's Education in the 21st Century," *Tenured Radical*, March 15, 2016.

A century earlier, the second president of Bryn Mawr, M. Cary Thomas had developed a formative vision for the college, as a place where young, white, Christian, well-to-do "ladies" like Faust, often from prominent families, would be given the rare opportunity to become serious scholars of the classics, science, art history. Others would wait on them while they nurtured their intellects and prepared to become formidable and influential leaders in a male-dominated world. A lover of exquisite things who displayed her wealth extravagantly on the campus where she lived with women partners, Thomas was visionary about the rights of white women, yet profoundly elitist and racist: a highly vocal and influential supremacist and eugenicist whose fierce opposition to class-and-race equity also infused her vision of the college. Specters of this vision still lace through shadows, blossom across the green expanses of this place.

Bryn Mawr alumna and historian Grace Pusey explains how inequities embedded in the college's history leave a profound legacy:

> Having an all-Black and predominantly female domestic staff served to reinforce and amplify students' status-markers of wealth and whiteness, and even Thomas' successors found that recruiting students from elite white families...and subsequently catering to their prejudices (and their expectations for a certain kind of lifestyle, sustained by Black women's domestic labor), proved essential to securing and maintaining the College's financial stability.[9]

9. Grace Pusey, "Response to 'Slippage' Essays from Grace Pusey," January 1, 2016 (4:42 p.m.).

Current support staff tread in the steps of others, whose labor and invisibility were thought necessary for an institution championing women's scholarship.

Now some students—more diverse by class, race, language, geography—call out these ghosts, underbelly of inclusion requiring exclusion; students and some faculty and staff speak the desire to change this place, to be in and of it.

The "Survey Highlights" of the 2009 Bryn Mawr Campus Climate Assessment reveal that "in the aggregate, social class is the category of identity that most clearly demarcates variation in the experience of Bryn Mawr's campus climate (particularly among undergraduate students and non-faculty staff)." Class shows up as most "problematic" in terms of a sense of "belonging," "a need to minimize or conceal characteristics," and the presence of "disparaging or stereotyping jokes or comments."[10]

In 2011 the college launches a yearlong, campus-wide initiative, Class Dismissed? Furthering the Dialogue about Class.[11] That summer first-year students are assigned *Class Matters*, a collection of *New York Times* articles purporting to analyze the "indistinct, ambiguous…half-seen hand that…holds some Americans down while giving others a boost."[12] In September, and again as fall turns cold, the students in Anne's and my classes complain that they've done the reading, but the college has "done nothing" with it.

Not entirely true. Six collaborative projects are selected by the Diversity Leadership Group and Diversity Council to "spark dialogue on the topic of class." Three will collect stories and generate dialogues, one relate stories to policy issues, another produce a documentary on staff and faculty contributions to the college. Our seminars will host a campus dialogue.[13]

Early in our seminars, students track stories that are less collectible: one follows a trail to her attic dorm room, reputedly haunted by a housekeeper who once lived there; others pursue traces in dorm "smokers" where students studied and talked while served by

10. Office of Institutional Diversity, "2009 Diversity Survey Highlights," Bryn Mawr College, 2010, 1–2.

11. Claudia Giananni, "Yearlong 'Class Dismissed?' Aims to Spark Discussion of Socioeconomic Class on Campus," *Inside Bryn Mawr*, May 3, 2011.

12. New York Times, *Class Matters* (New York: Times Books, 2005).

13. "Diversity Leadership Group Selects Six 'Class Dismissed' Projects for Funding," May 12, 2011.

others, in the bell-tower where seniors announce completion of their work.

The topic haunts, at this college where first-year students are suddenly "unclassed" by eating and living in spaces designed by and for well-to-do white women, "reclassed" by eating in restaurants rather than dining halls, by clothes on bodies and in closets, by décor on their walls and words in their mouths. As political analyst Sam Fulwood suggests, college education—long touted as an equalizer—may operate more as a billboard advertising, even exacerbating class differences.[14]

Early on, when Anne and I ask our students to "map your access to education," their very different trajectories to Bryn Mawr become visible: some with many, sturdy legs up, others with fewer, more tenuous supports. Cracks open among us. An international student writes of her shock at this divide: "i feel like i am an inhouse example of inclass/outclassed."[15]

During the semester, Anne, I, and our student consultants lay out classifications that don't hold, in a shifting, sliding effort to determine what determines class: How to label and compare? What about language, geography, education? The class is "about" class, the noun and its related verbs and adjectives, in all their permutations: grouped into upper crust and lower down, class can elucidate, complicate, detonate learning; can be crossed, or remain intractable, as we and our students face others' experiences and are caught short, puzzled, troubled. All are inflected in our expressions of class positionality in ways that, as Peggy McIntosh puts it during a campus visit, "Marx wouldn't understand."[16]

Class reading provokes sometimes troubling questions. From Richard Rodriguez[17] and Sandra Cisneros:[18] Is education about rejecting your heritage? Does class awareness separate you from family, heritage, even yourself? From the working-class women studied by Wendy Luttrell: Is talking about school "code for talking about class"? Why does education "make you somebody,"

---

14. Sam Fulwood III, "Race and Beyond: Income Differences Divide the College Campus in America," Center for American Progress, March 13, 2012.

15. Utitofon, "Polarized Access to Education," September 13, 2011 (2:32 p.m.).

16. Peggy McIntosh, "Coming to See Privilege Systems: The Surprising Journey," presentation at Bryn Mawr College, November 18, 2008.

17. Richard Rodriguez, "The Achievement of Desire" in *Hunger of Memory: The Education of Richard Rodriguez* (New York: Bantam, 1982), 43–73.

18. Sandra Cisneros, "From a Writer's Notebook," *The Americas Review* 15 (1987): 69–79.

and what about the value of real life intelligence?[19] bell hooks and Pedro Noguera provoke questions about how a white, middle-class teacher might engage in "transformative education" with non-white, working class students.[20] And intermittently throughout the semester, along with our students, Anne and I ponder Paulo Freire's directive to use education to "rewrite the world."[21]

Out of these multiple confrontations, I call up three encounters in what linguist Mary Louise Pratt calls the "contact zone…where cultures meet, clash, and grapple with each other, often in contexts of highly asymmetrical relations of power."[22] Each encounter highlights classed presumptions that get dug up and disturbed, instigating unexpected questions that are opened, shut, revisited. In the first, our students leave the suburban college classroom to enter an urban high school. In the second, we host an on-campus event, which is not attended by some of the people most intimate to our students' lives at college. In the third, we take up writing as a space where classed expectations can be examined and interrogated, as several students try out the Derridean notion of "welcoming…an act that entails acknowledging the other that haunts the self."[23]

Teaching that interrogates class structures and education in a college like this one spirals into complexity: the first semester writing seminar is tasked with helping students "master" the assemblage of skills, knowledge, and expectations that hold power relations in place. Enmeshed in class structures ourselves, while teaching students the skills to navigate them, we also look to interrupt, to teach "'against the evidence,' aspiring "to change the deadly tides of wealth inequality… and personal despair."[24] Amid the "level playing fields" and "savage inequalities" of our course description, we grapple for traction. What world-shifting work can we contribute to here?

19. Wendy Luttrell, *Schoolsmart and Motherwise: Working-Class Women's Identity and Schooling* (New York: Routledge, 1997).

20. bell hooks, "Confronting Class in the Classroom," in *Teaching to Transgress: Education as the Practice of Freedom* (New York: Routledge, 1994), 177–90; Pedro Noguera, *City Schools and the American Dream: Reclaiming the Promise of Public Education* (New York: Teachers College Press, 2003).

21. Paulo Friere. *Pedagogy of the Oppressed*, trans. Myra Bergman Ramos (New York: Continuum, 1990).

22. Mary Louise Pratt, "Arts of the Contact Zone," *Profession* (1991): 34.

23. Robert McRuer, *Crip Theory: Cultural Signs of Queerness and Disability* (New York: New York University Press, 2006), 208.

24. Cornel West, qted. in Jeffrey Duncan-Andrade, "Note to Educators: Hope Required When Growing Roses in Concrete," *Harvard Educational Review* 79, no. 2 (Summer 2009): 4.

Dreaming Class

It is a clear, bright day in mid-October. Twenty-some first-years—majority white, also brown and Black, from public and private, urban and suburban high schools and now all at this college—board a bus (though one misses it). One of our student consultants tells us to attend closely on our ride down the Main Line into West Philadelphia: Mark when we cross City Line Avenue, recognize when the walls, hedges, lawns, shops, and restaurants of the well-to-do are replaced by trolley tracks, cement steps, corner stores in a "food desert." She invites us to divide and class-ify, reminds us of power lines mapped over subtler differences: servants' houses in midtown Bryn Mawr, large elegant homes visible over the city line.

We disembark. Move easily or hesitantly through the entryway of a wide, squat building that houses two schools, get checked in by guards, then up a wide spiral into a large corner classroom where twenty-some high school students, all or mostly Black, sit interspersed amid desks and chairs they've left open for us. This is a small school described by the principal as one of the least selective of the district "special admits": there are fewer resources here, such as AP courses, electives, sports.

Fifty-plus cram into the classroom, not yet comfortable but alert, excited. Students talk and laugh with friends, glance at others. The college and high school teachers welcome everyone and explain our activity, the game of "Barometer," in which we will read statements aloud, asking participants to respond by locating themselves on a continuum from "agree" to "disagree." We ask for five volunteers from each school. The high schoolers put themselves forward quickly, the college students more tentatively.

I read out the first statement: People need to go to college to be successful. The high school students move quickly to "agree," college students to "disagree." The division is absolute. There is an intake of breath as I ask, "Why are you standing where you are?"

HAUNTING | 131

The high school students give the college folks a dubious look-over. Of course they want to go to college to become successful. Is this some kind of trick question?

The college students are in college. Fresh from reading Luttrell's *Schoolsmart and Motherwise,* they are passionate about the value of life intelligence gained outside school. But the high school students are putting considerable stock in just the sort of education being (modestly, but firmly) dismissed by those in college. The college students defend their position and enter a limbo, unlearning from the high school students what they think they know about themselves.

We continue this conversation in an on-line, college-based "diablog" (the college students already have usernames; the high school students enter as "guests," under the guise of names chosen from well-known African American figures):

SARAH GOODE (GUEST): I noticed that most Bryn Mawr students believed that you don't have to go to college to be successful, and all of them are in college…[25]

GEORGE WASHINGTON CARVER (GUEST): I think that if you go to college, you would have a better job, and life. But what really got me was the college students, most of them disagree the statement when they are in college be successful in life.[26]

J.NAHIG: Considering the majority of the Bryn Mawr students' responses to the question about college, I completely understand why you're asking "why are you in college"….I think it is easier for us to say that college isn't necessary, because we have (to a certain extent) a choice as to whether or not we are in college. Clearly we have the means in some way or another to attend college, and so we have the luxury of being able to consider a life without college without having to face that as an actual reality.[27]

LOUSE ARMSTRONG (GUEST): College is in some cases to be successful…. But there are thousands of people that have attended college at this day of times they can no get jobs.[28]

CHANDREA: I do see your point about the irony of us college students stating that one doesn't have to attend college to be successful. I suppose I chose to disagree with the statement

25. Sarah Goode, "I noticed that most Bryn Mawr," October 20, 2011 (12:08 p.m.).

26. George Washington Carver, "Do you need college to be successful life?" October 20, 2011 (12:04 p.m.).

27. j.nahig, "Consider the majority of," October 21, 2011 (5:37 p.m.).

28. Louse Armstrong, "Is college need to be successful," October 20, 2011 (11:56 a.m.).

because I was feeling pessimistic that day. My mom always told me that the higher up the educational ladder I go, the better for my future. But in today's economy we constantly hear about how college students graduate with loads of debt and end up jobless. It's a scary thought… And success has varying definitions. My mom had to stop attending her community college because she gave birth to me. The only thing she's got is a high school diploma, and I can see that that doesn't get much for her, so I work hard to get my degree from college and I hope for the best that there'll be a job waiting for me as soon as I step off of Bryn Mawr's campus.…[29]

In mid-November, the high school students come to our campus, where we get re-acquainted through the interactive exercise "Where the Wind Blows": "Everyone wearing the color red—go!" Students dart across the circle of chairs grabbing for a seat before they're called out. In small groups, questions deepen: Where do you feel most creative and alive? Where do you have the most to learn? To teach someone else? Then groups of two college and two high school students head out to explore campus through "one another's eyes."

Students are learning from and teaching each other, as the diablog makes clear. A high school student brings boldness and self-confidence, for example, which a college student desires to emulate:

> MAYA ANGELOU (GUEST): Something that i taught somebody in life is how to never worry about what people are saying about you.[30]
>
> NBNGUYEN: This is the thing I really want to learn from you. If you have time, please tell me how to do that…I am easily influenced by people's opinions. I try to be perfect so no one can criticize and look down on me. But I know, it's quite impossible to satisfy everybody's wants. Sometimes, I am not brave enough to make decisions for fear of mistakes and criticisms.… I wonder how you learned this skill.[31]

In a deeply classed system of education, the value of what these two students bring may be flipped: the high school student's

29. Chandrea, "In Response to Sarah Goode," October 21, 2011 (5:27 p.m.).

30. Maya Angelou, "Something that i taught," November 18, 2011 (12:45 p.m.).

31. nbnguyen, "This is the thing I really want to learn," November 19, 2011 (2:38 p.m.).

confidence, her willingness to dismiss "what people are saying about you" echoes the intelligence Luttrell shows working-class women gleaning from life. The college student's being "easily influenced by people's opinions" maps to a common value of higher education, learning to be influenced by others, to read, quote, emulate them.

Walking campus together, students' experiences of the space are altered by one another's perspectives:

> MARTIN L KING JR. (GUEST): I learned how to interact with strangers in a nice and pleasant way. Also that by us coming to their school and this being their first year, we took them to places that they have never been before on campus, and taught them new things about their school.[32]
>
> ZORA NEALE HURSTON (GUEST): Something I learned is that you can be apart of a community even if your new to it yourself. It becomes old to you once you share it with some other new people coming into the area.[33]
>
> HSBURKE: After walking around campus in groups on Tuesday, I realized how far I've come since I arrived at Bryn Mawr. Only three months ago, Bryn Mawr was completely new to me.... Now, as I proudly touted our campus to the [high school] students, I realized that Bryn Mawr has become familiar and comfortable, and that I feel a small sense of ownership: this is my home now....I was able to take a look at the campus through new eyes.[34]

A college student envisions the partnership as a bridge to new possibilities:

> SNATARAJAN: "I definitely loved having the [high school] students visit us because not only did we get the chance to show them some of our most favorite places on campus, but I was also able to learn about the hopes, dreams, and future goals of the students, some of which could potentially come to life on Bryn Mawr's campus in the future."[35]

Another, however, sees a disturbing specter:

> RAE HAMILTON: It hurts me to think of all the [high school]

32. Martin L King Jr. (guest), "I learned how to interact," November 18, 2011 (12:33 p.m.).

33. Zora Neale Hurston, "Something I learned is that," November 19, 2011 (12:34 p.m.).

34. HSBurke, "After walking around campus," November 20, 2011 (3:07 p.m.).

35. snatarajan, "This is the thing I really want to learn," November 19, 2011 (2:38 p.m.).

> girls who fell in love with Bryn Mawr, who might not be able to attend. It would be amazing to start some initiative program that would allow [these] students to come here instead showing something they can't have.[36]

At semester's end, when the classes meet via Skype to exchange appreciations and thoughts, the college students write collectively, then read,

> Thank you for calling us out on our inconsistency: a bunch of us [said] that college isn't necessary for success, but you pointed out that we are in college now; it was easy for us to say that college wasn't necessary…because we're in college…. Thank you for teaching us that it's ok to identify ourselves as what we aspire to be…

Reflecting on the semester's encounters, the college students talk about the "wisdom" and "maturity" of their high school partners, but also describe their "aspirations" as "heartbreaking": they have "the desire…a dream of college," talk about becoming pediatricians, nurses, college and professional athletes, but "don't take the next steps…" Identifying as "what [you] aspire to be" seems to play differently for some than for others. None of us—teachers, students, student consultants—knows much about where the high school students stand academically or financially. Although we speculate about how we might intervene, step into that gap of knowledge and resources to address a disconnect between dreams and means, we agree that we'd need more regular visits, stronger relationships, college visits…. A semester is much too short.

By the end of the semester, the clout of class difference is palpable: our classroom conversations reveal that even where class (and race) cross over, the college and high school students perform class differently. From their position inside an elite institution, the college students "negotiate [their] inherited and chosen identity toward where they are headed";[37] they also begin to look more clearly at their own complexly classed identities: one who works three jobs to stay here,

36. Rae Hamilton, "Hope for PHS students," November 27, 2011 (1:40 p.m.).

37. Julie Bettie, *Women without Class: Girls, Race, and Identity* (2003; rev. Oakland: University of California Press, 2014), 192.

several on leadership scholarships, another from an immigrant family stretched and anxious about their children's education.

Our students move on to various pursuits; most have now graduated. Samyuktha, who notes above her pleasure at hearing the high school students' dreams and goals, continues to work with the school. She reports that most of these students also have graduated; many went to community college or colleges in the area; some have since dropped out and have jobs, a few joined the military.[38]

Two high school students intern with Samyuktha to create a community garden, then visit her at Bryn Mawr to attend a poetry slam and other events. In their senior year, Samyuktha helps them with applications to colleges, including Bryn Mawr, where one yearns to go. But she is rejected, so devastated that she considers not going to college at all. Distressed, Samyuktha seeks counsel from the Education and Praxis Programs, which have supported the cross-school partnership. Along with Alice Lesnick from Education and Nell Anderson from Praxis, Samyuktha and I meet with several Admissions officers, but the situation proves intractable: the student's credentials aren't strong enough; what's done can't be undone; the college will try to offer more effective support in the future. Another meeting is planned, this time with the principal, and generates some shared goals, including more targeted collaboration on college admissions. This particular year was difficult at the high school, with no guidance counselors and little coaching for students about their applications; sharing this information is important to our collaboration.[39]

The two high school students attend community college, where they do well.

Although there is more outreach to students in Philadelphia, Bryn Mawr has yet to admit a student from our ongoing "community partner."

The college remains haunted by those who cannot get in.

Our partnership with the high school engages many of our

38. Samyuktha Natarajan, e-mail message to author, February 26, 2016.

39. Alice Lesnick, e-mail message to author, March 23, 2016.

students in sharing ideas, respect, even friendship; blurs the divide. Yet in their friendly encounters with the younger students, the college students inadvertently glimpse what Lois Weis calls the "class warfare" of college admissions: they have access, the high schoolers do not.[40] Being a "select" college means not admitting a number of students. Our efforts to use our educationally classed positions to invite others into dialogue are complicated and confounded by differences in access and unequal power relations. It is not only that the college students are in college now, at this elite institution, in part because the urban high school students are not. It is also that what is made invisible, unaccidentally occluded, are the ways that the college and high school students are mutually embedded in and essential to each others' positionings: each of our roles holds those of others in place. That these relationships can present as friendships, can be real and of value, renders the other dimensions of our interactions difficult to see, harder to get underneath.

Even so, the encounters between the college and high school students gesture toward new possibilities for both the younger and the older students. Valerie Walkerdine notes that what people conjure as possible is as relevant to mapping and making change as their actual landscapes. The maps our students imagine figure both individual desires and visions of greater equity. Although vision "must be enacted in the world of what is possible,"[41] moving imaginatively into that realm can help to create it.[42]

Growing out of this, Anne's and my work with our students, and Samyuktha's with hers, signal resistance to the strong undertow of things as they are, imagining into other possibilities…

I recount this story in major and minor keys: Desire and disconnection. Connection and critique.

40. Lois Weis, *Class Warfare: Class, Race, and College Admissions in Top-Tier Secondary Schools* (Chicago: The University of Chicago Press, 2014).

41. Walkerdine, "Using the Work," 761.

42. Maxine Greene, "Coda: The Slow Fuse of Change: Obama, the Schools, Imagination, and Convergence," *Harvard Educational Review* 79 (Summer 2009): 396–98.

Dismissing Class

Back on campus, our linked sections of "In Class/OutClassed" are designing a workshop to reach out to our own community. We craft this invitation:

> As part of the Bryn Mawr Class Dismissed Initiative we would like to invite you to participate in our workshop on Friday November 11th from 2:00pm-3:15pm in Rhoads Dining Hall; the workshop is titled Mapping Out Class. The Class Dismissed Initiative is an attempt to increase conversations about socioeconomic class on Bryn Mawr's campus as a result of a campus survey that revealed that class differences on campus are the most likely to produce feelings of exclusion among students, faculty and staff.
>
> The Mapping Out Class workshop will be an opportunity to have an open discussion on campus about an issue that is seldom talked about, but that is very present on our campus: socioeconomic class. In which spaces do we feel comfortable? How are class differences displayed on campus? Why do we feel excluded? We look forward to exploring this topic with a diverse group of students, faculty and staff and we want YOU to help us do it. In the workshop we will also look for ways to move forward and to envision a better Bryn Mawr. What can we do as individuals and as an institution to ease class tensions on campus?

Our class brainstorms an outreach strategy: students will invite people they know and want to know across constituencies of the college, in hopes of parlaying this event into a "diverse group of students, faculty and staff." Some who work in dining halls will invite co-workers; others look forward to inviting their housekeepers, with whom they feel a particular connection.

Although it's often a challenge to get folks out to events such as this, responses begin to come in, and—with excitement—we sense a mounting interest. But then first one, then another and another of our students report that members of the housekeeping and dining services staff have declined their invitations. Several students describe "a gate coming down" between them and those they thought they'd befriended. We problem-solve, meeting with the head of staff, who writes a memo excusing employees to attend our workshop during working hours. Still, only one housekeeper comes, a part-time student who has been in my class.

Even so, we pull off a highly successful event: well attended and taken up, with participants generating insightful critique and thinking toward next steps. Suggestions range from the clear, dry "Acknowledge me when I'm serving you—I go to this school too," to the acerbic "You have to get your…income tattooed on your forehead." There are specific recommendations:

> Please change international student orientation. Do not make students on financial aid stand up in front of others so that they must leave to go to a special financial aid session, when "wealthy" don't have to go to the session.

> [Talk] about issues from the beginning of each student's journey here—so all students are more aware and educated of the assumptions and prejudices we bring to campus and discuss how we can move forward together.

> Equalize the pay scale [for student jobs].

Many acknowledge the importance of discussions like this one, which "de-stigmatize the sort of class distinctions that dominate—unconsciously—the social imagining here at BMC," and help us "teach each other with no judgment." Yet absences speak loudly:

> I know this is the first year that class is really being talked about but I think the discussion needs to be integrated into the school's curriculum. Somehow, everyone needs to be forced to confront these issues because no matter how many optional conversations there are, the people who need to be there probably won't be.

> Respect for all levels of staff, especially such as dining, housekeeping, facilities. The folks who really keep the place going.

> More areas of interaction between faculty and (different levels of) staff. Allowing technical/clerical/utility staff to participate in community dialogue without fear of being fired. Allow staff on all levels to collaborate and get to know each other.

On-line, then in class, we debrief the workshop, highlighting both dialogues that happened and those that didn't:

> RAE HAMILTON: I invited people that I had constant disagreements/fights because of class. My original idea was for them to go to the workshop and maybe see my point of view better, yet I actually was one who learned a lot.[43]
>
> LISSIEM: Participating in the workshop was very challenging for me. It was very uncomfortable, but that's why we've having workshops like this in the first place![44]
>
> S. YAEGER: In many ways, the absence of housekeepers and landscapers from the workshop highlighted one of the difficulties in starting a discussion of this nature on campus. No matter how hard we work to be inclusive, there may always be a barrier between those in privileged positions, and those who are in positions of support. I wonder how we can bridge that barrier.[45]

These comments name a space of contradiction. Students note that we could have gotten the word out to staff members more effectively—made it clear that they could get released from work to attend—but also index tensions among staff members, acknowledge that "something else is going on with housekeeping": Staff members worry that they may lose their jobs or promotions if they speak out; the "head person is mean to them"; if they "step out of line," it would not be a "positive addition to their environment"; "you can attend but still have to get your work done"; "you don't know how catty people can be." Differences in age as well as class are signaled here.

Our group struggles not to deny complicity, to stay engaged. To understand these structures that classify and divide us, especially tricky since the work of the housekeeping staff overlaps with the work of mothers and with service work designed to be unobtrusive,

---

43. Rae Hamilton, "The Workshop," November 15, 2011 (3:52 a.m.).

44. lissiem, "Workshop," November 13, 2011 (10:47 p.m.).

45. S. Yaeger, "Some Thoughts on Our Workshop," November 13, 2011 (3:55 p.m.).

effaced.[46] A student reflects that if we invited support staff to other less formal events, like teas in dorms, this kind of invite wouldn't seem like such a big deal. Our position as faculty also occludes our vision: we might have extended our invitation through their organization, the Staff Association.

By inviting support staff to a campus dialogue, we presume shared community; by overlooking the unequal distribution, status, and visibility of labor, we inadvertently reproduce inequity. It is not only that the housekeepers' absence from our on-campus dialogue is, in part, what constitutes the experience of being served, as a member of the intellectual elite, by others. It is also that the positions of college students and housekeepers are interlocked, as luxury of study for the former is enabled by the work of the latter. M. Carey Thomas's vision still haunts, as the intimate, gendered connections between students and housekeepers discourage investigation of the very power relations we'd hoped to discuss.

Our student consultants join us in telling college administrators what we learned and what we suggest for moving forward:

> We had 70 some attendees; 3 were support staff. Inviting folks to "come have a conversation" generated a definite class-based response; many support staff are not comfortable w/ that sort of set-up.
>
> The notice to supervisors—to allow folks to take time to come—did not find its way to many (any?) staff members themselves. Housekeepers and other staff members said that their jobs could be jeopardized by their speaking out. And several housekeepers said that they "had nothing to say." Should we have framed our invitation differently-and-less-explicitly?
>
> Could "next steps" in this conversation include staging discussions among particular groups (folks in dining services, housekeeping, etc.) who would then "send some representatives" to a larger cross-campus conversation and "speak for" their constituent group? When people are on campus, they are professionals, representing the college. They have to consider what it means to be in their position and when honesty may put

46. Bettie, *Women without Class*, 198.

> them in an awkward professional position.
>
> If this workshop was truly valued, why wasn't it funded and advertised like [the semester's big event, a series of talks by] Judith Butler? How important is this Class Dismissed initiative?

In our report, we admit that our class was taken by surprise by the barriers to investigating class across constituencies on campus: the quiet, implacable structuring of roles in which only some of us are safely (and dangerously?) ensconced in positions of power. Our surprise is not so surprising: With the exception of living wage campaigns, the class divide on U.S. college campuses has been largely ignored. Alice Lesnick offers a sharp analysis of why this might be: that the very structure of educational systems teaches ranking, and so elucidates the staying power of these divisions:

> education at all levels too often amounts to teaching students to divide the world…by ranking different traditions, forms of work, and people. These lessons are not always the product of instruction; they result from the social organization of work.[47]

Our workshop and report—like other Classed Dismissed projects—are well received, with a reception at the president's house, upbeat coverage on college media, promises that this is a beginning. Some efforts follow: the college becomes test optional, a strategy that tends to increase applications from lower-income students; an Admissions officer pilots a cohort model to recruit small groups of lower-income students of color; "diversity conversations" continue to explore dimensions of identity including class.

Tensions and inequities remain, as investigated by first-year students in later writing seminars we offer; and much more extensively in the college's recent Community Day of Learning, "In/Visible: Class on Campus, Class in our Lives,"[48] where a day of workshops for all constituencies on campus includes sessions that cut broadly, others concentrating on the college, others on personal demeanor ("knowing the right things, carrying yourself in certain ways").

---

47. Alice Lesnick. "Teaching and Learning in Community: Staff-Student Learning Partnerships As Part of a College Education," *Journal of Community Engagement and Scholarship* 3, no. 1 (2012).

48. Emily Wells and Emily Schalk, "2016 Community Day of Learning Examines Issues of Class," February 25, 2016 (2:38 p.m.).

A century after Thomas articulated her vision of luxury and scholarship for select women, the Dean of the Undergraduate College, Karen Tidmarsh, confirms that a Bryn Mawr education "requires solitude, quiet, freedom from everyday responsibilities"—in order "to train a new elite, *an elite that will change the world.*"[49] This twist, in which the scholar becomes the world-changer, doesn't sit well. When I send a draft of this chapter to Anne, she writes into this discomfort:

> It's a gray and rainy day. I couldn't be more comfortable, sitting in a big soft chair, in a beautifully paneled room at the back of our farmhouse, reviewing the draft of a chapter about "encountering class" that Jody's just sent me.
>
> Rhoda Coffelt, who is cleaning here today, asks me if I can move into Jeff's study.
>
> So she can clean mine.
>
> This is less a ghost than an insistent presence. One that I rely on, in order to do my work. That unsettles me.

The word "school" is from the Greek "skhole" for "leisure." We begin to account, here, for some of the relationships that make that leisure possible.

It's unsettling, too, to realize that investigating class division on campus becomes a priority only when fissures among some of our students and the women who cleaned their dorms are revealed by our efforts to be "inclusive." Even that language presumes the possibility of completeness, and, as Martha Minow points out, suggests that we know the ways of working with difference that are best for everyone.[50] It also presumes straightforwardness—shared language and interests, equity of democratic structures—embedded in unstable social states. Teachers and students must disorient our gaze, reimagining with others across a spectrum on campus what it might mean to re-design life for-and-with the whole college community. A different kind of dialogue is needed,

49. Karen Tidmarsh, "The Highly Practical Liberal Arts," *Bryn Mawr Now* XXVI (Spring/Summer 1997): 7, italics added.

50. Martha Minow, *Making All the Difference: Inclusion, Exclusion, and American Law* (Ithaca, NY: Cornell University Press, 1990).

> ...contained in the assumption of neutral, impersonal writing styles is the lack of risk...we have lost the courage and the vocabulary to describe [the personal] in the face of the enormous social pressure to "keep it to ourselves"—but this is where our most idealistic and our deadliest politics are lodged, and are revealed.
> —Patricia Williams, *The Alchemy of Race and Rights*

> Writing instruction is a political process.
> —Julie Lindquist, "Class Affects, Class Affectations: Working Through the Paradoxes of Strategic Empathy"

one that questions the economic underpinnings of the college, and begins to imagine other landscapes into being.

As Gordon points out, even when hidden in plain sight, people can "achieve a measure of agency and possibility…refusing to be treated as if one was…fated to a life of…spectrality."[51] Following her here, we can read the decision of support staff not to attend our workshop less as absence than as agency, a choice about priorities, a refusal of our terms; a claim for approaches that differ from ours.

Classed admissions and classed arrangements on campus work hand in hand to fortify larger structures, as "selective" colleges cultivate greater access to power for the few, situating others outside of and in service to. Anne's and my own ambiguous location as continuing non-tenure track faculty comes into play here: we are both less vulnerable—in positions of some power vis a vis both staff and students—and more so—neither adjunct to nor on the academic hierarchy, shadows of "professors." Our positioning nudges us to question a "system that…limits our ability to find each other, to see beyond it and to access the places that we know lie outside its walls."[52] As we press our students and ourselves to encounter classed experiences and structural inequities, we work the tension between interrogating the system, and a yearning toward membership in it.

Writing Class

These encounters with high school students and misses with support staff take place within the framework of a first-semester writing seminar. And so it seems appropriate to turn now to the deeply classed nature of writing itself, both pronounced and obscured by entry into an institution and a course where learning academic writing is paramount.

My goals as a writing teacher hover and tangle: To teach the skills of conventional academic writing, what literacy educator Lisa Delpit calls "codes of power," to students who are diverse by class.[53] And

51. Gordon, "Some Thoughts," 15.

52. Jack Halberstam, "The Wild Beyond: With and for the Undercommons," in Stefano Harney and Fred Moten, *The Undercommons: Fugitive Planning and Black Study* (Brooklyn, NY: Minor Compositions, 2013), 6.

53. Lisa Delpit, "The Silenced Dialogue: Power and Pedagogy in Educating Other People's Children," *Harvard Educational Review* 58, no. 3 (1988): 163.

to help students learn to write in ways that take on conventional structures of language and power, becoming a source of power that can speak to power. And to open the space for those students to add their voices to the discourse, by taking up alternate forms of literate expression and offering us rich windows on different ways of being and communicating.[54]

Teaching college writing sits right at the hub of language, class, and power. As literacy theorists recognize, some students arrive still needing to learn conventions they'll be expected to perform throughout college, while others are already prepared to play with those forms. Delpit argues for the importance of explicitly teaching "codes or rules...for participating in the culture of power" to those who have less power, not to dismiss home languages but to amplify students' options.[55] David Bartholomae also notes the value of teaching students various forms of expression, including but not limited to discourses of power. He offers Patricia Williams' *Alchemy of Race and Rights*—a compellingly unconventional text from which we read in this final section of our course—as a text in which the "writing is disunified; it mixes genres; it willfully forgets the distinction between formal and colloquial, public and private; it makes unseemly comparisons...features we associate with basic writing, although here those features mark her achievement as a writer, not her failure."[56] How do writers show that they know they are playing with convention, and why does this matter?

Even listing these goals and questions reveals a split: Academic writing—a code of power—is conceptualized as distanced, impersonal, abstract, not as narrative or concrete. How to nurture a weave, a richer, more full-bodied set of possibilities? Understanding that "class is experienced in terms of affect, nostalgia, and desire," composition teacher Julie Lindquist coaches her working-class students in "narrative theorizing that enables consciousness of the particulars of class experience."[57] In this mix, class can operate as a source of power, integral to how and why people tell their stories.

---

54. Patricia A. Sullivan, "Composing Culture: A Place for the Personal," *College English* 66 (2003): 46.

55. Delpit, "The Silenced Dialogue," 163.

56. David Bartholomae, "The Tidy House: Basic Writing in the American Curriculum," *Journal of Basic Writing* 12, no. 1 (1993): 11.

57. Julie Lindquist, "Class Affects, Classroom Affectations: Working through the Paradoxes of Strategic Empathy," *College English* 67 (2004): 189, 194.

Literary critic Barbara Christian also insists that "narrative" can be a form of theorizing. Focusing on differences of race more explicitly than of class, she clarifies how splitting stories from ideas, academic from personal, is a political act, and how refusing this split carries its own clout:

> People of color have always theorized—but in forms quite different from the Western form of abstract logic…our theorizing… is often in narrative forms…in the play with language, since dynamic rather than fixed ideas seem more to our liking…the women I grew up around continuously speculated about the nature of life through pithy language that unmasked the power relations of their world.[58]

Lindquist and Christian suggest that narrative can be theory, that telling stories can help create critical spaces for reconsidering the locus and purpose of writing. Teaching writing can tease out nuanced, contradictory experiences of class, where stories and speculations, in all of their "variety, multiplicity, eroticism," are powerful, sometimes "difficult to control."[59] Telling stories can intervene in structures of power.

On the first of December, Anne's daughter Marian, an urban farmer and educator, comes to talk with our classes about a "class autobiography" she'd written a few years earlier, when she herself was in college. Marian's 'zine, "For what(ever) It'$ Worth: Reflections, thoughts, and suggestions on Class Privilege, Inheritance, and Inequity from a young white woman of wealth," is a frank interrogation of what it means to inherit a lot of money. Anne introduces her daughter: Mar and I are both taking a pretty big risk today—she to come as a guest speaker and facilitator to her mother's (!) classroom, me to come out to you all as the mother of a millionaire—and then we move into a silent discussion about class: moving around our classroom and commenting anonymously on large posted sheets with questions about key words—home, work, clothing, health, space, recreation, income, education. After we discuss this, Marian talks

---

58. Barbara Christian, "The Race for Theory," *Cultural Critique: The Nature and Context of Minority Discourse* 6 (1987): 52.

59. Christian, "The Race for Theory," 59.

about writing her 'zine, which infuses identity work with political analysis. Owning her membership in the "owning" class counters the debilitating "narcissism" of guilt and opens up her work in the world, as she asks, "What can I do with having money?"[60]

Students are intrigued by what Marian has to say, and curious, though uncertain, about the alternative ways she chooses to say it:

> JHARMON: in this [academic] process of editing, paring, and abstracting, how much of our voice are we deleting and muting? How much of ourselves do we take out of our own equation? Here, I'm thinking about Marion's zine and the way she kept it unedited. While it is messy and filled with typos, it reminds me of the journey of learning that Dewey alluded to in the beginning of the semester. It reminds me that this journey is just as important as the final product. Through Marion showing us an earlier work of what she hopes to accomplish, we understand her "unperfected" thoughts. Thus, we better understand her personal journey of knowledge, and from there we somehow relate and empathize with that journey and struggle...[61]
>
> MICHAELA: I have felt similarly—I often sit down...to write an essay, and feel like there are very specific points at which I am supposed to insert myself and my own voice, and others where I am supposed to keep quiet and let the facts speak for themselves—but how does that work? Don't I have to give light and interpretation to these facts?...I like Marian's zine, because it did show the less-polished side of thoughtful, provocative writing—but that could never be submitted for a grade in a college course. Can we encourage more students to take on projects like these? Or is it asking too much, given the high amount of academic writing each...college student...is assigned?[62]

What's happening in the space opened up by the clarity—paradoxically "messy" and "unperfected" in its texturing of struggle—of Marian's 'zine?

In acknowledging that "people are poor, in part, because of the concentrated wealth that I have benefited from," Marian opens the door to a personal way of going beyond the personal, a form of "narrative theorizing" from a position of power. Her 'zine reorients our

---

60. Marian (Paia) Dalke, "For what(ever) It'$ Worth: Reflections, thoughts, and suggestions on Class Privilege, Inheritance, and Inequity from a young white woman of wealth," self published, January 2009.

61. JHarmon, "Being Perfect," December 2, 2011 (2:56 a.m.).

62. Michaela, "I have felt similarly—I," December 3, 2011 (2:51 p.m.).

gaze, suggests how varied forms of writing might help unsettle our investment in classed ways of distinguishing ourselves.

Both to continue this unsettling and help our students imagine alternatives, we unbind our next assignment from conventions they've been working all semester to master:

> By 5 p.m. Friday (Dec. 9):
>
> writing assignment # 11, 3 pp. (or equivalent) "de-classifying" your writing for this class, going beyond the weekly 3-pp. papers you've been writing for Jody and Anne. What would you like to say to the whole Bryn Mawr community—or to the whole world??—about issues of class and education? What new format might you play with, to say these things? (Marian's zine may have given you some ideas....)

Not surprisingly, the confidence with which students take up these options is inflected by class.

We hear quickly from Chandrea:

> I was discussing my confusion on the next assignment we have to do for this class..., and my cluelessness reminded me of how dependent I am on writing academic papers. I remembered worrying, "What do you mean it doesn't have to be in the form of an academic paper?!"...I'm so used to writing papers in this class as well as other classes...That's all we did in high school! I mean, I could do a poster or something but I really am not that creative/artistic as I'd like to be. Maybe a slam poetry presentation would work for me because I think those kinds of things are fun.... I never expected to come to college and be told to do anything but write papers when it came to expressing my ideas...[63]

63. Chandrea, "Different Forms of Expression?" December 3, 2011 (4:56 p.m.).

Several days later, she returns to our public forum:

> This is a poster-collage that I did last night. I was pleased yet frightened with the finished project and I ended up running to my posse. They were really proud of me and wanted to do their own version of the poster-collage. I was inspired by Marian's zine and I remember being so amused with it because I could relate on so many levels - except that instead of being a millionaire, I decided to declare that I was FAR from that. I think I've always

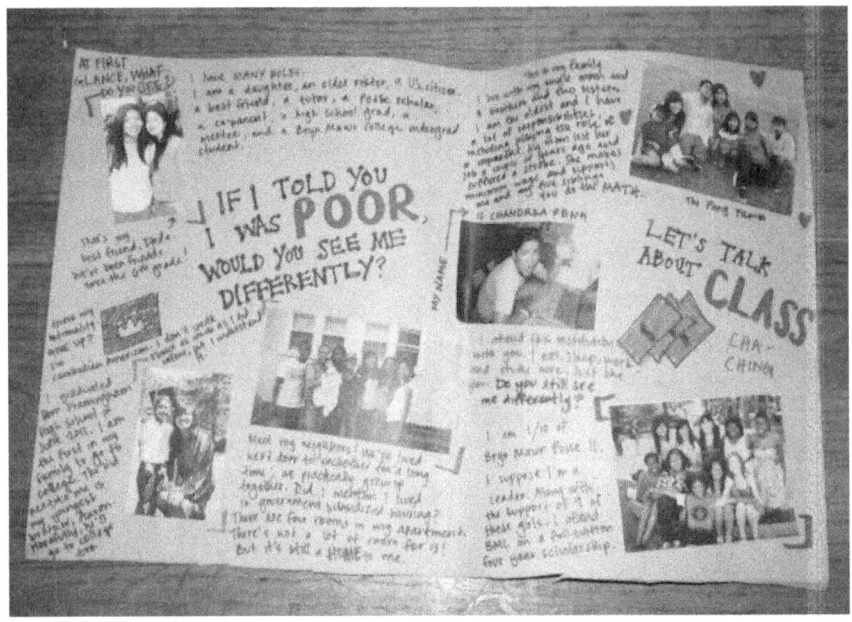

kept my socioeconomic status as a secret in high school and now that I'm in college, I'm deciding to own up to my status, just like Marian did. I'm actually thinking of posting it outside of my dorm because I don't know what else to do with it. But I don't know how the people on my hall will react or if they will react at all. I kept the class workshop in mind because we discussed broadening the audience when it came to talking about class. And my audience is the Bryn Mawr community as a whole. On the bottom left, next to the picture of me and my little brother it says: "I graduated from Framingham High School in June 2011. I am the first in my family to go to college. The kid next to me is my youngest brother, Aaron. Hopefully, he'll go to college too."[64]

Chandrea's poster plays with genre to invite and challenge viewers to examine our assumptions about who she is, and who we are. Her turn here from the conventions of schooled writing, revealing herself in relation to material goods, family, and friends, engages her in a creative act that maps her capacity to be in more than one place at the same time.[65]

Chandrea writes herself "poor." Another student, "Hummingbird,"

64. Chandrea, "If I told you I was poor, would you see me differently?" December 9, 2011 (5:34 p.m.).

65. Walkerdine, "Using the Work," 760.

also struggles toward a more complex cartography, in which she gets written as "privileged." Her final project for the class, which opens with a letter, is called "Classism v. Feminism and Why a Discussion about MTV Can Get Very Complicated Very Fast." It is set in a college dining hall, where a disproportionate share of working class students work alongside regular college employees.

> "Dear Bryn Mawr College Dining Services,
>
> You are all amazing people. To run this dining hall is like running the world. To deal with these dumb whiny bitches is too much! If they are trying to take the television out of the dining hall b/c they say that too many of the music videos objectify women, then they have meaningless and idiotic lives. You shouldn't take the dumbass bullshit from these privileged students. If they feel as though they are being objectified, they should write to MTV who shows the videos and, most importantly, the artists who produce the music. To complain about music videos and a television?! Most of the women, girls really, who complain, don't respect the spaces that they live in. They have no reason to complain about this place. Don't take the TV away. Rather, tell the snooty dumbasses to SHUT THE FUCK UP! YOU DON'T KNOW WHAT REAL OBJECTIFICATION IS!!!
>
> Sincerely,
>
> POSSE SCHOLAR"

> Confused? I was too.
>
> Actually, my range of emotions went from bewildered to outrage to confusion to (perhaps?) understanding and finally frustration. But this story didn't start out being about class.
>
> A few weeks ago Bryn Mawr College screened *MissRepresentation*. The documentary explores the ways women have been poorly portrayed by the media. My hallmates felt empowered by the film. My friend, Nina*, thought of the television in the back of Erdman dining hall and how the only channel is MTVU (the University/College version of MTV). She commented on the way the majority of the programming objectifies women. Nina

contacted Dining Services to see about having the TV removed. Dining Services said Nina would have to get a petition signed, as they didn't have the full authority to act on a request like hers.

Soon afterwards, two petition sheets were posted and I signed the one that read "I do NOT think MTVu improves my dining experience." As we were leaving, we took a look at the napkin notes and realized a debate was occurring.

Napkin Notes are a Bryn Mawr Dining Hall institution - pinned to a bulletin board for the dining staff to read. Students can request grapes at lunch, for example, thank Dining Services for a job well done. The MTVu conversation changed the Napkin Notes Board, though, because they were a conversation between students. When I first saw them, only two had been put up, both expressing a preference for ending the MTVu service. Nina and I were excited that napkin notes were being used to host a discussion. I wrote my own note to post on the board:

"I don't want MTVu in the Dining Halls, because I don't want to see degrading images of women while eating breakfast. We should be feeling empowered, not overdressed."

I felt good after adding my own voice. My friends agreed with my sentiment and commended me for writing. And then, a few days later, I saw the note we started with.

I was shocked and felt the accusations that those of us who disagreed with the presence of the TV were "privileged" were unfair and unfounded. I was also struck by how this conversation very suddenly became about class and not about gender. We had been labeled "snooty bitches" and we "[didn't] know what real objectification [was]." After the shock subsided, I was outraged. How dare she accuse me of being privileged because I didn't want to have to watch degrading images of women, in a women's college? Another note written in response to the angry note asked what gave her the right to conflate privilege with the ability to point out objectification. Then I reread the first note and noticed she'd identified herself as a Posse Scholar.

Posse scholars get a special scholarship based on their leadership skills. Scholars meet on a regular basis throughout their senior year of high school to discuss a range of subjects, including race,

> gender, and class, and they seem to be some of the most socially aware students.
>
> I decided to talk to my hallmate, another Posse Scholar.... To my surprise, she said she could understand both sides of the story. She explained that when she was growing up she watched MTV all the time. She could understand seeing a level of privilege in those who didn't watch MTV growing up. I was skeptical at first, but then thought about it. Could there be a classed difference in whether or not one grew up watching scantily clad women fawn over rappers? My hallmate also suggested the Scholar assumed our notes were directed to the staff—who work hard enough as is—instead of towards each other.
>
> So I'd come to (almost) understand the student's strong response. But if watching MTV as a child was, indeed, a sign of class difference, why did degrading women have to be a part of that? Every day, I felt as though I was being reminded that my job as a woman (or girl) was to be seen and not heard.
>
> I understand that removing a television won't stop MTV from showing videos that objectify women. I also understand that not everyone has the option to not view this objectifying media. However, I do think removing a TV which is currently owned by the MTV corporation is taking a step.
>
> *Name has been changed. Names on the Napkin Notes have been erased for anonymity.*[66]

Hummingbird's account traces her recognition of how different backgrounds can lead to different perspectives, and suggests how complex and fraught it is to navigate toward new understandings and actions. While Pratt's "literate arts of the contact zone," which we discussed early in the semester, feature the reach and risk of those on the lower end of power relations, Hummingbird's communication—also reaching, risking—invokes another source and purpose.

The way Hummingbird participates in the shared spaces of napkin notes and on-line dialogue suggests a confidence with putting forth her voice that may also be classed. She recognizes this as she reflects on her process: feeling "good after adding my

66. Hummingbird, "Classism v. Feminism and Why a Discussion about MTV Can Get Very Complicated Very Fast," December 9, 2011 (6:46 p.m.).

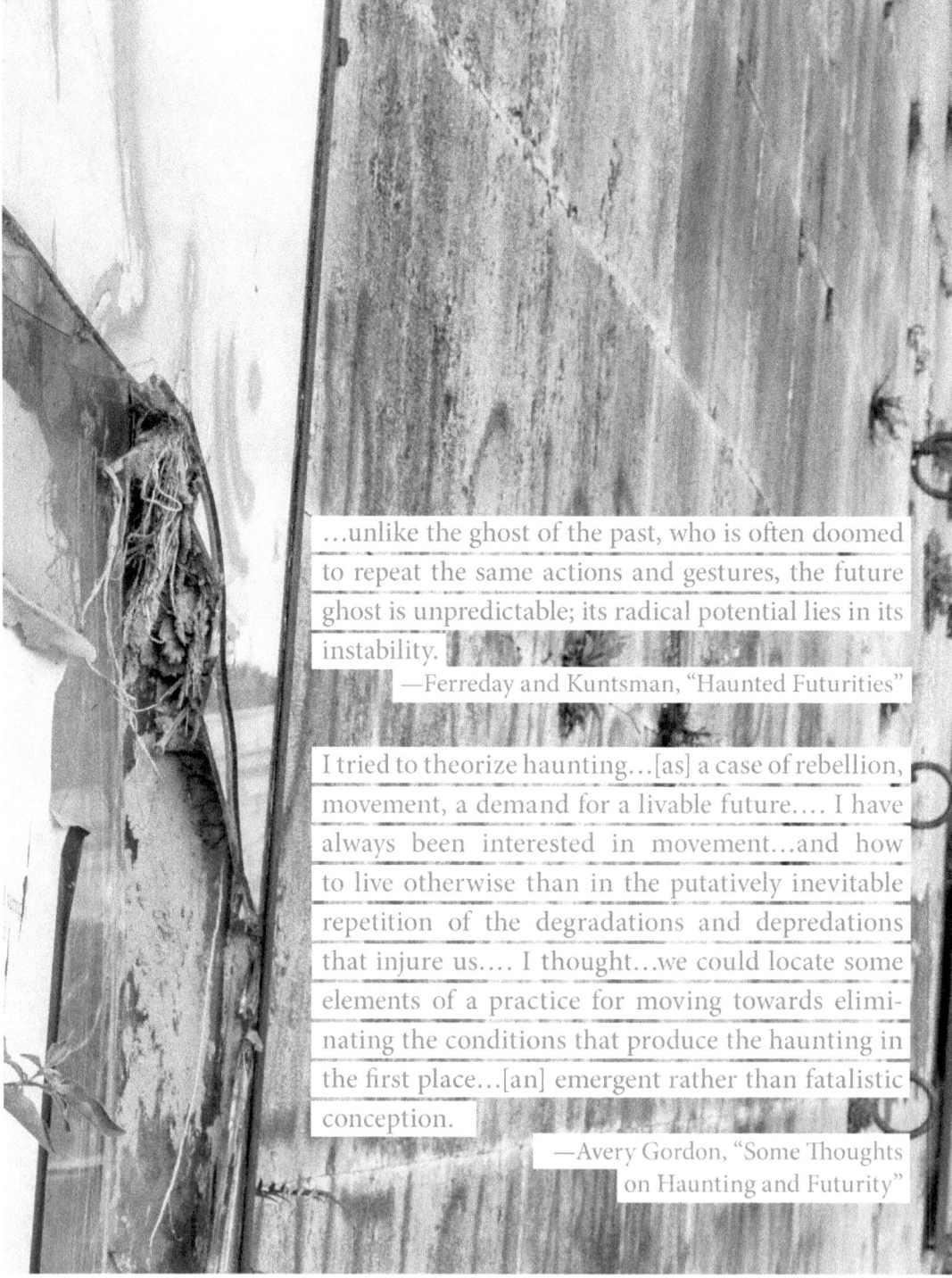

…unlike the ghost of the past, who is often doomed to repeat the same actions and gestures, the future ghost is unpredictable; its radical potential lies in its instability.
—Ferreday and Kuntsman, "Haunted Futurities"

I tried to theorize haunting…[as] a case of rebellion, movement, a demand for a livable future.… I have always been interested in movement…and how to live otherwise than in the putatively inevitable repetition of the degradations and depredations that injure us.… I thought…we could locate some elements of a practice for moving towards eliminating the conditions that produce the haunting in the first place…[an] emergent rather than fatalistic conception.
—Avery Gordon, "Some Thoughts on Haunting and Futurity"

own voice"; realizing that she's one of the "snooty bitches" being called out by a Posse Scholar who is likely "socially aware"; then asking, "Could there be a classed difference in whether or not one grew up watching scantily clad women fawn over rappers?" On the other hand, her queries throughout the piece use the middle-class convention of framing questions rather than making assertions; as Delpit notes, such oblique communication can betray discomfort with the power one holds.[67]

In this early moment in her college experience, Hummingbird tries to write herself into understanding another upbringing. Both off-line and on,[68] her writing generates a hot dialogue that includes "rage, incomprehension, and pain…wonder and revelation, mutual understanding, and new wisdom—the joys of the contact zone."[69] Hummingbird continues to struggle publicly, and to shift position:

> Last Friday (December 9th) I posted an opinion piece on the napkin notes and MTVu discussion…. When I wrote it, I knew it would be public—that was part of the assignment for our class. However, I didn't realize how quickly it would spread to be a topic of discussion. Even as we speak the MTVu situation is growing more and more complicated…. I no longer feel confident that removing the TV is our best option…. I think the school's best option right now is to host more discussions like the ones I've had with my friends—discussions which focus on sharing our experiences and thoughts on all these intersecting topics: gender, race, and class. Bryn Mawr is not a homogenous group and I think pushing on these tense topics can only help the student body and college grow as a whole.[70]

As Anne and I had done with the high school partnership and on-campus workshop, Hummingbird turns to dialogue as a way to generate learning and "growth."

From their differently classed positions, Chandrea and Hummingbird engage in narrative theorizing, calling on their experiences in transition to put forth risky thinking—not just to their teachers but to an audience that is both closer—in the dormitories where they live—and larger—on the internet. In her

67. Delpit, "The Silenced Dialogue," 284.

68. Comments, "Classism v. Feminism and Why a Discussion about MTV Can Get Very Complicated Very Fast," December 10, 2011 (2:39 a.m.)—February 2, 2012 (7:36 p.m.).

69. Pratt, "Arts of the Contact Zone," 39.

70. Hummingbird, "Gender, Body Images, and (M)TV," December 16, 2011 (12:25 p.m.).

description of a "contact zone," Pratt notes that "one had to work in the knowledge that whatever one said was going to be systematically received in radically heterogeneous ways that we were neither able nor entitled to prescribe," and calls for "a systematic approach to the all-important concept of cultural mediation."[71] Chandrea and Hummingbird occupy a contact zone, both in class and out of it, where their words shift meaning once exposed to others. I here lay their stories alongside one another, reading them as linked and mutually echoing, gestures toward futures that might surprise.

71. Pratt, "Arts of the Contact Zone," 39, 40.

Haunting the Future

In *The Communist Manifesto*, Marx & Engels called out the phantasmagoric: "a spectre is haunting Europe: the spectre of Communism"[72]—to signal the human capacity to change the conditions of our lives. More than a century later, my grandfather Joseph lived and died a committed socialist, leaving a spectral legacy that nuances my classed experience and propels my teaching: pushes me to ask what being and teaching this capacity to change lives might look like now.

72. Karl Marx and Freidrich Engels, *The Communist Manifesto*, 1848, rpted. in *The People's Cube*, February 26, 2009.

Avery Gordon muses that haunting can bring "a certain retrospective urgency: the something-to-be-done feels as if it has already been needed or wanted before, perhaps forever…and we cannot wait for it any longer."[73] In this final section, I speak to how this class on class might illuminate ways to approach the "something-to-be-done," with pedagogies of acting, reflecting, resituating, re-acting.

73. Gordon, "Some Thoughts," 5.

Alice Lesnick, who wrote so incisively above about education as de facto instruction in class hierarchy, also enacted an intervention in this dynamic: Her college-supported program, "Empowering Learners Partnerships," offered a philosophy and model for tapping into everyone's rich capacities, by connecting students with staff members as adult partners in teaching and learning. Partners learned about Islam, jazz, digital photography, social media, how to conduct online research; and developed greater awareness of each other's lives.[74] Although powerful for many participants, the program is no longer active: institutional support receded, and there was fear about staff vulnerability.

This reminder of the precarity of individuals as well as of institutional interventions calls up vulnerabilities exposed during "InClass/OutClassed": when students' own access became visible in relation to others' in our "Mapping Class Exercise"; when sharing their thoughts and hopes in public spheres generated push-back; when the high school student who dreamed of attending this college did not get in; when the housekeepers' susceptibility to censure may have kept them from joining our workshop. If, as Alice asserts, education inherently stratifies by valorizing academic work, and if challenging this hierarchy exposes both complicities and susceptibilities, then we must work differently. Generating integration from the belly of higher education means moving forth in and from contradiction, generating multiple tactics, interventions arising from diverse, shifting positions that include a recognition of people's precarities and positionalities.

In her introduction to *Tactical Media*, Rita Raley draws on the work of artist-activists to theorize alternative approaches to "revolutionary transformation": She describes how they "critique and resist the new world order but do so from within by intervening on the site of symbolic systems of power." These "campaigns comprise little tactics rather than bold strategies," Raley explains. "Critical Art Ensemble's understanding of power as diffused, networked, multiple, and a-territorial....'us' and 'them' are no longer permanently situated," rendering "the phenomenon of resistance fleeting, ephemeral, and subject to continual morphing."[75]

This description offers another way to read the forms of activism described in this chapter. Our students' work with high school students, their on-campus workshop on class matters, their interventions into the class presumptions of academic writing are all "little tactics," instances of "fleeting...resistance" that challenge a consensus

74. Lesnick, "Teaching and Learning in Community"; Alice Lesnick and Alison Cook-Sather, "Building Civic Capacity On Campus Through a Radically Inclusive Teaching and Learning Initiative," *Innovative Higher Education* 35 (2010).

75. Rita Raley, *Tactical Media* (Minneapolis: University of Minnesota Press, 2009), 11, 13.

reality that figures impact as large, lasting, widely recognizable, and exchangeable in discourse. These encounters arise and recede, shape-shift into others, ripple, submerge, erupt over time and across space.

Anne and I are teachers who hold radical beliefs in relation to social class, who are deeply troubled by the injustice of social class divisions—and who go to work every day on a campus filled with trees that surround majestic stone buildings, at a college that outsources the labor of maintaining this beauty. We are critical of the political and economic arrangements that make students who are lower-income, of color, of a non-traditional age, and/or of non-conforming gender less likely to be enrolled at this college; where those who serve the students have less power in the community than those who teach them; where conventional academic writing helps to maintain such class divisions. In a course aimed at cracking open presumptions about education and class, we also teach students to move through a system that keeps those presumptions in place. And yet this is a system where we ourselves thrive, as we have opportunities and resources to teach in ways that engage ourselves and our students in exploring alternative possibilities.

We teach to question and challenge the system we work within. Collaborate with colleagues and young people to access power to impact power. Practice not shutting down when we encounter institutional resistance. Wait for a moment to forge another path in—or out. Aim to be "accomplices" to our students, "compelled to become accountable and responsible to each other,"[76] in widening circles of writing, waiting, acting. Welcome hauntings as radical potentiality.

76. "Accomplices Not Allies: Abolishing the Ally Industrial Complex, An Indigenous Perspective and Provocation," Indigenous Action Media, May 4, 2014: 6.

INTERMISSION
WHEREFROM? WHO TO?

Settling in to work together on our new project, unbinding conventional assumptions of teaching and learning, buoyed up by our collaborative process—it's actually the pronouns that snag us first. We begin with the first person plural. It's the first—*and probably most repeated, though who'll do the count?*—word in our book:

> We write collaboratively as two experienced teachers....
>
> We draw on stories from our own teaching....
>
> we describe...
>
> we argue...
>
> ...seeking the sorts of spaces many of us both resist and long to explore, where our histories, nightmares, and desires "blow our covers" as rational subjects.
>
> —Anne and Jody, Introduction

As soon as we begin to share our work, friends write back,

> Who is "we" here?
>
> Here's a place where I don't know if "we" means the two of you or people in general: "We are all interconnected, and those interconnections are inexhaustible.... We think that we can actually learn...."

Drafting successive chapters, we begin to notice just how much that "we" *moves,* how slippery, shifting its referents.

Sure, sometimes it's just us two.

Sometimes it's a fairly comfortable extension: us and our students.

Sometimes it's our colleagues. Sometimes we try to reach way beyond those we know, make claims about, ask questions of, college teachers who attend conferences:

> Why are we reading, too much, too quickly, words that cannot be heard, understood, followed at such a pace? Why aren't we making space for back-and-forthing, for co-creation and exploration?
>
> —Anne, "Silencing"

Sometimes (as in those quotes bothering one of our colleagues, above), the claims are much grander.

Sometimes we risk speaking for radical educators:

> We are critical of the political and economic arrangements.... We teach to question and challenge the system we work within.
>
> —Jody, "Haunting"

All *learners, all humanity*:

> The persistence of this leakage...plays on a disquiet we work hard to keep at bay: the impossibility of fully knowing, containing, controlling our worlds, our immediate surrounds, ourselves.
>
> —Jody, "Leaking"

What Bruno Latour calls the problem of "how to tell" our common story continues to bedevil us.

We start working backwards. Re-thinking every "we" we've written. Re-writing. Cutting. Pruning.

Not wanting to over-generalize, determined to be more honest, to claim only what she knows experientially, I try switching over to "I."

There's a clarity here. The scope is smaller. The claims more manageable. The writing goes more quickly.

And almost immediately, I recall Virginia Woolf's indictment of the language of educated men:

> ...after reading a chapter or two a shadow seemed to lie across the page. It was a straight dark bar, a shadow shaped something like the letter "I." One began dodging this way and that to catch a glimpse of the landscape behind it.... Back one was always hailed to the letter "I." One began to be tired of "I."

Jody allows as how she doesn't really like the so-insistent "I." She wants to make claims beyond the biographical, say something more embracing of others. Explore what lies in that shadow, bring the "landscape behind it" to the fore.

Paula Gunn Allen lays out this process of looking for what has been background, aiming towards "equilibrium of all factors," the "even distribution of value among all elements in a field." As the focus of the action shifts, the "foreground slips along from one focal point to another until all the pertinent elements in the…conversation have had their say."

"I" sounds so certain. Doesn't much allow for the latitude of such possibilities.

> ...that nagging feeling that something is being left out of the way we know things.
> —Theodore Adorno, reprised in "Reassembling"

> We challenge the supposition of a stable self (one that knows itself, is secure in that knowledge, and able to make it transparently known to others).
> —Clare, Kevin, Jody, Anne, "Reassembling"

Can we begin in the personal, while reaching out behind and beyond it? Isn't it unconscionable, not to?

Gesturing towards what we-don't-quite-know? Speaking to the social, the political?

Modeling yourself on Claudia Rankine's wonderful language you decide to experiment with "you," to risk opening Chapter One of your book,

> When you ride the train in, especially when you are by yourself, you feel an almost physical body-pull backward.... What are you doing here? This question is in your marrow....

Some feel drawn in by this. Whatever your experience, you are now written into the story.

For others, it is disruptive, causes confusion.

> Why is this article in the second person?
>
> Did I enter here?

Your colleague feels strangely displaced, cut out by references to "your colleague with whom you've been in this every step," as "you follow your colleague's direction."

Others feel differently excluded. Later on in the essay,

> ...there is a sentence: "You know why you're here." As I read that sentence, I realized that I did not know why you are here.

Sort of the point, as our friend Joel Schlosser wonderfully explains in his own reading of *Citizen*,

> The "you" here has multiple functions: we cannot label these as Rankine's experiences, different from our own; if these thoughts seem strange to us we feel pressure with the pronoun to identify at least some commonality; these are not merely confessional lines because they address us so directly.
>
> In interviews, Rankine describes her use of the second person pronoun as an attempt to disallow readers from knowing immediately how to position themselves. Whereas the first person would have deactivated the scene by allowing for immediate identification or disidentification, the second person...forces the reader to consider how and why they might apply a racial identity.

While you are busy inviting your readers to re-consider who

they—and you—and we—are, y/our students are taking up another pronomial gambit, a profound expression of their own shifting explorations in gender identity, putting into circulation the newly emerging, increasingly popular-and-accepted form of the pronoun "they." Using the singular "they" marks their refusal to be confined to conventional gender binaries. Still hearing the term as plural, we stumble over the usage when they request it; writing this "they," we are also a little worried that our readers will think we don't know how to write, don't know our grammatical rules.

There's the shadow of another history here, too, which "proper" grammar polices: "they" so long embedded in "them and us"; too often, too obviously and uncomfortably used as the opposite of those on the inside: "we."

Those on the "outside" who, as Sara Ahmed makes clear, are welcomed by "us," those who feel at home, "on condition they return that hospitality…allowing institutions to celebrate their diversity."

No group gathers at Bryn Mawr these days without a round of introductions that includes names and preferred pronouns. One student risks challenging the practice: is gender so important? Is that really always how we want to be known and identified? Joel muses about stereotype threat: if we lead always with our gender, are we priming ourselves for certain behaviors, the risk of conforming to stereotypes about our social group?

> Some people find pleasure in aligning themselves with an identity.... But there can also be a horror in doing so, not to mention an impossibility.
> —Maggie Nelson, *The Argonauts*

Pronouns are tricky business.

Another friend, Eric Raimy, explains this in terms of linguistics, which distinguishes between "content" (verbs, nouns, adjectives, adverbs) and "function" words (pronouns, determiners, prepositions), which signal the structural relationships in sentences. The former are "open," the latter "closed," and the difference between them distributional: "you can create new nouns and verbs easily but it is very difficult, if not impossible, to create new prepositions, determiners, pronouns." Stephen Pinker adds, "function words form a closed club that resists new members. That is why all attempts to introduce gender-neutral pronouns...have failed."

Pronouns are hard to change.

This book is grounded in, arises out of, attempts to instantiate environmental claims about fluidity and porosity. It testifies to the absence of outsides, the limitlessness of connections.

> "Self" and "environment," "classroom" and "world," "teacher" and "student" are all transactional, malleable categories, imbricated in one another. Conceptualizing the boundaries of the classroom as permeable, we look to bring the complexity and unknowability of selves, and the complexity and unpredictability of the medium in which they live and learn, into the classroom and out again.
>
> —Anne and Jody, Introduction

In such a world, pronouns necessarily slip and slide. Are of uncertain referent.

As are we all.

Though some of us resist.

> I find that I want to know whose voice I'm hearing with "I" or "we" or "you."

The question of who is included, and how, is problematic, reaches beyond the pronomial.

As we finish drafting each chapter, we ask everyone who is mentioned by name, as well as everyone whose words we've cited at any length, to review what we've written, and let us know if (and if so, how) they want to be referenced. We invite each of them to write into the text, to add explanations, qualifications.

Our invitations are not comprehensive, though. Many of the lapses are underwritten by social and structural inequities. We don't ask Bryn Mawr administrators for their take on our stories of the college. Or request that the women serving time in jail review the text. Or the villagers, our artistic partners, who are developmentally delayed; could they understand what they would be giving permission for?

All these are nameless here.

We depend on their stories.

As we do on those of colleagues who respond.

Our friend Kristin Lindgren, who appears several times in the text, and enjoys how "fully peopled" it is, suggests that we describe the complicated process of asking people like herself to accede to our representations of them.

Writing, revising, sending out, listening, revising again is fertile—and challenging. A recent alum, completing her first year as a teacher, is excited to see what she calls the "time capsule" of her "first-year self, taking on hard conversations and paper assignments." Another student surprises us by their willingness to be represented in a state of open vulnerability. Yet another shares their concern about how white professors might gain from the use of their words, as a person of color. A colleague who suggests accentuating our marginal positioning at the college (which she shares), finds it less helpful on a second reading, not "porous" or "ecological" in the terms the book explores. Another disagrees strongly with how we tell a story in which we all play a part; another feels left out of our storytelling; quite a few express pleasure at their appearance here, and how we've represented their contributions to a larger story.

This plethora of reactions, many from readers who are characters in the tales we tell, incites a set of provocative questions from Ann Dixon, who has accompanied us throughout the inception and completion of this project:

> Who owns the story? Or to put it differently, whose story is it to tell? The author's? If so, who is the author: the storyteller, or

> the one who is the subject of the story? Does the publisher own the story? Or (by virtue of giving us money toward publication) does the college?

We're filled with pleasure, regret, and, always more questions, as we work through each instance of telling, knowing that it all is further grist for a collective mill.

> Good ecology uses everything, including banana peels, Pepsi cans, and emotions. We need to recycle everything we use, neglecting and throwing away nothing. Ordinary feelings you have while walking down the street are sacred.... To practice good ecology, we have to follow the neglected, the unpredictable, the numinous, and everything that catches our eye.
> —Arnold Mindell, *The Leader as Martial Artist*

Our open website invites further re-writing.

CHAPTER FOUR
SILENCE

...the image...forces things to stop for a moment. It forces the reader to reinvent breathing so that the eyes can again focus.... I was attracted to images...with an incoherence... placed in the text where I thought silence was needed, but I wasn't interested in making the silence feel empty or effortless the way a blank page would.
—Claudia Rankine, *Bomb: Artists in Conversation*

On Forcing Things to Stop for a Moment

Taking the image also forces things to stop for a moment. One of the things I love about making photographs is the bubble of silence that surrounds me, as I pause to look around, note what is there, attempt to capture a scene, a pattern, a surprising juxtaposition.

I snap the image that prefaces this chapter in El Yunque National Forest, taking a break from the National Women's Studies Association Conference, which was held in Puerto Rico, in November 2014.

I don't begin writing the words that follow this photograph, however, until eight months later, when I return, a little stunned, from two more back-to-back academic conferences. Each session, at each conference, is held in a windowless room, chock filled with presentations, read at breakneck speed, with little time for uptake, for reflection, for talking back-and-with, for absorbing, for taking in.

At the end of each day, at each of these conferences, I query the colleagues who join me for drinks and dinner: Why are we reading, too much, too quickly, words that cannot be heard, understood, followed at such a pace? Why aren't we making space for back-and-forthing, for co-creation and exploration? Attending to our needs for reflection, for apprehension, for uptake?

And why aren't we leaving these closed, indoor spaces for more open, expansive, troubling ones? I take some time off to explore the intriguing, even startling, sites around us: the Society for Disability Studies conference is held just blocks from the astonishing Civil Rights Museum in Atlanta; I spend hours there one afternoon, absolutely gripped by the narrative, reliving the history—both what I know, and what I have not experienced. Tears running down my face, I find it hard to leave that space-and-time, to return to the conference up the hill—which is also contributing to a vibrant contemporary civil rights movement. Ten days later, the Association for the Study of Literature and the Environment convenes in northwest Idaho, not far from both the Nez Perce Reservation and the original home of the Aryan Nations. Riding a bus into-and-through the reservation, guided by a Nez Perce elder, offers a different sort of interruption, not as immediately emotional for me, but one that also fills in, terribly, some of the silences of the history I have been taught. This makes it difficult for me, when we return to the conference venue, to sit still, in yet another closed room.

There is a lack of time in such settings; academics, engaged in pursuing-and-promoting our careers, need to carve out, of the little space available, efficient ways to demonstrate what we know to others in the field, who know other things.

And I do get very excited about this exchange of ideas, energized by quick-moving language.

But I want to talk here about our forgetting that silence, too, is resource. And source.

Spilling over with half-heard, half-caught ideas, frustrated with myself and my fellow-travelers for our failure to make time for silence in our gatherings, I here interrogate the "conference culture," pause to question why this particular subset of the human species, that of the academic conference-goer—of which I am an ever-eager, ever-curious, card-carrying member—finds it so difficult to surround our speaking with stillness.

Like my colleagues, I have a lot to say.

Am not humble.

Cannot be quiet.

When George Prochnik traces the roots of our English term, these humbling dimensions, both of being silenced and choosing silence, are highlighted:

> Among the word's antecedents is the Gothic verb *anasilan*, a word that denotes the wind dying down, and the Latin *desinere*, a word meaning "stop." Both of these etymologies suggest the way that silence is bound up with the idea of interrupted action. The pursuit of silence...generally begins with a surrender of the chase, the abandonment of efforts to impose our will and vision on the world...the pursuit of silence seems...to involve a step backward from the tussle of life...."What's silent is my protest against the way things are."[1]

I've spent my life mostly pushing back against "the way things are," and find it difficult to "surrender" to silence. It's very hard for me to stop the search for explication, for revising the current explanation; I'm always trying to get it "less wrong," always looking for the next (if never the last) word (and action). And yet (probably because this is so hard for me) I am also very much drawn to the practice of silence, and to the possibilities it opens up. That's what I'll be tracing in this chapter, as I excavate several layers beyond simple speechlessness, examining what silence might entail. Most obviously, space for reflection, for a fuller range of interpretation than quick speech might invite. Contrari-wise, help in acknowledging what cannot be said, even understood (so counter to the life of assured academic

1. George Prochnik, *In Pursuit of Silence: Listening for Meaning in a World of Noise* (New York: Doubleday, 2010), 12.

performance). Help in both re-thinking and re-working academic spaces to allow for these fuller, more uncertain slices of life. An invitation to look beyond the academic, even beyond the human, to the larger spaces we all occupy, to the unknown complexities that both inhabit and surround us, and the silences in which we might accede to that greater world.

I am guided in this direction, in part, by the masterful work of Eduardo Kohn, whose description of *How Forests Think* evokes a world of "other living selves—whether bacterial, floral, fungal, or animal."[2] Kohn reads dreams, too, as "part of the empirical," "a kind of real" that "grow out of and work on the world," and argues that "learning to be attuned to their special logics and their fragile forms of efficacy helps reveal something about the world beyond the human."[3] He also calls up the *"pensée sauvage"* of Claude Lévi-Strauss: "mind in its untamed state as distinct from mind cultivated or domesticated for the purpose of yielding a return." And he mentions all the "'mistaken' utterances" that so fascinated Sigmund Freud, "the defective performance of certain purposive acts," revealing "that which is ancillary to or beyond what is practical." Kohn's attention, via Lévi-Strauss and Freud, to thought "which resonates with and thereby explores its environment," an insight that gestures "quite literally to an 'ecology of mind,'" is key to my own.[4] But whereas Kohn's focus is on "the multitude of semiotic life," and how animals' varied interpretations of the world contribute to "a single, open-ended story" in which we all partake, my own interests ultimately lie more in what cannot be signed, or signaled, in what may exceed representation.[5]

Where silence falls.

2. Eduardo Kohn, *How Forests Think: Toward an Anthropology Beyond the Human* (Berkeley: University of California Press, 2013), 6.

3. Kohn, *How Forests Think*, 13.

4. Kohn, *How Forests Think*, 176–77.

5. Kohn, *How Forests Think*, 49, 9.

…where is space for educators to be vulnerable about their not-knowing?

—a student's comment

…silence…a terrifying moment for some teachers…something which instructors need to learn to "break"…it appears to be unproductive or damaging to self-development…numerous seminars about how to get students to talk, but none which deal with silence as a way to learn…implicitly understood in the humanities classroom to be a way to withhold information…an indicator of fear, boredom, resistance or ignorance.

—Julie Rak, "Do Witness: *Don't: A Woman's Word* and Trauma as Pedagogy"

On Learning a New Language

Going to academic conferences raises questions for me.

More extended and unstructured trips raise many more—and other kinds of questions about speaking and silence.

Most of these queries go unanswered.

From "Stranger in a Strange Land: Grokking in the Americas," September 11, 2006:

> I'm traveling in Central America with my daughter Marian and my husband Jeff. Marian has lived in Mexico, and is fluent in Spanish. Jeff and I have no experience either living or speaking in this part of the world.
>
> When we touched down in Guatemala City yesterday afternoon, the whole plane load of people burst into applause.
>
> MARIAN: "This expresses our gratitude to the pilot."
>
> ANNE: "Perhaps this suggests an uncertainty that we would be landing safely?"
>
> JEFF: "Are we one or two hours behind time?"
>
> MARIAN: "Parentals: There is one thing you need to know while living in a new country. You are not going to understand everything. Why people clap. What time it is."
>
> ANNE: "Inquiring minds want to know."
>
> MARIAN: "Your mind wants to know. Your mind needs to change."
>
> At this point, all the old women around us pull their suitcases down from the overhead bins, place them on their heads, and walk free-handed off the plane. Somewhat bewildered (how can they do this, without holding on?), we follow.[6]

6. Anne Dalke, "September 11, 2006," *Stranger in a Strange Land: Grokking in the Americas* (September 12, 2006).

As it turns out, Fall 2006 is a rough time for me; I don't manage very well. I loathe the loss of my voice in Spanish—and with it my ability to communicate with others. I feel as though I've surrendered any recognizable sense of self: I am no longer quick, sharp, eager to follow up any statement with a complicating question. Learning a new language is excruciating. Very slowly, I get the hang of just saying what I know (always so limited, so inadequate for what I want to be saying); what's far harder is engaging in on-the-spot dialogue, the give-and-take of wanting to say, and not having the words to speak. I'm very, very hungry to be able to talk—*really talk*—to the people I'm meeting.

But at our second language school, in Xela, Guatemala, I get off to a rough start with a new teacher, start crying because I can't find the words I need.

Not to be able to speak, for me, feels like death.

Yup. Pretty melodramatic.

I'm an extrovert. I love to talk with others, feel most alive when engaged in doing so. I enjoy college teaching so much because my days are structured around such encounters. My pleasure is well described by my friend Alice Lesnick (in dialogu*e—of course!*—with one of her students, who asks her what "fuels her creativity"):

> The primary thing is conversation.... I am very blessed to...work with many conversation partners, and I think of my work here as largely centered in...an exchange of language and ideas...it really floats my boat. Especially when the outcome is uncertain.[7]

[7.] Christina Stella, "the mawr you know: alice lesnick!"

The uncertainty is very important here. I'm far less interested in rants, sermons, even lectures that know where they are going. Like Alice, what I most enjoy is the back-and-forthing of an exchange that is exploratory, trying, collaboratively, to get somewhere, to figure something out: a text, a political or social question, an existential dilemma.

What I most like to do, what makes me feel most alive, most centered, most sure that my life makes some sense/is worth going through with, is being engaged with others, learning about how they understand the world, and trying out my perceptions on them in turn.

Part of this is just the joy of company-keeping. Part of it is feeling a sense of my own aliveness, called out by another. And a large part of it is the fun of finding out something new together.

So the most difficult periods of my life are those when I am not able to engage in this sort of collaborative dialogue.

I'm out of my element, away from what I do well, unable to flourish—even to function—in cultures different from my own, countries where "who I am," all I have come to be, seems to shift in meaning. I don't know my place, am not sure what my nationality, race, class signal. Operating as privileges in the U.S., here they dis-privilege me in some ways. I feel shut out, by a range of factors, from most of what is happening in Guatemala, Costa Rica, and Chile. I have just recently arrived in these parts of the world, and lack any facility in Spanish. Two of the countries in which I am sojourning have long histories of secrecy, decades of human rights abuses that I am only beginning to understand. The ghosts of Rios Montt and Augusto Pinochet cast long shadows; I often feel shrouded in darkness.

Silenced.

Unable to respond, acknowledging the limits of my capacity to intervene, provokes me to re-think some rather profound presumptions, about both who I am and how much agency I have to alter the world in which I live. I come to realize that, in many ways, my writing exercises and speaking lessons in the Americas, which feel so disabling to my sense of self, are concrete, personal demonstrations of the larger process of humans' telling one another stories of our experiences: not abandoning the search to connect, but acknowledging that we will never-never-never quite be able to do so.

I participate for several years in a Working Group on Language at Bryn Mawr, and one of the key ideas I learn there is the notion that humans use language, not to convey information, but to solicit feedback from others; not to tell them what we know, but to learn what we don't. This notion evolves from the analysis of linguists that what we say is never heard transparently, but rather always as an incomplete translation of what we mean. The stages of transmission are many: from what we feel, to what we think, to what we say; from what we say, to what we are heard to be saying; from what is heard, to what is thought, to what is felt by the one with whom we are speaking.[8]

Which is to say that the great pleasure I take in speaking is fueled in large part by my recognition of the inevitable limits of that activity, a realization that I never know, much less communicate, exactly what I mean. It is because I can never quite "connect" that I have to keep on trying to. And it is also because I can never quite "connect" that I have slowly come to appreciate silence, as marking that space and time where what cannot be said (in the moment, or ever) resides.

Silence refuses to valorize the quick uptake of language, allowing for the passage of time, out of which interpretation may emerge.

In part—and only in part perversely—because of my long resistance to being silenced, I become a member of the Religious Society of Friends, and slowly, but steadily, learn to take some solace in the practice of chosen, silent worship. All that is spoken in worship arises from and returns to silence, in which the words—themselves often faltering—can "grow," open up, have resonance. In Central Philadelphia Meeting this morning, for instance, someone speaks of "wood becoming fire," as an image of our "becoming what we attend to." This leads me to reflect on my own engagements: who-and-what I am drawn to, how that shapes who I am becoming, the work that I do. In such pauses between messages, I find connections between what is said, my own concerns, and larger ones. I learn to love that space of expansion.

I publish essays about the application of such practices to both the interpretation of texts and the dynamics of the classroom.[9] When I first design a new course on "The Rhetorics of Silence," in Fall 2012, I imagine offering my students a whole panoply of experience, of silence as a source of transformation, of active resistance

8. Language: A Conversation. Center for Science in Society, Bryn Mawr College. November 26, 2001–March 24, 2004.

9. Anne Dalke, "'On Behalf of the Standard of Silence': The American Female Modernists and the Powers of Restraint," *Soundings: An Interdisciplinary Journal* 78, 3-4 (Fall–Winter 1995): 501-19; Anne Dalke, "Silence is so Windowful: Class as Antechamber," in *Teaching to Learn/Learning to Teach: Meditations on the Classroom.* (New York: Peter Lang, 2002), 95-114.

that challenges how social meaning is made. I want us to engage in solitary and communal practices of silence; shared, dialogic, critical thinking about such experiences; reading and interpreting written, visual, and material texts about silence; finding effective, not only verbal, ways of expressing and acting in response to our emergent understandings—including the possibility of clearing some space not to articulate them—and the acknowledgement that there is much we don't, and won't ever, understand.

I want to explore silence, with my students, as an alternative space to observe, feel, think, and dream. I want to seek concrete applications in a variety of cultural expressions, drawing theoretical positions, and derivative practices, from cultural studies, feminist inquiry, linguistics, philosophy and religious thought. I think we might find educational theory and reflective practice of particular value, and I hope that the class can keep close to the bone in considering what is happening for us all, as teachers and learners of silence.

The deliberate practice of silence may accomplish more than increasing the range of things that *might* be said.

It may remind us that everything that is important *cannot* be said.

Bryn Mawr has taught me to speak in ellipses…Bryn Mawr…must have given me…the sense that…for everything you say…something…else is…left out.
—Elizabeth Catanese, "Some Thoughts on Teaching"

…silence…is an illusion. If we hear nothing…it only means we aren't listening hard enough…. The total absence of sound is never a possibility…silence is a…way of thinking…a way of imagining…a moment outside time…the possibility of pausing…proof that the decision to listen or not is ours. Proof that we are called to pay attention.
—John Edgar Wideman, "In Praise of Silence"

On Paying Attention

Predictably, the students begin my course on silence with the belief that speaking in class is an unmitigated value, that they are failing both expression and expectation when they don't talk. Enrollment consists, in large part, of sociology majors; a marked percentage of the students are Posse Scholars from urban communities, attending Bryn Mawr on leadership grants; almost all of them are activists, who begin the class with a heightened awareness of the damaging effects of silence—and a general resistance to the idea that silence might also have a positive valence. Most students are convinced that silence is a "bad" thing, that they—and the cultures they represent and care about—need to resist it, speak into it, intervene in its oppressive structure: "I was a shelved book...full of personal insights, suggestions, questions, and comments, but not opened or investigated."[10]

"Opening that book," however, in the form of public postings on our course website, provokes several painful encounters. Students begin to acknowledge differences among themselves: only some, for example, have had access to the kind of education that gives them the power to speak and write "well," as the term is conventionally defined.

Which means, on both sides of the equation? Further silence.

SASHA: I just shut myself down...because my writing is not even close to my peers extreme cohesive, poetic writing.[11]

DAN: After Tuesday's class, I felt so confused about my voice, about my place in the world and my privilege that I walked out of class in a daze, and ended up screaming in the woods.... After Thursday's class...I was flooded with doubts about how I speak and write...for some (like me) the extent of our privilege was articulated so loudly and clearly by hearing the stories and emotions of those who grew up marginalized by the culture of power.... I think the only thing I feel confident about is that it's about time for me to be quiet.... I need to listen so much more, and when I do speak, it should be as a listener. I feel kind of hollow—like I'm full of air and paradoxes, and nothing is true with a capital T.[12]

---

10. Dan, "Listening and Silence," September 9, 2012 (4:47 p.m.).

11. Sasha De La Cruz, "Paper 2," September 23, 2012 (2:29 p.m.).

12. Dan, "Silence, Air and Paradoxes," September 23, 2012 (1:19 p.m.).

OWL: When some classmates feel the need to silence themselves in order to allow others to speak it makes me feel as though I am "missing out" on intellectual diversity.[13]

13. Owl, "Keepers of Silence," October 7, 2012 (5:20 p.m.).

Throughout the semester, the silencing effects of speaking are—if not again shouted in the woods—repeatedly given voice, in both the classroom and our on-line forum. There's a shared need to defend turf through voice. And yet many of the students also speak-and-write of public silence, as the result of their own internal cacophony, a "noisiness inside" that prevents them from speaking:

CHANDREA: Instead of listening to what other people were saying and asking, I was too busy rehearsing what I was going to say.[14]

HS BURKE: I feel silenced because I just need space to think. Such heavy topics deserve a response that has been thought out. But there is no time for silence....I find it ironic that in a class about silence we are ALL SO LOUD....[15]

ERIN: As a foreigner come to a new country...I have to admit that...there were moments in class that I just can't process my peers' distribution.... Is talking always an active of exchanging intelligence or just a way of filling the blank?[16]

14. Chandrea, "Talking in a (High School/College) Class," September 16, 2012 (10:28 a.m.).

15. HSBurke, "Web Event #2: Silenced by a Lack of Silence," September 23, 2012 (9:53 a.m.).

16. Erin, "Silence and Talking," September 16, 2012 (5:20 p.m.).

In response to such queries, we practice allowing pauses between our speakings, remind one another to do this, choose sometimes to be still.

COULDNTTHINKOFANORIGINALNAME: I am asking that we use silence, one that is inviting, to leave room between thoughts so we can all process and ask clarifying questions. I genuinely want to learn and want to hear everyone's thought so please give me enough silence to do that.[17]

17. couldntthinkofanoriginalname, "Reading Delpit's Words through a Third Lens: Silence," September 16, 2012 (11:57 a.m.).

The site where these postings occur, our on-line forum on Serendip, also allows for silences between postings: it offers students both space to ignore what others say, and time to respond, without the pressure of being in the classroom together, without the expectation of an immediate response. We develop other practices, in-class and out: take turns opening each session with a structured period of silence; experiment with a range of written forms in which silence is marked; play with the "force of embedded silence: asterisks, gaps" in collages[18]; try out various forms of "blackout poetry," an exercise of eliminating all unnecessary words in a sheet of newsprint.[19] The students surround their visualizations and descriptions of silence *with* silence, reducing them to a single noun, verb, adverb. They rewrite essays into poems, culling the words with weight, the phrases with presence, letting the connections between them fall silent.

The books we are reading also repeatedly invite students to re-value such silences, to admit that they should *not* seek to clarify some of their confusions in listening, as well as in reading. Some gaps mark power differentials that need to be respected; some of them function as needed interventions in structures of privilege.

I, Rigoberta Menchu is instrumental in highlighting our need to acknowledge our limits as knowers. Prodded by Doris Sommer, who explains that "books can sting readers who feel entitled to know everything as they approach a text," that "the slap of refused intimacy from uncooperative books can slow readers down," my students and I have difficulty laying down our conviction that we "deserve to know." Sommer argues compellingly that Menchu's "inhospitality toward the reader" serves an important pedagogical function: it "merits a pause long enough to learn new expectations."[20]

> ISHIN: I am like others who assume that writing should be based in a "monolingualism" of sorts where all should be able to understand what is being said.... Sommer gave me a hard reminder.... There are certain gaps we just have to respect.[21]

---

18. Peter Elbow, "Silence: A Collage," in *Everyone Can Write: Essays Toward a Hopeful Theory of Writing and Teaching* (New York: Oxford University Press, 2000), 175.

19. HSBURKE, "Web Event #2: Silenced by a Lack of Silence," September 23, 2012 (9:53 a.m.).

20. Doris Sommer, "Advertencia/Warning," in *Proceed with Caution, When Engaged by Minority Writing in the Americas* (Cambridge: Harvard University Press, 1999), xiii.

21. ishin, "Oct12012S5: Universal Writing," October 2, 2012 (3:06 a.m.).

…for human beings, not to speak is to die.
—Pablo Neruda, "The Word"

…listen for the breakdown of syntax…. I am interested in the lack of words…in the gaps…not in what has been fully articulated, but in what is in the process of being articulated…in the very moment that the smooth-sounding words fail us.
—Anna Deavere Smith, *Fires in the Mirror*

On Learning Respect

Respecting what is not "fully articulated" comes hard, however. If students cannot understand an author or a speaker, they themselves feel disrespected, describe their experience as being "shut out," "slighted."

In mid-October, we welcome two visitors to class: my friend Mark Lord and his colleague Catharine Slusar share their in-process performance-and-production of Samuel Beckett's play *Footfalls*.

This does not go over particularly well.

> HUMMINGBIRD: I found the play we read for class today incredibly silencing and frustrating because I couldn't understand what was happening and what I could take from it. When I read the play last night, I got angrier and angrier because I felt like I was being shut out. I hoped the experience of watching the play might be more enlightening...I felt just as confused...at the end of it.... I still don't know what the theme of the play even is.... I feel as though I've missed out on something really important...a learning opportunity and that makes me feel like I've wasted time.[22]
>
> SARAH: AGREE AGREE AGREE! I was so frustrated!.... I don't know what happened.... I didn't get what was happening, if the mother was dead or alive, what the pacing/moving candle represented, who the characters were, what the random stories/anecdotes were about. I felt extremely shut out...[23]

22. Hummingbird, "Frustrated," October 23, 2012 (3:37 p.m.).

23. Sarah, "AGREE AGREE AGREE!," October 23, 2012 (4:23 p.m.).

Slowly and fitfully, however, some of the students come to recognize the presumption underlying such frustrations: their expectation that they have the "right" to know.

In one of our silent activities, the one international student in our class asks us to "read" and "make meaning" from a Chinese text. Having evoked a series of "inaccurate" translations, from classmates who do not know the language, Erin then refuses their request to translate the text, saying that it would "sound silly in English."

> COULDNTTHINKOFANORIGINALNAME: I still wanted her to translate it even if it did sound stupid in English.... I did feel like I deserved to know the English.... I felt slighted, as if I did have a

right to access Erin in that way. It did not feel good to feel like a foreigner in a space of my own discourse…did that mean it was okay if Erin did because she is not from America and therefore, should not deny me? AH:(! That's not a thought I am comfortable with at all.…we must first question why there is a need to know and what does that say about our identities and power?…was I unintentionally exercising power over her by requesting that I have access to her language?…was I pressuring her…to say yes and translate? By giving me that satisfaction, what would I have gained and what would she have lost? And by her saying no, what did that mean?…what good is keeping quiet…?[24]

The "good of keeping quiet" begins to emerge more fully during the last section of our course, when we shift focus from asking who holds power, and whether we owe one another explanation across such divisions, to whether we might learn better or differently if we engage systematically in the discipline of silence. This is less about the right to be silent, or respecting the silence of others, than about practicing silence as a different means of understanding. The texts we read at this point are religious ones, asking how we might open ourselves to insight that comes from some place beyond language, that isn't mediated by words.[25]

A number of the students are wary, however, of how this invitation might alter their sense of self. The concern now is less about who holds power over us than what we ourselves might be trying to keep at bay. Some students acknowledge Sister Joan Chittister's explanation:

> Silence frightens us because it…brings us face to face with ourselves.…tells us what we're obsessing about…reminds us of what we have not resolved…shows to us the underside…from which there is no escape.… Silence…shows us what we have yet to become, and how much we still lack to become it.[26]

COULDNTTHINKOFANORIGINALNAME: I fear my dreams—an internal, sometimes quiet, part of myself—because they are random, sometimes scary and realistic. I hate that even when I don't remember the dream, I wake up heavy with feelings, good

---

24. couldntthinkofanoriginalname, "Not Knowing Sucks, But Is Exclusion Necessary Sometimes?" September 20, 2012 (10:09 a.m.).

25. Sister Joan Chittister, "Seeking the Interior Life" (November 7, 2004); Juana Inez de la Cruz, *La Respuesta/The Response* (1690), trans. and ed. Electra Arenal and Amanda Powell (New York: Feminist Press, 1994); George Kalamaras, *Reclaiming the Tacit Dimension: Symbolic Form in the Rhetoric of Silence* (Albany: State University of New York Press, 1994); Caroline Stephen, "Selections from *Quaker Strongholds* (1890)" in *Quaker Spirituality: Selected Writings*, ed. Douglas Steeere (New York: Paulist Press, 1984), 239–58.

26. Chittister, "Seeking the Interior Life."

and bad. Perhaps I could control what silence represented to me during silence activities, or the noises that filled my silence, more than I could in a dream. I have no control over what I dream about and I am certain that has a lot to do with my fear of 'facing' myself.[27]

ISHIN: silence can have a certain…anxiety, unease, awareness to it…sometimes I would use it as a way to escape anxiety, but other times, I was forced to confront it, know it, and permit it to be a part of my state of being.[28]

HSBURKE: perhaps I am uncomfortable with the idea of free time because "it is silence that brings us face to face with ourselves," and that is something I don't want to see.[29]

Despite their fears about what falling quiet might reveal, some students also begin to acknowledge that rushing to "fill up" the silences in classrooms is failing to accept what John Wideman calls "the quiet interludes as breathing spaces, necessary reminders of… limits."[30]

SDANE: taking time for silence…can actually provide the crucial time and space to deal with some of the thoughts our heads are full with.[31]

Shaari is one of several who finds herself particularly drawn to the characterization of silence—offered by a friend of mine, a nun who visits our class at the end of the semester—as "pregnant, not empty."[32]

Silence grants a pause, for reflection, for questioning what it is we think we know—or even just to sit and hold what we hear, not explicitly interrogating ourselves or others. We can see that our evolving classroom exercise of allowing more time between speaking—what we start to celebrate as "wait time"—is also giving us practice in withholding judgment, along the lines of how Wideman describes his mother, who

> most of the time…held judgment in abeyance. Events, personalities always deserved a second, slower appraisal…. You gave

[27] couldntthinkofanoriginalname, "Wow…," December 9, 2012 (1:37 p.m.).

[28] ishin, "Anxiety and Practiced Silence," December 9, 2012 (6:30 p.m.).

[29] hsburke, "Hi Chandrea!," December 9, 2012 (11:44 a.m.).

[30] John Edgar Wideman, *Brothers and Keepers* (New York: Vintage, 1995), 237.

[31] sdane, "I really liked that quote," December 10, 2012 (12:55 a.m.).

[32] Sharaai, "Linda-Susan Beard's Visit," December 9, 2012 (8:59 p.m.).

people the benefit of the doubt...acknowledged the limitations of your individual view of things.... You tried on the other person's point of view.[33]

33. Wideman, *Brothers and Keepers*, 69.

These are our central challenges. Silence offers space and time to explore a range of possibilities—"autonomy, creativity, privacy, and bodily integrity."[34] But it can also mark impassable gaps between speaker and listener, writer and reader. Some of us encounter aspects of ourselves, in silence, which we would prefer not to acknowledge. Some of us feel shut out by texts with words we don't understand, that draw on cultural capital we don't share. Some of us acknowledge, and some of us may refuse to pay, the cost of laboring to understand such writing. Some of us eventually concede the impossibility of complete understanding, not only of ourselves, but of others: recognizing that if we speak only on their terms, or insist that others speak only in ways we can readily understand, we will limit our own stretch to say what we know, and to comprehend what they have to tell us.

34. Wendy Brown, "Freedom's Silences," in *Edgework: Critical Essays on Knowledge and Politics* (Princeton: Princeton University Press, 2005), 95.

> To effectively promote silence…involves…acute listening…asking what it was that people were trying to hear, and what it was that they were trying to block out…a reflection on what otherwise remains in danger of going unheard.
> —George Prochnik, *In Pursuit of Silence*

> …literature is important…as the place where impasses can be kept…questions…guarded and not forced into a premature validation of the available paradigms… giving-to-read those impossible contradictions that cannot yet be spoken.
> —Barbara Johnson, *The Feminist Difference*

On Guarding the Questions

Over the course of the semester, my students begin to acknowledge that attending to literature means that we need also attend more fully to silence, not merely as a mode to be overlooked or overcome, but as an alternative to language and thought that might open us to new possibilities. Acknowledging the recalcitrance and contingency of the medium of language, the disparity between what is experienced and what is possible to say, the students reflect on what happens in the rush to fill the silences that arise within and among spaces of academic exchange: the neglect of divergent forms of thinking, the failure to make space for others' thoughts, and our own, by being too quick to speak. Exploring the use-value of being quiet in classrooms, in writing on-line, and in reading texts suggests alternative forms of understanding silence, as "pregnant, not empty."

    I reach for this when I set up a "quiet gallery walk" for our discussion of Gayle Jones' novel, *Eva's Man.* I tape large sheets of paper on the classroom walls; each bears either an excerpt from the book, or a reflection, posted by one of the students, about her experience of reading the novel. I invite the students to get up, wander around the room, read each of the passages, comment on those that speak to (or provoke) them, wander again and—if moved to do so—comment again on the growing conversation. Then I have them cluster around the cluster of comments they'd most like to continue exploring…

    All this is done in silence.

    Imprisoned for the bizarre murder of her lover, Eva Medina Canada recalls a life tormented by sexual abuse and emotional violence.

    The disagreements about what we should attend to in Eva's narrative, and how we should respond to what gets highlighted in that selection, are sharp.

> COULDNTTHINKOFANORIGINALNAME: As I read the disturbing encounters Eva had with the men in the book, I couldn't help but sympathize with the guys…What were the stories of the males? What made them act this way? Who or what hurt them in the

past that led them to act out their personal abuse?... I see all characters involved as victims...all are apart of a cycle of abuse that goes on in cultures, communities, etc.... I think there is a larger conversation to be had...that touches upon male's oppression, sexism and internalized sexism in the African-American culture.[35]

OWL: I couldn't agree with you more! I especially found myself thinking about the "cycle of abuse that goes on in cultures, communities, etc." when Eva talks about her relationship with...her husband....[36]

JHUNTER: Personally, I don't need to know the men's stories as this is Eva's. Yes, they are in complicated situations, but I'd like to recognize that this is Eva's story, and I don't need to act as another psychiatrist.[37]

Surrounding the discussion with silence gives it space to play out. For us to speak, to listen, to disagree, to reflect. And again to be still.

Attending to silence expands the range of possible interpretation, gives us space to listen, really listen, to what one another has to say. It generally—and most particularly in this case—does not mean consensus. Deep listening, really deep listening, takes us beyond agreement.

According to John Wideman, who calls silence an "illusion"—insisting that "if we hear nothing," "it only means we aren't listening hard enough,"[38] silence functions as a method, a means to arrive at fuller understanding—and so at fuller explication. Silence, as figured in those interruptive images of Claudia Rankine, with which this chapter begins, enacts an aural and visual "blank space," a gap, an abyss that marks those uncertain teaching spaces, those moments of reading and talking when...

we don't know what we are seeing, what we are hearing—and so we do not speak. In the pause, we might notice the "negative space," not just, as Jennifer Roberts says in evoking "The Power of Patience," "a passive intermission to be overcome," but "a productive or formative force in itself."[39] Allowing for silence might mean taking more

35. couldntthinkofanoriginalname, "Reflections on Eva's Man," November 18, 2012 (3:33 p.m.).

36. Owl, "I couldn't agree with you," November 19, 2012 (1:08 p.m.).

37. jhunter, "Notes Towards Day 23," November 27, 2012 (11:37 p.m.).

38. John Wideman, "In Praise of Silence," *Callaloo* 22, no. 3 (Summer 1999): 547–49.

39. Jennifer Roberts, "The Power of Patience," *Harvard Magazine* (November–December 2013).

time. In Roberts' account, it's about looking at a painting for three hours. In my classes, as in my travels, it involves going inside the experience of silence, recognizing both the awkwardness of pausing, in a world wired for sound, and the fertility of doing so, the way in which space is thereby opened for…

something unexpected.

Most of us want to be recognized, to be intelligible—and allowing space for silence often means insisting that we forestall the desire to immediately be understood—or to understand: as we pause and acknowledge puzzlement, we refuse the pressure to speak. But such pauses can play an important role in our shared project of searching for understanding. As a student explains, during a second iteration of the course,

> there are not only opportunities lost to understand others when we shut out language that is not immediately accessible to us, but there are also lost chances to understand ourselves better. Sometimes we do not yet have the language or the means to come to important conclusions about ourselves; these methods or materials may be inaccessible to us at first. If we pause, listen, be silent, and perhaps speak to that silence, then there may be a whole new realm of expression to explore.

Over the arc of a long semester, and again with a different group of students, several years later, silence is at first only a physical phenomenon, the absence of sound: this is the definition that guides most of our structured silent exercises. Prodded by Wideman, and again by the great cultural critic Susan Sontag, we next explore the possibility that *there actually is no silence*, that even in the absence of speech, interpretation is always—somewhere, somehow—happening.[40] Eventually, we arrive at the counter notion that so terrifies me in Central America: that silence might mark, not only a profound failure to transmit meaning, but the absence of meaning itself. We struggle with what Samuel Beckett calls ultimate silence— the refusal of the universe to answer our deepest questions, with

40. Susan Sontag, "Against Interpretation," in *Against Interpretation and Other Essays* (New York: Farrar, Strauss & Giroux, 1966): 4–14.

"Every word…an unnecessary stain on silence and nothingness."[41]

Our orientation is, ultimately, ecological. We end up "looping" between speech and silence, knowing that, in a world of vast interconnection, something is always concealed. We begin to celebrate silence as a way of valuing what is not being shown, what exists—although it may not, at any given moment, be articulated.

[41]. Anne Dalke, "Notes Towards Day 13," October 11, 2012 (10:50 p.m.).

"Sound imposes a narrative on you," he said, "and it's always someone else's narrative."

—George Prochnik, *In Pursuit of Silence*

To be out is really to be in—inside the realm of the visible, the speakable...engaging in...dialogue about "personal" or "private" aspects of yourself...can make you TOO easy to understand...maintaining the liminal...position...means that you do not become "culturally intelligible." You can't be mainstreamed; your deviance cannot be absorbed...cannot be contained.

—Gayatri Spivak, *Outside in the Teaching Machine*

On Intervening

In March 2013, a few months after we conclude the first version of this course, three students and I are offered the opportunity to take what we've learned farther afield. We're accepted to present at a conference, "Silence…Silenzio," which is sponsored by the French Italian Graduate Society at the University of Pennsylvania. The conference call for papers describes silence as

> an act and experience that contributes to the way we perceive and live in the world. Silence can be deliberately adopted or forcefully imposed, political and/or aesthetic. It pervades society and cultural productions not only through its mute presence but also through its telling absence…silence renders apparent that which at first seems unutterable or ineffable. Silence can therefore say a great deal.[42]

The conference that ensues, however, does not focus either on the "unutterable or ineffable," or on what silence "can say"; it is centered, rather, around multiple critiques of enforced silences embedded in literary texts. My students and I spend a springtime Saturday listening to analyses of silences created by interpersonal relations and cultural trauma.[43]

These presentations are linked together by several presumptions running counter to those which have emerged during our fall semester of shared study: that silence means only the absence of words (other forms of communication—touch, eye contact, laughter—are scarcely attended to); that speaking is always preferable to being silent; that "authentic dialogue" is both possible and capable of facilitating political action. The more philosophic papers argue that we actually "cannot stop talking," whether guided by an understanding of the "inaudible whisper" of Heidigger, or the "open set" that is language in Lacan.[44]

Of the more than twenty papers read that day, only one gestures toward the possibility that language can be incomplete as a medium of communication, might inhibit awareness of something unspoken

---

42. Lisa Bromberg and Andrew Korn, Call for Papers, Silence…Silenzio: Annual Conference of the French Italian Graduate Society, University of Pennsylvania, Philadelphia, PA, November, 2012.

43. Natalie Berkman, "The Silence of the Interlocutor in Camus' *The Fall*"; Chris Bonner, "Staging a Dictatorship: Silence, Surveillance, and Theatri-cality in Marie Chauvet's *Colère*"; Carla Cornette, "Silence as Remedy: The Psychological Defense Mechanism of Silence in 'Mio Marito' by Natalia Ginzburg"; Jill González, "Silence and Memory in Guadalupe Santa Cruz's *Cita capital*"; Jenny Kosniowski, "Textual Silences and the Amnesty for Torture Committed during the Algerian War: Maïssa Bey's *Entendez-vous dans les montagnes…*"; George MacLeod, "'The Victim of His Victims': Silencing Survivors of the Genocide of the Tutsi in Rwanda in Immaculée Ilibagiza's *Left to Tell*" (all papers presented at the annual conference of the French Italian Graduate Society, March 16, 2013).

44. Sarah Myer, "Into Great Silence? A Lacanian Reading

or unspeakable. A look at *The Last Day of a Condemned Man* suggests that withholding narrative might both powerfully evoke the emptiness of the speaker's psychological state, and offer an intentional space for others to see beyond the moment of judgment, what is typically unseen.[45] Elsewhere, however—most forcefully during the keynote address with which the day concludes—we are urged to "resist silence," in literature as in politics. Christy Walpole ends the conference by encouraging all of us to speak in and against the "imposed silences" of political incarceration, of historical deletion, and—most particularly and climactically—those of the market logic driving university life. Walpole acknowledges the need for silence as a temporary strategy, a means of creating space for academic labor, of preparing for public speaking and writing, for filling in "empty blanks."[46] She does not invite us, however, to leave these blanks unfilled, nor does she explore the possibility that such emptiness might itself fill a need.

And yet all the sessions at the conference are filled with silences: the silence of those of us who aren't listening to what is being said; who don't understand French or Italian well enough to follow the talks presented in those languages; who disagree with the speakers, but don't speak up; the silence of those of us distracted by the cacophony going on inside our heads—or by the silence there.

At midday, my students and I offer a lunchtime intervention into this dynamic: a roundtable on the "pedagogy of silence" in which we explicitly engage in silent practices and explore their use-value, not as spaces of exclusion, but of abundance and possibility.[47]

Our experiment garners a mixed response.

Our own course on "The Rhetorics of Silence" has unsettled the norm of speaking in class, based on the linked assumptions that what is said is more important than what is left unspoken, that those who are speaking are guiding the class forward, while those who are silent are not contributing. My students and I open our conference session not by telling attendees these things, but by inviting them

---

of Samuel Beckett's *The Unnamable*"; Fredrik Rönnbäck, "The Sacred Word of Blanchot and Leiris" (both papers presented at the annual conference of the French Italian Graduate Society, March 16, 2013).

45. Melissa Verhey, "Noisy Silence: Wordlessly Reclaiming Voice in Victor Hugo's *The Last Day of a Condemned Man*" (paper presented at the annual conference of the French Italian Graduate Society, March 16, 2013).

46. Christy Wampole, "Quiet Impositions: On Involuntary Silence" (keynote address presented at the annual conference of the French Italian Graduate Society, March 16, 2013).

47. Anne Dalke, Sophia Abbot, Sara Gladwin and Esteniolla Maitre, "The Pedagogy of Silence" (roundtable presented at the annual conference of the French Italian Graduate Society, March 16, 2013).

to taste that experience, to feel their way into some possible positive uses of silence. Beginning our roundtable in silence has a particular value, we say, in the context of this academic conference, where speaking is so valued, and in the context of this particular conference, which purports to explore various dimensions of silence—where, ironically, we have been talking for hours about silence, and anticipate many more hours of the same.

We also try to suggest the value of silence in broader strokes, to offer the practice of stillness as a mode of "living differently."

Some in the room squirm, unsure what to do when the usual quick exchange that dominates in conference settings is set aside. Many of the participants find the experience destabilizing (although, not incidentally, the two exhausted conference organizers, who find it a welcome relief).

The discomfort continues throughout our session, as my students describe various ways in which attending to silence in our course has opened a range of possibilities for them. Drawing on her long-time experience as a "divergent thinker," who often finds herself distracted in classroom settings, Sara Gladwin asks for space in the curriculum "that allows what is traditionally silenced to enter the classroom." Sophia Abbot offers a pointed description of herself as a "typical outspoken student," who has learned to silence herself, and invites others to do the same, in the classroom. Esteniolla Maitre invites participants to experiment in a discussion conducted in absolute silence.

Investment in this exercise varies. Participants report feeling stripped of academic privilege, robbed of an opportunity to speak. Some experiment with gestures, or sign language; others simply give up trying to participate in the conversation. Many feel misunderstood, and all feel frustrated at not understanding what others were trying to "say."

Why, we ask, don't we attend to such silences? Why do we ignore them—or recognize them only by hurrying to end them, to obscure them with a quick and ready question? At what cost, to our own learning, do we fill up such spaces? And how might we intervene in such a process, open it up to alternative dimensions?

Trying to "give silence more space" seems to us a significant interruption of the range of vocal performances that constitute the genre of the academic conference, a way of bringing some of what we've learned about both the uses and limitations of silence, in an undergraduate course, into a primary site of graduate education.

It also feels appropriate to conclude our exploration in silence, so we end our session without trying to "sum up" what has happened.

> Words. Few. Very few. Inch worms across vast silences. After all that had happened.
> —Miguel Angel Asturias, *The Mirror of Lida Sal*

> There was a strange stillness.... It was a spring without voices.... On the mornings that had once throbbed with the dawn chorus...there was now no sound; only silence lay over the fields and woods and marsh.... The roadsides...too, were silent, deserted by all living things.... What has...silenced the voices of spring in countless towns in America? This book is an attempt to explain.
> —Rachel Carson, "A Fable for Tomorrow," *Silent Spring*

On Beyond Conferencing: The Stillness of the World

The same semester that I offer "The Rhetorics of Silence," I am also experimenting, for the first time, with a pair of courses—one version for first semester students, one for upperclasswomen—called "Ecological Imaginings." Sara Gladwin, who is enrolled simultaneously in both the class on silence and the upper-level eco-one, often finds ways to link them together, to carry insights from our interrogation of silence into our discussion of ecology, and, contrariwise, to translate the language of environmental studies into that of rhetorical silence. Listening to Gordon Hempton's podcast of "The Last Quiet Places,"[48] which documents the great difficulty of finding quiet in today's world, Sara recognizes a central pattern of her own education: she describes how she and many other children are taught to direct their attention in school, to close themselves off from both their own divergent and distracting thoughts and from their surroundings, "to let the environment fade into the background."[49]

Sara speaks about this dynamic at the "Silenzio" conference. I now follow her lead in finding my way back to the possibility of silence, not just as a placeholder for interpretation, a pause for gathering ourselves to speak more fully, but as a site for learning and teaching that might well not give way to words. Silence can serve as an invitation into more "ecological" habits of mind and body, which acknowledge how deeply embedded we are in larger structures we cannot name, direct, or control. As Eduardo Kohn makes clear in his study of *How Forests Think,* perception is always happening, and need not be—is primarily not—conducted, and often not even recognized, by humans.

Sometimes, in response to relationships of power (which can be oppressive and close off possibilities), silence marks a lack. Other times, in evoking things beyond human knowing (including the unconscious and the non-human world), silence can offer a kind of capaciousness. Acknowledging all these aspects of silence in

48. Gordon Hempton, "The Last Quiet Places" (May 10, 2012).

49. sara.gladwin, "Divergent Thinking," December 2, 2012 (5:24 p.m.).

the classroom means acknowledging the limits of understanding, redirecting education so that it is less oriented to knowing, more to being with the unknown.

During the conference of the Association for the Study of Literature in the Environment in Moscow, Idaho in June 2015, I attend an early morning session entitled "Out of Silence, They Emerge," in which the Mississippi poet Ann Fisher-Wirth evokes just this sort of orientation.[50] Troubled by our recent, seemingly intractable, season of racial unrest, Ann shares with us a passage from Faulkner's novel, *Light in August,* in which Joe Christmas articulates his own (unmet) need for silence, and imagines the peace it might bring:

> It is just dawn, daylight: that gray and lonely suspension filled with the peaceful and tentative waking of birds. The air, in-breathed, is like spring water. He breathes deep and slow, feeling with each breath himself diffuse in the neutral grayness, becoming one with loneliness and quiet that has never known fury or despair. "That was all I wanted," he thinks in a quiet and slow amazement. "That was all, for thirty years. That didn't seem to be a whole lot to ask in thirty years."[51]

Such diffusion is denied Joe Christmas—but it continues all around him. Ann reads us another "tiny unforgettable moment" from Faulkner's novel, in which Joe, en route to committing murder, is crossing the yard:

> In the grass about his feet the crickets, which had ceased as he moved, keeping a little island of silence about him like thin yellow shadow of their small voices, began again, ceasing again when he moved with that tiny and alert suddenness.... He walked without sound, moving in his tiny island of abruptly ceased insects.[52]

It is Faulkner's description, Ann says, of the lush environment in which "insects accompany humans"—humans who see one another as enemies, while the insects are so silently attentive and responsive to their movements—that forms the impetus for a project that attempts to capture a range of voices, including the "hatch-out of

---

50. Ann Fisher-Wirth, "Out of Silence, They Emerge" (paper presented at the biennial conference of the Association for the Study of Literature and the Environment, Moscow, Idaho, June 24, 2015).

51. William Faulkner, *Light in August* (New York: Vintage, 1932), 134.

52. Faulkner, *Light in August,* 94.

the 17-year cicadas" in the woods behind her house.⁵³ With the burgeoning economy in Mississippi, Ann says, has come the loss of such music, which, "as we wake, as we sleep, reminds us that we are embedded in this thick materiality of the non-human world." Ann hears the "spirit of place" in the voices of the crickets and of the people, whom she makes, in her poems, both equivalent and available to being understood by others.⁵⁴

Ann's poetry—as well as the silence that surrounds and holds it—inspires and shapes what-and-how I am now attempting to figure.

And also what I am risking leaving unsaid.

53. Ann Fisher-Wirth and Maude Schuyler Clay, "Mississippi: A Collaborative Project," *About Place Journal* 3, no. 2 (November 2014); "Mississippi: An Excerpt," *Bloom* (March 23, 2015).

54. Fisher-Wirth, "Out of Silence."

CHAPTER FIVE
UNBECOMING
WITH CLARE MULLANEY

"Unbecoming Women"

> If we refuse to become women, what happens to feminism?
>
> —Judith Halberstam, *The Queer Art of Failure*

During the 1900-01 academic year, a student using the initials E.T.D. published a short story in Bryn Mawr College's bi-weekly magazine, the *Fortnightly Philistine*. Entitled "The Crime," the narrative focuses on the experiences of a second-semester senior struggling unsuccessfully with the stresses and pressures of academic life. Apprehensive about the concluding assessments of her college career, she comes to embody such a state of fearful extremity that she is unable to complete her work. Although she proclaims that "I am in perfect possession of my senses. Nervous, yes; very nervous, very melancholy but not mad, no, no!," the story ends when "the unfortunate Senior, who had been an exceptionally good student...dashed her head against the corner of the table and expired, raving mad."[1]

We open our project with this story because it so acutely dramatizes our central theme: the dynamic relationship between intellectual achievement and mental disability. "The Crime," which riffs on Poe's "The Tell-Tale Heart," is explicit in its portrayal of a young woman's mind under pressure, so fearful of her inability

---

This essay was first published under the title of "On Being Transminded: Disabling Achievement, Enabling Exchange," in *Disability Studies Quarterly* 34, no. 2 (2014).

1. E. T. D., "The Crime," 7 (February 1, 1901): 2-4, Internet Archive: Bryn Mawr College Library, Special Collections.

to meet Bryn Mawr's standards of academic accomplishment that she eventually does violence to herself. We use the term "disabling achievement" to name this nexus of anxiety surrounding intellectual performance: it is our description of the mechanisms whereby aiming for achievement can have the "crosswise," or "transverse," effect of generating disablement. Because we believe that insistent emphasis on advancement, progress, and futurity—as well as institutional focus on preparing students to meet these demands—disables us all, we begin to craft here a space in which the structures of cultural achievement need not disable. We re-envision an institution in which no one need gain intellectually at the cost either of her own mental health, or of another's loss or failure. We end with a particular focus on the disabling quality of those time-pressures that structure, animate, and strangle academic life. Throughout, we traverse the tensions between institutionalizing disability studies and the field's promise of destabilizing the constrictions of normativity.[2]

2. See also Sharon Snyder and David Mitchell, *Cultural Locations of Disability* (Chicago: The University of Chicago Press, 2005), 192.

The 100-year-old story of "The Crime" serves both as dramatic backdrop and historical scaffolding for the disabling dimensions of women's higher education. The scene we set at our home institution extends into multiple larger, intersecting discourses of mental dis/ability, feminism, education, and queer studies. Fifteen years before "The Crime" was published, the founders of Bryn Mawr College had addressed head-on a particularly disabling understanding of "women's nature." Early proponents of the College were challenged by a contemporary belief about the distinctive frailness of female bodies, a view championed most ardently by Edward Clarke, a Harvard Medical School professor who began his study of *Sex in Education; or, A Fair Chance for the Girls* with a description of "closed bodily systems," which contained "only finite amounts of energy": For young developing women, studying pulled "blood, nourishment and energy away from reproductive organs that were in the fragile and critical stages of maturation."[3] Concerned that excessive study would divert a young woman's finite energy supply

3. Barbara Ward Grubb and Emily Houghton, "Building Muscles While Building Minds: Athletics and the Early Years of Women's Education" (September–December 2005).

from her reproductive capacities, inhibiting and threatening the health of generations to come, Clarke argued that only by avoiding college studies could a young woman "retain uninjured health and a future secure from neuralgia, uterine disease, hysteria, and other derangements of the nervous system."[4]

The second president of Bryn Mawr, M. Carey Thomas, whose vision was definitive in shaping the College's mission, spoke of being "haunted…by the clanging chains of that gloomy little specter, Dr. Edward H. Clarke's Sex in education."[5] In a 1908 address celebrating Bryn Mawr's "experiment" of offering women rigorous intellectual engagement that would not adversely affect their minds or bodies, Thomas proclaimed that the

> passionate desire of women of my generation for higher education was accompanied throughout its course by the awful doubt, felt by women themselves as well as by men, as to whether women as a sex were physically and mentally fit for it.… We were told that their brains were too light, their foreheads too small, their reasoning powers too defected, their emotions too easily worked upon to make good students. None of these things has proved true. Perhaps the most wonderful thing of all to have come true is the wholly unexpected, but altogether delightful, mental ability shown by women college students.[6]

Thomas countered Clarke's description of women's fragile biological structures by taking a stand against the social convention of intellectual isolation: young women, she claimed, had been "crushed by the American environment," not "enabled by circumstances to use their powers" because they had been "cut off from essential association with other scholars."[7] Although Thomas imagined an intellectual community in which such isolation would be reduced, one of the ironic outcomes of her vision has been the current perpetuation of what we see as isolating academic practices.

It is our hope to intervene, here, in the disturbing dynamics set in motion by the scholarly ambitions and attainments of women.

4. Edward Clarke, *Sex in Education; or, A Fair Chance for the Girls* (1873; repr., New York: Arno, 1972), 41–42.

5. M. Carey Thomas, "Present Tendencies in Women's College and University Education," *Educational Review* 35 (January 1908): 69.

6. Thomas, "Present Tendencies," 64, 70.

7. Helen Horowitz, "Women and Higher Education: A Look in Two Directions," Heritage and Hope: Women's Education in a Global Context, talk at Bryn Mawr College (September 23, 2010).

We use E.T.D.'s story, in the context of Bryn Mawr's founding, as paradigmatic of an ongoing, uneasy relationship between women's education and mental health, as we attempt to further refigure the relationship among individuals and institutions, personal narratives and larger theoretical claims. Our project is thus an extension of Thomas's, which took a stand against Clarke's vision of the female body as a closed system, in order to explore the possibilities that might lie in more open networks.

Although expressed in different language, disquietude about "feeble minds" is as prevalent in the early twenty-first century as it was in the late-nineteenth and early-twentieth. We no longer call unsettled minds "hysteric," but describe them instead with a range of DSM diagnoses, including "anxiety," "depression," "bipolar disorder," "OCD," "anorexia," and "bulimia." In "Revisiting the Corpus of the Madwoman," Elizabeth Donaldson argues that it is impossible to reconcile such "medical discourses of mental illness, which describe the symbolic failure of the self-determined individual," with "the competing discourses of democratic citizenship, in which will and self are imagined as inviolable."[8]

8. Elizabeth Donaldson, "Revisiting the Corpus of the Madwoman: Further Notes toward a Feminist Disability Studies Theory of Mental Illness," in *Feminist Disability Studies*, ed. Kim Q. Hall (Bloomington: Indiana University Press, 2011), 107.

The conflict Donaldson identifies between the individual and the communal, between medical diagnoses and their social implications, is also highlighted in our recent fundraising campaign, "Challenging Women: Investing in the Future of Bryn Mawr." In its review of the contemporary challenges "which Bryn Mawr must be able to prepare its students to meet"—

> to continue to advance as women in science; lead in the arts and humanities; prepare effectively for life in an increasingly global environment; build strong, diverse communities; use technology for teaching and learning; and *strive for balance between academics and other aspects of a modern, healthy life*[9]

9. "Challenging Women: Investing in the Future of Bryn Mawr," *Alumnae Bulletin*, Bryn Mawr College, Spring 2003, italics added.

—the language of the campaign bears witness, particularly in this last clause, to the continued uneasy relationship between academic achievement and health.

This dynamic is beginning to garner attention in the field of disability studies. Several years ago, Catherine Kudlick wrote a short article challenging the "normative ideas" underlying our conceptions of "academic competence," and questioning the "unhealthy forms of intellectual conformity" they entail.[10] Margaret Price's 2011 *Mad at School* was the first book-length scholarly text, however, "to broaden the field of DS and…the field's long-standing emphasis on sensory impairments," by focusing on mental disability in the particular context of the academy.[11] Price argues that "academic discourse," in its appreciation of rationality and reason, "operates not just to omit, but to abhor mental disability—to reject it, to stifle and expel it."[12] Drawing on her assessment of the ways in which educational institutions like Bryn Mawr continue to promote a profound distinction between intellectual work and mental disability, we suggest that they are instead dialectical, each constituting and negating the other.

Sharing both M. Carey Thomas's commitment to the academic achievement of women, and E.T.D.'s fears about the costs such achievement entails, we attempt here to open up possibilities both for enabling women and "disabling," or "undoing," what the category of "achieving women" entails. In advocating for a more open and collective system, we both resist Edward Clarke's closed one and welcome all forms of mental variety. In an era when the classification "woman" is under interrogation, and when women, however defined, can find their education at almost any academic institution, we suggest ways in which single-sex institutions like Bryn Mawr might better respond to the particularities of, as well as to the increasingly diverse and complex interactions within and among, their student bodies. From the particular location of feminist disability studies, we add to the ongoing deconstruction of "the unity of the category of *woman*" a range of questions about feminist valorizations of "individualistic autonomy."[13]

Bryn Mawr students call themselves "Mawrtyrs," as a punning expression both of their undying devotion to their academic work,

10. Catherine Kudlick, "A History Profession for Every Body," *Journal of Women's History* 18, no. 1 (Spring 2006): 164–65.

11. Margaret Price, *Mad at School: Rhetorics of Mental Disability and Academic Life* (Ann Arbor: University of Michigan Press, 2011), 5.

12. Price, *Mad at School*, 8.

13. Rosemarie Garland-Thomson, "Integrating Disability, Transforming Feminist Theory," in *Feminist Disability Studies*, 16, 34.

and of the profound ethics of this allegiance. In this essay, we call for a shift from "mawrtyr-dom" to a more open-minded, open-hearted way of thinking about intellectual work. To signal that shift, we employ a polygeneric form of writing, juxtaposing personal narratives with theory drawn from disability and queer studies. Using all of these voices to probe and ponder the others, we portray a messier world than the one described in Bryn Mawr's *Alumnae Bulletin*, one that replaces the binary constrictions of healthy and sick, sane and insane, with a more hybrid form: disarrayed, cluttered, toggling between disablement and enablement.

The protagonist of "The Crime," unable to be a "complete master of herself," fails to muster the characteristics needed to excel in a demanding academic environment. The leakiness and instability inherent in her madness, the "trickling, horrid drops" of ink that consume her "boiling brain," stand in contrast to the "stolid" buildings of the College,[14] which represent the sharply defined demands of academia that she cannot meet. Her unsteady movement enacts a form of "maddening" that results in disaster. We advocate, here, another version of her "waffling" and "wobbling," one with a different, and more socially useful, result. If we can resist "walling off" disability, we might prompt instead a form of interdependency defined by mutual vulnerability—and mutual desire.

In "The Crime," the protagonist's "horror of the appliances of study grew" until she had "a look of feverish intellectuality" that "no mere fleshly seeker of marks could rival." "An exceptionally good student" is thus "maddened" by the intersection of the College's demands with her own desires to achieve them.[15] Although her ostensible "crime" is that of stealing others' ink (in order to forestall the dreaded final exam), her larger fault is her failure to meet the institution's expectations of academic performance. Perhaps an even larger "crime"— etymologically: *"fault,"* or *"cry of distress"*[16]—is that of the College, which places those rigorous demands on her. A hundred years later, the "mad pride" movement speaks to this dynamic by stressing the

14. E.T.D., "Crime," 2–4.

15. E.T.D., "Crime," 3–4.

16. Douglas Harper, "Crime," *Online Etymology Dictionary*.

fruitful potential of mental variety and difference, and advocating, thereby, movement across presumed categories of disablement.

Dis-labeling Madness

> What if, like queerness, we began to preface disability less as an identity than an intensely generative methodology—a form of relation...an exchange embodied in the very crevices of breakage, the borderlines between abled-bodied and disabled worlds?
>
> —Clare Mullaney, "Brandy Snaps and Battlefields"

Like gay and lesbian liberation movements, which appropriated the once-abjected term "queer" for a new, proud self-identification, "mad pride" is a growing civil rights movement that aims at showcasing difference by re-signifying the term "mad," which has long been saturated in stigma. Efforts to gain justice for "madness" have since spread throughout the world. "International Mad Pride Day" is now scheduled yearly on July 14, because, in the storming of the Bastille, prisoners detained for being "mad" were freed.[17]

Multiple groups celebrate "mad pride." The Icarus Project challenges the distinct psychiatric divisions between "sane" and "insane" by commemorating the unusual and "spectacular" ways in which "information and emotion" are processed by those bearing the "dangerous gifts" of "mental illness."[18] MindFreedom also queries the social framing of difference, by using "sanism"—discrimination against those labeled as having a mental illness—as a new point of analysis. Replacing "disabled" with "dis-labeled," this group refuses to medicalize what they describe as "symptoms of life." The organization's president, David Oaks, points out that the term "mad" derives from the roots *"mei,"* meaning "to change," and *"mutuus,"* "done in exchange." Because these are also the roots for "motion,"[19] this etymological derivation helps celebrants of "mad pride" to

17. "Mad Pride—since when?" *Toronto Mad Pride.*

18. "The Icarus Project"; Alison Jost, "Mad Pride and the Medical Model," *Hastings Center Report* 39, no. 4 (July–August 2009).

19. David Oaks, "Let's Stop Saying 'Mental Illness,'" *MindFreedom International,* April 26, 2012.

mobilize madness: rather than a fixed, stable category, it signifies a state of variability.

Our work follows the trajectory laid out by MindFreedom. It draws as well on Bethany Stevens's interrogations of "transability," and on Judith Halberstam's use of the term "transgendered" to move beyond both "uniqueness" and "unilateral oppression, and beyond the binary division of flexibility or rigidity."[20] We offer here the kindred term "transminded" to suggest ways in which "mad" and "sane," long trapped in polarized mind states, might better be understood as related, variable, and productive mental activities. "Transminded" encompasses the inherent stretchiness of mental dis/ability, and suggests the ways in which its shape willfully molds both to and against others. We hope that this new term—not situated in psychiatry, more pliable than "neurodiversity"—works to queer the trope of madness: "transminded" is defined by expansion, rather than lack or impairment. It evokes multiplicity and diversity, as in Kate Millett's description of living with manic-depressive disorder:

> We do not lose our minds, even "mad" we are neither insane nor sick. Reason gives way to fantasy—both are mental activities, both productive. The mind goes on working, speaking a different language, making its own perceptions, designs, symmetrical or asymmetrical; it works…. Why not hear voices? So what?[21]

Those voices are not always tolerable, of course, and the experience of hearing them not always productive. We hope to alter the conventional valuing of "productivity," however, in our call for "transmindedness," a hybrid state that yields novel connections and perspectives. Building on the history in feminist disability studies of an ever-complexifying identity-based politics,[22] we nudge the field towards a methodology (*choose here your favored term to embody the act of querying normative assumptions*) for "queering," "cripping," or "maddening" what it means to be an intellectual woman in the early twenty-first century. In doing so, we move from nouns and their modifiers—*"queer womyn," "disabled activist," "madwoman,"*

20. Bethany Stevens, "Interrogating Transability: A Catalyst to View Disability as Body Art," *Disability Studies Quarterly* 31, no. 4 (2011); Judith Halberstam, *In a Queer Time and Place: Transgender Bodies, Subcultural Lives* (New York: New York University Press, 2005), 21.

21. Kate Millett, *The Looney-Bin Trip* (Champaign: University of Illinois, 2000), 315.

22. Cf. Garland-Thomson, "Integrating Disability," 3–47; Kim Q. Hall, "Reimagining Disability and Gender through Feminist Disability Studies: An Introduction," in *Feminist Disability Studies*, 1–10; Susan Wendell, "Toward a Feminist Ethics of Disability" (1989; repr. in *The Disability Studies Reader*, ed. Lennard J. Davis. New York: Routledge, 2006), 243–56.

"*smart lady*"—to verbs, from bounded identities to conditioned, and ever-conditional, actions.

Multiple scholars in disability studies have prepared the way for us here, by unsettling fixed identity categories. Robert McRuer's "crippin'," which replaces "cultures of upward redistribution" with "an accessible world,"[23] has been helpful to our thinking about replacing current conceptions of women's academic achievement, which are measured against the failures of those who do not conform. Lennard Davis's call for "The End of Identity Politics" has also been particularly productive for, and clarifying of, the feminist disability work we have been doing at Bryn Mawr. The states of "dependency and interdependence" Davis describes accord well with our sense of "maddening" as moving, fragmenting, and splintering; we draw on his de-stabilizing project as a way of thinking differently about— *queering, cripping, maddening*—what it means to "identify."[24]

Leaking beyond conventional patterns and schemas of being, "madness" forges a non-linear trajectory, an un-straight path. We turn now to describe how re-thinking madness within a more flexible frame has helped us to refigure, and reimagine, achievement and disablement at Bryn Mawr.

23. Robert McRuer, *Crip Theory: Cultural Signs of Queerness and Disability* (New York: New York University Press, 2005), 71.

24. Lennard Davis, "The End of Identity Politics and the Beginning of Dismodernism: On Disability as an Unstable Category," in *The Disability Studies Reader*, ed. Lennard J. Davis, second edition (New York: Routledge, 2006), 241.

Exploring Alternative Feminisms

> We are all nonstandard.
> —Lennard Davis, "The End of Identity Politics"

We have nurtured several "transminded" initiatives on our campus over the course of the past few years, each one shifting our understanding of "madness" from an anchored category to a more open, mutable one. Anne first began to engage this dance of disabling achievement in a small Faculty Working Group on Assessment, where a year-long conversation about varieties of academic appraisal and evaluation led to an appreciation of the wide diversity of our students, and multiple discussions about how better to recognize and evaluate their work. Slowly this conversation shifted to imagining educational structures that might allow more space not only for the various modes of student achievement, but also for life's interruptions and challenges.

Because a recent study of the "campus climate" had made it clear that the portfolio of the ideal Bryn Mawr woman—an ambitious, capable, and high-achieving student—emphatically excluded mental illness (and with it multiple, valuable forms of human and academic expression), we began to explore the possibility of bringing a discussion of student mental health to the faculty floor. The Advisory Council to the Faculty Chair thought the topic important—but also dangerous enough that it needed to be handled with extreme care.

The prospect of a faculty-wide discussion evoked a range of fears: of naming the problem, of being called to be responsive to and responsible for it, and of making some serious mistakes in trying to respond. In the initial stages of our conversation, the Advisory Council conceptualized "mental illness" as a distinctly medicalized category, encompassing a small number of students whose conditions threaten our shared academic work. Concerned that faculty "don't like uncertainty," and did not feel competent to deal with the range of student needs and challenges, the Council proposed that a panel of mental health professionals might advise faculty how to "deal with this kind of diversity," and so guide our thinking about strategies of inclusion.

It was challenging even to label this topic: saying that we wanted to "address the mental health needs" of our students already framed the conversation as being about a medical problem. Over the course of our planning discussions, however, the Advisory Council became eager to facilitate a process that might help the campus move beyond the paradigm of trying to "fix" those students who are challenged by our classrooms. The productive large-group conversation that eventually ensued in late March 2012 was not framed by the topics of "illness" and "disability," but presented rather as one in a sequence of discussions about "meeting the needs of our diverse student body."

Those who teach in classrooms were joined in this conversation by athletics faculty, deans, and staff members from the Health Center and Office of Public Safety. A member of the Graduate School of Social Work prepared us for the conversation by sharing some statistics and offering three frameworks to help us begin thinking specifically about mental illness: we could understand it as a medical issue, the result of biological malfunctioning; as a social construction that serves to maintain the status quo (Ray McDermott and Hervé Varenne argue that the culture of schooling creates particular syndromes that then need accommodation);[25] or as "desire-based," a formulation that replaces the language of "damage" and deficit" with the complexity, contradiction, and self-determination of lived lives.[26]

We began with writing and then speaking in small groups, before gathering together for a wide-ranging discussion reflecting on what the institution rewards, and at what cost: how to begin talking about ways in which the culture at Bryn Mawr contributes to mental health problems for everyone on campus, *including staff and faculty*? The distinct identities of the "mentally ill" and the "healthy" began to blur as we considered structures that might better enable us all.

Margaret Price explains that discussions like these often fall into two clearly divided camps, with those personally affected by issues of mental disability set against those concerned with "falling standards" and maintenance of the academy's drive for "able-mindedness."[27] Our intervention in that distinction meant naming the dialectic in which each "camp" undergirds, and so defines, the other. "Protecting standards" predicates achievement on the existence of a population who cannot meet those goals; advocating for the "disabled" sets that distinct identity against those who are "enabled." Both acts of "exclusion" are caught within what Lennard Davis identifies as the "larger system of regulation and signification" which disables us all[28]—a system that Bryn Mawr faculty and

25. Ray McDermott and Hervé Varenne, "Culture as Disability," *Anthropology and Education Quarterly* 26 (1995): 323–48.

26. Eve Tuck, "Suspending Damage: A Letter to Communities," *Harvard Educational Review* 79, no. 3 (Fall 2009): 413.

27. Margaret Price, "Killer Dichotomies: Ir/rational, Crazy/Sane, Dangerous/Not," University of Michigan Press Blog, February 14, 2012.

28. Davis, "End of Identity Politics," 240.

staff will continue to interrogate in the months and years ahead.

Multiple student activities are also aimed at ending the culture of silence and shame surrounding mental illness on campus. This is a particular focus of Active Minds, a national organization founded in 2000, which now has chapters on over three hundred college campuses. In the spring of 2010, when Clare first began serving as one of the co-presidents of Bryn Mawr's chapter, we could not seem to build up our membership, and our events were poorly attended. We imagined a dynamic and interactive community that could replace the normative public discourse about strength and autonomy with discussions about shared vulnerability, but we were finding it very difficult to talk openly about feeling weak, frustrated, vulnerable, tired, *irrational*. It seemed to us difficult, if not impossible, to create "mad spaces" amidst the Bryn Mawr culture of achievement.

Bryn Mawr is mostly welcoming to those who are gender variant: a range of identities are explored and celebrated, among friends, in courses and student groups; organizations pertaining to bodily variety, gender identity, and sexuality have a large presence on campus. Active Minds had been trying for several years to promote a similarly inclusive environment for all types of minds, but mental illness carries a particular stigma at Bryn Mawr, serving as the shadow side of the strong, independent, and productive women the students are striving to be. Although gender variance may destabilize the traditional notion of a "women's college," it does not threaten the image of the "intellectual sister" that is so essential to Bryn Mawr's vision of itself and others' vision of it. Raising questions about the mental health costs of this intellectual work complicates this vision tremendously—although we are arguing here that doing so can offer a richer, more creative version of what an "intellectual sister" might mean.

In keeping with the character of Bryn Mawr, where intellectual work is so highly valued, we began connecting activist objectives with more theoretical ones. With Anne as our faculty advisor,

A black poster board, featuring an arrangement of post secrets, in many different shapes and colors, on display in Bryn Mawr's campus center. Photo by Clare Mullaney.

29. anneliese, "The Slippery Brain Sodality," June 25, 2009–November 8, 2011.

we formed a network linking the "top-down" organization of "Active Minds" with the "bottom-up" structure of "The Slippery Brain Sodality," a group composed of individuals with "brains that change states frequently/rapidly," who were rethinking existing approaches to stigmatization, cultural dependence, and the very basic contrast of "health" with "illness."[29] We also created a documentary entitled "Stomping Out Stigma," featuring students and faculty talking about their experiences with mental illness on Bryn Mawr's campus. Modeling our video after the "Pink Glove Dance," a YouTube sensation created to raise awareness of breast cancer, we asked each of our participants to wear a silver crown, as they danced in their dorm rooms and shimmied in their offices, physical education classes, and gymnastic practices.

We followed the campus premiere of the documentary with a panel discussion that explicitly aimed to break down the conventional distinctions separating the personal from the theoretical, and mental health from mental illness. The panelists included Anne; another professor who specializes in film studies, and has lived with depression; and two psychologists from our on-campus Child Study Institute. Our conversation centered around the unhealthy demands for performance to which Bryn Mawr holds its students, and the high standards to which these student "Mawrtyrs" hold themselves. We discussed the widespread student culture of "passing" as abled and achieving. One student described the professors as "another species" of "accomplishment and achievement," who were unable to understand her struggles. We challenged the divisions separating those who achieve from those who fail, the capable from the incapable, the mentally fit from the mentally ill, acknowledging that all of us operate on a spectrum of difficulty and possibility.

Our most successful venture in this regard was an event, suggested by our national organization, called "Post Secret." Placing a blank index card in each student's mailbox, asking her to write, draw, or "craft" a secret, we collected over two hundred responses for display in the student center. We were heartened to learn, from a survey we conducted later, that many students felt grateful to have suppressed, often shameful, experiences pulled to the surface, to see what they knew reflected in the words of someone else. In contrast to the closed system of Edward Clarke, our Post Secret project figured an open structure that highlighted multiple forms of mental variety. Each postcard was detached from the person who wrote it, intermingled on the display board with secrets of very different types. The link between behavior and identity was thus disrupted, as was the hierarchy of importance governing the relationship of different secrets to one another. Stories of severe mental illness appeared next to sillier tales; the network of secrets was utterly horizontal in its distribution.

The aesthetic form we created, with postcards separate yet connected, was that of a collage. Halberstam terms this mode "self shattering," because it models the depth of interdependence and "interbeing" in individual trajectories, and so challenges the "deeply disabling" mode of the self-sufficient individual.[30] By connecting all parts, we featured a collective representation, which may have made individual authors of the postcards feel less vulnerable: they could see that these were perturbations they did not have to absorb on their own. The scattered world we put on display illustrated, too, what we mean by the act of "maddening": unsettling the distinctiveness of dis/ability.

30. Halberstam, *Queer Time*, 136, 139.

Our understanding of what we accomplished in this project is still incomplete, as are the possibilities that might be revealed by its further iterations. For instance, a student in Anne's Non-Fictional Prose class, who posed some questions on-line about the viability of the Post Secret initiative, queried the degree to which "anonymity allows the truth, or facts, to become clear." She troubled in particular the "truth claims" of the display: "I wonder how many of these are true, how many are exaggerated truths for the sake of public recognition/publication"?[31] Transforming a "closed system" of shameful secrets into an open form of posting is a means of advocating extension and claiming lateral space. But what other dangers—and possibilities—lie in open networks?

31. FatCatRex, "Anonymity, Authenticity and Healing: Secrets of Truth-Telling Revealed," October 29, 2010.

We have learned a lot from our several years working with Active Minds, both about the strong fears that animate any conversations around questions of mental difference and dis/ability on campus, and about our own preferences for activism with a clear theoretical base, which both understands why it is acting, and is savvy about the limitations of that action. We have also recognized our particular investment in forms of activism that refuse to privilege the needs of one group over those of another, and signal as well the instability of any category that we might use to separate ourselves from others. We acknowledge, too, the fluidity of the categories we have used to separate parts of ourselves from other parts: the "capable" from the "mad," the "achieving" from the "failing," the enabling from that which disables.

Our largely practical discussions with faculty, as well as our advocacy activities on campus, have certainly complicated the project of disability studies at Bryn Mawr, where it has become much more than a mere call for accessibility: not a one-way request, but rather a multiply-positioned, "transminded" exchange. We are now dreaming together about a more capacious vision of what it might mean for us to create a shared community out of these multiple interacting parts. The cross-disciplinary approach we see emerging is that of community intent on expanding itself, combining creative, literary, educational, political, psychological, sociological, and scientific perspectives.

Some of the actions we envision have a pragmatic dimension: establishing chapters of Active Minds on each of the five "sister" campuses (Bryn Mawr, Barnard, Wellesley, Smith, and Mount Holyoke), with representatives convening each year to discuss past events and plan future ones; reaching out to the first-semester students who are facing the challenge of leaving home; creating a website for this population that not only lists the symptoms of various disorders, and valuable resources for treatment, but also information about the fluidity of identity, as described by disability studies, crip studies, and mad pride activists. We imagine more on-campus events like "The Female Orgasm Project" co-sponsored by Active Minds and Rainbow Alliance (an LGBTQ advocacy group), which showcased the usefulness of conceptualizing our identities as multiple and positively intersecting (*"orgasms are good for mental health!"*).

Other projects might focus on larger, perhaps-surprising questions, such as the disabling quality of our current conceptions of time. In accord with such possibilities, we turn now to speculate on the degree to which all preoccupation with achievement—itself dependent on futurity—is inherently disabling.

Unbinding Time

Consider, for a moment *(what is a moment?)*, these three images on the opposite page—one visual, two verbal—each replacing the inexorable "train track" of linear time, and its anxious measurement in school settings, with the possibility of communicating with the past (and future?). Visualize, for a moment *(what is a moment?)*, the enabling vision of a "loopy" universe. Or of one molded to us and holding us up. Or—even better—moldable *by* us to (better) sustain us all. Re-visualize, for a moment *(what is a moment?)*, the time in which we are teaching and learning, not only as sequential but also as iterative, not only as measured but also as experienced, not only as outer but also as inner. Imagine, for a moment *(what is that moment?)*, a form of education that is less driven by the clock, less bound by the conventional rituals of school time.[32]

> Timing clearly enters into the measurement of educational achievement…through the numerous forms of timed testing in which performance is evaluated in relation to material grasped in a specific segment of time…the quality of reflection is conditioned by its temporal organization, and so, too, is the quality of imagination.
>
> —Hope Jensen Leichter, "A Note on Time and Education"

A review of the past several decades of publications in *Teachers' College Record* turns up very few articles that acknowledge, as Hope Leichter did in 1980, the way in which "all educational experience… is organized in time." Leichter's observations, that the "assumptions about time and timing" that "pervade educational theory and practice" "often remain unexamined," and "alternative modes of temporal organization ignored,"[33] remain as true now as they were when she conducted her study over thirty years ago.

The adoption of business values and practices in educational

32. Cf. Joseph Cambone, "Time for Teachers in School Restructuring," *Teachers College Record* 96, no. 3 (Spring 1995): 517.

33. Hope Jensen Leichter, "A Note on Time and Education," *Teachers College Record* 81, no. 3 (Spring 1980): 360.

Matt Johnson, *The Shape of Time*, 2009. Bronze. 52 x 52 x 40 inches. Photo: Joshua White/JWPictures.com. Courtesy of the artist and Blum & Poe, Los Angeles/New York/Tokyo.

A tire, looped and twisted in a shape resembling a three-dimensional figure-eight, sits on a concrete surface. Each loop intersects with the other, forming a three-pointed structure.

Life + art is a boisterous communion/communication with the dead. It is a boxing match with time.

—Jeanette Winterson, *Why Be Happy When You Can Be Normal?*

What does time look like? I think of two hammocks, one an individual human can feel on the body, and one vast.... Universe as hammock? The holding and the mesh and mold ability seem key.

—Alice Lesnick, E-mail

administration has been extensively documented in Raymond Callahan's classic study of *Education and the Cult of Efficiency*, which denounces the latter as an "inadequate and inappropriate basis for establishing sound educational policy,"[34] and accordingly recommends changing the nature of graduate work in educational administration. Our own very compatible intervention involves re-thinking the role of standard "time" in education writ large.

U.S. educators long ago turned to factories as a model for designing schools;[35] the newly technologized, standardized, and purportedly "objective" testing regime has more recently given rise to subject-specific chunks of time, administered to students in age- and ability-specific groupings.[36] In now bringing this particular—*and profoundly disabling*—dimension of educational practice into focus, we challenge the belief that the purpose of education is to turn out children at a standard pace, with a measurable set of skills. Current education policies such as No Child Left Behind and Race to the Top demonstrate the persistence and intensification of narrowly quantifiable learning and measurable results. These days, the only learning that counts is countable. The drumbeat of "time on task" and measurable achievement locks students into a system in which one very particular kind of productivity is maximized.[37] These procedures are of course not limited to K-12 institutions. Ellen Samuels explains, for instance, that graduate student education at the University of California at Berkeley "is structured by an administrative construct called, with no hint of irony, 'normative time,' referring 'to the amount of time it takes ideally for a student in a particular discipline to complete a doctoral degree.'"[38] Alison Kafer has also more recently challenged the normative and normalizing expectations of pace and schedule by evoking a "resistant orientation" to "productivity, accomplishment, efficiency."[39]

We join Samuels and Kafer in our argument that the heavy drivers of time and a narrowly productive status quo fail to match the complex world we learn and live in.

---

34. Raymond Callahan, *Education and the Cult of Efficiency: A Study of the Social Forces that Have Shaped the Administration of the Public Schools* (Chicago: The University of Chicago Press, 1962), viii.
35. Jeannie Oakes et al., "Schooling: Wrestling with History and Tradition," in *Teaching to Change the World*, 2nd ed (New York: McGraw-Hill Higher Education, 2006), 6, 22.
36. Oakes et al., "Schooling"; Diane Ravitch, *The Death and Life of the Great American School System: How Testing and Choice are Undermining Education* (New York: Basic Books, 2010).
37. Jean Anyon, "Social Class and the Hidden Curriculum of Work," *Journal of Education* 162, no. 1 (Fall 1980): 67–92.
38. Ellen Samuels, "Cripping Anti-Futurity, or, If You Love Queer Theory So Much, Why Don't You Marry It?" Paper presented at the Society for Disability Studies Conference, San Jose, CA, 2011.
39. Alison Kafer, *Feminist, Queer, Crip* (Bloomington: Indiana University Press, 2013), 40.

In 1931

> —eighty-one years ago—
>
> Salvador Dalí etched his final strokes on *La persistència de la memòria*...

And so we recommend some alterations in educational practice—as well as in discursive form (you'll begin to notice now a few of our poetic experiments, interspersed in this text, in slightly smaller font, in hopes of interrupting the "flow" of things....)

> What would academia look like if we built in more interstices, more time when 'nothing' happened?
>
> —Margaret Price, "Ways to Move"

> ...the aim is to slow down... truly theoretical reflection is possible only if thinking decelerates...finding anomalies, paradoxes, and conundrums in an otherwise smooth-looking stream of ideas.
>
> —Timothy Morton, *Ecology Without Nature*

"Slowing down," learning to teach and learn in what Thomas Berry calls more "comprehensive dimensions of space and time,"[40]

> ...the three withering clocks were thought
> are thought
> to be a symbol of the unconscious,
> its violent collapse between
> time
> and
> space...

we here interrogate the "time-bound": our academic attachment to conventional understandings and measurements of time, and of its concomitant anxieties. In educational practice, suspending modern temporality

> ...the arrows begin to waver;

---

40. Thomas Berry, "A New Story," in *The Dream of the Earth* (San Francisco: Sierra Club Books, 1988), 123–37.

> 7:55 grows
> annular…

means questioning our attachment to the clearly demarcated limits of conventional, linear time, which moves only—*and quickly!*—in one direction, in order to be measured, and to enable us to measure ourselves against one another.

> no longer fixed and pointed,
> but adaptable,
> molten…

Our work with Bryn Mawr's Active Minds has made it clear to us that such time-based measures of achievement are problematic, as is our attachment to an understanding of time that undergirds such measurements.

> …saturated within this liquifying temporality
> the Coast of Catalgonia
> droops.…

We need a more relaxed, *hammock-like* way of thinking about what happens in educational practice, one in which the shared time we occupy in classrooms gives "space" to a more capacious sense of phenomenological time, one in which past, present, and future are intertwined.

Joseph Cambone, one of the few educational researchers who has written about the effect of time in school reform, observes that "time is largely a collective subjectivity—an agreed-upon convention that allows us to structure our lives temporally." We need to place ourselves in the same place at the same time; we need to be "on time" so we can be together "in time." Given the extent of such arrangements, "to restructure people's time," as Cambone acknowledges, "is actually to restructure their thinking and being."[41]

Re-structuring our shared subjectivity in this way would involve "re-doing" our conception of time in ways that acknowledge what

41. Cambone, "Time for Teachers," 513–14.

we all know, but continually forget: that the most profound experiences of our educational lives happen "outside" measured time, moving freely across the dimensions we conventionally distinguish as "past" and "future."

> …the horizon caves in and our sense of futurity softens to a miry evanesce & v a p o r . . .

Reading texts written hundreds of years ago, or speculating about future possibilities, we continually cross the borders of the conventional rituals of school time, those "strong boundaries" of the socio-temporal that demarcate "the beginning and endings of periods, school days, and school years."[42]

42. Cambone, "Time for Teachers," 517.

> …time, like the melting Camembert cheese that inspired Dalí's art, becomes s p o i l e d . . .

Cambone asserts that such boundaries "cannot be transgressed without incident."[43] It is our counter-assertion that the most profound academic work is actually *constituted* by such transgressions, emerging through temporal leaps, beyond standards, beyond measured expectations.

43. Cambone, "Time for Teachers," 517.

> The point is to go against the grain of dominant, normative ideas…the only ethical option…is critical and self-critical…the guiding slogan is: 'not afraid of non-identity.'
> —Timothy Morton, *Ecology Without Nature*

> So I read on. And I read on, past my own geography and history, past the founding stories…. The great writers were not remote…. Time is not constant and one minute is not the same length as another.
> —Jeanette Winterson, *Why Be Happy When You Can Be Normal?*

Many disability studies scholars include time in their systematic "cripping" of normative assumptions about human experience. "Crip time" has several different meanings: the term has been used to describe "pre-programmed" time, the sort of scheduling that seems entirely overwritten "with other people's voices."[44] It has also been used, contrariwise, and much more extensively, to signal interventions into such programming: accommodations, "a flexible standard for punctuality," the need for "extra time"[45]—although negotiating such accommodations is always "tricky against the normative ebbs and flows of legitimated knowledge production."[46]

The concept of "crip time" could also conceivably be used in a third sense, to identify the possibility—the profound *need*—for some time that (as an anonymous reviewer of this essay observed) is "just plain wasted...sometime we are just 'doing time'—in depression, in illness, in times when there is nothing really beyond surviving to do." Although the field of disability studies has evoked, and advocated for, the variability of "crip time," it has not wrestled directly (so far as we know) with this notion of wasting time. Like the women's movement, and the women's colleges like Bryn Mawr that emerged from it, the disability movement seems particularly, and somewhat paradoxically, invested in a narrative of "overcoming" particular impairments, in order to be taken seriously in the academy. The field hasn't yet offered us, we think, the tools we need to interrupt the narrative of academic achievement, to find a space where nothing happens, to discover gaps in which normative time is ruptured, suspended.

And so we gesture, here, toward some of those possibilities that lie in empty and "unproductive" time.

...do the gossamer clocks meld or resist?

protest

or conform?...

44. Anne McDonald, "Crip Time."

45. "Crip Time," *Dictionary of American Slang*.

46. Borderdwelling, "The Ph.D. and Normative Time," Brooke's Blog, July 4, 2012.

> Does the demonstration of coherence indicate a stronger mind?
>
> —Margaret Price, *Mad at School*

Does getting your work in on time indicate a stronger mind? (Or: why is punctuality so important?)

Margaret Price has conducted an extensive analysis of the ways in which the academy's structuring of itself around schedules—placing importance on appointments, deadlines, the completion of timed tasks—excludes and discriminates against those with mental disabilities; she shows how the demands of academia can exacerbate symptoms which may be manageable in a less stressful environment. It is relatively easy for a college to imagine accommodating physical disabilities, Price argues, but much harder for a place that prides itself on mental accomplishment to envision accommodating mental diversity and difference—to adjust, in particular, to the altered *pacing* that differently-minded minds might require.[47]

As an alternative to current time-based arrangements, Halberstam advocates other temporal models. Her concept of "queer time"—the outcome of "imaginative life schedules, and eccentric economic practices," of "non-normative logics and organizations" of activity—invites us to imagine "other logics of location, movement, and identification," to mark out "willfully eccentric modes of being."[48] Our own interrogating—*querying, queering, cripping, maddening*—of educational time accepts Halberstam's bid to re-conceptualize what time looks-and-feels like. Of particular use in our attempts to make the academy more welcoming of difference, and more able to acknowledge multiple modes of failure and achievement, is Halberstam's proposition that we step out of "the logic of capital accumulation," to live and work "on the edges of logics of…production."[49]

In 1873, Edward Clarke was concerned that the education of young women would inhibit and threaten the health of generations to come.

47. Price, *Mad at School*, 25–57.

48. Halberstam, *Queer Time*, 1, 6; cf. Samuels, "Cripping."

49. Halberstam, *Queer Time*, 7, 10.

> …is what is lost in time gained in an intransigent standstill?…

In this decade, Halberstam is inviting another generation of young women to break away from "repro-time," to embrace alternative logics that don't simply *reproduce* what has been done before. She thus addresses the two-fold fears of Edward Clarke, that educated women might fail to bear both biological and intellectual fruit. In imagining an education system that does not reproduce old-fashioned understandings of time, and thereby reproduce old divisions among various kinds of "mindedness," we also attempt to correct both of Clarke's "mis-conceptions."

> …angular rocks give way to curved conditionings…

We imagine a form of schooled time marked less by tests needing to be passed "in time" and "on time" than by an understanding that we are all "held up by" a hammock-like, loopy, iterative structure.

Can we imagine a college semester that isn't organized according to conventional temporal logics?

Can we imagine academic time that isn't organized by semesters?

Schooling restructured in such time might involve a "spiral curriculum," fostering re-examination of a subject "in different forms at different stages."[50] Or perhaps, following GrayandGrey, it will evoke "some other shapes":[51]

50. Leichter, "A Note on Time," 368.
51. GrayandGrey, "Some Other Shapes," March 27, 2009.

Glenda León, *Jardín Interior IV/Inner Garden IV*, 2003. Digital C-print. 80 x 120 cm. Courtesy of the artist.

A pair of images: the left one features two clusters of strings, one labeled "possible pasts," the other "possible futures"; these are bound together by a single thread labeled "this moment." The right image shows a field containing small differently-shaped flowers, some looking like bows, others like pinwheels.

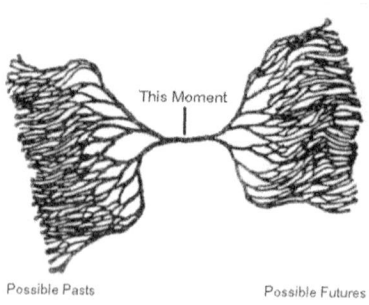

In sharp contrast to Edward Clarke's characterization of the "closed bodily systems" of nineteenth-century women, which contained "only finite amounts of energy," we've been experimenting here with very different representations: of the fluid "self" of the contemporary woman, of her relationship to others in an academic environment, and of the various forms her prose—*our* prose—might take. We have been trying out what might emerge if we break through the barriers crucial to keeping a system "closed."

...drip drop,
tick tock...

We have played here with the possibilities opened up by "maddening," or "montaging," academic writing, interrupting the conventional, sequential form of argumentation with images, snips of poetry, and quotations, not woven seamlessly into the whole, but rather creating "holes" within it.

Being "transminded," to our minds, not only refuses the binary of mental health and illness, acknowledging the mutability of a spectrum of identities, the shifting "self,"

...a dissolving persistency
a phase ensconced   i n v a r i a n c e   and contradiction...

but also invites different forms of "composition" than the conventional representations of "coherence."[52]

52. Cf. McRuer, *Crip Theory*; Price, *Mad at School*.

> I live life in slow motion. The world I live in is one where my thoughts are as quick as anyone's, my movements are weak and erratic, and my talk is slower than a snail in quicksand.... I communicate at the rate of 450 words an hour compared to your 150 words in a minute—twenty times as slow. A slow world would be my heaven. I am forced to live in your world, a fast hard one.... I need to speed up, or you need to slow down.
>
> —Anne McDonald, "Crip Time"

We have moved from a fictional story about a young woman, maddened over 100 years ago by her efforts to complete her studies at Bryn Mawr, to an alternative tale that re-positions our apprehensions about productivity and achievement within larger temporal arrangements. Edward Clarke was concerned both that women's intellectual work would be insufficient, and that it would interrupt their ability to reproduce. In the founding of Bryn Mawr, M. Carey Thomas and her cohorts countered that anxious narrative. Now, in a time when it is still a challenge for women to have children and academic careers, we again attempt to re-write that story, querying the disabling effect of temporal demands, in search of a quirkier temporality in which we might all flourish. This more pliant time might include a range of unexpectedly "stretchy" forms: surely more lenient deadlines, but perhaps also more defined structures, for flexible minds that need tighter bounds. For some of us, more open, exploratory configurations would provide finer spaces for flourishing; for others, clearer access to what is needed, and more transparency about expectations, might provide the necessary "mesh," a much-needed "hammock."

Setting "madness" in motion has meant our moving words and images around on the page, in demonstration of an open, and "open-minded," system. Beyond this essay,

> ...dream in undefinable moments,
> inclusive instants,
> slivered seconds...
>
> time as a hammock, inherently stretch-y like the "transmind," offers us dilation, heterogeneity, resistance to rhetoric.

"Achievement," in a world so conceived, needn't imply completion; it might instead gesture, as we do here, towards what is incomplete, even uncomplete-able...

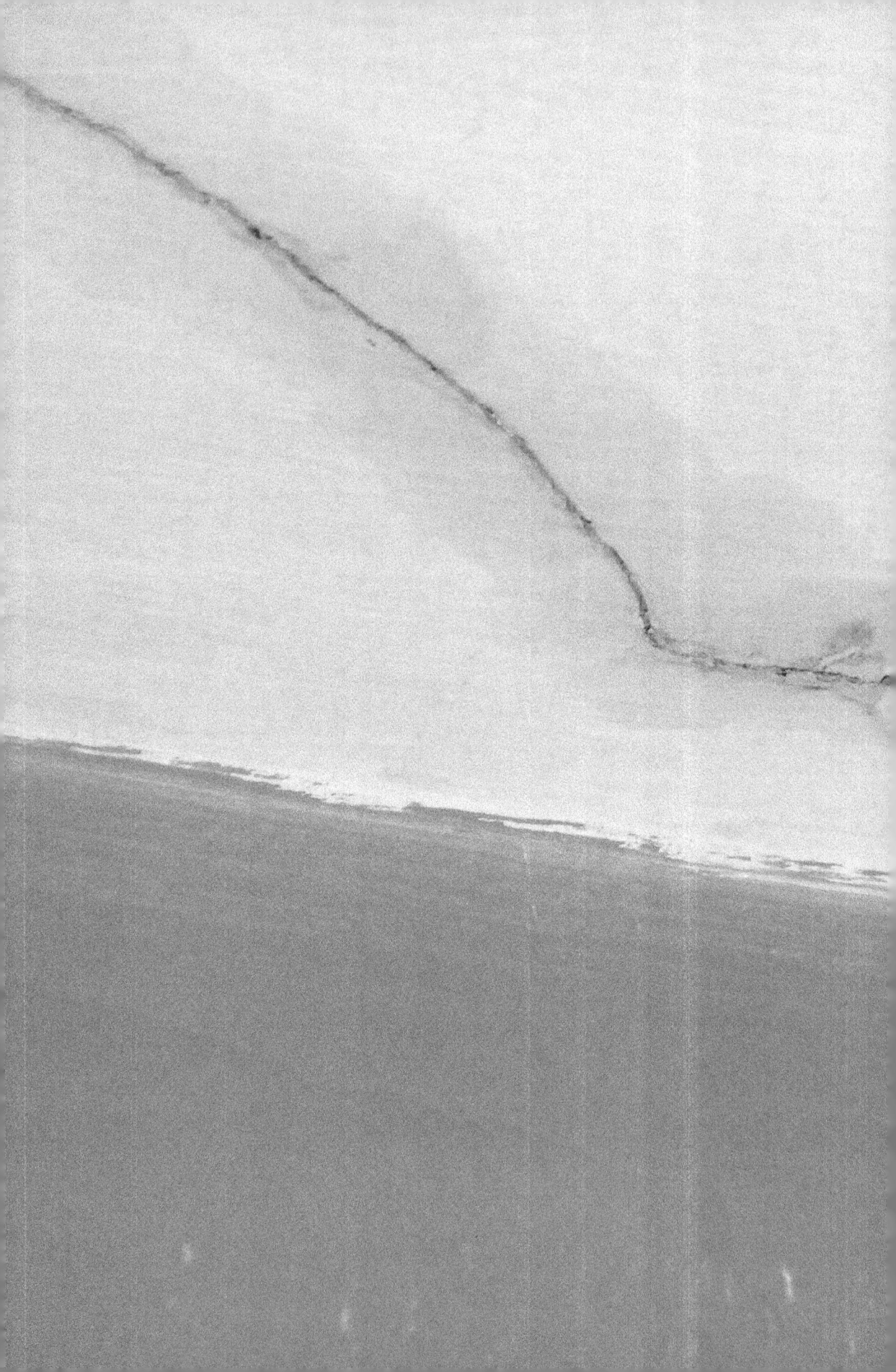

New Crack with Water Damage, Aaron Gustafson, CC-BY. https://flic.kr/p/ABgEd

CHAPTER SIX
LEAKING

Wading into Dark Waters

Moscow, Idaho in June: it is very hot, even at night, not air-conditioned in the dorm where I'm staying for an environmental humanities conference. I'm thinking: fans. On a bright Saturday afternoon, I get a call from my husband in Philadelphia: it's pouring here, he says, watching a leak track across the second-floor ceiling. As he arranges pots underneath, we hit a panic note as homeowners: what if the ceiling collapses in our new home?

A leak in the roof brings on a special kind of attendance and anxiety: a reminder that the outdoors is always potentially indoors, the elements never truly at bay. If you don't do something and soon, the ceiling softens and the leak spreads; water always finds a way through.

This everyday worry permeates the installation series *Dark Waters*, C. Rhee's response to Hideo Nakata's Japanese horror film of that title:

> My art installation…began as a carefully placed drip from my studio ceiling, at the time located in a trailer (the sort used in overcrowded public schools) on a university campus. The moment water seeped through the ceiling, the leak marked the school site as an everyday space of possible horror and dysfunction. Constructed yet also really seeping water, the leak caused visitors to question whether the space was an artwork or a living, breathing problem. It was this disturbance of certainty into openings for horror and anxiety that became the heart of the Dark Water works.[1]

[1] Eve Tuck and C. Rhee, "Exemplar Chapter 33: A Glossary of Haunting," in *Handbook of Autoethnography*, ed. Stacey Holman Jones, Tony E. Adams and Carolyn Ellis, (Walnut Creek: Left Coast Press, 2013), 639–58.

The persistence of this leakage, the deliberately evoked unease about whether it is "artwork or a…problem" play on a disquiet we work hard to keep at bay: the impossibility of fully knowing, containing, controlling our worlds, our immediate surroundings, our*selves*.

The concept of leaking evokes these differentially situated vulnerabilities, an image of environmental threat and a historical repository for remnants that do not disappear, even as we hurry to plug or patch them over, trying to protect boundaries, to cordon off a separate, coherent self. As evoked in this book, learning demands a different scenario: happens not in containers but in gaps, cracks, places of leakage, in the spaces *between* our actions and our conscious understandings, where who we think we are and what we think we know recedes, maybe even dissolves—and so opens unexpected portals in our psyches and our relationships: enticing, and dangerous. Rhee's installation helps me think about academic institutions as spaces where borders do not hold: the outside cannot be kept out, the visitor too involved with the leakage; where, as a Black man puts it to white teachers, "if I am not what I've been told I am, then it means that *you're* not what *you* thought you were *either*!"[2]

Half a century later, in a letter to his son, Ta-Nehisi Coates again highlights the false, dangerous belief in boundaried selves by repeating the phrase "people who believe they are white."[3] Leakage beads through the cracks in classrooms, in colleges visibly riven at this moment when young people here and across the country are calling out the hauntings of these spaces, buildings named for those identified as racists, colonizers: how is it possible to teach in, of, about these ambiguous and haunted spaces—for *all* students and *for* social justice?

In their "Glossary of Haunting," Tuck and Rhee probe the nature of haunting, warn us to resist "righting wrongs." As an educator, I take this personally:

2. James Baldwin, "A Talk to Teachers," 1963; repr. in *The Price of the Ticket, Collected Non-Fiction 1948–1985* (New York: Saint Martin's Press, 1985).

3. Ta-Nehisi Coates, *Between the World and Me* (New York: Spiegel & Grau, 2015).

> Haunting lies precisely in its refusal to stop. Alien (to settlers) and generative for (ghosts), this refusal to stop is its own form of resolving. For ghosts, the haunting is the resolving, it is not what needs to be resolved. Haunting aims to wrong the wrongs, a confrontation that settler horror hopes to evade.[4]

[4.] Tuck and Rhee, "Glossary," 642.

I am struggling with how to teach to and for students in varying positions in relation to settling and colonialism, vulnerability and trauma. Without the seduction of trying to "right wrongs," what might it mean to teach for social justice? Tuck and Rhee unsettle even this question: "Social justice is a term that gets thrown around like some destination, a resolution, a fixing.…The promise of social justice sometimes rings false, smells consumptive, like another manifest destiny."[5]

[5.] Tuck and Rhee, "Glossary," 647.

In this chapter, I reflect on how the concept of leaking might help me and others, pedagogically, to work from and with students' and our own vulnerabilities; to use the often unwelcome seeping through of what we don't know and may well fear as a font for learning; and, in light of this, to reconsider what we teach *for*.

Metaphorically, political leaks show us how leakage can exacerbate fragmentation within communities, even as new possibilities emerge. Geologically, boulders split by ice allow water to seep in and freeze, shattering the core. Not often (ever?) desired, leaks are inevitable; dangerous, disruptive, potentially transformative.

I look at these processes in teaching and learning, first through "enactments" in a Multicultural Education class, then through a session in a prison and its aftermath back on the college campus. In each of these spaces boundaries are asserted, riven, realigned, sometimes opening the way for deeper engagements, sometimes demanding a fortitude that some among us—students and teachers—may not have, at least individually. Leakage into pedagogy is also in play here, as I and my co-teachers look to diffuse authority while also finding ourselves taking it up in unexpected ways.

Throughout, I explore what kinds of learning can happen

> Vulnerability is intrinsic to our humanity: the human person is contingent and inter-dependent: we are born in a state of total dependency and will die in a state of radical vulnerability.
> —Timothy Kearney, "The Transforming Power of Vulnerability"

in "a site that is simultaneously a ruin and a remake, is haunted and haunting, is horrific and very plain…"[6] Where a "ruin" might become a "remake."

[6] Tuck and Rhee, "Glossary," 646.

Vulnerability

Judith Butler begins her work on the possibility of solidarity founded in shared loss and grief with the recognition that to be human is to be vulnerable; to be in relationship and thus susceptible always to "breakage," to being "undone" by one another. This shared vulnerability—from the Latin "vulnerare," "to wound, hurt, injure, maim"—cannot be evaded or "willed away"; it emerges from our state of inherent relationality with the world. Even so, Butler acknowledges, "the condition of precarity is differentially distributed";[7] even in our wounding, we are not equal.

[7] Judith Butler, *Notes Towards a Performative Theory of Assembly* (Cambridge: Harvard University Press, 2015).

How to develop a pedagogy that recognizes and works with these precarious conditions as sites of learning?

Classrooms are spaces where people may choose to take risks with our thinking and feeling; where immersion in words, images, interactions may call up difficult experiences or memories; where trauma of an individual or collective kind might be revisited, perhaps occluding choice. These are spaces haunted by ephemera clinging to walls, texts, and exchanges, where "triggers" might touch off re-visitings or new visitations of histories that continue to reverberate in the present.

Linguistically, wounding links vulnerability with trauma. Originally from the Greek, trauma came to signify a "surgical wound," and then psychic wounding,[8] experienced individually or collectively as a response to occurrences so intense and overwhelming that they return often unexpectedly in horrific memories and dreams.

[8] Ruth Leys, qted. in Rachel Spear, "'Let Me Tell You a Story': On Teaching Trauma Narratives, Writing, and Healing," *Pedagogy* 4 (Winter 2014): 60.

Teachers and learners bring our wounds to the classroom, which is far from hermetically sealed. Recent debates have swirled around "trigger warnings," the practice of alerting students to material that might re-ignite their experiences of extreme vulnerability or trauma. In *Inside Higher Ed*, a group of seven humanities professors, including a colleague at Bryn Mawr and another at nearby Swarthmore College, argue that "Trigger Warnings are Flawed": because teachers cannot know what material will trigger students, content warnings are necessarily incomplete, even misleading, "making promises about the management of trauma's afterlife that a syllabus...should not be expected to keep."[9] Strikingly, and ironically, this essay shifts the locus of vulnerability from learners to teachers, with the caution that faculty who teach about social injustice are the most likely to be marginalized.

Feminist disability scholar Angela Carter points out that, for those whose lives are impacted by trauma, considering its impact on pedagogy is not a choice. Rather than short-circuiting academic freedom and critical thinking, Carter argues that acknowledging trauma is "an imperative social justice issue" in our classrooms.[10] As Alison Kafer notes, "It's hard to imagine a trauma that is not in some fundamental way attached to relations of power."[11]

Recognizing trauma as extreme woundedness that can act to open up or shut down new learning, I acknowledge radical differences among students' experiences that pose differential challenges to individuals and sometimes to us as a group. I probe this node of systemic oppression, vulnerability, and trauma as un/bounded categories that split and elide, as singular and shared experiences of "radical vulnerability" and interdependence.[12]

A friend and colleague with expertise in the treatment of trauma asks what happens when my prison classroom triggers difficult, sometimes traumatic responses for incarcerated women, then I leave and they return to their cells. Another friend and colleague notes that this question of "what kind of responsibility one has if one takes up these kinds of radical pedagogies" applies also to our college students: "Are there *ir*responsible practices that emanate from the pedagogy you embrace?" I'm reaching here to address

---

9. Elizabeth Freeman, et al., "Trigger Warnings Are Flawed," *Inside Higher Ed*, May 29, 2014.

10. Angela Carter, "Teaching with Trauma: Trigger Warnings, Feminism, and Disability Pedagogy," DSQ: *Disability Studies Quarterly* 35, no. 2 (2015).

11. Alison Kafer, *Feminist, Queer, Crip* (Bloomington: Indiana University Press, 2013), 18.

12. Timothy Kearney, "The Transforming Power of Vulnerability," *Irish Theological Quarterly* 78, no. 3 (August 2013): 245.

such real, hard questions, with a pedagogy that both recognizes our radical, shared vulnerability and relationality as inevitable, and draws on these as a source of learning.

Enacting

> Long post ahead. Short version: if you're not a person of color (this applies to all of you, not some imaginary person off in the distance), you should rethink engaging with the trauma of people of color, especially in academia and the arts, if you are not ready to hold space for them to engage with or and work through it on their terms. Your terms don't matter if you are not from that population.
>
> —Whitney López, Bryn Mawr '15

Built like a fortress, Bryn Mawr is maintained through a complex history dependent on the labor of others. A classroom where I often teach is on the second floor of a building named for Joseph Taylor, whose will established a Quaker college for women.[13] Constructed of local stone to look like a castle, Taylor Hall is steeped in the mustiness of creased spines and more than a century's worth of young women exercising their minds. This space is a palimpsest where "traces of the past…bleed through." I love teaching in this classroom, with its material history tracked in deep splintery wood and tall thin-paned windows, chair rails identified by a student who recognizes what she's seeing and decodes for others, including me; its old-fashioned closets abetting our connection with worlds beyond: once stacked with blue exam books, now housing various technical aides. But leakage tints these walls, "prior writing ghosted through to the surface."[14]

Places are themselves a form of pedagogy: ones that hold and challenge us, although we may not recognize them as such. Elizabeth Ellsworth explains how we experience a place of learning not only

13. "A Brief History of Bryn Mawr College," Bryn Mawr College, 2016.

14. "This Is a Palimpsest (calicult)," *analepsis*.

in terms of knowledge but also physically, as we rest, pace, laugh, discover: "Our experiences…arise not only out of our cognitive interpretations of the building's allusions to historical or aesthetic meanings but also out of the corporeality of the body's time/space as it exists in relation to the building."[15]

In her efforts to unearth the history of Black women at Bryn Mawr, Grace Pusey notes the bodies missing from the buildings: the near invisibility of African American domestic workers in the archives and the near absence, until recently, of African American students in the college. The "Black at Bryn Mawr" tour, created by Grace and Emma Kioko, takes visitors through servant tunnels that "manifested the supposition that [domestic laborers] were to do their work without being seen or heard.…African American domestic laborers were forced to participate in their own erasure." Pusey calls on women's historian Michelle Moravec's concept of "unghosting" to highlight why such absences can be as significant as presence.[16] The call to "unghost" is a methodology for reinscribing stories erased from history. This work nudges me to ask: what to do *pedagogically* with such ghosted pasts and contemporary manifestations?

In my Taylor Hall classroom, I've been experimenting with such allusions and relations by using a strategy of "enactments" with my Multicultural Education students. These dramatic scenarios are complexly layered, moving through textual, bodily, and architectural surfaces. Emerging from and across our readings and students' writings about themselves and others, about the college and other life contexts, this strategy excavates, intervenes in, films over other, older scripts that nonetheless bleed through.

The first day of class I ask the 25 or so students to gather themselves into "diverse" groups of 4–5; we brainstorm dimensions of diversity in the room, and I ask that they include some people they don't know; groups form through a kind of speed dating. For the next three weeks they write, read, and discuss weekly blog entries in response to this sequence of prompts:

15. Elizabeth Ellsworth, *Places of Learning: Media, Architecture, Pedagogy* (New York: Routledge, 2005), 4.

16. Grace Pusey, "'Unghosting' African American Women's Labor History at Bryn Mawr College, 1880–1940," unpublished manuscript, 2015, 6, 9, 10.

WRITE AND POST BY SUN. AT 5: something that happened in your past (in school, neighborhood, family…)— you were part of it or witnessed or in some way had direct contact with—that troubled/s you, raises questions for you about culture/multiculturalisms/diversity/in relation to equity/in relation to power, even if you're not exactly sure how. Tell the story in terms of your perspective when it happened; then feel free to add any comments/questions from your perspective now.

WRITE AND POST BY SUN. AT 5: something that happened this year in/around the Bi-Co—you were part of it or witnessed or heard about it (in the air)—that troubled/s you, raises questions for you about culture/multiculturalisms/diversity/in relation to equity/in relation to power. Tell the story in terms of your perspective when it happened; then feel free to add any comments/questions from your perspective now.

WRITE AND POST BY WED. AT 5: something that happened this week in/around your life, including (but not limited to) the Bi-Co—you were part of it or witnessed or heard about it—that troubled/s you, raises questions for you about culture/multiculturalisms/diversity/in relation to equity/in relation to power. Tell the story in terms of your perspective when it happened; then feel free to add any comments/questions from your perspective now.

After reading and responding online to each other's entries, the groups use our texts and discussions as lenses for talking further about their stories, evolving issues and crossovers. A few weeks in, I alert them that they'll be using their entries as source material to develop an "enactment"—a dramatic evocation of a story or composite of stories from their blogs, which will invite the full class to engage in key issues or dilemmas the group has been processing. Groups develop "scripts" and perform for the class for 5-8 minutes; I usually ask them to do this twice. The first time the rest of us watch; the second time we are invited to enter or intervene: as a "thought bubble" by standing behind a character and speaking what we think that character is thinking; as a character, tapping out a player and deliberately shifting the action; or, in the midst of the scenario, calling out "freeze frame" to raise a point of discussion.

As we're stirring these experientially-based investigations, we're also reading theorists and educators: Stuart Hall, Ann Berlak, Sekani Moyenda, Paul Gorski, Kevin Kumashiro, Elizabeth Ellsworth.[17]

After each enactment, I ask the "audience" to speak first from the position of one of the theorists, before speaking as themselves. "Speaking as" another is a way to step away from the person we believe ourselves to be; speaking "as oneself" may then stretch, perhaps even surprise. Prising open a fissure between what we know and who we are can become a site of leakage, of disquiet, of learning, for "enactors" and "audience."

Enactments involve demanding intellectual and creative work: the performing group has to think hard about the issues they take on and the kinds of questions they want their audience to engage; as audience, class members need to deepen their understandings of theorists to embody them in dialogue with one another; participants prepare, and also deal with the unexpected.

This exercise tends to be highly engaging, to signal and at the same time puncture coherence, to engender troubling moments that unfurl in dining halls and living rooms. Students find themselves writing and sometimes "playing" characters from their lives with whom they don't share aspects of their identities that feel important to them, or whose perspectives or values might disturb or even horrify them. A white student's story of her friend group spurs her group's enactment, and she takes up the role of a character mocking Asian students. Afterwards, she talks about how bad it felt to do this, how she hasn't been able to shake off "speaking as." In enactments, the world leaks into the classroom, the classroom back out into the world, opening up new relationships but also creating raggedy edges with friends or family. In an enactment cutting between quick sketches of a Chinese student's experiences in college and a series of phone calls with her mother, we witness what she doesn't share

17. Stuart Hall, *The Multicultural Question* (Milton Keynes, United Kingdom: Pavis Centre for Social and Cultural Research, The Open University, 2001); Ann Berlak and Sekani Moyenda, *Taking It Personally: Racism in the Classroom from Kindergarten to College* (Philadelphia: Temple University Press, 2001); Paul Gorski, "Working Definition," *Critical Multicultural Pavilion*, edited and updated April 14, 2010; Kevin Kumashiro, *Against Common Sense: Teaching and Learning Toward Social Justice* (New York: RoutledgeFalmer, 2004); Elizabeth Ellsworth, *Teaching Positions: Difference, Pedagogy, and the Power of Address* (New York: Teachers College Press, 1997).

with her mom: a cacophonous cultural remix at the college, then a humiliating body search at the international airport. Soon thereafter, this student stops attending classes. Worried, I reach out, but don't hear back, and weeks later learn that she's withdrawn from the college. Not saying this was because of the enactment.

But like the dropped ceiling leakage into "a site that is simultaneously a ruin and a remake,"[18] enactments hover, bubble, dissolve. Sometimes they call out phantoms that do not easily settle or "appease." And they call me and my students to bear witness to each other and ourselves in our shared precarity.

Over the years, I try out various versions of this activity, learning also that each class and group takes up the project differently. One group addresses the issue of dislocation into another persona by using a strategy from the Alternatives to Violence Project in which characters visibly step into and out of their roles at the beginning and end of the enactment. In one class the "audience" hesitates to jump in and intervene during enactments, preferring instead to locate their probing analytical discussions afterwards; in our debrief at the end of the project, we discuss this as a gesture of maintaining respect for the struggles being represented "on stage"—in doing so, were the students resisting "leakage"? Rather than presuming a "right" way to take up enactments, we acknowledge that this is delicate territory in which we are each and collectively threading our ways; hesitation might constitute a crack in the flow of the plan, a crevice of curiosity.

This year's class jumps in from the get-go, intervening in planned and unplanned ways and sometimes questioning premises. Their risks rivet and seduce us into moments of disconcerting exposure.

18. Tuck and Rhee, "Glossary," 646.

Controversy, Raw and Uncivil

The school year began with two seniors from the south taping a Mason-Dixon "caution" line across their hallway, then mounting a Confederate flag outside their dorm room. Their actions catalyzed a storm of campus reactions, media coverage, and in-and-beyond-classroom conversation, and overlap with the non-indictments in the deaths of Michael Brown and Eric Garner. It was a charged fall.

As Anne tells this story in "Slipping,"[19] it ends in December. But now it's February, and many are not "over it." In our enactments, one group uses their diverse positions to dramatize the "Confederate flag incident."

Several of their pre-enactment posts set the stage:

> STUDENT A: It was the night of parade night when it first occurred, the night when I realized that racism and oppression truly exist on my campus...on the night that we, freshmen, were celebrating the beginning of our college careers; two signs that symbolized African American oppression and degradation existed on this so called "liberal" college.... This event...made me realize that our colleges are a representation of this country that we live in. That "the land of the free and every man is equal"... in reality is just an ideology that helps certain groups feel good about them while keep the minority tranquilized and tolerate what is happening in this county and also in our colleges.[20]
>
> STUDENT B: [In] a facebook group [about the Confederate flag incident]...thousands of comments from alums (and a few comments from current students) poured in over a number of weeks....Overall, issues of POC safety and historic racism were routinely ignored in favour of...personal attacks or counter-attacks; primarily white voices drowned out the POC voices, and alums spoke over students.[21]
>
> STUDENT C: During the Confederate Flag incident, I was told by a lot of American friends that I should join the protest because I should feel offended. Their saying is not new to me, because it was not the first time since I came to America that people kept telling me I should have been angry and should have taken actions against discrimination. People told me I should not be

19. See Chapter 8, "Slipping."

20. "Parade Night," February 1, 2015 (5:37 p.m.).

21. "Bryn Mawr Bigotry," February 1, 2015 (1:52 p.m.).

quiet after I was told a joke about my race, although I found the joke very entertaining myself. I was told to join the protest before I knew what was really going on because I should be offended as a person of color.... It's not that I will never be offended by racism. I will. But when I'm offended, I think I'm able to tell. And the most hurtful racism is not being joked about my race but being told again and again that I should be easily wounded because of my race.[22]

22. "Trust Me, I Can Tell," February 1, 2015 (3:16 p.m.).

Shades are down, a Confederate flag fills a large screen at the front, a blue-taped Mason-Dixon line cuts our classroom in two.

Timeline/Draft of "script":

> 1. Pull up the image of the flag on the projector screen, Student E will lay down tape on the floor as though it's a Mason-Dixon Line. He will stand on one side, and Student A, B, C, and D stand on the other.
>
> Student A will speak about her feelings about seeing the flag.
>
> Student B will speak about the alumni's reactions to the flag.
>
> Student C will speak about what it is like to feel obligated to feel offended.
>
> Student D will speak about what it is like to watch everything happening from Haverford's campus.
>
> Student E will speak as though he is a "generic white male," and read segments from the articles authored by white Haverford male students about the issue.
>
> Everyone will move toward the center of the room and take up a piece of the tape. Someone will turn off the projector screen.
>
> We will all sit in a circle, as though in a silent vigil.
>
> Student E will stand and read from the senator's email [hate mail threatening student protesters and valorizing the students who displayed the flag] [SHOULD WE DO TRIGGER WARNING????]
>
> The other [female] students will hold hands then proceed to lie down, like the "die-in"s of Black Lives Matter. Student E will walk away and avert his gaze.

SCENE

Afterwards, unscripted, players converge for a group hug, before taking their seats. The room is hushed. We do not run this twice: We are witnesses to testimony that feels singular. I begin post-enactment comments by asking group members if they want to speak.

> STUDENT A: It was scary to reenact this Confederate flag incident. I don't feel safe on this campus—it's dark and quiet at night, I come from New York City where it's light and there's people all the time. Walking alone at night after the email [threatening students on campus] was scary....Reenacting this took me back to all that.
>
> STUDENT E: I had such a feeling of separation and vulnerability across the Mason-Dixon line while we were up there. Really needed to hug my group when it was over.
>
> STUDENT C: It was hard for me to share this, I've had trouble with this since I came here, people telling me how to feel about who I am.

Others add their perspectives, speak immediately not as theorists, but themselves:

> But shouldn't she have gone to the demonstration even if she didn't connect with the issues? People should learn about the flag and its relationship with racism, with lynching. Innocent people died because of that flag. Learn about it, march, and have that response now. I agree...but if it's not bringing up constructive emotions, you shouldn't feel forced to go! We can't go to an extreme, excluding experiences from the conversation.
>
> You always have to consider what your place is in a movement.

Student C is now quiet, perhaps surprised to have taken this risk and then be called out just as she'd feared. The other student continues: there are really no excuses not to participate in this protest; perhaps she is not surprised to find herself once again taking a hardline position that seems to push away students of color.

A mental, emotional adrenaline freezes us, in various states of intimacy, alliance, wariness, disaffection, as my next class drifts in, backs out again. Wanting to intervene in many ways at once, I do not remember what—if anything—I said. In writing about moving classrooms "From Safe Spaces to Brave Spaces," Brian Arao and Kristi Clemens recommend "controversy with civility,"[23] but this very interconnected space feels raw, uncivil. This enactment has leaked through the boundaries that structure the exercise. I am moved and shaken; deeply uncertain about how we move on through the very dangers we have been studying.

After break and through the semester, this enactment remains, seeping into the woodwork and discomfiting us with a stain that is yet elusive, an edge of threat discernible in sudden raised voices, silences. My experience of this classroom, haunted by the absence of Black servants and students of color, now further twisted as I host classes that also create traces that haunt…

Tattooing Scar Tissue

Prison teacher Anna Plemons warns educators against a "progress narrative" of teaching and learning, proposing instead that teaching be more like "tattooing scar tissue": teaching writing especially involves "taking it slow, making design choices that work with the material reality of the landscape, and understanding that some tattoos are meant to hide older skin stories."[24]

Plemons uses the human body as a site to talk about writing, where layers of the past bleed through to texture versions of the present; her approach highlights the complicated ways people "make sense of many nuanced, complicated, relational contexts… acknowledge the furrows, folds, and taut patches which co-author meaning."[25] As with the palimpsest, the action and image of "tattooing scar tissue" suggests a teaching process guided by scrutiny and deliberation—some measure of control punctured by elements of inquiry and volatility.

Teaching and learning through enactments similarly involves participants in working with and across our mind and bodyscapes;

23. Brian Arao and Kristi Clemens, "From Safe Spaces to Brave Spaces: A New Way to Frame Dialogue Around Diversity and Social Justice," in *The Art of Effective Faciliation: Reflections from Social Justice Educators*, ed. Lisa M. Landreman (Sterling, VA: Stylus Publishing, 2013), 144.

24. Anna Plemons, "Tattooing Scar Tissue: Making Meaning in the Prison Classroom," Talk at Washington State University, March 27, 2015.

25. Plemons, "Tattooing."

layering over events, places, people; acknowledging gaps, leakage, hidden stories; inquiring into this messy relationality: tracings and hauntings of the past, silent elisions and splittings of the present, new possibilities.

My colleague's question about *ir*responsible pedagogy shifts, for me, into a query about whether and how pedagogy recognizes and impacts relationships: with living people, also ghosts, places, things. Reorienting this question redirects my attention to powerful bonds within the enacting group, to the relationship between current students and institutional leakage, to hovering, unspoken questions that both preserve and eclipse the distance between international and domestic students, to our connections with airport security, flags, unknown correspondents.

These questions provoke new ones: How might the concerns—of the (white) student about who perceives themselves as part of U.S. racism, of the (Asian) student who reveals her distance from this, and of the (Black) student who exposes her fear in this enactment—bleed into one another, perhaps opening up new ties? In conversation with a friend, I realize too how many of these enactment stories involve Asian students, who are outside the dominant U.S. Black-white paradigm; perhaps this also represents a leakage, one that I need to work with more deliberately.

As groups design their performances, enactments allow glimpses of what's beneath, what gives rise. Teaching toward this vulnerability requires working for students to feel seen and heard, not "safe," perhaps, but accompanied in shared unpredictability—by me and by each other.

To acknowledge: my questions about how to stay with this work in times of unease and division; my authority that may propel and also inhibit what students choose to risk. And to desire: from tenderness, and from our learning, new connections.

Resisting, Re-enacting

The enactments in the last section ask participants to exercise porosity as they move into and out of personas. The ritual designed by the Alternatives to Violence Project for entering and exiting roles suggests that consciously *choosing* to set aside the selves we believe we are can create a semblance of safety. But this process can still engender surprises, call up unexpected responses, invite what had been unconscious to leak into consciousness. Anna Deveare Smith, who creates performances evoking multiple participants in a complex situation, describes "the obvious gap between the real person and my attempt to seem like them. I try to close the gap between us but I applaud the gap between us." In this space, she works with the "uneasiness we have about seeing difference displayed,"[26] as a gap of vexation, provocation, learning.

Part of what makes enactments powerful is their *un*safety: the dialectical tension between intentionality and the triggering of the unconscious can evoke other times and places, move into re-enactment and out of control. When wounds open and leak into consciousness, the brain can call up traumatic memories, display these as if real. It is critical—and difficult—to create a pause, hold the space between conscious and unconscious, recognize the wounding as *not* current and open up room for learning in the present moment.

Such questions take on a particularly strong valence when college students and faculty enter a prison to facilitate and participate in a book group with women who are incarcerated. In crossing the boundary between outside and inside, between "students," "faculty," and "inmates," we enact roles other than those of our accustomed selves. In the course of this enactment—less formal, and not signaled as such—a session fragments, falls apart. The experience leaks into re-enactment for various of us in various ways. We try to learn from the cracks that open within and among us.

Fifteen students take linked courses with three professors in a

26. Anna Deavere Smith, *Fires in the Mirror* (New York: Anchor, 1993): xxxvii–xxxviii.

> We are vulnerable to claims for which there is no adequate preparation.
>
> —Anne's notes from Judith Butler's talk

> The ghost demands your attention. The present wavers....a traumatized person or society is stuck in a past that repeats as a present that can never end. I tried to theorize haunting...[as] a demand for a livable future.
>
> —Avery Gordon, "Some Thoughts on Haunting and Futurity"

360° cluster called "Arts of Resistance,"[27] which also involves a praxis placement at a women's correctional facility. At least two of the students describe themselves as having dis/abilities, three as having variant gender identities. At least a quarter use trauma-related language and stories to describe their experiences as members of their racial/ethnic/cultural groups; at least a third identify themselves as having experienced personal trauma.

How much of what happens is about how the intimate structure and intense engagements of the 360° invite more disclosure, more leakage, than is usually "allowed" in classrooms? How might revealing such intimate aspects of our lives inspire us to patch up, crack open, allow our experiences to bleed into each other's?

To "create fearlessly, boldly embracing the public and private terrors that would silence us, then bravely moving forward even when it feels as though we are being chased by ghosts"?[28] In Danticat's call to find courage in vulnerability is an intimation of a pedagogy of "moving forward" when we might want to turn and run, guiding us to pause, listen, turn, and begin to "imagine…what ghosts might want from us."[29] This is a way of being, learning, and teaching that values aliveness and presence, and also risks absence and overwhelmingness; teaching here is not about treading lightly but about bringing radical attention and care.

There are two levels of pat-down as we enter the jail. The first, usually by a woman guard, often one who knows us, often relatively light; the second performed after we've gone through the two heavy metal doors that must be electronically opened, passed the backs of our hands under ultraviolet light to verify that we have been stamped, handed over our papers and books. This second pat-down is less predictable, more often performed by a male guard, more insistent, more disruptive for our students.

> He felt my boobs, he asked if I was wearing a bra and told me to put one on.

27. "Arts of Resistance." 360° Cluster, Bryn Mawr College, Fall 2015.

28. Edwidge Danticat, *Create Dangerously: The Immigrant Artist at Work* (New York: Vintage, 2010), 148.

29. Les Back, "Haunted Futures: A Response to Avery Gordon," *Borderlands* 10, no. 2 (2011): 3.

> Because it was a guy and it brought everything back. I was upset the whole time we were there and after, I didn't want to go back.
>
> My breath was coming too fast, and I couldn't breathe.

The pedagogical decision to take young people into jail is fraught. Places *are* pedagogy, and this is a place of horror, of assault. Students choose this placement as part of their college experience; and yet, do they know what they're choosing, really? When the passage itself is so troubling? As Alice Goffman reminds us, in this country the passage into adulthood is burdened, differentially precarious: college for some, prison for others.[30] When we make the decision to offer jail as an option for young people in college, we confirm and confound those forked paths.

Students' earlier experiences of trauma leak into the jail classroom. One recalls: "It was to relinquish bodily autonomy to the hands of someone who I didn't know, so they could pat me down and deem me and my peers and professors 'non-threatening.' It was watching my peers being frisked and feeling helpless to stop it, and knowing that I was next…getting in was harrowing almost every time."[31] Weeks in, the appearance of a particular male officer in the entry area reminds them of their abuser. Sometimes during class they go numb, disconnect; later, when we are talking in our college classroom about what has gone on there, they realize that they don't remember. My friend with expertise in trauma talks to me about disassociation. I discuss options with the student: the possibility that they not go in, that they try tracking the class by writing. They try this, and begin to remember.

From our first passage inside, our group confronts the ambiguity of who we are in relation to mass incarceration, and to the women inside. While none of us has been imprisoned, we are also different from each other in our relationship to incarceration. One of us is haunted by a psychic assault from a correctional officer, who tells her not to forget that as a Black woman she too could find

30. Alice Goffman, "How We're Priming Some Kids for College—and Others for Prison," TED Talk, March 2015.

31. Joie Waxler, email message to author, April 16, 2016.

herself inside "wearing the blue." Others struggle with their privilege, including seeing officers as protectors. Some students describe feeling "relaxed," "freer" during jail sessions than on campus. There's less expected of them there, away from college demands, and they too may expect less of those inside—a monstrosity we name. "When you are not the 'monster' in prison, you can forget that you're the monster surviving life by stepping over those other lives to get your morning coffee."[32]

More than halfway through the semester, one of the professors and many of our students are given a tour of the correctional facility. This makes freshly palpable the atrocity of imprisonment, the separation of "us" from "them": "Whenever a person wearing an orange jumpsuit, or blue hospital-looking clothing walked by, the warden stopped, instructed a guard to escort that person around us, seemingly trying to cut-off all natural and desperate communication between the people wearing the jumpsuits and those who had the privilege to study them."[33]

One afternoon we are up in the Education section of the jail, waiting for the people in the class to be sent from their units. I've gone down the hall to check with the co on duty, and a student follows me out, they're breathing hard and fast, in the midst of a panic attack, I ask, should we leave the jail? But outside our area, beyond one of four sets of electronically locked doors, they see the male officer who evokes their abuser. A tiny room, the library, empty and open, and we go in. We sit. Talk about him a minute, then about making things with clay and paint, about feeling materials with our hands. Their breathing slows, and we re-enter the classroom, where on this day women arrive in a kind of tumble of chaos, upset, resistant to the representation of prison life in our text. It is the hardest session we've had. We open, some of us, like a wound—raw, leaking—while others shut down, pull back. (And yet on this day too, a bond happens between a college student and an incarcerated student, who for the first time stays in the room for the whole session.)

32. Anna Deveare Smith, *The Pipeline Project, a Work-In-Progress*, dir. Anna Deveare Smith, Penn Museum, University of Pennsylvania, Philadelphia, PA, May 5, 2015

33. "Locks Don't Cure; They Strangle—Prison Tour Reflection," November 14, 2015 (5:39 p.m.).

We are discussing *Brothers and Keepers*, John Wideman's memoir about the life and imprisonment of his younger brother, Robby. The college student who opens the class uses the word "escape" three times, in as many sentences, to describe the pressure put on both Robby and John to leave Homewood, the Pittsburgh neighborhood where they grew up. My shoulders tighten with associations about which neighborhoods are presumed "bad," needing "escape." Although John writes about Robby and about their relationship, and includes Robby's own words, several object that it's John's story. Robby's gone missing.

We miss too. We can't get going on a conversation, a single speaker revving up. When the student facilitators break us into two groups, one to talk and one to write, the first is dominated by a woman haunted by her drug usage, telling her story—perhaps in relation to Robby's—over and over, on a loop. The writing group also splinters, with a woman, usually engaged, first withdrawn today, then talking, weeping to the huddle around her.

Later, one of our students describes this woman haunted by the act of "protection" that now separates her from her children; describes too her own effort to connect, her feeling of helplessness, and the intervention of "Christal," an incarcerated student:

> "Liana" came in...and seemed visibly distressed. She took a seat next to me and...said that she was "depressed today" and preferred not to write, instead sitting quietly. I asked her if she wanted to go outside and talk...Her eyes filled with tears as she began describing her children to me...She showed me a photograph of two of them, all milk-teeth innocent smiles and wondering eyes making funny faces for the camera. She whispered so softly that I could barely hear her, about how painful it was to be away from them, to be unable to mother them. "Horrible things happen in the world. Rape happens, people hurt other people... I was only protecting what was mine. I feel like I repented enough. I'm trying to leave everything to Him"—she pointed at the Bible in in her arms—"but it's so hard." I tried to think of something, anything substantial to say...but what could possibly alleviate

> the pain? I settled for just squeezing her hand as tightly as I could. I told her that her feelings mattered, and she was important, that she would always be a mother to her children…
>
> And then Christal joined us…her first reaction was the polar opposite of mine. "I get where you're coming from, but crying isn't helping you. Indulging isn't helping you. When we're here, we lose a little bit of ourselves every day. We can't be whole. But giving into that is not the way to go. You have to do what you can to live while you're here. You can't give up. Crying won't do anything for you right now."
>
> Class ended at that moment. Liana, still brimming with tears, had to get up. I let go of her hand, gave her a long hug.
>
> In this world, on the outside, sometimes we can allow ourselves to fall apart. We do not have the threat of constant surveillance on us, the shame that comes from it.…If the women in prison allowed themselves to succumb to the intensity of their feelings, they would fall apart, and it would happen in shame, without privacy. The most that they can do is pull themselves together, even repress their emotions, carry on. They risk losing even the small pinch of humanity that prison allows them, the last bit of honor that they have left. "Let go," Christal kept saying, "crying doesn't help. Nothing helps except moving forward."[34]

34. "Sunday Post," November 15, 2015 (5:14 p.m.).

Our student's acceptance of Christal's response as more attuned to Liana's current experience highlights her sense of not-knowing, of control leaking away. The session ends feeling so chaotic and unhappy that we can't even debrief as we leave, taking the class into our evenings and weekends.

On Sunday another of our students articulates the experience of "losing control…indulging [our] humanness" and, through this, opening up the space for a "defeat" that is also a "delayed triumph":

> I'm sitting here in Hot House, as I do every Sunday, attempting, as I do every Sunday, to put into eloquence an incredibly complex experience fraught with intense emotion, unwanted analysis that so often feels nothing less than disingenuous, and so many human lives that have no place in this coffee shop.

I'm miles away from the prison, days removed from one of the hardest book groups we've had yet, and stratospheres away from the lives and experiences we try to fit into that classroom every week. And here I am, sitting in a coffee shop, as college students do, carrying out an assignment, as college students must, and enjoying a slightly overpriced Hot House breakfast that my multiple jobs allow me to indulge in. This analysis, or reflection, has no place in here. It doesn't fit into this suddenly impossibly small little shop, filled with people pressing hands, mumbling and murmuring light conversations, sharing laughter and anecdotes and histories and human moments that simply don't exist in the same way at the prison.

But then, isn't that what was shared in the prison on Friday? An incredibly human experience, of failure and breakdown of structure, of raw, vibrant human emotion that we (or at least I) have been so wary of in that space? All of a sudden, the humanity that we have been trying to grapple with in class, attempting to impose and perhaps imagine into that classroom space, came crashing through that room in a way it hasn't before. Clattering against chairs and tables were personal triumphs and failures, stories that needed to be shared and held, and tears shed, and hands grasped and tissues exchanged, and a chaos that was not at all chaos but unfettered human need at the crux of it all.

I too indulged my humanness this past week. Long held back emotions and fears and histories and harms came barreling at me so violently this Friday that there was nothing else for me to do but let it momentarily wash me away. Perhaps in defeat, perhaps in delayed triumph. For whatever reason, this was the week that I lost the control I had held so tightly to for so long. My front lines were obliterated and my defenses shattered and in the chaos and confusion of that moment I was allowed to be held. And the color returned to my whitened knuckles, and the fists I had clenched for so long relaxed and released in utter exhaustion and acceptance at the loss of the control I had clung to like a rope, dangling me over the abyss, hoping beyond hope that rope would hold and keep me from falling. But I did fall, or maybe I just let go. Maybe it was what I had needed all along.

Maybe the perceived chaos of this last class was what we needed to fully acknowledge what it is that we are doing. Not our

> purpose necessarily but the physical and practical aspects of the fact that we are going into a medium security prison and engaging in conversation on difficult topics with individuals that we would most likely never interact with in our daily lives. And in acknowledging our privilege, and in talking and talking and musing and analyzing and reflecting about the imbalances and injustices and structures and theorists and theories, we constructed a sense of control that we never really had or deserved. I think that illusion was broken this past week. And I think that's okay.[35]

35. "Sunday Post," November 15, 2015 (11:58 a.m.).

I talk with my husband, a therapist, who reads the session similarly: for awhile people struggle to bring their least neurotic, most highly functioning selves into a group, trying to *be* the self they want to appear as, to be, but in the approach to intimacy, in the search for acceptance of our whole selves: the reveal. I begin to see the session less as a disaster, more as leakage between the conscious and the unconscious, a testament to the intimacy of the group. Especially in such a tightly controlled space where we released some controls. What now? I say, wanting to believe. And glimpsing too how what happens in jail clarifies the pulsing of vulnerability and resistance in our college classrooms.

Even as things "fall apart," a student's post reminds our group of connections:

> Book group yesterday felt discombobulating, frustrating, and important....I got into a conversation with one of the women about Brothers and Keepers. It was hard for her to focus on the book, she explained, because it hit so close to home. The narrative and description of the prison in the story led her mind to wander to her own impending release next February, and how she was committing to change her actions so she wouldn't be returning to the prison for the fourth time. This turned into a conversation about her crime, which transformed surprisingly naturally into a conversation about my life. "Do you have a boyfriend?" she asked. I hadn't been asked this question in years— and when I explained why, she laughed, insisting that she didn't want to assume anything but it was "pretty obvious." Suddenly

> excited, she hurried out of the room and returned with pictures of her girlfriend—"See, doesn't she look like a boy, like you??"... Now, outside of class for a day, I'm still grappling with my gut feeling that that conversation was all that really mattered. I know that we came into the prison with educational purposes to some extent, intending to focus on reading and writing. But I can't help but feel like those are only useful in our case in the gateways they provide into personal and honest conversation and moments of connection.[36]

36. "Sunday Post, 11/5 (A little early)," November 14, 2015 (1:49 p.m.).

Tuesday I open class with excerpts from these posts. As we begin to process all this emotionality and uncertainty, a number of us admit to anxiety about going back inside; we consider leaving *Brothers and Keepers* behind.

But the next Friday in jail we return to a short, rich discussion of this text, shaped by a woman inside: she focuses our attention on a passage in which the author describes the men inside in terms of their predatory gaze at his adolescent children; she argues that his language reveals that it is *he* who is the sexual predator. We are none of us all or only what we seem. We write and share poems about "Where I'm From," putting forth selected aspects of our selves. Anne points out that we are focusing on positive, even nostalgic memories, rather than fuller, harsher versions of our stories. There's uncomfortable laughter. Are we still performing "best selves"? Several of us begin again.

In the theater of the prison we enact the unlikely possibility of connection: As college professors and students seek to become more than ourselves, to reach for selves that are braver, more expansive in a place that may feel frightening and foreign (even if also, sometimes, paradoxically relaxed and freer); to connect with human beings there. Women who are incarcerated, for the first or many times, headed home or upstate, with more or less support for surviving on the "outside," and more or less experience with college, also seek to become more than themselves, to reach for selves that are braver, more expansive, to connect with professors and students who enter and stage this space as a college classroom. Although not named in these terms, this too is an enactment, in which we are susceptible to re-enactments arising from our own lives and our readings, writings, talk, and physical presence together. And in the space between enacting and reenacting, between known and unknown selves and others, leakage can startle and unbalance us, spark fear and also deep inquiry in its unforeseen textures and bleed-throughs.

Bearing Witness

This cluster of classes takes me to some of the hardest, most unanswerable and vulnerable places I know; pushes hard against my capacity to understand others and self; leaks into my pedagogy, leaving me with a rawness, a deep uncertainty about what it means to teach and learn in such circumstances. My co-teachers and many of our students articulate such feelings. When we enter the prison, we encounter an extreme edge: the vulnerability, sometimes trauma of the people inside; a visceral encounter with the social, political trauma of mass incarceration. As I hear from students, this triggers a reencounter with self: How/can I stay, listen? What can I understand, or not, how can I respond? Some look not only to us but also to each other with these questions. Authority seeps, circulates.

While the jail "triggers," brings our shared vulnerability to the fore, rendering it intensive, defining, we also bring our own hauntings, relationality, mortality. So it is that in the midst of the semester I undergo a psychic and physical wounding as I am diagnosed with a small but fast-moving breast cancer. Within weeks I undergo a minor surgery that heals and also wounds, leaving me with a scar and disturbing questions. Exiting the clinic, I walk 11th Street strung up with awareness of the ultimate vulnerability "that emerges with life itself," "precedes the formation of 'I'"[37]—and attends our exit from living. This precarity strangely anchors me in a remembrance of all we don't know of one another as we pass on the street. Heightening

[37.] Judith Butler, *Precarious Life: The Powers of Mourning and Violence* (Brooklyn: Verso, 2006), 310.

the visibility of circumstances of radical vulnerability can carry peril, elation, potentiality.

When Anne reads the trauma novel *Eva's Man* with our students, one arranges an alternative assignment, trashes the book in their dorm room, then removes it utterly from their space; others say they struggle with being a "traumatized scholar" in the classroom; a third is "so glad I read this book, it changed my life."

We are in our 60s, some of our students not yet 20. It is astounding to be working together, figuring our way through precarity.

Roger Simon and Claudia Eppert share a framework they've developed working with students who bear witness to trauma: witnesses must listen, remember what they hear, recognize its importance; acknowledge that although they are outsiders to this experience, these "memories of violence and injustice press down on [their] sense of humanity." And they must take action: carry the stories they've heard into other contexts, retelling narratives as a way to exert agency and provoke protest to injustice.[38] In this framework, witnesses are not just repositories but also actors, with an invitation—or an obligation—to bring what they have learned to bear on others, to make an impact. For our students, and for us, this is oddly inclusive, offers us a position of strength, of some efficacy.

In line with this call, my co-teachers and I are now asking our students to find ways of communicating publicly what they are learning from our prison work. Initially, our students resist: like us, they are often unsure about what they are doing in the prison. Early on, we invite in a creative consultant who has long made art that renders the Prison Industrial Complex visible to those outside it. She proposes that our students use the writings of women inside as the central texts for their public project, but they push back hard on what seems to them a self-interested, even dishonest agenda: soliciting and exhibiting others' lives for still others to view feels antithetical to what they are trying to do: build trust and mutuality, as they lead a reading and writing group. And so begins a variegated

38. Roger I. Simon and Claudia Eppert, "Remembering Obligation: Pedagogy and the Witnessing of Testimony of Historical Trauma," *Canadian Journal of Education / Revue canadienne de l'éducation* 22, no. 2 (Spring 1997): 178.

dance of fits and starts as the students resist and engage in research and expression. Right up to the day of the exhibit, in the most central and public space on campus, many of us vocalize uncertainty about whether this will come off, what it will look like.

As several of the students explain, they are struggling to recognize the trauma of mass incarceration in the "forced vulnerability" of those who are incarcerated, in the dehumanization of enforcers, and in their own involvement:

> Witnessing the day-to-day interactions of a high-ranking prison official and inmates…while the PIC has its detrimental effects on incarcerated peoples, it also has effects on those in positions of power in that system.[39]
>
> I tried to think of something, anything substantial to say.…We do not have the threat of constant surveillance on us…[40]

As Simon and Eppert gloss this experience: absorbing "something absolutely foreign…may call into question what and how one knows" and so bring oneself to the edge.[41]

Leaving their sense of themselves as knowers behind as they immerse themselves in a shared humanity with those who are incarcerated may be particularly jarring in light of the charge to know, to achieve, even to make a difference. And yet it is from these questions and this edge that our students act: move hesitantly, resistingly to share their learning.

Their exhibit is astonishing. "Freedom Forgotten: Works of Silence and Resistance" sets forth words, images, and actions of incarceration earlier and now, of Asians, American Indians, Black, Latinos, white people. And draws others on campus into consideration of how identities and locations create one another: an empty hoodie floats over pastoral calm; a carved book insinuates words by incarcerated transgendered people between the lines of the DSM-V, where "gender dysphoria" is newly offered as a diagnosis; a sculptured torso is pierced with wire and etched in words and

---

39. "Prison Reflection," December 17, 2015 (6:14 p.m.).

40. "Sunday Post," November 15, 2015.

41. Simon and Eppert, "Remembering Obligation," 180.

prisoner ID number; text magnified from the minutes of the Student Governance Association exposes racial issues on campus, in counterpoint to images and words that have excluded American Indians, via both education and criminalization.[42]

In the hours of mounting the exhibit, and in the days of its visibility, skeins stretch between college and prison: invite into consciousness the hauntings of these apparently separate institutions; and in this way gesture—in what students later describe as a "flash mob exhibit," "less exhibit than invasion in the lives of people at college," "a labor of love"—welcoming ghosts.[43] Later too, students say, Now I have to open up this conversation in my [Chinese/Indian American/conservative] community. The work we do at home has deep emotional ties, I don't know yet how to do this. We glimpse our own and others' frightening tenderness, throw up protective gear, pierce the skin, and etch ink over and through our scars. Students leave, show up again, for now: Stakes are high.

In our final meetings with our students and their last written reflections about classes, both in jail and on campus, they speak of their own processes, where they will go with this work. Four will return to work in the jail next semester, the decision of one especially surprising, given her report of trauma and even paralysis. Several say they will not return—this work is too painful and without clear enough benefit. No one says it was easy. And some of it is very hard to listen to: it can be painful, discordant to hear students' vulnerabilities inside the larger networks of our shared precarity. A few struggle with whether this experience was *too* difficult, hindered their learning. We talk with each other about our own struggles: the receptivity and investment, the releasing and reengaging of authority that this kind of teaching has asked of us.

Still, one of our students writes of the day things fell apart inside: "This was the experience that stood out to me, this was the experience that I will take with me in anything I do after this 360, not just in abolition and prison work, but in my life as an individual, made

---

42. "Freedom Forgotten: Works of Silence and Resistance (Some Photos and Commentary)," December 13, 2015 (7:51 a.m.).

43. Tuck and Rhee, "Glossary," 654.

LEAKING | 267

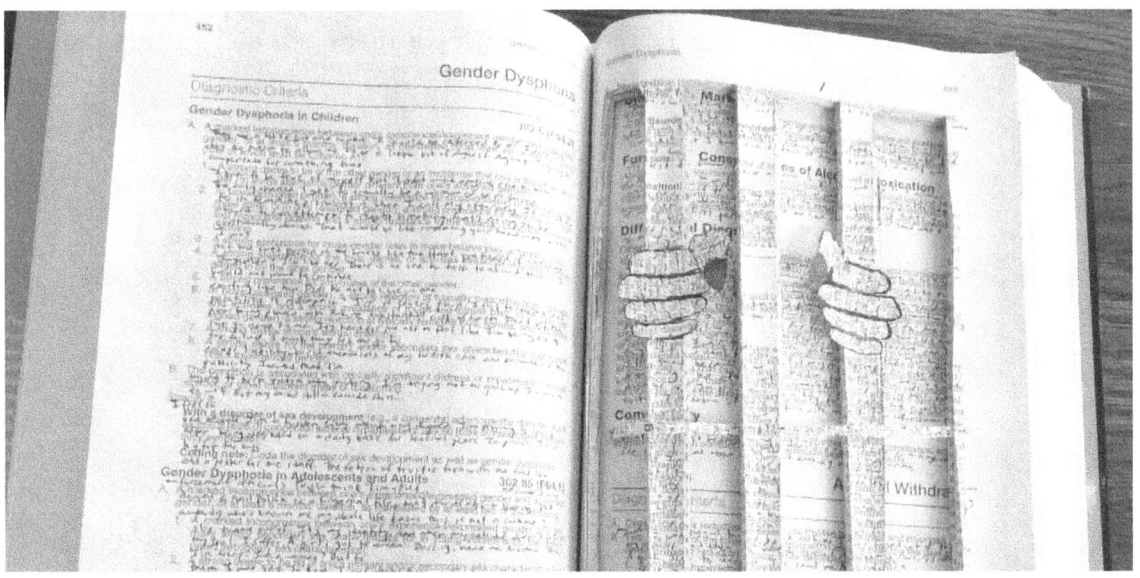

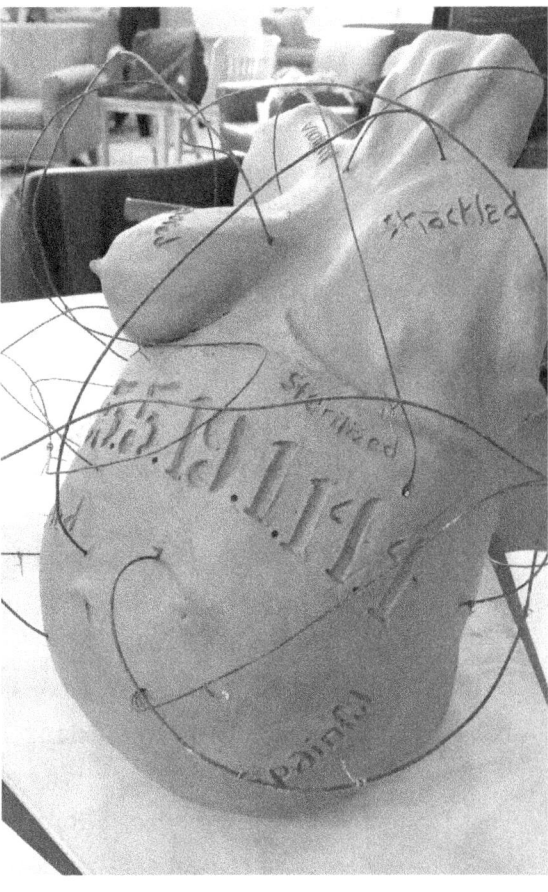

up of all of the experiences and people and words and lessons and moments I have ever been part of."[44]

> 44. Joie Rose, "The Last One (Prison Reflection)," December 15, 2015 (7:45 p.m.).

Teaching Relationally

> Inseparable from grief and rage is a profound, wrenching, far-from-sentimental affirmation of the beauty and wonder of nature, of human life.
>
> —Sharon Welch, *A Feminist Ethic of Risk*

In the oldest Italian Tarot deck, the Wheel of Fortune shows four figures, each in a quadrant of the cosmic wheel around a blindfolded figure at the center. Moving clockwise, the text translates from the Latin: "I do reign," "I have reigned," "I am without reign," "I will reign"; or, more loosely, "I act," "I have acted," "I am acted upon," "I will act." This cyclical view of time resonates for me both ecologically and experientially: in a dialectic of living and learning I see myself and my co-travelers in these cards, as we enact, let go, are acted upon, move to enact. Each stage is haunted by the others, as Gordon suggests, altering "the experience of being in linear time," "the way we normally separate and sequence the past, the present and the future."[45] Acknowledging the porosity of time, the fluidity of temporality, cues the recurrence of trauma, where narratives of extreme vulnerability are inadvertently tripped, or invited in as part of a reparative process.

45. Gordon, "Thoughts," 2.

In moving toward a pedagogy that is responsive and responsible to the complexly recursive and interrelated strata of our lives, I am helped by one of Anne's students, whose study of trauma led him to an "invitation to consider the (im)possibilities of radical vulnerability," to create "dangerously under such conditions, wherein the personal narrative is a political act of resistance."[46] Leakage into our dwellings, spectral presences, scars puckering our skin are all powerful reminders that none of us is separate, nothing we do finished,

46. samuel.terry, "Matter," May 11, 2014 (3:08 a.m.).

that radical vulnerability can be a source of connection, learning, consequence.

Butler writes of coming into being *as* interbeing, and of relationality as responsibility:

> I am wounded, and I find that the wound itself testifies to the fact that I am impressionable, given over to the Other in ways that I cannot fully predict or control. I cannot think the question of responsibility alone, in isolation from the Other; if I do, I have taken myself out of the relational bind that frames the problem of responsibility from the start.[47]

In this vein, "leak" shares antecedents with "lack," a term Jacques Lacan uses to signify a shared human hunger for full existence that impels us toward each other.[48] Articulation of this lack, and of the desire that fuels it, can be frightening, and also can cast skeins of connection, drawing us together. In our work together, this may emerge as a quickening when students realize that the "personal" and the "academic" are not ultimately separate: in the wordless connection of the Confederate flag group; in the struggle to respond to Liana's pain; in the flash of the students' exhibit.

Leakage, though seldom welcome, is always a possibility. It will seep through, softening edges, sometimes eradicating boundaries; this can induce withdrawal to a drier, safer space; can also catalyze insights, connections. My co-teachers and I share and draw on the lack that is also desire, as we look for ways to accompany our students, release the reins of separation and control, attend closely to and respect the gaps between enacting and re-enacting. As represented in the Wheel of Fortune, acting is haunted by absence, desire by lack, strength by leakage. Authority leaks, becomes a lack that may be experienced as a wound and also gives rise to desire.

To be responsible, pedagogy must know itself as happening in the midst of vulnerability, relationality, and unpredictability; it would be irresponsible to assume otherwise. Responsible pedagogy must include multiple points of entry, access, exit, and interconnection:

47. Butler, *Precarious Life*, 46.

48. Jacques Lacan, "The Direction of the Treatment and the Principle of Its Power," in *Ecrits: A Selection*, trans. Bruce Fink. (New York: W.W. Norton & Company, 2002), 215–70.

no guarantees, but a commitment to bringing a discerning, loving presence that supports others in work that can be scary, messy, overwhelming, and also compelling and deeply connective. This work is specific and real, grounded in desire and in daily efforts at recognition. Touched always by what is leaking and haunting, past and still present, recognition and response-ability can move us toward each other, prompt us to reach, and take up what we don't yet know.

INTERMISSION
WHY WE WRITE AS WE DO

We depend throughout this book on the work of other scholars, rely on their words and ideas to think with-and-through, to take us deeper in. We smile, shake our heads at Bruno Latour's fatherly caution that a "paper that does not have references is like a child without an escort walking in the night in a big city it does not know: isolated, lost, anything may happen to it." And yet we do draw heavily on theory, seeking and struggling with and reveling in it to expand, elucidate, test the limits of our own experiences. Turning to others' thinking gets us mired, helps us see things in new ways…

Some readers enjoy following these "escorts," find the references compelling:

> I liked it when the theorizing interrupted the storytelling, because then I felt like you were telling me what the point of the stories was.

Others worry that they lose us in these abstractions:

> The citations disrupt the reading in ways that almost seem to undermine…the very emotional and personal accounts…

> I felt like you weren't there!…so I didn't believe what you were saying.

Others testify to a loss, not of us, but of themselves. Feel shut out:

> I'd be more engaged if I had a sense all through that I was a member of the intended audience, and that the ideas would lead to some connection to my experience….I remain the reader who finds the abstractions dense.

> I have dipped into it a few times and gotten stuck each time…sections pulled me in and I found them very engaging but, as they

> went on, increasingly difficult to understand and therefore a little intimidating, both intellectually and politically....Has anyone else said that? I want to be able to push past that.... I don't know if this is a priority...talking your readers through the content...

As we write and re-write, the titles of our chapters morph. In our initial proposal, each title figures an identity: we line up race, gender, social class, even as we acknowledge the leakiness of each. In a later version, each title names a place: the classroom, the jail, various field sites. Eventually we find ourselves shifting from

> understanding less as a noun (an ascribed set of traits) than a verb, something through which we move (again and again), both in and out.
>
> —Clare, Kevin, Jody, Anne, "Reassembling"

Moving from selves, to sites, to ways of being. And doing.

David Bohm explains that the edgy field of eco-linguistics focuses on how language structure influences and shapes our thinking, how conventional English usage—such as the usual ordering of subject-verb-object (as in "Anne calls the class to order")—invites, even forces, us to imagine a world made up of separate entities that are fixed and static. Eco-linguists like Andrew Goatley experiment with changing such common structures, giving a more prominent role, for instance, to the verb, making sentences more reflective of unbroken, undivided movement ("Called to order, conversing happens..."?).

Slowly, our verbs themselves begin to shift, from root forms to present participles.

Gerunds take over, become subjects, complements, objects of sentences.

Titles. Entitled. Titling.

Moving from past to present tense.

> …it's by writing…by stepping back a bit from the real thing to look at it, that we are most present.
> —Alison Bechdel, *Are You My Mother? A Comic Drama*

Experimenting with presenting everything in the continuous present.

> …altering "the experience of being in linear time," "the way we normally separate and sequence the past, the present and the future.…Acknowledging the porosity of time, the fluidity of temporality.
> —Jody, "Leaking"

And so puzzling some readers:

> The most common source of confusion is the shifts in time.…I find the present tense confusing—clearly these events were in the past.…
>
> …this way of presenting past events as they unfolded needs to be set up more clearly.

Or less?

> Seeking a more relaxed, hammock-like way of thinking about what happens in educational practice, one in which the shared time we occupy in classrooms gives "space" to a more capacious sense of phenomenological time, one in which past, present and future are intertwined.
> —Clare and Anne, "Unbecoming"

We add some dates. Take out others. Mix it up.

Time-play is allusive. Sometimes incoherent or lacking a clear referent. Like some of our photographs.

> All those images that *force things to stop for a moment.*
> —Claudia Rankine, reprised in "Silencing"

Elusive, evocative; not clearly directional. Or directive.

> I wonder if there is a place to explain the contexts you include in this book, what led you to them, why you choose them for inclusion in the narrative.
>
> …because of the complexity you have come to, I wonder if…you might acknowledge/explain your style in some way—help readers ease into the eloquent but many-edged sentences; the framing of your work and this project uses the somewhat postmodern (or beyond that?) language of partiality, complexity, etc., which might be a little overwhelming for some readers….do readers need some prep for entering the space (made) of this language?

Maybe we need a map. Another friend, Betsy Reese, cautions that

> Any map is selective. Not just a reduction, but a distortion, of what it represents. Looking at the world from one vantage point, losing the advantages of another.

Can we be so direct and explicit about what we are up to? Do we always *know* what we mean?

Do we lose, thereby, the evocative? The peripheral glance? Our own sense of on-going discovery?

Can we put into writing some form of

> design for access, not knowing what we don't know about our [readers and their] needs? How might…we acknowledge the unpredictability of uptake, the possibility of being taken unaware? Can we reimagine accessibility…as ambient ubiquitous interface, shaped by surrounding social forces?
>
> —Clare, Kevin, Jody, Anne, "Reassembling"

Can we write more simply? More accessibly? Do we *want* to?

> Doris Sommer says that "books can sting readers who feel entitled to know everything as they approach a text," that "the slap of refused intimacy from uncooperative books can slow readers down." She argues that such inhospitality serves an important

pedagogical function for the reader, meriting "a pause long enough to learn new expectations."

Pausing.

> The world asks us to be quickly readable, but the thing about human beings is that we are more than one thing... We are multiple selves. We are massively contradictory.
> —Ali Smith, "An Onion of a Novel"

> Less oriented to knowing, more to being with the unknown.
> —Anne, "Silencing"

A central story in this book is the unpredictability of what happens, when a range of unconsciousnesses, unknown to one another as well as to themselves, gather in a classroom. In letting dreams "interrupt" the narrative, we try to model in language what we experience while teaching and learning. A friend muses,

> I've had some training in dream analysis—but the sense I was making, or thought I was making, of the dreams didn't fit with where you went afterwards. I felt dumb: didn't know what was going on, or what I was supposed to do with this.

Can you experiment with this text as a space where your own un/conscious has voice? Might you play, as Katherine Hayles suggests—skim, scan, select what you want to read—let the rest go for now?

Slow down….?

> What about having two doors into the text….a sort of reader self-navigation? One for those who, like me, feel invited by narrative and find theory very hard work, and one for those who think theoretically and find their interests engaged with a rousing theoretical start? And make it clear which is which, and make it possible to get well into the book through either door?

Each of these intermissions offers other forms, other doors—to what we've spoken here, to other directions you might take, to deep time, the greater whole.

SECTION III
RELATIONS

Sketch based on *Anne and Jody Go to Work* (photo taken by one of our long-term students, Sasha De La Cruz, February 25, 2014).

CHAPTER SEVEN
BEFRIENDING

On Being Friends

ANNE: March 16, 2016. I am sitting at the bedside of my three-month old granddaughter. Jules was admitted to The Children's Hospital of Philadelphia, a week ago, with bronchiolitis. Since then, we've been in a cascade of disaster and despair: she's put on oxygen, and moved to the ICU; diagnosed with two viruses—RSV and Rhino. The next day: a breathing tube through her mouth, a feeding tube through her nose, a central line into her neck, a catheter threaded through her urethra. She's on some wonderful, terrible sedatives: midazolam and fentanyl (a friend tells me Michael Jackson died from this). There's a secondary diagnosis of pneumonia, then septic shock.

I try breathing with her.

I can't.

I cry. Pray. Try, again, to breathe. Sit helpless in a darkened room, watching this child, whom I love so much—unbearably, love more. She's so still, so near to slipping away. I feel myself in another universe, one where time, too, is still. What is going on outside doesn't matter. And what is going on outside is horrific: bombings at the Brussels airport and subway station.

Much of the medical lingo swirling around my head is indecipherable. Don't want to understand it. Can't bear not to.

Turns out, this is an exceptional site for writing. Where there is no future. Where nothing matters but what I can do nothing about.

You offer to visit, but are not allowed up here. It's respiratory season, especially harsh in Philadelphia this spring. Each week, you come as far as you can: to the hospital lobby. We talk there about our writing: what you've drafted and I've now read; what I've drafted and you're responding to. No escape from the tubes and monitors on the fifth floor, but extension, elaboration.

Another monitor, another lifeline.

This is what friendship feels like.

After a week on the respirator, the doctors begin decreasing Jules's sedation, hoping to encourage her to start breathing more on her own. The switchover happens much too quickly; they increase her medication again, try a step-down drug—dexmedetomidine. When they scale back again, Jules goes into severe withdrawal. This is (I hope) the worst day of my life, holding my granddaughter, who has fever, chills, diarrhea, twitching, shaking, an exaggerated startle response…it's a horror.

The symptoms of withdrawal are milder the next day, the day following…the central line comes out; we "graduate" to the regular floor. Jules is now getting morphine and ativan, as well as some of her formula, through a feeding tube. There's debate about how slowly to wean her from the last round of drugs; a balancing act.

I'm writing less now: Jules is more awake, sometimes fretful. The medical care is less intensive; more is asked of me.

You come again. We talk writing, re-writing, caretaking. Befriending.

JODY: You are there, at the hospital: deeply, attentively, constantly.

We sit at converging angles on couches in the lobby of CHOP, saturated in afternoon light and cafeteria smells. Speak of diagnoses and medications, of our grown children and other things too until our laptops flip open: This hard chapter on befriending: what is too difficult or potentially hurtful to say, what risks might we take? What to say about the tangle of friendship, politics, working for change in the college and in related spaces of prison, city schools, "the environment"? And other chapters: how are we each situated in relation to "disability," to learning, to the overall themes of this book? How to describe Bryn Mawr in terms of the strong draw of a women's college—the powerful sense of what is possible intellectually, imaginatively—for certain women in particular times? Drew Faust writes about this, you tell me; raised like you in western Virginia: rural, land-owning, Christian. A Jew from a recently middle-class family of immigrant, urban roots: this stretches me.

Then, always, you head back up into the sprawl of this hospital; I wander out into rain, dazzling sun, surprising March warmth, onto the crowded bus that takes me down South Street.

ANNE: March 26. Jules goes home. The calculations: 18 days in the hospital, 6 rooms, 10 roommates, 8 tubes, 4 courses of antibiotics, uncountable medical professionals and procedures—not to mention at least 45 cafeteria meals.

I care for her in the mornings. My afternoon and evenings become again my own.

What I take home with me are the dreams.

Jules has a huge growth on her forehead—a luminescent ball, which looks bizarre, though the doctors assure us that it is benign. The next night there is a contest to measure either her intake of milk or output of urine; my cousin and her husband (a four-star general, winner of contests) get this right; they are ½-an-ounce closer than me. This morning I dream that the hospital is located on the streets of Brooklyn. I am sitting in a car with Jules, when I see three white-coated men coming down the street—these must be the doctors on rounds. I jump out with the baby, hoping to get their attention, thinking that there must be a better way to manage all this. And somehow I lose her in the crowd…

It is such a relief to wake up.

When I sleep again, all my children and grandchildren have fevers; they are all in the same hospital room. My husband Jeff and I are doing the caretaking; it seems pretty calm. In another dream—one of those early morning awful ones—there's a tsunami: I stand, with someone else, atop a cliff, looking down at thousands of bodies on the beach and in the ocean.

I dream that Jeff and I go to fetch Julia from the hospital. They won't let us take her, because, as grandparents, we don't have the right "certification." When we walk into the lobby, we find my parents sitting there, both in wheelchairs. I think, How can I manage them *and* the baby?

And then this: My friend Kristin Lindgren—a disability studies scholar who knows deeply the emotional ups and downs, the moving forward and backward of extended hospital stays, and who has accompanied me, in waking life, through this latest crisis—has missed a plane flight. Wasn't she supposed to travel with us? Or come visit us? I am outside with others, working in Jeff's orchard. We look up to see a very large plane, very close up, heading down: it is in flames, clearly going to crash. I am afraid, at first, that it is going to hit us. It doesn't.

But I know that Kristin is in that plane.

The literal dreams are easier to assimilate than the symbolic ones—that huge airplane, that tsunami.

As my unconscious continues to process the past few weeks, I try to write, again…

that this book is a collaborative project, of two experienced teachers, advocating for a form of sustainable pedagogy that flourishes amid diversity and disequilibrium.…

Wondering: what happens to this argument, when the uncontrollable is not chosen, but thrust upon me this-a-way: unwanted, unasked, unawares…?

Have I reached, here, the limits of the form of exploration you and I celebrate throughout this book, come to its edges, acknowledged what I do when what is unanticipated just gets too scary? Threatened by an illness that seems genuinely dangerous my family and I turn—turn gratefully—to medical authorities.

There are risks in opening up and challenging institutionalized arrangements: disrespect, a failure to acknowledge expertise, the "tyranny of structurelessness."[1] My experiences in the hospital prod me to ask now what the horizons are of the risks we advocate elsewhere: of acknowledging—even embracing—both complexity and unpredictability.

When might a radical disruption in a space of teaching and learning feel too dangerous, too hot to handle? When might that cause you, me, colleagues, and students, to turn to the expertise of others for guidance, even salvation? And what does it mean to acknowledge that, in some instances, we ourselves are "the experts"?

What happens when a similar sense of edginess, even threat, emerges between us? There are risks that friendship can shield us from, offering companionship when times are tough. But there are also risks within friendship itself. Friends can be both vulnerable and threatening to one another. Because of what we know—and so can say, and do.

The day before Jules goes in the hospital, you send me a draft, saying that you think it's "close." I struggle with what you've written, finding it hard to enter, tripping over gaps in the argument. In a hurry, en route to other meetings on campus, I send you a long—and sharp—critique. As I mail it, I feel satisfied that I've met that obligation and can move on to others—but soon after, start to question: was I too hurried, not careful enough in what-and-how I wrote?

I check my e-mail several times that afternoon, worrying about how you're reading my response. A couple of your notes seem curt. I worry some more. I don't sleep well that night.

JODY: We have both been writing hard. Every day, or nearly. With joy, frustration, astonishment, grit, questions, questions, words,

1. Jo Freeman, "The Tyranny of Structurelessness," talk presented at the Southern Female Rights Union, Beulah, MS, May 1970.

and images. On a windy afternoon over our cups of hot caffeinated froth, we talk each other through the forests of words, ideas, sometimes push hard: What are you saying here? Can you go further, deeper, so I'm really feeling it? Can you write into that explosive class, those students, that fruitful tension of love and institutional change? What are we doing with the images in this chapter?

I'm sitting on my front stoop when I get your response to my latest draft. There's a lot, and I read quickly till the end: you say I sound like I'm recommending exactly what I've dismissed M. Carey Thomas for doing: valorizing the middle class, the college degree. My shoulders tighten. I know we'll have to talk this through—and I also want to turn away from this conversation.

The next morning deep blue, gorgeous.

ANNE: Almost as soon as we meet, at a coffee shop in Old City, I ask, did my note upset you? You say, Yes. This is going to be a hard discussion. I say (really anxious now): let's start there. No, you say, let's talk about some other things first…we find a bench down the street, in a churchyard, in the sun. You tell me of a great dance performance you went to over the weekend. I say that Jules is sick, en route to the pediatrician this morning; we talk about other family matters…

…and eventually (I think, maybe, when you feel we've softened the ground enough, reminded ourselves of the wide and thick net we share, a condition of critical befriending that will carry us through this rough patch…?) you say, Okay. Let's talk about your comments on my chapter.

It's very hard for me to hear, then, that you felt disrespected, that I wasn't acknowledging the difficulty of what you were trying to do: writing about the beast from the belly of the beast. That my response made you—for the first time, and this is a blow for us both—not want to write.

This, too, is what friendship feels like.

Bench, Lisa Campeau (2012). CC-BY. https://flic.kr/p/bMqBfR

You actually seem okay about this—have worked through your anger and resentment before we meet—but now I am shaken, feeling very sorry to have rocked the til-now-so-steady boat of our friendship. I apologize, and again. We talk through why I may have written you this way: not feeling good about my own writing, thinking I may have lost direction. Pushed, discouraged, unable to go "deeper" in the way, the week before, you'd asked me to. Coming to read your writing from those spaces of your critique, my discouragement. And then—always those disabling time-pressures of academia[2]—responding too quickly, wanting to get my comments to you before other obligations intervened. Not trusting the flourishing of this work "amid diversity and disequilibrium," amid "the interconnected and unbounded" ecology of writing and living: not quite believing that, in time, you'll find your own way through this text; that the stretched-out process of our shared reading and writing, the hammock of our friendship, the holding, the mesh will support this…and so misstepping, overreaching.

I'm still apologizing when Katie calls. She's taking the baby to the emergency room. Can I come with her…? We get up too quickly. You fall, in your chair, off the unsteady little platform where we've been sitting, and land on your side. But you shrug it off, keep me company as I buy a salad, walk me to the corner, go on talking about the draft of this chapter: where it's thick enough, where it still seems thin to you…

I know you're talking just to keep us going. I'm grateful, though at that moment the details of what you say about my writing are too hard for me to hear, much less take in.

We miss Katie as she drives through the intersection. She's parked on a corner where I can't see her. I am anxious, distressed to have kept her waiting…

Over the weeks ahead, you come, again and again, to the hospital. You say that my critique turns out, after all, to be helpful. I am still sorry about what happened between us, wishing I'd taken more care. It feels like I've created a rift, that there is now a crack…

---

2. See Chapter Five, "Unbecoming."

This, too, is what friendship feels like.

JODY: On the train platform, debrief classes, meetings with students, connections with colleagues. Or drive back down I-95 from the prison, processing: the women who didn't show up and those who did, our students as teachers, the forever vexing questions of this work inside. Slather the mosquito netting in 100% deet oil, pull it over my bed in the whitewashed room of the Simli Center in Dalun, Ghana, then lean against the rounded stone of the rotunda to plan with partners in Alice's project. Meet up at Good Karma with our friend and co-teacher, Joel Schlosser, discuss his writing about a book we've taught together, Claudia Rankine's *Citizen*: as white people, who are "we" when Rankine uses "you"?

With Josh, Giovanna, Caleb, Rachel—colleagues, students, friends—we design a roundtable, "Pedagogies from Below," delving into "diverse identities, fear and love, despair and activism," for a largely white, highly professionalized, conference space on the environmental humanities. Debrief over barbeque and beer; ride the winding crevices of the Nez Perce, across luminous Idaho prairies. At an international gathering of feminists, join with Sue and Romarilyn on a panel about our prison work, from outside and in; slip into private receptions, discover walls alive with birds in the Old San Juan evening, ride lush, twisting roads through the rainforest outside the city.

These, too, are touch and taste of friendship: fed by shared desires and pleasures, tensions and risks; feeding a reaching out, reaching toward.

On "Refusing the Academy of Misery"

JODY AND ANNE: This chapter begins in deepest love and deepest fear. A beloved baby, struggling amid a loving, and frightened, family of friends, in a mighty hospital right at the limits of its powers. On the worst day, in the other world of illness and hope, where, amazingly, writing also happens.

Anne's dreams re-play these scenes. Who is "here," who not? Who is on the margins, and speaks from "there"? How to figure the relationships among a sick child, frightened parents, family, friends, medical advisors…?

How, also, to figure the relations among friends in such a site: comforting, but perilous, too…?

And what might such questions reveal about our on-going life in the ecotone, where danger and possibility, work and play, family and friends meet and comingle?

Searching for expansive ways to think-and-write about friendship in the academy—the shifting sites of connection, trust, risk, depth, change, where cracks within and between us call up play and work, ruptures and delights; reaching across conventional boundaries and warnings into shared political efforts, back again to places of personal pain and anxiety—we find wonderfully resonant an invitation from Stefano Harney and Fred Moten, who ask how we can

> think about it in a way to help us organize ourselves to make it better here?…How come we can't be together and think together in…the way it should feel good?…. Everybody is pissed off all the time and feels bad…that's the insidious thing, this naturalisation of misery, the belief that intellectual work requires alienation and immobility…. Enjoyment is suspect…. I believe in the world and want to be in it…. in the joyful noise of the scattered, scatted eschaton, the undercommon refusal of the academy of misery.[3]

3. Stefano Harney and Fred Moten, *The Undercommons: Fugitive Planning and Black Study* (Brooklyn: Minor Compositions, 2013), 117–18.

Our co-teacher Joel Schlosser identifies the "undercommons" as the site where acts of befriending can flourish, outside narrow social structures and legal contracts; he includes relationships among faculty and students. Engagement beyond what is dictated by strict professional transaction is susceptible to unscripted, open-ended encounters:

> Aren't we really theorizing an art of resistance? Resistance to the structures of hierarchy that result in mere collegiality as well as

unfriendly student-teacher relationships??...practicing friendship among colleagues resists collegiality and aims to remake the academy of misery; practicing friendship among students resists assessment and judgment and aims to remake the anxiety-ridden and insecure classroom. In both cases the practice of friendship seeks to replace paradigms of productivity—producing knowledge, producing learning (the "banking model," focused on achievement) with ...[what] is unpredictable, happens in fits and starts, can be a great source of pleasure.[4]

We seek out others who have similarly testified to the "collaborative creation of new relationships in marginal spaces." Mark Kingston, for instance, draws on Foucault's late, obscure work to argue that "putting this concept of friendship into practice...constitutes a form of localised resistance," "a challenge to the excessive normalisation of relationships."[5]

Acknowledging our own shared positioning—long-term, not tenured at the college—we try out Foucault's understanding of friendship as a site where gay men can choose to stretch assigned roles, working together to build new forms of relationship, of potentially resistant, politicized engagement.[6] We know from experience how the dialectical play of intimate relationships within established social structures can tease out opportunities for astonishment, inversion, disruption of the everyday order of things.

We also try on the related concept of "positive marginality," first put forth by Clara Mayo, which describes how people in borderline social locations call on their differences as a source of critical appraisal and activism: among friends, "critical watching and reframing of life experiences" can be used to enact an intimate politics, bring about the "subversion of social institutions."[7]

And we puzzle through contradictions: ways that befriending is not always a site of positive marginality or resistance, not necessarily a place where radical politics is enacted and productivity refused (*consider the shared writing of this book*). Although we like the word "pleasure," that too is also not always the case (*we have to stretch*

---

4. Joel Schlosser, e-mail message to authors, March 2, 2016.

5. Mark Kingston, "Subversive Friendships: Foucault on Homosexuality and Social Experimentation," *Foucault Studies* 7 (September 2009): 7.

6. Kingston, "Subversive Friendships."

7. Ruth Hall and Michelle Fine, "The Stories We Tell: The Lives and Friendship of Two Older Black Lesbians," *Psychology of Women Quarterly* 29, no. 2 (June 2005): 177–87.

hard to meet one another, in the hospital, at the café…). Like other relationships, friendship can be troubled, troubling. Precarious.

Early on in this writing, Joel points out that, as a keyword, "friendship" is actually too noun-like, too "fixed" to evoke the sort of unpredictable, hazardous process we're trying to uncover here. The verb "friending," which suggests movement, works better—but is also now associated with the casual "liking" that occurs on Facebook.

The more archaic "befriending" sounds less trendy, evocative of actions stretching far back in time. That history carries a preface with a tail of other meanings. We like the first—"cause to be"[8]—because of its deliberate quality. The O.E.D. says that the prefix "naturally intensifies the sense of the verb," adds "the notion of 'thoroughly, excessively.'" "Be-" is "a living element," "renders an intransitive verb transitive."[9] All active.

But then "befriending," too, begins to unpeel.

Sounds like it's about beginnings—and yet we are using it to evoke on-going, mutable experiences of being and doing in relation.

Our friend Mark Lord asks, "Is befriending different than 'becoming friends with?' Seems like one is for people of unequal status, the other for peers. If such categories apply." In Mark's reframing, "befriending" sounds not "just" like reaching out, but reaching out to someone below or beneath oneself—and yes, checking the dictionary again—the O.E.D. calls it the act "of a Samaritan," places it "in areas of social work."[10]

Since we are using the shifting locations of margin and center as ways to understand relationality, this is a troubling development. Joel reminds us that the "good Samaritan," who helped the stranger in the parable, was himself excluded, marginal. Each of us seeks and offers succor from different places, for different reasons, trips over and triggers various power differentials.

Eventually, we decide to stick with the term "befriend," precisely because it is fraught. Because the actions of befriending are fraught: in reaching out to others, we make ourselves vulnerable—to their

8. Vocabulary.com, s.v. "befriend."

9. Oxford English Dictionary, s.v., "be-prefix."

10. Oxford English Dictionary, s.v., "befriend."

losses, and to losing them. Judith Butler writes movingly about this in her book *Precarious Life*, which finds in human attachment the source of our fundamental fragility, "sees us as vulnerable to the loss of the other, to grief in the sundering of emotive bonds."[11]

Making a new friend may also mean not reaching any further, excluding others outside the "friendship circle." (*We fret about those we may have left out here.*) Inclusion and exclusion are always in motion, never fully or finally realized.

The sort of befriending we attempt to understand and describe acknowledges such losses and limits—but also always urges us toward surprise. The uncertainty of what can emerge among friends evokes possibilities beyond what is already known. And so, with Jack Halberstam, we refuse the institutional "call to order," the conventional "distinction between…chatter and knowledge,"[12] looking instead toward the never-predictable uptake among and between us. We join Eve Tuck, too, in her call for a moratorium on "damage-based research," reaching with her towards forms of inquiry and activism that spring from "desire," the complex web of lived, living with, dreaming toward.[13]

We locate our looping narrative in acts of befriending that are constituted by the emotions of vulnerability and passion, as well as by reflections on them that assume a form of "bifocality," attending, as Lois Weis and Michelle Fine note, to both "structures *and* lives."[14] We examine the relationship of public to private; how our emerging relations as allies, accomplices, conspirators, collaborators re-figure our classrooms, the college that hosts them, the space that stretches wide beyond the campus. We invest in one another's flourishing, in the institution that binds us, in the world that holds us all; we also acknowledge the interlacing tensions, ambiguities, ambivalences that characterize these. The synergy of befriending, institutional and world commitments unsettle, and so re-generate, one another.

11. Rosemarie Garland-Thomson, "Misfits: A Feminist Materialist Disability Concept," *Hypatia: A Journal of Feminist Philosophy* 26, no. 3 (Summer 2011): 599; see also Judith Butler, *Precarious Life: The Powers of Mourning and Violence* (London: Verso, 2004).

12. Jack Halberstam, "The Wild Beyond: With and for the Undercommons," in Harney and Moton, *The Undercommons*, 8–9.

13. Eve Tuck, "Suspending Damage: A Letter to Communities," *Harvard Educational Review* 79, no. 3 (Fall 2009): 409–27.

14. Lois Weis and Michelle Fine, "Critical Bifocality and Circuits of Privilege: Expanding Critical Ethnographic Theory and Design," *Harvard Educational Review* 82, no. 2 (June 2012): 174.

ANNE: May 28, 2015. Alice, Jody, and I have planned a three-way, day-long retreat for ourselves. Eager to work together in a range of modes, we meet at the Spruce Street Harbor Park on the Delaware River Waterfront, gather around the monolithic stone at the park's center, start slowly with movement—stretching, opening.

Lots of silence. Some writing, reading out. Eventually, we begin to speak, of what's on our hearts, what's happening at home. Then, beyond: Alice's summer community-based work in Dalun, Ghana; Jody's and my going into prison in North Philadelphia each Friday. Taking space to talk about what each of us is up to, really hearing what we're doing and dreaming into. It's a different mode of talking, looser, longer.... Our focus shifts to the college: what's happening there, where we feel discouraged, where there's hope, what we imagine shifting, how our own re-imaginings might contribute to that.

Thinking deeply with one another, with a kind of freedom and passion of questioning—about what we understand of our work, as it has been, also some of what might be. I have been inspired by the Democratizing Knowledge collective at Syracuse University,[15] which conceives of itself as both a sanctuary and site of risk-taking for those in marginal positions.[16] Alice and Jody join me in considering what the concept of "democratizing knowledge" might mean for us, and perhaps for others, at the college....

Along the way, we wander into Queen Village, find our way to a neighborhood café for lunch, end the day in Jody's living room, where we stretch again, re-configure.

Alice writes then,

> I think of our collective as a kind of weave or grid—hammock-like, that can light up with insight, energy, and support as the occasion demands.... We have slid, winged, glided, and otherwise shape shifted from a posse to a collective to a coven.... I remember at the start of our retreat feeling ah, I am with other witches who know what to do. Such a great feeling.... To our collective dreaming, I want to add, strongly, an alum presence....

15. "Democratizing Knowledge Project: Developing Literacies, Building Communities, Seeding Change," The College of Arts and Sciences, Syracuse University.

16. Chandra Mohanty et al., "Transnational Challenges to Global Empire: Cultivating Ethical Feminist Praxis," panel presented at the annual conference of the National Women's Studies Association, San Juan, Puerto Rico, November 2014.

> one of my main interests is to raise the vibration and power of an electric grid that already connects us with many alums on this wheel with us.[17]

17. Alice Lesnick, e-mail messages to authors, May 22, 2015, August 8, 2015, August 25, 2015.

ANNE: It hasn't been so easy, though, for us to get to this place, has been unsteady en route.

We stumble, as we plan to gather, realizing that the time we've set aside for our small retreat conflicts with a larger faculty workshop. When Alice first shares her desire "to go deep, tap root, and be more deeply oriented, and dis-oriented as needed, thereby," I confess that I "am very much drawn to the retreat we've planned for us three. I am also very drawn to [the Environmental Studies Retreat], which is scheduled for the same day, and where (I say) institutional intervention is happening/can happen/where I can help make it happen. And of course I don't want to have to choose between these!" "Feeling mixed herself in a coupla different directions," Jody names our honesty and risk-taking.

This is a painful exchange, sorting, shifting, eventually re-scheduling, recognizing that different facets (some of them unseen, maybe unknowable even to ourselves) are differently tangled, for each of us, with multiple other webs of commitment and connection. The plan for our three-way retreat is more easily changed than the institutionally scheduled one, but this very flexibility makes our arrangements seem tender, more vulnerable. As if we are struggling to be whole in an institution that fragments us.

JODY: By the time we three meet again, the following spring, Anne's granddaughter is scarily sick. It is a lovely, warm and windless March morning. Growing out of individual pursuits, and the interest we take in one another's, we do tai chi and yoga stretches in Rittenhouse Square before Anne goes to the hospital. Alice and I walk to Fitler Square. On leave, writing and doing yoga, I'm already worrying about what I'll lose when back on campus; feeling time as a zero sum game. But Alice has a different way of seeing this. Her insight captivates and teases, as we amble up a narrow, cross-cutting street, one of those where another century feels just beneath your steps.

And later the three of us, at a table on Sansom Street sharing hummus and beer—the delight of running into our friend Joel and his wife Sarah in their dark shades. Then coffee as we continue to probe what snags, intrigues: Anne's and my recent difficulties in co-writing, and in making the move from teaching only at the prison to also working with people returning to the community. One of Alice's close partners in Ghana has elusive, troubling medical issues; another doesn't yet have the money to finish her schooling as a community health worker; two are coming here to visit in April, she hopes, if they can get visas.

When we first talk about creating a different kind of space for our friendship, one with a more deliberate intention to support the work we do in the world, we have lots of questions: Will we invite others to join us? How public is our vision, how much about "institutional change"? Alice talks about wanting an intimate space, in which we might have the time and the ease, trust with each other and ourselves to more fully cultivate the various branches of our work, our particular, variegated visions. Might institutional tasks include more of the juicy now of our work and loves?

With Anne and I on leave—*writing this book*—we still have a presence on campus. The provost asks Alice and two students to speak about a departmental diversity initiative that we've been involved with, first at a chairs' meeting, then at a gathering of the full faculty. When the "project dorm room" competition is featured on the college website (*"Judges are looking for…ingenuity, and style…the interesting and creative ways that residents have decided to work with limited means and spaces"*), we strategize about what seems a troublingly classed event. Alice raises our shared concern on campus, initiates some dialogue there.

An e-mail goes out asking for nominations for an award, for staff members "who are hard-working, humble, kind, dedicated, enthusiastic, approachable, considerate, and willing to go over and above expectations." *"Humble?!"* Anne writes. *"Institutionalizing humility?"* Alice begins to track this, through relationships with people variously positioned on campus, wending her way through the institutional web. We see how the intersection of fancy dorm rooms and humble servants reprises the college's long history, in which, as Grace Pusey writes, "white women could be groomed to inherit a role...ruling over men and women of color."[18]

These are the varied and complicated textures of our own locations and connections: befriending various others in a range of settings, discovering tensions and potentials. Our befriending is contiguous with something instrumental, inviting different intercessions that intersect with individual and communal growth. We explore how such arrangements might operate too in working groups, classrooms, programs: spaces where the intimate can vex the political, the political irritate the intimate, giving rise to new possibilities in public and private spaces, as well as troubling the formulation that sees them as separate.

Re-envisioning the university both as a site of misery, distancing, and separation, and as a site of connection, resistance, and surprise, we share here stories that entail laughter and energy—also frustration and anger—as we try to pull ourselves beyond ourselves, to shift how intellect and feeling intertwine, how knowledge is authorized and shared. In these contexts, we understand befriending as intimate, holding, public, political. Succor and risk. From the "chatter" of these gatherings that move out of and back into institutional structures emerges a dance of order, resistance, desire, divergence, reordering.

18. Grace Pusey, "'Unghosting' African American Women's Labor History at Bryn Mawr College, 1880–1940," unpublished manuscript, December 5, 2015, 5.

298 | STEAL THIS CLASSROOM

Burning Ghat, Varanasi,
India (2016)

"Offering a Strange Hope"

ANNE (JANUARY 2016): With five other family members, I am traveling in northern India. The dynamics among us, as we move together, are always complicated, sometimes fraught. Without street signs or maps, each of us takes up differently the challenges of negotiating the small alleys of Varanasi: some of us distressed by not knowing where we are, others excited to see what we might find.

I am feeling vulnerable, especially disoriented as we make our way from the ghats, the stairs to the Ganges where washing and worshipping take place, to those that are sites of ritual cremation. I have never seen anything like these ancient, sacred, crowded sites of transition from life to death.

Who am I here? What is my relationship to what is going on around me? How can I be open to what is happening, curious about and respectful of what stretches so far beyond what I find familiar?

JODY AND ANNE: In Spring 2011, under the aegis of TLI, the college's Teaching and Learning Initiative, we join Alice and three other colleagues in a series of conversations about "assessing assessment."[19] Alice calls this group our "posse." Anne shares a poem by Kim Stafford, naming us "kindred in this work." We're a little giddy at our regular getting together, write e-mails to one another beforehand, long postings on Serendip after we gather.[20] Our discussions range quite broadly, as we think contextually about what education is, how to deliver and receive it, what we want our students to get better at. We are motivated by the tension we perceive between nurturing and evaluating thinking, the difficulties grading poses to teaching and learning relationships, its artificiality as a measure of the work of problem-solving, the need to open students' minds to ways of working and valuing their work that go beyond standardized forms so potent in this era. As we experiment in such directions within a competitive structure, we wonder just how far we can

[19] Teaching and Learning Institute at Bryn Mawr and Haverford Colleges.

[20] "Assessing Assessment" (2011–2012).

go. What would it mean, for us as teachers, to be fully empowered in this institution?

We have particularly rich conversations seeded by Margaret Price's new book, *Mad at School,* an analysis of the conflicts between academic structures and the experience of learners and teachers with "mental illness,"[21] and a recent *New Yorker* piece by Paul Tough, "The Poverty Clinic," about a new, holistic approach to public health and poverty, which makes education a focal part of "treatment."[22] Both prod us to think hard about what we are assessing, and why. Does the very structure in which we are embedded instigate mental health problems? How-and-why is it essential that students be able to "make manifest"—that is, to publicly reveal—what they have learned? How might we work toward a more diverse range of manifestations?

We talk about the possibility of evaluation on the level of the group, rather than always focusing on individual accomplishment. We consider a "pedagogy of surprise" (to what end?); discuss (and dismiss) "gatekeeping for weakness"; worry about the insistently time-driven dimension of assessment. We take the risk of sharing and discussing our own teaching evaluations—students' responses to a set of questions standardized throughout the college that can nonetheless feel surprisingly intimate, teaching us and exposing us in the rawness of our professional lives.

Paying attention to the mental health of both students and colleagues, we now see, is one aspect of treating each other as friends.

We join a tradition of educators who organize into groups of "critical friends" to meet regularly, engage in structured inquiry, and work collaboratively to improve their teaching.[23] This concept of a "critical friend" originated in education reforms of the 1970s, where it arose out of, and represented an expansion of, critical pedagogy and self-appraisal, a "marrying of unconditional support and unconditional critique."[24]

We're trying to ride this tension between supporting and challenging one another, the paradox (as articulated by Zen teacher

Shunru Suzuki) that we are both perfect just as we are and "could use a little improvement."[25] We engage a dialectic of risk and trust, as a cluster of friends "who *unsettle* formerly settled matters like what's important to learn, how much learning should teachers press for, and how will they know that learning has been achieved."[26] We begin to conceptualize ourselves as "allies" in an effort to critique and change the institution.

"Allies" doesn't quite capture it, though. Anne's daughter Marian leads us to an article that challenges the commodification and exploitation of ally-ship in the "activism industry," which calls such support and solidarity a means of perpetuating colonialism—and offers the alternative of being an accomplice, "a person who helps another commit a crime," becoming complicit in a struggle towards liberation.[27] This term delights us, less for its explicit "criminal" associations than for its multiple etymological layers: deriving from the Latin *complicem*, "partner, confederate," and *complicare,* "fold together" (as in "complicate"), with echoes, too, of "accomplish."[28]

As our labor takes on an explicitly political tone, we ask what roles we might play in fostering more democratic directions in the college: creating an environment in which our students could conduct their own assessments, as reflective meditative communications, for example, "presenting" themselves in ways that make most sense to themselves. In July, Alice and Anne publish an essay advocating for institutional structures that do not predetermine goals and measure how well we have achieved them. Without room for surprise, we argue, education is denied, and distorted by the loss of one of its central energies: the circulation of the gifts of chance and serendipity.[29] In October, following a conversation at the faculty meeting about expanding the college-wide course evaluation form, Wil and Anne write the provost to explain how our group has been imagining alternative ways of assessing the growth and development of students as members of an intellectual community. The provost responds with "encouragement and support" for our

25. Shunryu Suzuki, *Zen Mind, Beginner's Mind* (Boulder, CO: Shambhala, 2011).

26. Joseph P. McDonald, "Uncommon Common Principles: A CES Big Idea," Coalition of Essential Schools, 2016.

27. "Accomplices Not Allies: Abolishing the Ally Industrial Complex," May 4, 2014.

28. *On-Line Etymological Dictionary,* s.v. "accomplice."

29. Anne Dalke and Alice Lesnick, "Teaching Intersection, Not Assessment: Celebrating the Surprise of Gift Giving and Gift Getting in the Cultural Commons," *Journal of Curriculum and Pedagogy* 8 (2011): 75–96.

conversations—along with a clear statement of satisfaction with "more traditional forms of assessment" and "the way the system is working."

There are other tensions, gaps, as we try to extend our circle: We invite Margaret Price, whose work so stimulated our thinking, to meet with us. Our unstructured conversation veers into difficult territory: One of us asks a question that seems to offend. Several of us press into that difference, another looks to soothe, as the shared value of marginality—students' and now our own—turns prickly, divisive. In a later session Margaret explains that "kairotic spaces" like this one, pairing spontaneity with high levels of professional and academic impact, intersect problematically with mental disability: "when expectations are less clear, I find it very difficult…I don't know how to perform."[30] The broad, ever-present challenge of assessment bedevils relations with colleagues as well as with students.

No one's given us a toolkit, which makes the process of staying in relationship a demanding one. We suggest roles to one another, or choose them ourselves, fumble our way towards them. Gaps emerge among us. Some of us want to stretch beyond our original directive, to initiate a broader conversation about mental health issues among faculty and staff. Alice refuses to do this labor in and for the college; contending with a difficult family situation, J.C. also pulls out of the group, choosing to preserve energy for direct contact with students.

Four of us brainstorm action steps for sharing what we're learning and questioning with the broader community: a workshop for interested faculty colleagues, presentations to campus groups, recommendations for revision of assessment practices? A small group, we seek a larger center for our work, one that attends to the mental health of both faculty and students, rather than depending on a fiction that those who are struggling are somehow "outside" a system that is flourishing. After months of negotiating with the agenda-setting committee, we bring a discussion of campus mental health to the November and March faculty meetings. We select Sara who, as a

30. Anne Dalke, "structure!" February 10, 2012 (9:30 a.m.).

social worker, is best positioned to initiate the conversation. The special meeting is well attended, with lots of engaged discussion. Notes are made and distributed. In April, Sara and Anne talk with the members of the Dean's Office about fortifying the support structure; in late summer, the Dean reports on a range of new initiatives. Two years later, Sara, Jody, and Anne join a "rump group," as an unofficial Advisory Committee on Campus Community Health, which meets regularly with the president to discuss the campus climate and pilot a few interventions. A year after that, Sara and Anne are elected to serve on the Trustees' Task Force on Student Health and Counseling Services, which recommends some changes in the way health care is offered on campus.

Creative irritation takes form, is brought to fruition, then reified. As our ideas become institutionalized, it feels to us that the more exploratory and imaginative aspects of our shared engagement recede, and we notice that our interest wanes. We have been bringing an awareness of complex interdependency into our shared institutional lives, eliciting fragility, vulnerability. As our initiatives are realized administratively, we also find them "called into order"—shaped, streamlined, the social and political risks of disarray managed and contained. Like friendship, a structure that moves from being unsettled, into stability and out again, institutional change also cycles through periods when new ideas come into being, destabilize, then revise the status quo, cohere.

As the institution shifts, and each of us assumes a new role in relation to the college, the befriending that fuels such ideas also takes new forms. Alice and we are named "term professors," a public ranking more aligned with responsibilities we've been assuming over the past number of years. Sara becomes tenured; she and Anne collaborate on a new 360° on "Identity Matters."[31] J.C. is soon to retire; Wil leaves to work as a viticulturalist and winemaker.

Intersecting, colliding, dispersing, reorganizing—friendships, interventions, and institutions are all mutable over a long time frame.

31. See Chapter 7, "Slipping" and Chapter 9, "Reassembling."

As Ta-Nehesi Coates observes, "nothing about this world is meant to be.... This is not despair. These are the preferences of the universe itself: verbs over nouns, actions over states, struggle over hope."[32]

We can see how such shifts, in positions, relationships, and institutional dynamics, may be enacting what Sheldon Wolin calls "fugitive democracy," how a focus on moments rather than forms, "an ephemeral phenomenon rather than a settled system," offers "a strange hope" rooted in the "multiplicity of differences bound together in any given point."[33] And yet, in suggesting the structural exclusion of the very thing we wish to cultivate, such fugitivity is also limited in its reach. We are stretching, still, to acknowledge the ways in which friendship might also be institutionalized, not just an interruption of things-as-they-are, but a means of renewal, built into the fabric and structure of the college.

"The Work of Improvisation"

ANNE: My family and I arrive at an old hill station in West Bengal. We are staying at The Windamere Hotel, a rather astonishing, and very disturbing, remnant of what was once a boarding hall for English and Scottish tea planters. On a hill above the hotel, we are further astonished to find a cluster of shrines, where Hindu priests are chanting prayers, and hundreds of Buddhist prayer flags flutter among the trees. In the valley below, we find the Tibetan Refugee Self-Help Center.

How do I locate myself, and the work I do in a small liberal arts college in the U.S., in relation to the multiple histories and current activities which give structure to this place where I am traveling?

Where is center? What marks the margins?

ANNE AND JODY: After several decades of teaching, we are drawn into the field of Environmental Studies. We conceptualize this as an extension of our work on identity matters and social justice, and

---

32. Ta-Nehisi Coates, *Between the World and Me* (New York: Spiegel and Grau, 2015), 71.

33. Isaac Villegas and Jason Rust, "Fugitive Democracy: Sheldon Wolin and Contemplating the Local," April 25, 2006.

Shrine on Observatory Hill, Darjeeling, India (2016).

find ourselves curious about the various ways in which identity *and* environment—identities *in* environments—shape one another.[34] A program emerging across three linked colleges and multiple disciplines, Tri-Co Environmental Studies seems a space where friendship and institutional change might intersect in generative ways: still very much in a process of being carved out, it appears to us as another "crack" in the solidity of our institutions, in the disciplinary structure of the academy, in the academy's separation from the "real world." What new potentials might grow here?

Unlike our assessment posse, which grew out of friendship, the Environmental Studies program arises from the intersections of institutional affiliation. How we identify institutionally is not necessarily aligned with personal connections, and programmatic arrangements often involve staking out some territory. In these processes relationships can become complicated, both between faculty and students, and among faculty members themselves. It quickly becomes evident that differences will both nourish and challenge this creative vexation.

At a workshop, a Swarthmore colleague gives an account of a "pedagogical apocalypse," the "slow unraveling of shared interests in last year's senior seminar." Half the students are "hard-core green fundamentalists," who form their own class to "do politics." The other half wants to talk about Native American spirituality, "living in harmony." How might the split between politics and spirituality be differently understood? How might activists work with others less passionate or "learned" than they? The students who leave fail to engage others. Later, we hear a different account, from the colleague who directs the work of the students who have withdrawn: all are women, half of those women of color, who are saying "no," in part, to the longstanding Environmental Studies tradition of guidance by white men.

We find this split especially intriguing, because it reprises a tension present throughout this book: we, too, move between forms of teaching and learning that explicitly seek political change, and those

[34]. "Changing Our Story," Fall 2015; 360°, Spring 2014.

that seek something less tangible, in moments of revelation beyond what is usually visible in classrooms. We are drawn to both dimensions of change, always looking for how they are, or might be, linked.

Although "diversity" is named as one of the challenges of Environmental Studies, very little time is given, in our shared planning sessions, to unsettling either dominant narratives or hierarchical structures.[35] A large proportion of a morning's discussion devoted to "strengthening programs" is spent talking about how to ensure job security. We are interested in working with others to build this program, but frustrated that the conversation doesn't reflect our developing sense of risks and possibilities: an orientation toward developing and enacting a vision for change that might challenge rather than just pursue greater institutional stability, in the interests of promoting the Environmental Studies values we've been discussing: "holism, synthesis, fluidity, adaptability, agility, advocacy, outreach, creativity, community engagement, experiential learning, silo-busting…."

When the Environmental Studies faculty gathers for what's billed as "the family meeting," there is much celebration of co-teaching and other forms of critical friendship: A number of colleagues agree that they learn a lot more "than they ever do teaching alone," that the "work of improvisation" this compels is "a huge stretch, a vertiginous experience," a "high wire act" of "standing on the margins of our discipline looking for common discourse." The discussion is less centered around the growth such friendships might foster, however, than deep in deliberations committed to institutional stability. We bristle at the push-back against teaching our students to be activists, to being activists ourselves. Good work is being done to move the colleges toward environmental sustainability (*projects on geothermal energy, going "trayless" in the dining halls, converting our light bulbs to* LEDs, *reducing building operational impacts…*), but there's no calling the institutions to accountability in terms of seeking more equity within, or permeability of, structures.

35. Cf. Zoé Samudzi, "We Need A Decolonized, Not A 'Diverse', Education," March 11, 2016.

It occurs to us now that Environmental Studies could include befriending among the interaction of elements it studies in any given location, read friendship as part of the environment. Following the psychological conception of "the universe in process" (as described by Daniel Palmer), with objects understood "as more or less persistent regions in an onslaught of spatio-temporal change,"[36] we see movement across the permeable membrane of self and environment, organism and medium, as we re-conceptualize the shifting relationships of befriending and institutionalizing, experiencing both actions as transactional, malleable, imbricated in one another. The acts of befriending and institutionalizing are joined in what Timothy Morton calls "the ecological thought": a "collectivity of weakness, vulnerability, and incompletion."[37]

As Environmental Studies seeks both to stabilize itself within the colleges, and to have an impact on them, friendships do emerge, weaving in and out of this para-institutional context, both taking up and resisting the drive toward stability. Fed by shared fears and longings, we find ourselves in a new web of affiliation. Some of us admit frankly to one another the overwhelming challenges we face. Students are terrified by what they learn in these courses—they are the first generation "to get it," and they get it worse as they become more knowledgeable. Can we resolve their "sense of out-of-controlness," offer tools and emotional strength to help them deal with what we are teaching? We connect with Josh Moses, who snags our attention by admitting that his own "meager knowledge" is surpassed by the changes we are seeing, that he feels ill-equipped to help students adapt to changing facts. Moving outside of the "knowing tent," opening to precarity, fragility, possibility. Trying to offer them an expansion of both moral and imaginative possibilities, Josh takes lots of risks in the classroom and outside it, offering field courses, for instance, where, as his syllabus explains, much of the time is spent in the city, "subject to contingencies that classrooms are sheltered from—weather, late trains, human and animal interference, getting

---

36. Daniel Palmer, "On the Organism-Environment Distinction in Psychology." *Behavior and Philosophy* 32, no. 2 (2004): 317–47.

37. Timothy Morton, *The Ecological Thought* (Cambridge: Harvard University Press, 2010), 127.

lost, broken buses." His classes require a new degree of flexibility from students, and he urges them to approach these challenges with an adventuresome spirit.

Another new friend is clear that the work of Environmental Studies calls us to institutional reform. Giovanna DiChiro refuses to separate "social" from "environmental" problems. She takes on directly the problematic structural issues in how universities operate ("from the top," following "orthodoxies"), arguing that one of our interventions should be to change our colleges, from the corporate model of hiring, to the security of tenure, to "what counts" as research and science; if we don't respond more effectively to what's happening in the world, others who come after us will have nothing to study. Let's ask every department what their motivation is for what they teach, help them reimagine this space to identify the competencies people now need. Like Josh, Giovanna envisions a robust, socially critical environmental education, one that involves lively collaborative action research.

We make dates to go on talking with Josh and Giovanna, get some generous Tri-Co funding for the four of us to have dinner together in South Philadelphia: share questions about community partnerships; pause over our differing experiences with a touted figure in the field; acknowledge our uncertain, perhaps diverging desires and trajectories. With two of our students, we co-present a panel for the Association for the Study of Literature and the Environment. The colleges support our travel expenses. The institutional structure is paying for us to develop new friendships, which we hope may open up the institutions in turn, as well as some of the larger structures beyond them.

Observing that professionalization suppresses "any attempt at passion, at stepping out of this skepticism of the known into an inadequate confrontation with what exceeds it and oneself," Harney and Moten ask whether "the critical academic [is] then not dedicated to…the impoverishment, the immiseration, of society's cooperative

One of thirteen architectural instruments at Jantar Mantar, an astronomical observatory built of concrete in the 18th century, to predict the times and movements of the sun, moon, and planets. New Delhi, India (2016).

prospects."[38] It is precisely against such impoverishment that we here position ourselves, by arguing for friendship motivated by passion, destabilized by vulnerability, and steeped in the complexities of institutional engagement. A non-centralized program such as Environmental Studies offers a structure for puzzling over the shifting positions and variable strengths of margins and center. It also offers a site where relationships can grow, vexing structures, creating opportunities for collective action.

[38. Harney and Moton, *The Undercommons*, 39.]

Crossing the Border

We share a draft of this chapter with Ann Dixon, an alum and IT consultant at the college. Her many years of work on Serendip have provided an online ecosystem for our teaching and, more recently, for our drafting of this book; we live and work in a technological place she has built. Ann pushes us to look more closely at our focus here on friendships among faculty, who may be marginal in some ways, but in many others not nearly as much as staff members, those she calls "the 'doers' who keep the place running."[39]

[39. See Chapter 2, "Haunting."]

Describing herself as a "borderland person," Ann is an exception in this narrative: a good friend, colleague, and co-worker who is not a member of the Bryn Mawr faculty. Recognizing how our friendship with her marks some of the limits of our account, we are troubled by the ways in which our stories reprise the hierarchies of value inscribed at the college. We recognize the relative rarity of friendships among faculty and staff members, of relationships that go beyond exchanges at work, that might entail meals, movies, walks off campus, lead to other kinds of understandings, actions, possibilities.

We recognize too that the assignment of institutional roles may constrain the development of any relationship that exceeds such roles: structured expectations guide where we put our time and energy, calling us into some friendships while inhibiting others. Our friend Michael Tratner observes that befriending is not simply an open-ended encounter between two people, but shaped—both enabled and constrained—by the identities and experiences each of us brings to the exchange. Friendship is itself a structure: in large part a reaction to, and expression of, surrounding social structures, including institutional positions. Friendships may interrupt such structures; contrariwise, the formal structures of classrooms and institutions may break into, and break through, the existing structure of friendships.

> You befriend a colleague, take walks in the woods near campus, get together for a meal with both your families. Enjoy driving together into the city, for a meeting with colleagues who live downtown. Work together in a summer program for K-12 teachers; write together about your pedagogical experiments; celebrate the publication of the article that emerges. You are on sabbatical, selecting small carvings to bring back for her; she knits you a scarf. As she moves up through a series of administrative positions at the college, it slowly becomes harder for you to find time to hook up. One summer morning, snatching a conversation on campus, you hear yourself sharing a new idea about how this place might run differently, also hear her musing about how much effort it takes just to keep things going around here. You realize that the sort of brainstorming you used to do together has become more difficult, the stretch between your roles hard to overcome.

Befriending may be insurgent, a potential place of connection and instigation, of possibility and change. It may also raise difficulties, as personal differences, tensions between work and life commitments, or alterations in institutional status interrupt emerging relationships.

Possibilities and problematics emerge, too, in your close working relationships with students. The discussions of the assessment "posse" turn quickly to students' growth and development; you invite students to present with you at conferences; develop your prison teaching program with students. While they are here, students help you carry the energy of collaborative work both inside and outside the college. You are continually investing in people who are buoyant, open, courageous....

And this too is complicated: what does it mean when you collaborate, over years, to design a program with students, and yet have to enter their final grades; when you find yourselves negotiating with colleagues to help a student make it through; when relationships with some become markedly distinct from relationships with all?

> You work closely with a young woman during her years at the college—as your student, yes, and also over time as your teacher, then friend. A woman of color serving as your TLI consultant, she coaches you to bring your white identity explicitly to your classroom discussions of urban education, as an invitation, no an insistence, that white students fully engage, rather than just listening—which she sees as a way of putting students of color onstage. After she graduates, you stay in touch, meet for coffee when she's in town, co-present at conferences. She returns to work in the Admissions Office, arriving just as the college—again—rejects applicants from a local urban partner school.[40]

In follow-up meetings with her supervisor, in which she is positioned to represent the college's policies, you worry about how to challenge such practices while also respecting the delicacy of her position, and honoring your friendship. It's a long time before you can talk together about this.

As you call out and tangle with the details that exemplify the larger issues that make up our current campus culture—strategies for diversifying hiring and curriculum, changing policies on student financial support and staff wage equity—you appreciate the aptness of Grace Pusey's description of her own work, excavating the hidden history of the college:

> It's like the proverbial village where everyone who drinks water from the well gets terribly sick—we can either develop treatments for people's symptoms, quarantine people we think are infected/who we think are spreading the disease, do our best to manage the epidemic and minimize its harm, or we can all walk over to the well and ask "what the heck is in this water???"[41]

Working not in the proverbial village, but in the space of "surveillance, control, and dehumanization"—also love, possibility, and

40. See Chapter 3, "Haunting."

41. Grace Pusey, "Response to 'Slippage'" Essays, January 1, 2016 (4:42 p.m.).

challenge—that is American higher education today, you are not alone in wanting to inspect "the water" closely, and also not alone in calling on friendship to rejuvenate what feels like an "impoverished relational fabric."[42] Hunt and Holmes highlight "the intimate and everyday practices of allyship" that are exemplified at "the level of interpersonal relationships."[43] You join them in acknowledging the already-knit-togetherness of the intimate, the collaborative, the public, the political.

The passion that fuels befriending can not only survive, but incite, multiple other forms of institutional work. As one of the interlocutors of Derrida's politics of friendship observes, this dynamic "functions across the border separating private from public."[44] Its complex, intersecting quality—simultaneously liminal and central—renders befriending always in motion, dialectical, never complete. Co-teaching, collaborating at project sites, co-presenting at conferences, reassessing, envisioning—such activities embody the intimate and institutional dimensions of border-crossing that is the ongoing, variable practice of friendship.

Unlike Harney and Moton, who claim that the "only possible relationship to the university today is a criminal one,"[45] you see friendship as opening alternative relationships to the academy. Centered in desire, commitment, and a willingness to risk, friends can navigate "the way out…in the wall against which we are living,"[46] rendering porous the boundaries between love and politics, private and public, what is personal and what is institutional.

You celebrate—and want to extend opportunities for—threading friendship from the edges into and through the college where you work. Befriending itself is fragile, unstable: when you make friends, you open yourselves to love and support; also make yourselves vulnerable. Befriending winds itself in and through the commonplace of campus, conference site, prison, hospital, museum, park, café, where "every point in the local, every event of ordinary life, bubbles with deep flows that may take us into undiscovered worlds of promise, into hopeful futures."[47]

---

42. Foucault, quoted in Kingston, "Subversive Friendships."

43. Sarah Hunt and Cindy Holmes, "Everyday Decolonization: Living a Decolonizing Queer Politics," *Journal of Lesbian Studies* 19, no. 2 (March 2015): 156.

44. David Wills, "Full Dorsal: Derrida's Politics of Friendship," 2005.

45. Harney and Moten, *The Undercommons*, 26

46. Albert Camus, "Create Dangerously," lecture at the University of Uppsala, Sweden (December 14, 1957).

47. Villegas and Rust, "Fugitive Democracy."

Befriending has an intransigent power, is resilient even in damaged and damaging circumstances. It's also very, very complicated. Animating this chapter are many stories, of many sorts of friendships, which flourish, stumble, fail, sometimes re-gather.

> You befriend multiple co-teachers in your cross-disciplinary endeavors. They bring into your conversations excitement about teaching and learning, insight from other disciplines, tantalizing questions about art, politics, power. You are differently positioned—in life and at the college—which impacts how able each of you feels to take up and challenge structures at the college, prisons, museums, gardens, school programs....
>
> A friend adept at prison education is located uneasily at the college where she is finishing her doctorate and co-teaching with you. A long-time friend and colleague with whom you share valued life affiliations diverges from you in pedagogical practice. A friend whose deliciously barbed cynicism buoys you at lunch has very different commitments about the direction of the college. A friend who shares your pedagogies and political commitments is ensnared in the demands of their department, then free.

In this border zone, neither this nor that, the structures of both relationship and institution are malleable. Working in friendship is living in an ecotone, on the edge that Rachel Carson calls

> a strange and beautiful place...an area of unrest...an elusive and indefinable boundary...changing with the swing of the tides, belonging now to the land, now to the sea.... it is a world that keeps alive the sense of continuing creation and of the relentless drive of ...that intricate fabric of life by which one creature is linked with another, and each with its surroundings.[48]

48. Rachel Carson, "The Marginal World," in *The Edge of the Sea*, 1955, posted 2016.

Evan Vucci, *Confederate Flag Wavers Greeted President Obama in Oklahoma* (2015). Image Courtesy of the Associated Press.

CHAPTER EIGHT
SLIPPING

Slipping into Something More Comfortable

> You should be aware that failure is a distinct possibility. That was so freeing.
>
> —Benjamin Wallace-Wells, "The Hard Truths of Ta-Nehisi Coates"

Yesterday, "Confederate flag wavers greeted President Obama in Oklahoma."[1]

1. Arlette Saenz, "Confederate Flag Wavers Greeted President Obama in Oklahoma," *Good Morning America* (July 16, 2015).

Today, as I take my usual morning walk—several miles looping out of the farm and back again—I, too, am "greeted" by three new displays of the stars and bars.

Later, driving into town, I see three more.

I was raised in the Shenandoah Valley of western Virginia. I have been a college teacher in the Philadelphia suburbs for more than thirty years, but I still spend many weekends, and most of my semester breaks, in the South. I return, too, for several months each summer.

Writing now from this site, I am trying to puzzle through what has changed (or not), both in this rural southern county, and on my suburban northeast campus, since I first crossed the Mason-Dixon line, which I naively thought separated one from the other. In doing so, I find myself tracing a variety of ways in which institutionalizing diversity generates a backlash, as deliberate moves to create inclusive structures provoke pronounced displays of further exclusion—sometimes conscious, sometimes very much not so. Alexis de Tocqueville famously signaled the former, when he observed that "inequality is enshrined in mores as it disappears from laws."[2] His focus, in 1835, was on the ways in which customs and conventions slow the pace of legal change, making abolition more difficult.

I focus here on a second, often unconscious, form of resistance that I'm calling "slipping": an act of associative misspeaking that may be more iterative, more complicated—and potentially more hopeful—in its effects than the one Tocqueville described. I imagine the ways in which, if such slipping is endemic to learning structures, like my college, it might also be generative of their evolution. Such imaginings lead me to query a range of concepts often advanced in diversity work: those of "restoration" and "repair," of offering "hospitality" to "strangers." I ask also about the dangers of anonymity and privacy, about the counter-need and concomitant dangers of transparency and disclosure. Like other processes explored in this project, slipping is well characterized as a form of "ecological" thinking and acting: diverse, unruly, and fertile; conditional, uncertain, and incomplete—an unending process, very much dependent on the unexpected.

Asking in particular what it means to engage in such actions in the "contact zones"[3] that are intentional communities, I juxtapose the small town where I grew up with two institutions in the northeast: the small women's college in the Philadelphia suburbs where I teach, and a nearby land-based village designed around the needs of adults with developmental disabilities. In fall 2014, some of my students got to know some of the residents here, by joining them for

2. Alexis de Tocqueville, *Democracy in America*, trans. Henry Reeve (1831; repr. Gutenburg e-book, 2013).

3. Mary Louise Pratt, "Arts of the Contact Zone," *Profession* (1991): 33–40.

a week of work, and also by engaging in "the act of slow looking" needed to compose visual portraits of their lives.

The college and the village both seek "to sustain a community diverse in nature and democratic in practice,"[4] but are certainly challenged by the difficulties of doing so. At each—in the terms supplied by Sarah Ahmed, in her study of racism and diversity in institutional life—a "holding pattern" has become "intrinsic."[5] With the help of both Ahmed and Ta-Nehisi Coates, whose rising voice charts his "sense of the futility of individuals confronting the structure of white supremacy," his "pessimism about what can be changed," his doubt that "the future will be better than the past," I acknowledge the strength of what he calls "the long arc of history."[6] But I testify also to the inevitability of its constant disruption.

It is precisely such unpredictability, and its surprising lessons, which catch me off-guard again and again; it is also such unpredictability that reminds me of the possibility of undirected change. In the village, the developmental disabilities of community members, and the lack of acquired "filters" that these entail, make slipping likely. Amid the rigorous academics at Bryn Mawr, slipping is just as inevitable, but often unnoticed; its potential has certainly been little unexplored.

Over ten years ago, I first heard the concept of "slipping" formulated, by a student, as a messy, slow—indeed, inevitable and unending—process. Emily Elstad, who studied "Big Books of American Literature"[7] with me in Spring 2003, wrote at the conclusion of that semester about the importance of attending to the gaps that open up when we misstep, misspeak. Emily's essay, entitled "Slipping into Something More Comfortable," anticipated much of the current discourse about embracing difference, acknowledging a "racial unconscious" that needs to be—indeed, cannot avoid being—brought into the open, in order to be addressed.[8] Beginning with an explanation offered by a local congressman, of a "slip" made by the mayor of Philadelphia, in addressing the NAACP—

4. Bryn Mawr College, "Mission" (1998).

5. Sarah Ahmed, *On Being Included: Racism and Diversity in Institutional Life* (Durham: Duke University Press, 2012), 185–86.

6. Benjamin Wallace-Wells, "The Hard Truths of Ta-Nehisi Coates," *New York Magazine*, July 12, 2015 (9:00 p.m.).

7. "Big Books of American Literature" (course offered at Bryn Mawr College, Spring 2003).

8. Marguerite Rigoglioso, "Unconscious Racial Stereotypes Can Be Reversible," *Insights by Stanford Business* (January 1, 2008).

> The Brothers and Sisters are running this city! Don't let nobody fool you: we are in charge of the city of Brotherly Love. We are in charge! We are in charge!
> —John Street (Spring 2002)
>
> You're speaking your mind and sometimes you slip. We all slip.
> —Lucien Blackwell, in response to Street's comment

—Emily went on to draw on a range of classroom experiences, to argue that political correctness, or our fear of "mis"understanding, anticipates offenses that can

> never be predicted, and that if we do not allow ourselves to "slip," we cannot learn the truth about what we think or the truth about how others feel about what we think. "Slip" can mean "to slide or glide, esp. on a smooth or slippery surface; to lose one's foothold" or "to break or escape—a person, the tongue, lips." These definitions imply that what we bring to verbal "slippage" is involuntary, which suggests that in "slipping" somehow we access our unconscious, or what we "really mean." Other definitions of "slip" include "to fall away from a standard; to lose one's command of things," and "to pass out of, escape from, the mind or memory." These notions of "slip" posit a new state emerging from the act of slipping, a temporary loss of control that yields both a personal, subjective truth and a changed state that has moved away from "a standard" and into new thought and order. Instead of chastising people for "'slipping," for describing the way in which they honestly think about the world, perhaps we should consider the meaning behind words spoken in moments of "slipping" and really think about how they speak to our world. Thinking metaphorically, sometimes only by slipping and falling to the floor do we notice that there is something down there that needs to be cleaned up.[9]

At sites like Bryn Mawr, where many members have made intentional commitments to create an inclusive community, I've been learning how an unintentional "slip" might function, as Emily

9. Emily Elstad, "Slipping into Something More Comfortable," paper written for English 207: Big Books of American Literature, Bryn Mawr College, (Spring 2003).

explains, to remind us that "there is something down there that needs to be cleaned up." This making of messes, and then cleaning them up, never ends, but I also see how this process can function as an ongoing impetus not to settle in, a noting and questioning that can precipitate action and change.

Cleaning up is, also, not the only—sometimes not even the most useful—thing that can be done with a mess. What about exploring it? Painting with it? Surrounding it with silence? Meditating on it? Accepting it as the condition in which we live?

It is precisely the payoff, for institutional structures, of slippage, of the associative sort of thinking that isn't seeking a particular end, and so tumbles into new—sometimes murky, sometimes illuminated—spaces, that I highlight here.

Unbinding

I re-start my story (where I start most of them): in a classroom, in the recent past. In Fall 2013, I offer (as I have many times) an introductory course at Bryn Mawr College called "Critical Feminist Studies."[10] This is an English class that focuses on questions of representation, and queries what it might mean to "unbind" feminism from what Wendy Brown calls "the big bang theory of social change." We follow Brown and other poststructuralist feminists in locating the "conditions of gender" not somewhere "outside," where we can seize and eliminate them, but rather internally, in "deep processes of identifications and repudations only intermittently knowable...even less often graspable."[11] This re-conception—which also seems to me ecological, insofar as it acknowledges the permeability of self and environment—shifts our paradigms for transformation, not only theoretically, but experientially. Among us.

Among the twenty-five students enrolled is a queer woman from Texas who writes, early on,

10. "Critical Feminist Studies" (a course offered at Bryn Mawr College, Fall 2013).

11. Wendy Brown, "Feminism Unbound: Revolution, Mourning, Politics," in *Edgework: Critical Essays on Knowledge and Politics* (Princeton: Princeton University Press, 2005), 115.

> I honestly grew up in a box. It was a box with walls of expectations. I was never comfortable in that box. Yet it was not until I was old enough to think for and make significant decisions by myself that I began to question and tear apart my box. I wish I had begun this process earlier because I know now how much of an impact those walls had on me as a person. Our childhood molds us, but it does not make us who we are.[12]
>
> I just changed my avatar name because my previous name was too identifiable as me…the distance is necessary because I do not perform…the same for everyone because I am afraid of the conservative, close-minded society I come from…I do not want my resignification…to be revealed preemptively. I am not ready to face the music if certain people happen upon this forum…I would rather do it in my own way and in my own time.[13]
>
> I've moved around quite a bit during my 20+ years. I never felt connected enough to a place to call it home, I also never trusted a place enough to call it home.[14]

As we transition into the second half of the semester, the syllabus shifts from "engendering ourselves" to "engendering our institutions," and the student re-directs her focus from her own emerging identity to that of the college:

> …there are many cases where Bryn Mawr with its "progressive" and "open-mindedness" has stifled the cultural identities of students.… The student body at Bryn Mawr has become a close-minded place, focused on the advancement of certain cultural identities. Bryn Mawr like any other cultural hub has norms: white, queer, upper middle class, atheist, liberal, etc. If one does not conform to these norms, they are looked down upon, there exists societal pressure to conform to the cultural identity of Bryn Mawr.… Bryn Mawr is above all else a sisterhood, a home, a community, and we must foster this sense of togetherness, by coming together and not isolating and discrimination against the variety of cultural identities which exist on our campus.[15]
>
> I propose a mandatory seminar for first years…comprised of small, randomly-selected groups who will discuss and investigate the role of gender and sexuality at Bryn Mawr. I believe this

12. "Breaking Down Boxes," September 7, 2013 (3:51 p.m.).

13. "Avatar Name Change," October 6, 2013 (9:04 p.m.).

14. "What is home?" November 6, 2013 (12:41 a.m.).

15. "Web event #2: Bryn Mawr: Community? Empowered? Sisterhood?" November 14, 2013 (11:56 a.m.).

seminar is important for fostering inclusion, and will open dialogue within the community.[16]

She closes the semester with a prediction of individual change that will have implications for the college:

I will never hide behind the expectations of others again.... I take from this class a greater understanding of myself...accepting, and being proud of who I am.... This semester I unbound myself...just as the flowers use the wire as vines to grow up, I am going to use the bounds that once held me to blossom.[17]

Two semesters later, the student and her roommate, who is from Georgia, hang a rainbow flag out of one of their dorm windows. They also display a Confederate flag, first in the hallway and then—after dorm residents and deans seek its removal—from their second window. They also lay some duct tape, which they label "Mason-Dixon Line," in the passageway leading to their room.

Multiple dialogues—as well as lots of protesting, and lots of posturing—ensue. The media—first local, then national—picks up this story.[18]

Sara Ahmed writes, "The media is crucial...as the interface between an organization and its publics."[19]

Much of what happens is the result of this interface, the ways in which what is (not only) "outside" drives what is (not only) "inside" the campus. We can't clearly demarcate what we say from what is being said about us; it isn't possible for those of us who live and work here to speak to one another in ways not framed by media coverage. Many students record their experiences digitally; inside and outside are increasingly, visibly, permeable.

How to make sense of these many narratives being generated, off-campus, on, and in-between?

What do they call for, by way of response, continued dialogue

---

16. "Final Web Event—Addressing Exclusiveness at Home at Bryn Mawr: A Seminar," December 18, 2013 (11:03 p.m.). Student's banner image from "Unbinding."

17. "Unbinding Myself to Blossom," December 19, 2013 (5:50 a.m.).

18. "Students Rally After Confederate Flag Display," NBC10, Philadelphia, PA (September 19, 2014); Dave Huber, "Confederate Flag at Bryn Mawr College Dorm Causes Uproar," *The College Fix* (October 5, 2014); Susan Snyder, "Confederate Flag in Dorm Roils Bryn Mawr Campus," *Philadelphia Inquirer* (October 6, 2014); Katilin Mulhere, "A Flag and Race at Bryn Mawr," *Inside Higher Ed* (October 6, 2014); Andy Thomason, "Confederate Flag Raises Controversy at Bryn Mawr College," *The Chronicle of Higher Education* (October 6, 2014); Steven Conn, "Callous or Callow: Waving the Confederate Flag at Bryn Mawr College," *The Huffington Post* (October 7, 2014); Eric Owens, "Tolerance and Diversity Cause FREAKOUT Over Confederate Flag at Fancypants Women's College," *The Daily Caller* (October 6, 2014); Nicole Lopez et. al, "Petitioning Bryn Mawr College" (October 8, 2014).

19. Ahmed, *On Being Included*, 143.

and learning? And what are the sites where such conversations might be most productive?

An unlikely space for any sort of important-or-productive speaking is the monthly Bryn Mawr faculty meeting. And yet, in mid-September, as the president is describing various interventions—she proposes, for instance, that we devote one day during the spring semester to "campus professional development"—I find myself on my feet, trying to puzzle through, in public, some of my most pressing questions. In the company of more than a hundred colleagues, I ask how much power I-and-we have to direct the course of action here:

> I was raised in the rural South, and have long quipped that the longest trip I ever took was crossing the Mason-Dixon line.
>
> This week I have been thinking that I hadn't gone far enough.
>
> Several of the student leaders are in my classes, and I have been spending lots of time, in class and outside, dealing with what has happened here. Colleagues and I have been talking about our role as faculty, thinking together about curricular changes that might address some of the gaps in our students' education, how we might have failed to teach them…
>
> But this morning I learned that one of the students who displayed the flag had taken my introductory course in Critical Feminist Studies. I spent this afternoon re-reading her papers, and I began to see how the ideas of identity, intersectionality, representation, and signifying, which I had been talking about in that class, might have been taken up very differently than I intended; the uptake was quite other than what I meant.
>
> And so—as we plan these educational interventions, and I am all for them—I also want to add a note of humility: we do not know how our students will make use of what we give them. The gap between intention and uptake can be huge—as they struggle to make sense of their identities…and as we struggle to make sense of ours.

I am interested in how we might carry this idea forward institutionally, in how to incorporate such awareness into the structures in which we teach. The wise advice of the educational theorist Elizabeth Ellsworth, regarding the unpredictable "uptake" of our "teaching positions," is not to try and control the responses they evoke, but rather to activate, explore, even celebrate the multiple subject positions that are called into play in such pedagogical exchange. It is an ongoing challenge for me to join Ellsworth in embracing varied uptakes—which then can, perhaps, be revised—as diversity, unruliness, and fertility enter (and leave!) the classroom, in the guise of hunger, desire, fear, "ignor-ance."[20]

20. Elizabeth Ellsworth, *Teaching Positions: Difference, Pedagogy, and the Power of Address* (New York: Teachers College Press, 1997).

The Act of Slow Looking

In this intolerable season, not only has the Confederate flag been on display on the Bryn Mawr campus, but non-indictments have been handed down in both Missouri and New York.[21] College administrators begin to organize a Community Day of Learning, "designed to illuminate and consider the benefits and challenges of living and learning in a diverse community."[22] As I participate in the planning, I am feeling troubled by Sara Ahmed's observations that "diversity management" might function as a way of "containing conflict or dissent," "a discourse of benign variation" that "bypasses power as well as history." I recognize how easily the language of diversity can be "mobilized as a defense of reputation," "a means of maintaining privilege." "The discourse of diversity," Ahmed prods, "is one of respectable differences...used not only to displace attention from material inequalities but also to aestheticize equality."[23]

21. Ryan Grim, Matt Sledge and Mariah Stewart, "From Daniel Pantaleo To Darren Wilson, Police Are Almost Never Indicted," *Huffington Post*, December 3, 2014 (5:15 p.m.).

22. "Campus Comes Together for Community Day of Learning," March 20, 2015 (1:06 p.m.).

23. Ahmed, *On Being Included*, 13, 151.

My immersion in the residue of history, of its continuing action in the dynamics of power, continues unabated as fall 2014 unfolds.

This semester, along with Kristin Lindgren, a colleague in Disability Studies, and Sara Bressi, who teaches in the Graduate School of Social Work and Social Research, I have co-designed a cluster of courses modeled on an intersectional approach to identity. Focusing, in particular, on those identity categories of "humans being" that may seem non-normative, we read, view, and create a range of representations, asking what stories we tell, and what images we construct, about ourselves and others—and how we might revise them. What are the possibilities, what are the limits, and what roles might others play in these re-imaginings?

A central event in this work is a co-curricular project conceptualized and led by artist and curator Riva Lehrer. During an extended stay at the nearby intentional community that includes adults with intellectual disabilities (called "villagers" by the other community members, who are known as "householders"), our students share in meals, participate in work assignments, and are welcomed into many other aspects of daily life. Among the group of villagers selected by the Volunteer Coordinator (based on their interest in the project and their capacity to pursue it), each one works closely with a college student to create a portrait that represents them both realistically and symbolically. Our students, in turn, complete drawings and portraits of their village partners. At semester's end, the villagers visit Bryn Mawr, where they tour the campus, see the dorm rooms of their student partners, have lunch together, and exchange completed drawings and portraits.

At least that's the plan.

The reality—of an active world, shaping and being shaped by active subjects, constrained by the limits of time and energy—turns out to be considerably more complicated.

Tobin Seibers describes disability as a "body of knowledge."[24] His concept of the interactively-constructed self helps to highlight one very challenging dimension of our experiences at this dynamic farming, gardening, and handcrafting community, which is spread across hundreds of acres of farm, gardens, and woodlands. The bucolic site offers a local model for intentional, ecological living; it is filled with the pleasures of easy access to the natural world, and fueled by sustainable human actions, such as dairy farming, fruit and vegetable gardening, weaving, pottery-making, bread- and cookie-baking.

24. Tobin Siebers, "Returning the Social to the Social Model" (paper presented at the annual conference of the Society of Disability Studies, Minneapolis, MN, June 2014).

There is much here to enjoy and admire in this community; Riva compares, for instance, the sensory deprivation of being hospitalized with the multiple delights offered by the village.

Here "invisible people" are accepted as "social refugees," made visible and useful. And yet, as one of the long-term householders also explained to us, "this is a community place, not a people place"; she means that individual empowerment is valued less than communal harmony—and such harmony comes at a number of costs, including those of diversity of race, class, and ability. The community does not offer a political or empowerment model of disability. It is insular, and strikes us, when we visit, as largely unaffected by time, modern technologies, and the demand of creating access for villagers whose families cannot afford the substantial fees for living here.

The three evocative photographs on the next page were taken at the community by Rebecca,[25] one of the students in our course cluster.

Her role in capturing these images is a reminder that there is always someone behind the camera.

In mid-October, when we arrive at the village, one of our students is assigned to shadow a villager who tells her that she doesn't like to be with people who look like her. Her saying so is a challenge to Riva's vision of how we will "build the project around the concept of portraiture as relationship," how "the act of slow looking fosters encounters that unfold differently from, or raise productive difficulties about, standard power relationships...of age, race, gender, and able-bodied and impaired."[26]

Many of the villagers lack the social filters which conventionally refuse to name, or look aside from, such differences. The villager who says she doesn't like to be with people who look like our student, for instance, makes a very direct statement of personal preference and bias. In challenging our shared project of "slow looking," the villager seriously queers some of the presumptions underlying it, forces my re-consideration of some of its standards. Is "seeing past

25. rebeccamec, "Fall Break Photos," December 2, 2014 (19:19 p.m.).

26. Riva Lehrer, "Consent to Be Seen" (proposal for a panel on "The Ethics of Representation: How Context Matters," to be presented at the Society of Disability Studies, Atlanta, GA, June 2015).

SLIPPING | 329

Pictured is a large, open field. At the center is a piece of farm equipment, which is distinctive in having two seats; the sky, which is filled with lowering clouds, takes up half the picture.

Displayed here is a photo of a living room highlighted in red and blue. A circular table sits in the center, on a braided rug; three chairs surround the table, each with a braided cushion. There is an upright piano on the left; sunlight enters through two windows in the center; a sideboard on the right is covered with games.

Seated in the center of this photo—of a garden of herbs, and of blue and orange flowers—is a person, back to us, wearing a broad-rimmed hat, an orange shirt, and blue pants and scarf, who appears to be weeding. We catch only a glimpse of the side of their face, as they look down at their task.

stereotypes" our goal? Is forming friendships in such a short time, across such vast distances, a viable aspiration? Have we allowed enough time for this experience to unfold? If we haven't, is it unethical? The finiteness of our end time feels powerful here.

All this is distressing to me and my co-teachers. We face Ellsworth's unpredictable uptake. Brown's unbinding.

In trying to make pedagogical sense of what happened here, I draw on an essay by Eli Clare, who visits my class on "Ecological Imaginings"[27] at Bryn Mawr the following semester. We read and discuss Eli's "Meditations on Disabled Bodies, Natural Worlds, and a Politics of Cure," which begins with a walk through a restored tall-grass prairie, and invites us to think from that place about the concept of "restoration," of "undoing harm," rebuilding a system that has been broken. It is an action that—while acknowledging that such a return will always be incomplete—is rooted in the belief that the original state was better than what is current.[28]

Eli argues that this metaphor (like all metaphors) falls short, as a means of thinking through the concept of "cure," if we imagine it as a mandate of return to a former, non-disabled state of the individual body. The desire for restoration is bound to loss, to yearning for what was thought to have been—but sometimes such restoration is not possible. In Eli's story, as in many others, the original non-disabled body has never existed; such an account arises from imagining what the (normal, natural) body should be.

We discuss the limitations of this concept for those who are disabled, for those who are marginalized in other ways. Eli's essay is a critique of the concept of a "restored" and "restorative" world, like that of the village community, and of the limitations placed on the possibilities of our engagement there. Eli says to us that "disabled bodies, like restored prairies, resist the impulse…toward monoculture."[29] In the creation of retreats for disabled bodies and minds, we need also find a way towards more varied acts of resistance to the monocultural.

27. "Ecological Imaginings" (course offered at Bryn Mawr College, Spring 2015).

28. Eli Clare, "Meditations on Disabled Bodies, Natural Worlds, and a Politics of Cure," 21.

29. Clare, "Meditations," 19.

For starters: markedly absent in my account so far has been an elaboration of the experience of the villager whose "unfiltered" dismissal can be heard as a conduit for prejudicial feeling. I don't know much about the reach and limits of the villager's mental capacities, except that she knows enough to say what she doesn't like. The villager is paired with another of our students, Amelia, for the remainder of the week. Although the "success" of this substitution may well reflect and reproduce certain forms of privilege, the two of them are able to share a number of meaningful interactions over the course of the week.

The photos Amelia selects to figure her relationship with the villager are interactive: the two are seated close to one another, both smiling broadly. Amelia's text—which is illustrated with colorful images of the natural world, of people and food—also witnesses to the pleasures of time "slowing down," of "calm, comfortable" days when the only expectations are "being present and getting to know one another."[30]

Amelia's pastel drawing of the villager captures her at work in the pottery studio:[31] she has one hand on a vase she is making, while she looks up at the viewer, as if, in the midst of her work, she has been called out by another—called, perhaps, into relationship.

But perhaps the most profound image of such knowing is the doubled portrait of Amelia and herself that the villager creates.[32] This pictures two figures, one in a dress, one in pants, who seem together to be carrying a bag; pants, dress, and bag are all colored the same shade of blue. Behind the shorter figure lies the ghost of an earlier sketch; the artist seems to have changed her mind about how tall she wants that figure to be....

I now imagine that ghostly figure as the villager's first partner, who—due to a whole panoply of larger dynamics—is excluded from, and yet continues to haunt, this pair. The failure of that earlier relationship arises—not entirely deterministically, but not incidentally, either—from a range of conventional stereotypes, from historical

30. abradycole, "Zine Page," December 18, 2014 (10:29 a.m.).

31. abradycole, "Villager Portrait," December 14, 2014 (11:25 p.m.).

32. abradycole, "Drawing," December 14, 2014 (11:26 p.m.).

332 | STEAL THIS CLASSROOM

Amelia's portrait of the villager (top);
Villager's portrait of Amelia and herself (bottom).

and structural barriers to acknowledging one another, forming a working partnership, much less a friendship. In the village, which is intentionally shielded from the outside world, the student and the villager are unable to come to know one another as my co-teachers and I hoped they might. The villager is direct about her disinclination to work with the student—although there may be some complicated answers to the question of what it means for an adult with intellectual disabilities to make these statements.

Even as I bring into view her portrait and one of the images she created, the villager herself also remains something of a ghostly figure in my account. Silence surrounds my story of her, a silence that (as I explain more extensively in Chapter Four) both acknowledges my limits as a knower, and offers a space for questioning what it is I think I know about what happened here. Given the complexities of access in this process, how do I now understand our collective project of "ethical portraiture"? And (how) is it possible for me to provide an ethical account of what happened among us?

Eli Clare ends his own meditations on "disabled bodies and natural worlds" with a return to the tall-grass prairie, not "a retreat but the ground upon which we ask all these questions."[33] I, too, have a range of related questions about the complex valuing of difference as a form of both cultural and ecological diversity, and about how we might make such difference palpable and available.

Do my co-teachers and I need to return to the village, either with these students, or with another class, to keep on working through our partnership? Are different sorts of relationships possible among us?

Might a more active politics of difference enable us to move beyond our desires for restoration—of impairment, of a relationship, of a community, of a campus, of an eco-system?

33. Clare, "Meditations," 24.

Taking Up Residence

> ...if diversity is to remain a question, it is not one that can be solved.
>
> —Sara Ahmed, *On Being Included*

> ...how can I, can we, stay with the trouble...?
>
> —Donna Haraway, "When Species Meet"

The structures I want to alter, the silences I want to break, have been a long time a-building—not only at the village, but also at Bryn Mawr, where I have little interest in restoring the college's history. Drawing on Dean Spade's description of institutions like Bryn Mawr as "political projects," and the questions of "who gets to learn, and what they learn there," as "deeply political questions,"[34] Monica Mercado decries the founding of influential universities as part of the larger colonial project of unsettling Native Americans, clearing the land of people who lived there, replacing them with white settlers—who, in turn, founded institutions of study, "not for the enslaved or the replaced," but for white men. Colleges such as these, Monica maintains, are "part of the arsenal of European imperialism"; all the leading universities promoted and profited from slavery, racism, and colonialism. The earliest of these were playgrounds for wealthy boys, where ideas about race were "made and taught." Created as "bastions of white upper class women," the Seven Sisters Colleges followed this model, denying to African Americans the education they made available only to "a certain kind of woman." The histories of elite institutions like Bryn Mawr are histories of intense privilege and wealth, and of the hierarchies they create and maintain.[35]

Racism remains insistently present-and-active at the College, as it does elsewhere in the country. And much of our current work to unseat such campus hierarchies seems to me problematic, paradoxical, enacting the dream of restoration, grasping for a time that never was, and never can be. Sara Ahmed is prescient here, once

34. Dean Spade, talk at Barnard College, April 2014.

35. Monica Mercado, "A (Short, Incomplete, and Often Invisible) History of Race and Higher Education" (paper presented at the Bryn Mawr Teach-In on Race, Higher Education, Rights and Responsibilities, Bryn Mawr College, November 2014).

again, cautioning that diversity can be offered as a narrative of repair, as what allows us to "recover" from racism. She cautions that such recovery is not possible:

> Diversity is often imagined as…a way of mending or fixing histories of being broken.… diversity enters institutional discourse as a language of reparation; as a way of imagining that those who are divided can work together; a way of assuming that "to get along" is to right a wrong. Not to be excluded becomes not simply an account of the present…but also a way of relating to the past. Racism is framed as a memory of what is no longer.[36]

[36. Ahmed, *On Being Included*, 164.]

Searching for an alternative to "restoration," "repair," and "recovery"—seeking for a way, in other words, to "stay with the trouble," while not settling for-or-in it, I realize that the sort of "slippage" we encountered at the village is not confined to those with intellectual disabilities. It happens all the time, everywhere—including at communities like Bryn Mawr, where many members have been identified as "intellectually gifted." More importantly, Emily Elstad's essay suggests that such "slips" offer the college a way to move beyond old forms of failed engagement, in which those of us who "belong" welcome (or refuse welcome to) those of us who have more newly arrived. And where those who belong, my friend Alice Lesnick adds, have to keep showing that they do, in an ongoing performance, never "one and done."

As we construct and re-construct ourselves during our college years (and for decades thereafter), as we construct and re-construct the institutions within which we live and work, the differences within-and-among us are always in motion. Ahmed is once again helpful here, calling out how each act of inclusion, each gesture of hospitality, re-figures an old—and yet somehow always new-and-surprising—exclusion:

> To be welcomed is to be positioned as the one who is not at home…treated as guests, temporary residents…welcomed on condition they return that hospitality by integrating into a com-

mon organizational culture, or by "being" diverse, and allowing institutions to celebrate their diversity....this very structural position of being the guest, or the stranger, the one who receives hospitality, allows an act of inclusion to maintain the form of exclusion.[37]

37. Ahmed, *On Being Included*, 43.

If each new inclusion reactivates old exclusions, how to speak with one another about such divergences? (How) is it possible to construct a classroom space, a campus, a county or a country, which can hold them all?

I get a chance to work through these questions the next semester, when I offer "Ecological Imaginings," a course structured around the premise that "the real, material ecological crisis...is also a crisis of representation...a failure of narrative."

Not so surprisingly, the narrative that holds this course together falters. Ahmed again: "solutions to problems are the problems given new form."[38]

38. Ahmed, *On Being Included*, 143.

One of my experiments here is to ask each student to take a turn at selecting our class site. I hope this will result in our meeting outside more often, and so engaging with a range of interesting eco-pedagogical questions: how attentive should we be to the distractions of wind, sun, rain, birdsong, and the voices of others nearby? How much space and time should we give to those interruptions not on the course agenda? I take my inspiration from a student who enrolled in the first version of "Ecological Imaginings," and challenged me to "expand the net of attention" in class. Sara Gladwin asked if it were "ecologically literate" to teach and condition children to filter out divergent thinking," to teach them "not to pay attention to their surroundings, to let the environment fade into the background.... maybe the environment would be better protected," she posited,

> if instead of reprimanding the student whose eye has been caught by whatever can be seen from a classroom window, we were to give that student the opportunity to go outside, to broaden their thinking horizons. Maybe we would be able to expand our

concept of importance, give focus to what has been consistently pushed into the backgrounds of our imaginations.[39]

The weather is pretty miserable in the Philadelphia area this winter and spring, so we don't get outside very much. We do relocate twice a week, however, in various buildings around campus.

On April 21, we gather in the common room of Radnor dormitory, which was the site of the stand-off around the Confederate flag. Radnor has also long been the site of the biggest party of the school year (and, as a result, also the site of occasional shutdowns, and fairly frequent disciplinary action); in short, it is the dorm that students, faculty, and administrators are least likely to associate with schoolwork. The common room has been well-decorated, with lots of Christmas, Halloween, and flower lights hanging at the entrance, above the fireplace, along all the walls.

The week before, we read Terry Tempest Williams' memoir, *An Unspoken Hunger*.[40] In its aftermath, a member of this class writes,

> our classes in academic institutions feel a little like going to church on Sundays: there are so many powerful, moving, ecological thoughts, but in the end we all leave the building and go home.... There isn't much space made for intellectual thought to be brought into tangible practice. It's not just the question of how we can effectively educate people, but also the question of how we can provide spaces and practices that embody thinking in doing.... It is scary to be vulnerable and honest with ourselves and each other.... Because in doing so, we realize that we have so much to sacrifice and let go of.[41]

Sitting in a circle in the Radnor common room, I ask class members to take turns reading this passage aloud. Midway through the course of this exercise, one of the students looks around the room, and says suddenly that the lights make her uncomfortable, because they remind her of Christmas—and she is not Christian. In response, another of the students immediately offers to turn off the lights. When she does this, the others seem to me disappointed,

39. Sara Gladwin, "Divergent Thinking," December 2, 2012 (5:24 a.m.).

40. Terry Tempest Williams, *An Unspoken Hunger: Stories from the Field* (New York: Vintage, 1994).

41. "Earthquake Aftermath," April 17, 2015 (8:05 p.m.).

but—glad not to have to negotiate this division, which has caught me off-guard—I quickly re-direct our attention back to the text at hand.

Immediately after class, however, another student writes in our course forum:

> I do want everyone to feel comfortable [and safe] in all of the spaces we share.... i think it's important for every member of a community to be heard. so i'm also uncomfortable with a majority giving in to the wishes of a minority. every voice is not heard and respected in that situation either. consensus based decision making seems impossible on the scale of this entire campus, and too time consuming for our classroom, but i wonder if we can make a little more space for it in our lives.[42]

42. "consent/consensus," April 22, 2015 (10:22 p.m.).

Recognizing this as a call to "make a little more space" in our class, I start our next session with the observation of yet another student that "thinking ecologically" has ceased, for her, to be about the environment, and more about collaborative and interactive process.[43] Following her lead, I say, we need to talk about our interactions, about how, in particular, we might adjudicate differences such as these that have arisen among us. The student who originally objected to the lights says that they are an explicit reminder of "Christians killing Jews"; one person's "Christmas" lights have become another's "Holocaust." The student who posted says that she, too, is Jewish, but finds the lights a comfort; they make her feel that she belongs at Bryn Mawr. Yet another student observes that seeking "consensus" among these views might limit the range of our knowing. I posit that this tension is one we'd also seen in the fall, when the display of a Confederate flag by two Southern students, declared by them a sign of "home," was read by most others on campus as an unequivocal symbol of racist segregation.

43. Purple Finch, "Teach in Thoughts," April 17, 2015 (12:52 a.m.).

We all slip.

The structures with which we surround ourselves are slipping, too. As Monica's "(Short, Incomplete, and Often Invisible) History of

Race and Higher Education" makes clear, these institutional structures are actually built on slippages.

The incorporation of racial diversity was not part of the original vision of Bryn Mawr; the views of its second president, M. Carey Thomas, who re-designed and re-directed the college's mission, were both exclusionary and supremacist. According to research conducted by my friend and colleague Linda-Susan Beard, Thomas's letters and speeches entwined "feminist ideology with talk of racial hierarchies," her "views about Negroes and Jews" particularly discriminatory.[44]

Coates: "America begins in black plunder and white democracy, two features that are not contradictory but complementary."[45]

It takes most of our class time that day, but the students eventually arrive at a quantitative judgment: that one student's pain outweighs the slight loss of pleasure experienced by the others.

I am very glad that we have this conversation. In directing the students outside the classroom, I had asked how much space and time we should give to interruptions not on the course agenda. Instead of the distractions I'd anticipated—"of wind, sun, rain, birdsong, and the voices of others nearby"—we have been brought back inside, to attend more directly to our interactions with one another.

Of course I also have the contradictory thought (which may well have occurred to you while reading this account) that, in focusing on how we handle differences among ourselves, we very well might be deflecting the even more overwhelming questions raised by the texts I assign for discussion this week: excerpts from Naomi Klein's new book, *This Changes Everything: Capitalism vs. The Climate*,[46] and from Joanna Macy's reflections on *World as Lover, World as Self: Courage for Global Justice and Ecological Renewal*.[47] These books ask us to reflect, respectively, on the mounting dangers of climate change, and of the storage of nuclear waste. We set these reflections aside, in order to talk about community making.

And yet. The two projects are closely intertwined. At semester's

44. Linda-Susan Beard. "The Other Bryn Mawr History: The M. Carey Thomas Legacy" (talk at The Community Day of Learning: Race and Ethnicity at Bryn Mawr and Beyond, March 18, 2014).

45. Ta-Nehisi Coates, "The Case for Reparations," *The Atlantic* (June 2014).

46. Naomi Klein, *This Changes Everything: Capitalism vs. The Climate* (New York: Simon and Schuster, 2014).

47. Joanna Macy, *World as Lover, World as Self: Courage for Global Justice and Ecological Renewal* (Berkeley: Parallax Press, 2007).

end, one student writes a manifesto about this relationship:

> The slow, amorphous, complex entities of climate change and environmental disaster upend conventional ways of teaching and learning. To grow empowered and thoughtful students, environmental education needs to provide shovels for us to dig deep into the way systems are set up, the way we live, as well as to inculcate a rich ethic of stewardship based on empathetic, compassionate encounter with both world and self.[48]

48. "Manifesto for Environmental Studies," May 13, 2015 (6:45 p.m.).

As I and my students stumble and slip, re-framing, re-shaping and unsettling the systems in which we operate, I hear our work well described, once again, by Sara Ahmed:

> We come up against the force and weight of something when we attempt to alter the conditions of an existence...when we do not "quite" inhabit the norms of an institution.... When we are... held up by how we inhabit what we inhabit, then the terms of habitation are revealed to us. We need to rewrite the world from the experience...of "being stopped"...from the point of view of those who do not flow into it.... Diversity work...can describe the effects of inhabiting institutional spaces that do not give you residence...being made into a stranger...not being at home in a category that gives residence to others.[49]

49. Ahmed, *On Being Included*, 175–77.

The student who felt "stopped" by those Christmas lights, which "made her into a stranger" at Bryn Mawr, writes up what has happened. In doing so, she records what we said in class not as statements made by individuals, but as "a collective undertaking":

> I tried to not assign opinions and emotions to people, but instead see this discussion and conflict as a joint issue/problem that... we all must confront.... In this exercise, I am claiming people's ideas...not as my own, but as unowned, and flowing in through, between the collective.

I find what she calls her "political, social, racial, gender writing experiment"[50] a wonderful, concrete example of using language to reflect a more interactive and collaborative way of thinking-and-enacting,

50. "Class Observation/Notes," April 24, 2015 (12:53 a.m.).

one in which each of us assumes a role, not of insider or out, familiar or strange, but all co-habiting, re-shaping our institutional "residence" as we do so.

Conversations continue afterwards among pairs of students. Some of the differences among us are exacerbated, as classmates recognize how much their interests diverge, and they choose not to work together on their final collaborative projects; other differences among us get smoothed over during these last stages of the course. Slipping generates a range of different outcomes here than it did in the earlier course. I have a couple of ideas about why. It may be the (random?) capacity of this particular group of students to come together. It may be (more likely?) because the structure of this latter course invites the students to focus more on environmental matters than on individual ones. It is most likely because we are working long-term together over the course of the semester—rather than just visiting for a week, as we did in the village—that enables us to make productive use of the inevitability of messy slips in the classroom. We have an ongoing relationship, an ongoing commitment to working it out together, which gives us time to attend to, and clean up some of, the messes we make.

Staying with the Trouble

> Diversity would be institutionalized…when it ceases to cause trouble.
>
> —Sara Ahmed, *On Being Included*

In early December, I join a march that begins on campus, centers on a "die-in" in the center of town, and continues to the Haverford College campus, a mile away.

Although most of the media coverage, this time, is local, not national,[51] I am heartened to be there.

At the faculty meeting the following week, I stand again, to say how glad I was to join so many of my colleagues in the

---

51. Pete Bannan, "All Black Lives Matter 'Die In' Held in Bryn Mawr During Evening Rush Hour," *Main Line Media News* (December 8, 2014); David Chang, "Protesters for Mike Brown, Eric Garner March Through Main Line," NBC10.com (December 8, 2014); Justin Finch, "College Students Join Together for 'Die-In' Demonstration on the Main Line," CBS *Philly* (December 8, 2014); Kenneth Moton, "Die-In Protest Reaches the Main Line," ABC *Action News* (December 9, 2015).

342 | STEAL THIS CLASSROOM

"All Black Lives Matter 'Die In' Held in Bryn Mawr During Evening Rush Hour," *Main Line Media News* (2014).

demonstration; of how, during my thirty-three years at the College, I've never participated in an action that left campus to take a stand, as this one did; of how proud I am of our student organizers, of their professional demeanor…and that I've also been distressed to hear of an interaction, over the weekend, between a white member of our Campus Safety staff, and several Black students, both residents and guests. I understand that the encounter involved racial profiling. I have questions about valorizing confidentiality, both in this incident, and in the procedures that were followed in the confrontation over the Confederate Flag.

When sanctions are not made public, I say, the public story becomes one of non-action.

Told that these are "personnel issues," not public matters, I recall C. Wright Mills' definition of "the sociological imagination," "the vivid awareness of the relationship between personal experience and the wider society."[52] I want to shout about the ways in which "personnel" issues are always structural, about how institutional racism enables and covers personal assault, about the danger and downside of anonymity and privacy, about the counter-need for transparency and disclosure.

Instead, I send the provost an article about the "fateful pairing" of rape and anonymity, in which Geneva Overholser asks,

> How do you size up a problem that's largely hidden?…. Without data and transparency, the issue has…a hard time gaining footing…. When the crime is not reported, and no one is named, how do you get the data?…anonymity…prevents the public from fully engaging with the problem.[53]

I pair this with two testimonies to institutional racism, recently posted by Black members of the Vassar faculty, Kiese Laymon's "My Vassar College Faculty ID Makes Everything OK,"[54] and Eve Dunbar's "Who Really Burns: Quitting a Deans' Job in the Age of Mike Brown."[55]

Several months later, I meet with the provost and several other faculty leaders; we plan for on-going diversity training of faculty

52. C. Wright Mills, *The Sociological Imagination* (London: Oxford University Press, 1959).

53. Geneva Overholser, "Rape and Anonymity: A Fateful Pairing," December 11, 2014.

54. Kiese Laymon, "My Vassar College Faculty ID Makes Everything OK," November 29, 2014 (1:56 p.m.).

55. Eve Dunbar, "Who Really Burns: Quitting a Deans' Job in the Age of Mike Brown," December 2, 2014 (12:10 p.m.).

members, which may unsettle new members of the community, may further unsettle the community itself.

This makes me hopeful.

At the same time, back in Virginia, the local paper is running an article about the "sudden visibility of Confederate flags," "long scorned as a symbol of racism and hatred," now "enjoying a resurgence of popularity...in Shenandoah County," "festooning...front porches and pickup trucks as never before."[56]

I can't leave the farm without noticing a pair of walkers, each toting a flag; a biker towing an over-sized one; many trucks with six or more a-flying. Driving a few miles south, I enter one festooned neighborhood; a few miles north, another.

And now I wonder: in communities formed less intentionally than Bryn Mawr, like the one in which I was raised, and to which I repeatedly return, what other opportunities for renewal might exist, what slips between intent and action, between action and reaction?

"The sociologist travels at home," Peter Berger quipped, "debunking" and "unmasking"—"with shocking results."[57]

Pushed, I acknowledge that there may be some resemblance between the orientation of those who fly Confederate flags, and my own attitude, in faculty meetings and classrooms up North: feeling a compulsion to ask my questions aloud, refusing to accept what I read, or to settle for what I'm told, feeling pressed to share these refusals, to speak out, and so to push others...

"Don't tread on me."

Don't tell me what to think.

I begin to imagine what dreams might lie behind these flags.

In the rural South, as in the suburban North, there are desires for restoration.

But there are surely also—and simultaneously—other forms of dreaming that are less "domesticated," an associative sort of thinking that isn't seeking to reprise what was, or any other particular end. *In How Forests Think*, Eduardo Kohn describes his own

---

56. Keith Stickley, "Confederate Flag: Heritage or Hate? Old South Symbol Gains Popularity Here," *The Free Press* (July 30, 2015).

57. Peter Berger, *Invitation to Sociology: A Humanistic Perspective* (New York: Bantam Doubleday Dell, 1963).

learning, in an Amazon forest, in these terms:

> to become aware of…associative chains of thought…and then…to learn something about the inner forests these thoughts explore as they resonate through the psyche. Freud, of course, wanted to tame this kind of thinking…. But…there is another way…we might see these associations as thoughts in the world—exemplars of a kind of worldly thinking, undomesticated…by a particular human mind and her particular ends…the semiotics of dreaming…involves these spontaneous, self-organizing…associations in ways that can dissolve some of the boundaries we usually recognize between inside and outsides…when the conscious, purposive daytime work of discerning difference is relaxed, when we no longer ask thought for a "return".… Dreaming may well be…a sort of thought run wild—a human form of thinking that goes well beyond the human…a sort of "pensée sauvage"; a form of thinking unfettered from its own intentions and therefore susceptible to the play of forms in which it has become immersed.[58]

In Kohn's formulation, such an "unfettered" form of thinking is the activity of an individual, relaxing into an awareness of her web of connections with the world. I am suggesting here that such kinds of associative thinking might operate as well, and well, on a group—even on an institutional—level.

"Things are not what they seem," Berger advises, "Social reality turns out to have many layers of meaning. The discovery of each new layer changes the perception of the whole," can "fly in the face of what is taken for granted."[59]

How might the college, *as institution,* dig into these layers of meaning, seek out an active politics of difference based on what is found there, make it palpable and available? What political motions might unsettle the established structures, keep them ever off balance, ever renewing and renewable?[60]

58. Eduardo Kohn, *How Forests Think: Toward an Anthropology Beyond the Human* (Berkeley: University of California Press, 2013), 177, 185, 188.

59. Berger, *Invitation to Sociology*, 23.

60. Cf. Sheldon S. Wolin, "Norm and Form: The Constitutionalizing of Democracy," in *Athenian Political Thought and the Reconstruction of American Democracy Democracy,* ed. Peter Euben, John R. Wallach and Josiah Ober (Ithaca, NY: Cornell University Press, 1994), 29–58.

CHAPTER NINE
REASSEMBLING
WITH KEVIN GOTKIN AND CLARE MULLANEY

Never at ease or in complete control.
—Christine Sun Kim, "Partial Thesis Statement"

ANNE: This chapter opens in a place between.

Not a classroom, or a conference hall—it's an art space. October 2012. I've just arrived, late on a Friday evening, at Haverford College's Cantor Fitzgerald Gallery, for the opening of yet another astonishing event initiated by my friend Kristin Lindgren. The work of nine disabled artists is being showcased here, in a provocative exhibit that aims to demonstrate that "we do not yet know what bodies are, nor what bodies—all bodies—can or should do."[1]

The highlight this evening is a performance by Christine Sun Kim, a deaf artist who declares that she is "allowed to make sound," to "reclaim it as her property," although she is never "at ease nor in complete control of sounds she makes," knowing that they violate conventional etiquette about what noises are permissible. In my class earlier this week, Christine had asked provocative questions about ownership, negotiation, and translation ("I have no access to the files I make; if I am making sounds I can't hear: do they belong to me?") and—describing her deep sense of interdependency—called herself "a collaboration whore." This evening she's conducting an astounding experiment with "sound as texture." The

Derived from a presentation, with Kevin Gotkin and Clare Mullaney, at the June 2014 conference of the Society of Disability Studies.

1. "What Can a Body Do?" Exhibit curated by Amanda Cachia, Cantor Fitzgerald Gallery, Haverford College, October 26—December 16, 2012.

gallery is overcrowded; I have trouble seeing the performance, in which Christine is making vibrations visible in paint.[2]

But then I see Clare. Delighted with the opportunity to catch up after a long gap in our own collaborations on access initiatives at Bryn Mawr,[3] we also seriously violate "sound etiquette" by turning our backs on the performance, in order to share stories about what each of us is up to now. I tell about my new courses (including the one Christine just visited, which focuses on "the rhetorics of silence").[4] Clare introduces her new friend and colleague, Kevin Gotkin, with whom she's initiated a Disability Studies Reading Group at the University of Pennsylvania, where both are graduate students. Eager for more shared engagement, we agree to meet again soon.

When we do, I invite Jody to join us; like me, she's an alum of Penn's Graduate School, with some family experience of disability, but little knowledge of the field of Disability Studies, which intrigues her. Like me, she's also just delighted to be talking with grad students again: so close to us in intellectual and life interests, so far from us generationally. Graduate school is much more focused on quick professionalization than it was back in the day, and Clare and Kevin are on career trajectories very different from the sort of nonlinear tracks Jody and I have both been traveling for so long.

Happily engaged, we agree to meet again. And again. Much of our conversation is fueled by what we are learning together about Disability Studies. Kevin works on the intersections of technology and disability in the field of Communication; Clare is using Disability Studies as a methodology for reading nineteenth-century literary texts. Jody and I are finding in Disability Studies a profound extension of the thinking we've been doing about "unbounded" teaching, as we follow the intermeshing of everything deep into the varieties of the human unconscious, as well as into "outside" spaces of uncertainty, incompleteness, and conditionality.

Each of the four of us feels deeply drawn to what Kristin Lindgren calls the "inventiveness, creative interdependence, and artful

---

2. Christine Sun Kim, "Is Unlearning Sound Etiquette" and "Partial Thesis Statement."

3. See Chapter 5, "Unbecoming."

4. See Chapter 4, "Silencing."

navigation of the built environment" required by the "daily lives of most disabled people," wanting better to understand the ways in which "variability in human form and function…give rise to creativity and new knowledge."[5] Each of us has also had a somewhat fraught relationship to the field of Disability Studies, has been concerned that we may not fully fit (or be seen as not fitting) within its borders. Elizabeth Ellsworth's observation that, if "perfect fit" were possible, it would in fact guarantee that no learning would happen,[6] along with Rosemarie Garland-Thomson's explication of the many ways in which "misfitting can be generative,"[7] enables us now, however, to see this nagging issue of our "fit" as both a clue to emerging directions in Disability Studies, and a crack where we might enter.

In line with the work of Garland-Thomson, and the larger argument of this book, Clare, Kevin, Jody, and I here posit the notion that "disabled enough" thinking—the sense that only some of us fully fall within the category of "disability"—obscures the true creative wellspring of what it means to embody both physical and cognitive difference. In his film, "The Rupture Sometimes" (which was playing at the Haverford exhibit), Kevin observes, "It is the gradations, shades and registers—all the things that mark both differences and similarities—that open up disability into a capacious intellectual brain space."[8]

Throughout this book, Jody and I similarly query identifiable, claimable categories, predictable "uptakes" in teaching, learning, living: the spaces among us, the gaps Ellsworth identifies between perception and cognition: unconscious yet palpable in their diversity, unruliness, and fertility. In this chapter, Clare and Kevin join Jody and me in arguing that attending to a world of unpredictable, inexhaustible interconnection, as well as to (temporary or longer-standing) experiences of fear and pain, constraints and limits, shifts not only our orientation toward classroom interactions, but also our understanding of a wide range of academic and activist

5. Kristin Lindgren, "The (S)paces of Academic Work: Disability, Access, and Higher Education" in *Transforming the Academy: Faculty Perspectives on Diversity & Pedagogy*, ed. Sarah Willie-LeBreton (New Brunswick: Rutgers University Press, 2016), 114.

6. Elizabeth Ellsworth, *Teaching Positions: Difference, Pedagogy, and the Power of Address* (New York: Teachers College Press, 1997), 44.

7. Rosemarie Garland-Thomson, "Misfits: A Feminist Materialist Disability Concept," *Hypatia: A Journal of Feminist Philosophy* 26, no. 3 (Summer 2011): 604.

8. Kevin Gotkin, "The Rupture Sometimes," YouTube video, 27:44, September 19, 2012.

fields that do not explicitly define themselves as either psychological or ecological.

As a way of experimenting with this sort of re-orientation, the four of us draw connections among wild internal diversity, unruly classrooms, and the fields of study in which we position ourselves, tracing a variety of fluid passages between sites of learning and disciplinary formations. We try out, in particular, the implications of thinking ecologically in the field of Disability Studies, which seems to hold real promise for understanding what it means to be humans in relationship with the environments in which we learn.

We are well accompanied in this exploration by an emerging group of "crip ecologists," who work across the fields of disability, queer studies, and ecocriticism to think through the interchanges of environments and bodies in radical ways. As a noun, "crip" shortens the word "crippled," claims it as a proud identity. As a verb, "cripping" has a much larger reach, is used politically "as a way to re-imagine conceptual boundaries, relationships…cultural representations, and power structures."[9]

Crip ecologists think evolutionarily, of all life as adaptive to the environment.[10] Acknowledging that some bodies are more durable, others more vulnerable, crip ecology is not a minoritarian discourse: it understands all of us to have a certain eco-enmeshment. Everyone is porous, permeable, allowing the outer world to flow through us.[11]

As materials for understanding, crip ecologists draw out wanted, unwanted, known, unknowable intimacies with ourselves and all that surrounds and interpenetrates all types of human bodies.[12] Approaching "nature through the lens of loss and ambivalence,"[13] crip ecology conceptualizes humans as vulnerable, embodied beings interacting with environments: affected by the places we inhabit, simultaneously leaving our imprint on these locations.

---

9. Emily Hutcheon and Gregor Wolbring, "'Cripping' Resilience: Contributions from Disability Studies to Resilience Theory," M/C Journal 16, no. 5 (November 6, 2013).

10. Cf. Mel Chen, Animacies: Biopolitics, Racial Mattering, and Queer Affect (Durham, NC: Duke University Press, 2012); Kevin Gotkin, "The Norm___ and the Pathological," DSQ: Disability Studies Quarterly 36, no. 1 (2016).

11. Levi R. Bryant, "Stacy Alaimo: Porous Bodies and Trans-Corporeality," Larval Subjects, May 24, 2012.

12. "Welcome to Crip Ecologies!" Composing Disability Conference, March 2016.

13. Alison Kafer, Feminist, Queer, Crip (Bloomington: Indiana University Press, 2013), 142.

J. Stimp, *Muddy Tire Tracks 1, Comana Natural Park, Romania* (2015). CC-BY https://flic.kr/p/AbKkNa

Keeping the question of who we are permanently open.
—Judith Butler, "Toward an Ethics of Cohabitation"

In October 2013, Clare and Kevin lead a workshop for the students in Anne's Critical Feminist Studies course. Building on our discussions about accessibility, they call this a "crip classroom," and experiment with pacing the discussion—going as fast, then as slow as possible—as they introduce the students to the concepts of "crip time":

> Within the disability community, many use the term…to signify a flexible approach to temporal demands.… As Alison Kafer explains, "Crip time is flex time not just expanded but exploded; it requires reimaging our notions of what can and should happen in time.… Rather than bend disabled bodies and minds to meet the clock, crip time bends the clock to meet disabled bodies and minds."[14]

14. Lindgren, "The (S)paces of Academic Work," 121.

"Bending time" by enacting varied pacing in the classroom, Clare and Kevin "enable" me and my students to experience some of the problematics of such an intervention: Going slow enables some students, disables others; going fast, ditto. Switching back and forth confuses us all. In our first shared experiment in access configuration, we realize that giving everyone in the room as many accommodations as possible can quickly become overwhelming—and may not be effective. Where, here, are the limits of accommodation? When-and-how might "accessibility" become "excessibility"?[15]

We'd like to do a better job at this.

The following week, Clare, Kevin, and I attend a conference on "Disability Disclosure in/and Higher Education," organized by Stephanie Kershbaum and Margaret Price at the University of Delaware.[16] The conference models a variety of approaches to access. Stephanie and Margaret report that they

> worked to reduce and eliminate fragrances...offered a quiet room...assembled a schedule that provided ample down-time opportunity...provided photographs of conference spaces accompanied by crowd-sourced descriptions; and...integrated interaction badges...to provide a means for participants to nonverbally signal their preferred level of interaction.[17]

This impressive range of interventions also marks, however, the impossibility of full access, as conflicts arise between those who require multi-sensory modes of access and those who find them distracting, those who need guide dogs and those who are allergic to them, those who request the assurance of safe spaces and those who recognize the unpredictability of triggers. Stephanie and Margaret themselves reflect on a number of other "inaccessible elements" in the event, raising "vital questions about the range of bodies and minds 'allowed' in academia": those present are "overwhelmingly white," "healthy and well enough to travel...can afford to spend three days in a rarefied space engaging in intellectual and social conversation, and...can procure institutional funding or other financial support."[18]

15. "Notes Towards Day 13: Cripping and Excessability," Critical Feminist Studies, Bryn Mawr College, Fall 2013.

16. "Disability Disclosure in/and Higher Education," University of Delaware, October 2013.

17. Stephanie Kerschbaum and Margaret Price, "Perils and Prospects of Disclosing Disability Identity in Higher Education," March 3, 2014.

18. Kerschbaum and Price, "Perils and Prospects."

Nearly a year later, at the June 2014 conference of the Society of Disability Studies, Jody joins Clare, Kevin, and me on a panel reflecting further on some of the problematics of disclosure and accommodation.[19] The four of us perform our various vulnerabilities, privileges, and interdependencies through multiple modalities. We theorize accessibility, in front of videos of us telling stories from our lives. We are all also knitting, a practice that enacts a kind of "absent" presence of mind, while allowing us to hold in our hands the richness of the threads we are trying to weave together here. In doing so, we are, in part, celebrating accessibility, the way knowledge blossoms when we tear down barriers and fiercely commit ourselves to inclusion. We are also demonstrating how Disability Studies nuances our understanding of identity politics, challenging what we mean when we talk about self and social world as stable entities. Joining the field of Disability Studies in building an expansive notion of access, we are also querying a key presumption underlying that concept. We wonder how our multi-modal performance invites some in, others not; whether our very efforts to communicate with multiple, diverse beings in the room might itself be overwhelming, non-communicative.

As commonly defined and pursued, access requires a stable self and world. Much of the scholarship now bridging queerness and disability,[20] however, refuses to "crystallise" identity in any specific form, and so brings analytical pressure to bear on "'the open mesh of possibilities, gaps, overlaps, dissonances and resonances, lapses and excesses of meaning where the constituent elements…can't be made…to signify monolithically.'"[21]

This sort of thinking has a long history. Theodor Adorno anticipated it, for example, when he offered the term "nonidentity" to describe the slippage between a concept and the material of that thing: "What we may call the thing itself is not positively and immediately at hand."[22] Nonidentity, Adorno said, accounts for that nagging feeling that something is being left out of the way we

19. Jody Cohen, Anne Dalke, Kevin Gotkin and Clare Mullaney, "Intervening in the Accessible: Reassembling the Social in Disability Studies," panel at the Society of Disability Studies, Minneapolis, MN, June 2014.

20. Cf. Robert McRuer, "Cripping Queer Politics, or the Dangers of Neoliberalism," *The Scholar & Feminist Online* 10.1–2 (Fall 2011/Spring 2012).

21. Eve Sedgwick, qted in Annamarie Jagose, *Queer Theory: An Introduction* (New York University, 1996), 99–100.

22. Theodor Adorno, *Negative Dialectics*, 2nd ed. (London: Bloomsbury Academic, 1981), 5.

know things—what Jody elsewhere calls "haunting."[23] No concept *(no person, no thing)* is singular or unified; no word exhausts the thing conceived. There is a chasm between reality and the language we use to grapple with that reality. Nonidentity is "heterogeneous" to all concepts, and "negative dialectics" is the method Adorno gave us for attuning to that "remainder."

We find Adorno's concept of nonidentity, as that which always escapes from the inadequate container that is language, useful as a means of problematizing the process of giving access. At a time when contemporary disability theory is offering competing ideas about how we should conceptualize "identity" (for example, Lennard Davis tolling the "end of identity politics"[24] while Tobin Siebers calls for identity politics "in a new register"),[25] we are taken by a term, *non*identity, that at first seems to negate identity altogether, but in fact provides the basis for a positive affiliation across difference. A serious attunement to nonidentity gives us a route to re-conceptualize accessibility, as process that can be pursued when none of us fully knows, nor can fully express, either who we are or what we need. In Disability Studies, a field that is so deeply invested in identity, we relish a concept that allows us to think of our being bound together by what exceeds conventional identity categories *(the disabled, the temporarily able-bodied)*.

Nonidentity is a key insight in ecological thinking, too. In a world filled with "fundamentally uncanny and unfathomable" entities, Timothy Morton observes, "life is non-identical to itself."[26] Beginning with such a concept of nonidentity, a more fluid, unbounded version of the self, invites us to acknowledge both the implacable particularities of individual impairment and a more "relational ontology," with flux and flow as the intermediaries of power. Agency becomes tied up, entangled in the twisted social world. Attending to such synergies bears an ethical force; in the language of physicist Karen Barad, it demands a "responsibility for the reconfigurings of which we are a part."[27]

How then to take up that responsibility? How to design for access?

---

23. See Chapter 3, "Haunting."

24. Lennard Davis, "The End of Identity Politics and the Beginning of Dismodernism: On Disability as an Unstable Category," in *The Disability Studies Reader*, ed. Lennard J. Davis, 2nd ed. (New York: Routledge, 2006), 231–42.

25. Tobin Siebers, "Disability and the Theory of Complex Embodiment—For Identity Politics in a New Register," in *Disability Theory* (Ann Arbor: University of Michigan Press, 2008).

26. Timothy Morton, "Practising Deconstruction in the Age of Ecological Emergency," in *Teaching Ecocriticism and Green Cultural Studies*, ed. Greg Garrard (New York: Palgrave Macmillan, 2012), 162.

27. Karen Barad, *Meeting the Universe Halfway: Quantum Physics and the Entanglement of Matter and Meaning*, (Durham: Duke University Press, 2007), 91.

What does it mean to acknowledge the problematics of disclosure, the unpredictability of uptake, the likelihood of being taken unawares?

At the conference, we reimagine accessibility not as replacement or retrofit, more as an ambient ubiquitous interface, which cannot readily be pinned down. Our ruminations about the impossibility of full access draw on our own experiences, as well as on many contemporary theorists, within and outside of Disability Studies,[28] who work their way beyond the conceptualization of a stable self in a stable social order.

In critiquing the too-ready legibility of disability, the four of us look not to redefine the concept of access, but to re-imagine its structure; we do so by following the many ways in which Disability Studies is reshaping what we know about both identity and sociality. Our unravelings do not take access or accommodation lightly. We are not disregarding the ways in which access can make a difference in an ableist world; we are also not claiming that Disability Studies stops where the category of disability does, that disability itself has clear edges. Wanting to see Disability Studies cited in all the domains it is poised to reinvigorate, we enact some of this reach, critically examining what gets called identity, experimenting with how far out these categories might stretch.

Disability is not its own self-identical thing; there are strong differences among those who are assigned, or choose, that identity.[29] Crossing the dividing line between disabilities that are stable *enough* to request predictable accommodations, and those that are not, means challenging presumptions about knowability, both of who we are and what we need. It means that access will always be not-entirely-known. There are no guarantees in this unpredictable process: a clarity of uptake not assumed, the outcome of calls for accessibility ultimately unreliable.

Clare, Jody, Kevin, and I situate our alliance in several connected and disconnected positions, telling stories of our own various disablings and enablings, from the perspectives of "selves" working our

---

28. Leo Bersani, *Homos* (Cambridge: Harvard University Press, 1996); Judith Butler, *Notes Towards a Performative Theory of Assembly* (Cambridge: Harvard University Press, 2015); Davis, 231–42; Jay Dolmage, "Universal Design: Places to Start," *DSQ: Disability Studies Quarterly* 35, no. 2 (2015); Robert McRuer, *Crip Theory: Cultural Signs of Queerness and Disability* (New York: New York University Press, 2005).

29. Cf. Judith Butler and Sunaura Taylor, "Examined Life," YouTube video, 14:23, October 6, 2010.

relations to the field of Disability Studies and "others" who im/possibly exist outside it, as well as from cracks within and between all these. We find our mode of residence in the crevices among disparate locales: spaces that are both personal and scholarly, pragmatic and abstract, real and imaginary. We're interested in how voices intersect in moments of "access," and figure here a continual shift in perspective, one grounded in our conviction that the self is never fully situated, thoroughly placed, or entirely anchored.

Eugene Kim, *Village of the Arts and Humanities* (2007). CC-BY
https://flic.kr/p/GAYg5

Part of what I am is the enigmatic traces of others.
—Judith Butler, *Precarious Life*

CLARE: My story begins with a pair of gloves acquired only months ago. It had been an especially cold winter, and I was rummaging through my family's disparate collection of winter accessories in search of warm gloves. I stumbled across an old pair of my great aunt's, which were given to her by my mom only a few Christmases before she passed away. They're quite stiff, and it's obvious they have hardly been worn. My aunt had received them right when her outings began to dwindle, when driving and traveling had become all the more difficult with age.

When I first held the gloves in my hands I felt close to my aunt. I imagined her ten fingers snuggly encased within their fleece lining and was comforted that mine, too, would be similarly enclosed. I stared for moments at a particular mark on the left glove. Mary (or "Auntie M" as she affectionately liked to be called after Dorothy's aunt in the *Wizard of Oz*) was a heavy smoker. I remember sitting on the front porch of my grandmother's home in Scranton, Pennsylvania when I was about five years old, and suggesting to M that I would stop sucking my pacifier, as per a desperate plea from my dentist, if she promised not to smoke. It was then, at a young age (although too old, I'm certain, to be resolutely attached to my pacifier) that I was already placing myself within an economy of exchange, one in which our own vices, our own mechanisms for coping with an uncertain world, would be swapped for the other.

The mark on the glove seems to be the result of the accidental stumbling of her cigarette, in which its sultry tip had briskly touched the garment's exterior, gently melting some of the little puckered holes decorating its surface into a soft imprint. The blot emerged, in my minutes of recollection, as a story of an un-narrated moment—one that wasn't disclosed until the aftermath of Mary's death. The glove enacted a crumpling of time; it allowed, if only momentarily, past and future to touch.

I lost the glove one evening as my family was forced to evacuate a burning restaurant. The restaurant ended up being fine, and I wasn't so much worried about the lost glove itself as I was about Mary. It was the doubleness of the displacement, of my aunt and now her object, which distressed me the most. And yet, there seems to be something about clothing that is much more about distance than intimacy, about loss rather than gain. In the end, this un-pairing of the glove seems fitting. When my "Auntie M" passed, we were literally unpaired, our treasured dyad ruptured.

My sister has always staunchly insisted that she won't wear dead people's clothes. In my work on textiles, I've come to the conclusion that all clothes are the product of ghosted or dead bodies, which is precisely why I find them so compelling. As Karl Marx would have it, the commodity always obfuscates the touch of its producers. Our clothes, then, are never our own. As much as cloth is about belonging—about obtaining the proper fit—it engenders absence as well as presence, injury in addition to reparation.

I am left with one glove rather than two, a glove that now has very little "use value" without its other mate. My hope was that Mary's glove might be found when the snow finally defrosts beneath the warmth of an arriving spring. But maybe it's better that the lost glove remains lost. Both in scholarship and life, I've been invested in probing the gap between fabric and flesh, cloth and body, and I wonder what possibilities exist in this empty space. I'm sure "M" would have loved the story about her glove being left behind during my family's evacuation from a restaurant with nothing more than a clogged hood in their kitchen. I can hear her giggle. That makes me smile.

What this story reveals for me is how narratives congeal around the hybridization of subject and object. In reconsidering how I've shaped this personal narrative, I wonder in what ways I have mimicked myself to and against my analysis.

In one of my graduate seminars, we've been talking about "writerly" fidelity. The class discussed how we see this made legible in the mimetic relation between self and object of study. This "fidelity" or faithfulness to ideas might be said to surface in theoretical texts that introduce personal narratives where the individual voice "ruptures" more traditional, objective theorizations. And yet, I wonder, is any act of writing—or any mode of articulation—really intimate, with self and object thoroughly sutured? To write is to exteriorize; thoughts flow from the channels of the mind to the tips of the fingers, finally surfacing on paper or screen. We might say that the self is always "othered" in the very process of writing, that to write is to perform a splitting or severing of identity. So much of who we are is dependent upon mediation and the difficulties that ensue in these processes of translation.

And so, I rethink the way I tell this story of my aunt through her garment. The gloves mediate my own grief and stand in, if temporarily, for her absence. They bind aunt and niece across time and the chasms imposed by death. The story is one of recollection and recursivity, of returning to consider where the self lies in its disappearance, in memory, narrative, and the things we leave behind.

Residing in the Intersection

JODY: I, too, use fabric to trace an intersection—in a collection of cloth figures that both connect and distance. In her essay "Reviewing Eve," Nancy Miller describes an installation Eve Sedgwick created in the CUNY Grad Center English Dept. lounge. Sedgwick used cloth figures she had made—stuffed forms dressed in blue leggings and tunics, draped with woven cloth, hung from the ceiling—and distributed a screed she called "in the bardo," about the "between-state" that immediately follows death. In Tibetan, "bar" means in-between, "do" means suspended, thrown. Miller explicates this:

> the figures' strongest representational ties are to the disorienting and radically denuding bodily sense generated by medical imaging and illness itself, on the one hand; and on the other, to material urges to dress, ornament, to mend, to re-cover and heal....the wordless figures invited us to meditate on the process of coming to terms with the contours and accidents that shape any given life.[30]

I use this installation to evoke my sense of self, emerging from "the contours and accidents" that have shaped my life. I'm someone who tends to see and present myself as (relatively) "normal," "stable," a "coherent self." I speak from the vantage point of "outside disability," although also striving to be inside it, to better understand.

When I mark myself as "normal," I not-incidentally conjure you as with me in this, or not: as abnormal. As Ray McDermott and Hervé Varenne suggested some years ago, "no ability, no disability; no disability, no ability"; likewise, no "normal" without "abnormal."[31] When I claim "normal," I tap into the you waiting in the wings to be called forth as somehow, well, fucked up. More recently, Lennard Davis has argued that "all groups, based on physical traits or markings, are selected for disablement by a larger system of regulation and signification."[32] And what if your "trait or markings" are not perceptible, are mental or cognitive rather than physical, or physical

---

30. Nancy Miller, "Reviewing Eve," in *Regarding Sedgwick: Essays on Queer Culture and Critical Theory*, ed. Stephen Barber and David Clark (New York: Routledge, 2002), 222.

31. Ray McDermott and Hervé Varenne, "Culture as Disability," *Anthropology and Education Quarterly* 26 (1995): 323–48.

32. Davis, "The End of Identity Politics and the Beginning of Dismodernism," 275.

but not visibly marked; what if you are not externally recognizable?

I write this, knowing all the while that this is a painting over of cracks and crevices, some dark corners, limits, and scary places that I've visited not-so-willingly at particularly challenging times in my life, and some that I've not visited. At times, I've longed to go there, to these places, but also haven't wanted to be there; except maybe for brief spurts like under the influence of hallucinogens. So yes, I have always been both resistant and strongly drawn to darker, scarier, unknown, and unknowable places—in myself and in others—and these "places" are actually anywhere: to be found right beneath my feet, gazing down into the depth of grimy sparkle in a city sidewalk.

When I was coming up in the square-plotted walled-in suburb of my childhood, I was fascinated by and intensely drawn to the worlds of people then labeled "handicapped" and "mentally ill": read their stories voraciously; sought out these "others" in my work as a teenager with other teenagers then called "blind and multiply handicapped," and later with the heavily gated and sedated so-called "chronically mentally ill" at St. Elizabeth's, where I fantasized that I could take home (?!) an older woman with multiple diagnoses with whom I was—how can I say it but, in love.

But now I ask myself, how "outside" was this when this "otherness" lurked, yes, right in my own family—my grandfather and uncle suicides, my aunt and cousins profoundly depressed and diagnosed with "psychoses" of various kinds and taking (or not) various cocktails? And here's a wall: my own parents seeing and presenting themselves as "the stable ones," and my mom in a constant tension with my aunt over this intense splitting, even now with my aunt many years gone.

In his focus on disability as the physically marked—what artist Riva Lehrer describes as "the great billboard of bodily truth"[33]—Davis does not attend to those mentally "marked" by "accidents of brain chemistry," as my daughter recently termed her state of

33. Riva Lehrer, "Jarred: Self Portrait in Formaldehyde," talk presented at the Chicago Humanities Festival, November 11, 2014.

being. And if not accidental but plotted somehow, then where in my family album of mental markings are the genomes, and what does this signify?

Telling stories about race, Davis writes, "Eugenics told us one thing about race and genes, social construction told us quite another; but if race is not in the human genome, how then are we to make sense of "genetic markers for disability, defect, and disease?"[34] *If* difference is genetically marked, what then of the differences of mind, perception, interaction that characterize the (how many) mental differences detailed exhaustively in the DSM VI? And what difference does this make, or: what does the story of genetic marking do here? And to what work might it lead me?

Some years ago I had this dream: I was lying in a bunk bed next to my daughter. She must've been about sixteen years old. Someone else was in the bed with us too, a male, shadowy. I was just waking up, turning toward her when S opened her mouth and bared a set of large, sharp, and frightening teeth, animal teeth.

At that time S had been diagnosed (first by herself, then by a psychologist) and was dealing with OCD. Being her mom put me face to face, scarily right up close to this "other-ness": We are in our living room and she's entering a panic attack—obsessing on a girl in high school who said *something*, I don't remember what; she scissors off her new dreadlocks and then screams at her shorn head, frightening my son in the next room; yet another teacher is telling me how silent she is. Most unnervingly, we are travelling and she is convinced we're being followed, doesn't feel safe in our hotel room, or on the beach at our favorite pond, or really anywhere; we are at a profound home place for me—very beautiful, and so even more frightening. The darkness is in the beauty in a way that I had been inviting and fighting all my life.

In order to be S's mother, I need to find in me the capacity to face the parts of her—and myself—that are NOT "normal," "coherent," "stable." To acknowledge in myself the cracks between my aunt and

---

34. Davis, "The End of Identity Politics and the Beginning of Dismodernism," 266.

my mom, the gaping holes left by suicides, the internal emptiness of the "strange stranger," as eco-critic Timothy Morton describes the self.[35] The non-negotiable demand of this is the greatest gift anyone could have given me. A gift that rescues me from the seductiveness of the ordinary, opens me to the wildness often relegated to animals; that makes searingly evident how we are all implicated in the web of difference, of disability, each "role" dependent upon another.

The postmodern view of identity put forward by Stuart Hall[36] and others might suggest that the question of a link between my daughter's make-up and my own is differently relevant when we see it in the context of partiality and hybridity. Davis takes this notion further, arguing for a "dismodern subject…whose realization is not autonomy and independence but dependency and interdependence…all humans are seen as wounded…impairment is the rule and normalcy is the fantasy."[37] Access, then, might bear re-visioning: what to value, what to desire?

In describing a presentation featuring photographs of jarred fetuses as "specimens of disabled bodies," Riva Lehrer talks about a "narrative stripping": "biography is peeled away until nothing is left but naked diagnosis." A person with spina bifida, she has "no spina bifida elders, to show me how to live."[38]

Now recognized and diagnosed more widely, OCD does seem to run in my family, where many of the cousins deal with this mental "marking." My daughter is the elder, a position that has both challenged and strengthened her as she has become an advisor—on therapy, medication, and daily life. And I am also in this flux, my learning self colliding with her realities, the trash that taunts her on the streets, other material stuff that she interacts with daily—stuff that now enters my realities. And so we are all networked, though so little is understood about what it might mean to have this marking or that; still, the genetic story helps me here to know my humanness, my connections with what is visible to me and what I don't yet know.

I query, again, the construct of "accommodations." If "dis/ability"

---

35. Morton, "Practising Deconstruction in the Age of Ecological Emergency," 160–61.

36. Stuart Hall, "The Question of Cultural Identity," in *Modernity: An Introduction to Modern Studies*, ed. Stuart Hall, David Held, Don Hubert and Kenneth Thompson (Indianapolis: Wiley-Blackwell, 1996), 596–631.

37. Davis, "The End of Identity Politics and the Beginning of Dismodernism," 276.

38. Lehrer, "Jarred."

is indeed, as we have posited, a web with all of us implicated, then it seems problematic to conceptualize "accommodations" in terms that rely so strongly on a notion of "regular," what some people can do that becomes the standard against which "others" cannot.

Play theorist Stuart Brown asks when fidgety-ness became ADHD.[39] This is a schooled designation, too-often raced, classed, and gendered, too-frequently used to contain and isolate boys of color.

What if instead we looked to these children as leaders, who could show us the constrictions of the classroom, help us discover what's possible in their rough play? What could we learn about access that would meet Davis's "ethic of liberation" for all of us?

If on some level we are strangers, not only to each other but also to ourselves, and if at the same time we have a capacity to discover this, to become if only for a moment less estranged, it seems problematic that people with "disabilities" should be positioned to do this, to go deep, while others ride the "normal" curve. For instance, as I trace this "stranger-ness," this incoherence of self, back through my mom's family, up through my daughter, and into my own self, a different question emerges for me: whether and what I or any of us does with this potentiality. And if it were understood that this is the question and a possibility for all of us—if, for example, we were to recognize all that is going on in a space, say a classroom, that is *not* "readable" or even necessarily knowable by others or by oneself—our orientation to questions of "access" might also shift dramatically.

In her remembrance of Sedgwick, Nancy Miller writes,

> Opening the door to the past as the necessary preliminary to change is never easy, but here it's not the past tense of memory that hurts the most. [And then Eve herself:] "No, the harder part is telling it now; choosing now to thread the viscera of the labyrinth of
>
>> what I didn't know,
>> and when I didn't know it,
>> and what that felt like."

---

39. Stuart Brown, "Play, Spirit, and Character," *On Being with Krista Tippett*, June 19, 2014.

>...Eve explicates what love means to her: the connection of an intimacy without which "both your soul and your whole world might subsist forever in some desert-like state of ontological impoverishment."[40]

[40. Miller, "Reviewing Eve," 218–19.]

And so it is critical that when S bares her animal-teeth, I turn not away but toward her, grafting "abnormal" and "normal," living out relationality, reveling in the interdependence that Sedgwick calls love. Access—to one another and to ourselves—then becomes a process that we are always starting again and over, reassembling. The bed that my toothy daughter and I share (with a strange male) is a space of unease and promise, a space where we re-create access in our continual willingness to re-engage and re-enter—to teach and learn with each other.

Living out Relationality

KEVIN: Jody's description of "access as a process of reassembling" puts me in mind of the work of anthropologist Kathleen Stewart, who, in *Ordinary Affects*, attempts to capture the slow ooze, a "dragging undertow" of affective contemporary experience. Stewart borrows from Raymond Williams's formulation of "structures of feeling" to find forms of life woven in and through everyday moments. The ordinary has "the quality of a continual motion of relations, scenes, contingencies, and emergences," Stewart writes. Ordinary affects are "things that happen."[41]

To register affective "contact zones" for analysis, Stewart writes in the third person: "I call myself 'she' to mark the difference between this writerly identity and the kind of subject that arises as a daydream of simple presence."[42] In so doing, the researcher-subject is not so much in pursuit of anything more definitive than herself as a point of contact. She looks, waits, performs, imagines. Ultimately, she suggests what a scene might offer.

I experiment.

He experiments.

His family moved to Tokyo from New Jersey when he was five. One night, there was an earthquake. It was either the offshore Sanriku earthquake in December of 1994 or the Kobe earthquake of January 1995. With his family members, he took turns sitting in a recliner chair in their living room because the springs in the seat transferred the dull shaking they couldn't feel standing around. He remembers thinking that they should get under the tables like he practiced at school, but no one sensed the urgency like he did. He hadn't grasped yet that danger could have gradients. That's not what the drills at school were designed to convey, anyway.

Developmental psychologists say that a number of crucial things begin to happen between the ages of five and six for neurotypical children like this one. The child will learn to reason, follow rules,

---

41. Kathleen Stewart, *Ordinary Affects* (Durham: Duke University Press, 2007), 2.

42. Stewart, *Ordinary Affects*, 5.

and be fair. He will begin to understand space and time, color, sorting, and organization. He will be able to tell a story. He may begin to have organized, continuous memories. But all that we do not know: How does something like an earthquake *shake up* what the child knows? What do the chancy adventures in a foreign city do to who he later became?

His mother was reading him a bedtime story on the couch. She had just eaten a banana. With a flare of whimsy that was impressive for the working mother wrangling two young kids in a foreign city, she asked how fast he could run to the trashcan and back before she started the story. He made it to the kitchen. He remembers turning the corner on his way back. And then he remembers sitting on the counter some moments later with blood coming down his face.

He had tripped somewhere down the final stretch. His big toe might have snagged on the carpet and his face went crashing into the corner of the coffee table. His eyebrow had split open. Later he was told that if he had tripped on a piece of the carpet inches away, it would have been his eye itself, not the brow.

The self unstable. More disabled.

His mom likes to tell the story of him on the way to the emergency room. He asked whether he looked like a football player. He turned to his mom with cautious glee and asked, "Isn't this a little exciting?"

There was a decision to be made about the cut. The doctors could stitch it up and he would lose most of the eyebrow, or they could put what's called "butterfly bandage" over it, which is a small adhesive strip that stretches over a thin laceration to hold it together. Stitches would ensure a clean and fast healing process but with more scarring. A butterfly bandage would mean less scarring, but also less certainty that he wouldn't accidentally open the wound again, which was already on a fairly active part of the face. His mom wanted him to have an eyebrow. He got the butterfly bandage.

Twenty years later as he reads and writes, he rubs his fingers over his scarred eyebrow, where there is a thin line of hair missing. This is not a conscious habit, just a repetitive motion while he's thinking. But when he remembers the scar he pauses to think how it must look: twenty years later and he's still feeling to see if it's healed.

Who is the child with a butterfly bandage? This question is less important than the ordinary affects this scene tells of. Disability is an apparitional affect outside of its identity formation. That is, we know something about disability even when it is not an identity we inhabit. Disability Studies has long insisted on the universality of "temporary able-bodiedness." In recent years, disability scholars, dissatisfied with being treated as the youngest kid on the identity politics block, have made the case that disability urges us to reconsider all identity formations as more mutable than we allow. In "The End of Identity Politics," for example, Lennard Davis writes, "What we are discussing is the instability of the category of disability as a subset of the instability of identity in a postmodern era." If identity politics rely on a legible distinction between who does and does not occupy certain subjectivities, disability is that which cannot be made to function in a system of exclusion. "Rather than ignore the unstable nature of disability," Davis continues, "rather than try to fix it, we should amplify that quality."[43] A "dismodernist" identity politics, beyond a postmodern one.

43. Davis, "The End of Identity Politics and the Beginning of Dismodernism," 26.

Lingering in the fracture, the broken.

Imagining a crip identification, despite the fear that privilege will flood a minority category and displace our sensitivity to differentially distributed power: Can the child with the butterfly bandage be said to have registered a crip moment?

Robert McRuer inaugurated what he calls "crip theory" by leveling unlikely identifications at the heart of how an orientation to disability might be a necessary strategy to resist neoliberalism's mishandling of marginalized subjects. After describing the ordinary affects of his partner, he asks readers to imagine their crip identification:

> Crip theory might function as a body of thought, or as thought about bodies, that allows for assertions like the following: if it's not even conceivable for you to identify as or with Brazilian, gay, immigrant workers with multiple sclerosis, then you're not yet attending to how bodies and spaces are being materialized in the cultures of upward redistribution we currently inhabit.[44]

44. McRuer, *Crip Theory*, 76.

To be injured or to be diseased is not to be disabled. But it does mean that one must reckon with how disability makes a productive problem for ideologies of ability that make able-bodiedness seem invisible, natural, or normal. One experiences the stakes of disability whether or not one *is* disabled. Crip moments abound, exposing able-bodiedness as fragile, tentative, and ultimately impossible.

The butterfly bandage is an epistemological as well as experiential frame. The butterfly suture incorporates repair and precarity into dynamic balance. Stitches provide certainty that a wound won't open, but only by making more incisions. The butterfly suture never promises certainty that the wound won't open again, but it's not as if healing is less important. The butterfly bandage keeps things delicate. The butterfly itself suggests a certain gentleness and sensitivity. It encourages you to check your wound often, to make sure things are progressing okay.

As Bruno Latour says, critique as the humanistic *modus operandi* has "run out of steam,"[45] because its openings require too many punctures. Strong interventions have tradeoffs. The repair one enacts when announcing that "excluded here is any account of X" is fleeting and unsustainable. What the critical impulse needs is some attunement to the new experience of a laceration, a way of letting the body (of thought) heal into its new state.

45. Bruno Latour, "Why Has Critique Run Out of Steam? From Matters of Fact to Matters of Concern," *Critical Inquiry* 30, no. 2 (Winter 2004): 225–48.

Attunements to New Lacerations

ANNE: When we present an early version of this chapter at the 2014 conference of the Society for Disability Studies, Riva Lehrer asks why we begin our challenge to access in "ambivalence, rather from the space that is implacable." In giving our attention to the ambivalent interfaces of bodies and environment, she queries, are we refusing to acknowledge the reality of impairments that cannot be accommodated?

We know that many impairments cannot be accommodated. Can we enlarge our language and that of Disability Studies to accommodate this? I am re-tracing these questions, as my husband Jeff and I move slowly across a boardwalk, snaking through a bog in Canaan Valley, West Virginia. It is a rainy afternoon in August, and the walkway is slick. We know this, and are taking it gingerly, when, on an incline, I start to slip…and can't stop. Seen from outside, the scene must be hilarious: I slide, and slowly turn, before landing (surely with a plop!) on my back, in the bog. Experienced from the inside, though, there is no room for laughter. As I slide, inexorably, and turn, inflexibly, I feel a pain—excruciating, in my right knee. When I try to get up, it's totally non-negotiable: I cannot put any weight on my leg. And there it is, in a moment: the implacable.

Implacable, too, are my needs over the next few weeks, as I am displaced from agile mind to immobile body, as I hobble, and ice, and ask for assistance from Jeff who is, in turn, (un)fairly implacable in his judgment of what needs I (think I) have, what needs he thinks need meeting. We negotiate, or I do without, when he will not accommodate.

That fall, I return to Bryn Mawr, moving with less pain, although still using a cane—and encounter an agitated warning from our new access coordinator: all needs must be met. Or else. In a steadily rising tone, she writes me about the college's legal obligations to a student who has told us of her needs too late for us to accommodate them all:

> Part of the responsibility for this is [the student's], however, legally the college would be found at fault, should she be so unhappy and decide to pursue it legally….[that the student] did not contact me until very late…in no way gives the college "wiggle room"; in the eyes of the Office of Civil Rights and the Department of Justice, colleges must be ready, yesterday, to have all materials ready for students who need accommodations …. There is to be no lag time or wait time for the student in terms of receiving materials in the appropriate format.[46]

46. E-mail message to author, September 5, 2014.

And yet, it turns out, there is nothing implacable there. Getting to know the student, introducing her to the administrator who is scanning our documents, we together work our way through the syllabus, identify what needs to be re-scanned to be made audible, agree to do so on a workable timetable.

A month after the administrator, my student, and I reach accommodation, Riva arrives on campus, to serve as the creative consultant for a cluster of courses, a 360° I am co-teaching on "Identity Matters."[47] When Riva first comes to my class, she asks us all to begin to imagine—and then to draw—the "invisible body of desire": what we would look like, if we were completely unbound by any restrictions? What could we do as an entity, if all constraints—gravity, time, whatever holds us back from being whatever we might be *(everything implacable?)*—were lifted?

To get to this place, she asks us first to think to our last vacation, our last really enjoyable time—

I was on vacation when I slipped and tore that ligament— and then back to a longer vacation, a time freed from responsibility and obligation, centered around what we always wanted to do—and then even further back, to the seventh grade, when we were beginning to dream about what we wanted to be. How were these states connected? Where did they make a "turn"? When did our desires change? What might have happened in our lives, if we had gotten to do completely what we wanted to do when we were twelve?

All constraints lifted, all choices totally open: what powers do we have? What are our minds and hearts good at doing? Peeling back from the everyday to much older motives: what moves us now at the essential level? "Build a body that lets you be that entity," Riva says (as she has done, in a self-portrait called "At 54").

Her invitation is a way to enter students' psychic spaces, to seek, under their own direction, what they most long for—in the language of crip ecology—"to open up desire for what disability disrupts."[48]

And so it is really Riva who articulates, first at the conference, then in my class, the tension that animates this chapter: the stretch between what is implacable, cannot be negotiated, and what is

47. See Chapter 8, "Slipping."

48. Elizabeth Chandler, "Cripping Community: New Meanings," *No More Pot Lucks*, September 5, 2013.

Riva Lehr, *At 54*. Acrylic and collage on paper, (2013). Copyright Riva Lehr. Image courtesy of artist.

desired: flexible minds, bodies, social spaces. Mobile. Unbound. Pliable. Placable. Changing the circumstances in which the self finds herself. Mediating between what is necessary and what is impossible, what is wanted and what is do-able. In flesh and feeling, both constrained and reaching.

The swing between implacability and desire, between what cannot be negotiated and what can be dreamed, is ever on-going, always inviting renovation. I learn these lessons—the need to attend, the difficulty of doing so, the im/possibilities of responding appropriately, the invention of new possibilities—again and again throughout the following semester, as Riva and I co-teach "Identity Matters" with Kristin Lindgren, who directs Haverford College's Writing Center, and Sarah Bressi, of Bryn Mawr's Graduate School of Social Work and Social Research. Partly because of our topic, partly because of the structure of profound engagement that a 360° entails, partly because of the particular mix of individuals who gather to share this project, the work of this cluster makes transparent the on-going, back-and-forth, ever-unsettling and unsettled process of access and accommodation in teaching and learning. We desire. Adjust. Long for something more or else. Recalibrate. Thread in and out of our shifting environment.

For the twelve students enrolled in this particular group of courses, who represent a variety of classes, races, genders, and dis/abilities, the focus on "identity matters" makes this project intensely personal from the get-go. Fed from multiple directions —the students' own investments, and ours (Riva's creative exercises, Kristin's course on disability, Sara's on aging, mine on feminism)— we give extended attention to the interpersonal dynamics of accessibility and accommodation, hold repeated discussions about how we speak with one another, how we listen to what was said, how we might grant respect to every class member. Wishing. Stumbling. Wanting. Exhausting. Aspiring. Up and through the semester's end: on-going negotiating of constraints and longings. Our group effort constitutes another instantiation of "crip ecology," shifting our environment as it shapes and shifts us.

Our classroom is filled with desires—all compelling, all legitimate—and incapable of being fulfilled in the same place at the same time. "Accommodation" is an "assembling" and re-assembling that never settles, is never fully accommodated.

Throughout this essay, we move from speaking of "access," which signifies a capacious, radical vision of the equal participation in society of persons with disabilities; to describing "accommodation," which signals more narrow, specific strategies (such as extra time for testing, or large print texts). We also evoke the concept of "universal design," which, as Jay Dolmage observes, "often usefully syncs with" accommodation, but also critiques that model with a more profound sense of "the actual, tricky, ongoing negotiations of classroom practice," a recognition that there will never be a "grand solution."[49]

Our own relationship to each of these orientations also shifts from that of critique to syncopation and back again. For instance, we accept Jay's description of universal design for learning as offering "places to *start* thinking, doing, acting and moving," always aware that any teaching strategy that offers a "good solution in the classroom" will also inevitably create "conflicts of access."[50]

My students' postings form a collage of such conflicts: different, often competing, capacities and checks, needs and wants.

> HUMMINGBIRD: I appreciated the energy our classroom discussion had today. I appreciate the passion, openness, and sincerity many of us brought to the classroom space. I also noticed some of us did not have the space to bring that passion, openness, and sincerity. There were interruptions, raised voices, and comments over each other. Can we work to maintain that passion and energy, and to also incorporate pauses in between our voices? Can we work on scanning the room and noticing when our peers are making an effort to interject but not finding a way? Can we try to be more aware of each other? Allow each other to finish

49. Dolmage, "Universal Design."

50. Dolmage, "Universal Design."

our thoughts before jumping on? Checking in with our peers to make sure we haven't skipped over a voice?[51]

Another student, who is a McBride (one of a cohort of women over the age of 24, who did not complete college immediately after high school), reports on the "unexpected invisibility of being a McBride":

> KHINCHEY: my insecurities as an academic are reinforced through the narrative that I 'don't belong' in the Bryn Mawr community with my non-normative timeline and my inability to succeed as a student in my first go at college.[52]

Realizing that such anxieties frequently lead her to bring her personal experience into class discussion—and that these are significant expressions of her longing to belong—she challenges Hummingbird for using the privilege of upper-class politeness to silence her, refusing her the right to speak in her accustomed mode.

Other students, largely silent to this point, also begin to write about their experiences of the in/accessible:

> I too share a lot of these same feelings. I suffer from anxiety and I don't feel comfortable always saying that out loud. My anxiety has shaped me into someone who tends to be a listener within the classroom…and a talkative person outside of the classroom. I really appreciated the conversation we had today and although I don't believe we should have a fully structured course that includes hand raising or using cards, I still would appreciate more space to be who I am. [A classmate] brought up the idea of not wanting to have to shrink within the classroom and while I do agree with that, I am also grappling with the idea that the classroom only has so much space (our space being our time). One person taking up a lot of space causes another to take up less. I know that I don't speak up that much within the class and it has always been a struggle for me. I am a victim of emotional abuse which included a lot yelling and chastizing that silenced me as a child.[53]

The student consultant we've engaged through Bryn Mawr's Teaching and Learning Institute[54] reports that one-or-some students

---

51. Hummingbird, "A Plea for Space," October 2, 2014 (5:27 p.m.).

52. khinchey, "On Still Not Having All the Answers," December 18, 2014 (11:23 p.m.).

53. "Thoughts about our talk and invisible diablities," October 8, 2014 (1:35 a.m.).

54. "Teaching and Learning Institute at Bryn Mawr and Haverford Colleges."

think that I should intervene more in class, to keep people from getting cut off, and/or direct the discussion more. Knowing we disagree on what "respect" sounds like, and also that different ones of us prefer different pacings, I propose that we share this labor: asking for some other voices in the conversation, being more aware of what's going on, not so caught up in what we want to say that we don't look around, pay attention to others' body language, making sure—especially if we've already spoken—that others aren't wanting to speak before we speak again; try a breath in between. These gestures—pushing ourselves to speak if we haven't, pushing ourselves to be still if we have already talked in any given session—are all forms of accommodation, ways in which we and our environment continue to respond to one another.

We expend much effort before recognizing the essential incompletability of this project. We can't achieve the total access we desire—*and* we can't stop trying to.

At semester's end, Hummingbird testifies that her contributions in class aren't taken up in the way she expects. Her story is a tangle of not being able to understand, and of not being understandable, of her "words taking on meanings" she doesn't intend. All of this in the context of love—of a deep, familial longing for connection:

> HUMMINGBIRD: Not too long after we discussed deafness and Deaf culture in Kristin's class, I dreamt that I had become entirely deaf. Friends and family members were speaking to me, but I couldn't understand what they were saying. In the dream, this deafness had occurred months before and I'd been taking a sign-language class in response. But when I tried to communicate with my family and friends with my elementary level sign language, I couldn't fully express my feelings. When I spoke aloud, they told me I sounded entirely different and couldn't understand me. I could think clearly what I wanted to express, but I had no way of expressing it. I felt entirely cut-off from the people I loved.[55]

55. Hummingbird, "Communication?: a Self-Reflection," December 18, 2014 (8:54 p.m.).

In early November, we are trained into a more disciplined practice of speaking and listening. We attend a public performance of "Two Women Talking," by Bryn Mawr alum Monsoon Bissell and her good friend Benaifer Bhadha; then an all-day workshop, just for our group, on their "narrativ" method. Learning how to implement careful listening: to clear our minds of obstacles that might prevent us from being fully present and receptive, as we prepare "listening bowls" to catch one another's stories. A student explains the first step: "Imagine that the words coming out of your mouth are filling a bowl. In order for your words to be received well you must 'clear your bowl.' Simply name all the things that may hinder you from listening." Another student elaborates: "Take a moment and think about…the space you offer up when you agree to listen to someone. We all have a variety of bowls (shallow, deep, tall, wide), and we are offering up our biggest bowl when we are most ready to listen."[56] During the weeks after, we are able to put such exercises to repeated good use in class. I am particularly heartened when some students who have been in conflict organize their own "listening conversations," and report back that they've learned to "widen and deepen" their bowls.

And yet, as the semester draws to a close, two other students, who are very angry with one another, are telling the same story: each posts something on-line that gets no response, and so feels invisible, not listened to. Two others tell counter-stories: they read their classmates' posts, have no words to respond. I observe that we all have been, and have had, sustained silent readers throughout the semester. Sometimes we don't realize this: we *are* being seen, listened to.

When we gather for our last class, I invite the students into a closing ceremony, designed by Alice Lesnick, which figures this understanding. Calling attention to the beautiful bowl I have set in the center of our circle, "fragile but capable of holding whatever we put in it," I instruct the students to place in the vessel something they want to leave there; then, on a second round, to demonstrate

56. Final Booklet, December 9, 2015.

and articulate what they are carrying out. To do this in an embodied way, considering the shape and weight of these things....

I say, drawing on a powerful image offered by one student, that the bowl "has been here all along, and it isn't yet filled." I see it holding the fear of another student that our upcoming public listening conversation "isn't focused where our priorities should be, on police brutality," the sense yet another has of "being suffocated by too much information," the apology of a fourth for a lack of presence, the awareness of a fifth of "our continued shared martyrdom," even a sixth student's "feeling bad that they're not feeling bad."

The "listening bowl" marks the fullness of possibility, without insisting on its full realization (which probably, anyway, can't be found in words...). Learning what is wanted is a process. The bowl is both a metaphoric way for each of us to attend to what one another has to say, and—without choosing one mode of access over another, or ever reaching full accommodation—it figures a means of experiencing the material classroom, intermittently, as an "imagined community."[57]

This, again, is ecology "cripped," unsettling what we think we know in favor of interruption and disturbance, unveiling new imaginings that unfold in how we live our lives, enact our selves, interact with all that surrounds and moves through us.

There are, to be sure, cracks in this bowl. But there's a sufficiency here, too—and a space to hold it all. Longings deeply linked with the capacity to imagine otherwise. Filled with failure that is also, always, a mark of desire. A "holding environment"[58]—not as permanent, but as a space of learning, to return to as needed.

57. Benedict Anderson, *Imagined Communities: Reflections on the Origin and Spread of Nationalism*, rev. ed. (Brooklyn: Verso, 2006).

58. Cf. D.W. Winnicott, *Maturational Processes and the Facilitating Environment: Studies in the Theory of Emotional Development* (1957–1963; rpt. London: Karnac Books, 1996).

Sufficiency—and a Space to Hold It All

CLARE, KEVIN, JODY, ANNE: In telling these linked stories, we challenge (at least) four suppositions:

1. of a stable self (one that knows itself, is secure in that knowledge, and able to make it transparently known to others);
2. of family members (who they are, what they need, what they can make available for the shared project of building a life together);
3. of students (who they are, what they need, what they can make available for the project of shared learning); and
4. of what accommodations we require (can request not only of our institutions, but also of one another, in class and out) and be satisfied with what emerges therefrom.

We draw, throughout, on the insights of Disability Studies, on the

Mike McGuire, *Green Cherry Tree at Georgetown University, Washington, DC* (2017). CC-BY https://flic.kr/p/To5RAG.

ways in which crip ecologists, in particular, speak from-and-to the cracks, drawing out wanted and unwanted, known and unknowable intimacies with ourselves and our environments, destabilizing—and so recognizing as unending—the process of accommodating.

In bringing together Disability Studies and various related "ecological imaginings," we start not with identity but rather the spaces between, underneath, and outside. The human body and mind do not end at the fleshly contours surrounding the self; no being is hermetically detached from the physical world. As Stacey Alaimo explains,

> humans are the very stuff of the material, emergent world…profoundly…transformed by the recognition that the very substance of the self is interconnected with vast biological, economic and industrial systems that can never be entirely mapped or understood…environmental ethics…denies to the "human" the sense of separation from the interconnected, mutually constitutive actions of material reality…what is supposed to be outside the delineation of the human is always already inside.[59]

These "mutually constitutive" interconnections are not just about frustration and deprivation, but also a space of promise and possibility: forever, and exasperatingly, something to be desired.

Starting with the disabled "subject," the movement for Disability Rights created a visible community to advocate for much needed rights. Activist efforts to pass the Americans with Disabilities Act in 1990 worked in tandem with The Disability Studies bibliography published in *Radical Teacher* in 1995,[60] which many cite as a crucial moment in conceiving of the field's coherence, and which was chock full of sociological titles. In both theory and action, disability was re-defined from an individuated, shame-inducing experience to a socially-maintained structure built around able-bodiedness. At that point, in both academic and activist sites, "social" was a crucial word in defining what "accessible" meant. By naming and holding stable what was meant by "social," Disability Studies conceived of "access" as a goal.

59. Stacy Alaimo, *Bodily Natures: Science, Environment, and the Material Self* (Bloomington: Indiana University Press, 2010), 20, 23–25.

60. Simi Linton, Susan Mello and John O'Neill, "Disability Studies: Expanding the Parameters of Diversity," *Radical Teacher* 47 (Fall 1995): 4–10.

But conceptualizing disability as bounded, its inherent fluidity circumscribed, forecloses the myriad ways in which individuals thread in and out of disabled states, based on various contexts, environmental presences, networks of care. Following these connections, we now reorient ourselves to less bounded, ever-shifting forms of relationality.

In *Reassembling the Social*, Bruno Latour, long known for his foundational work in science studies, charges that sociologists have, for far too long, been using the term "social" to signify a stable set of affairs: something too static, too material, too cordoned-off from other domains of interaction for it to be useful in answering questions about the actual social world. For Latour, the social is momentary, a fleeting collection of agencies, which can be only glimpsed according to a Heisenberg-like principle that figures various elements as rapidly changing assemblages.[61]

What Latour does with the word "social" is similar to what Disability Studies is now doing with the word "accessible." Just as Latour argues that sociologists made the "social" too sealed-tight to be useful, Disability Studies is recognizing the limitations of making accessibility too tensely committed to sanctioned forms of accommodation. If accessibility, like sociality, can only be caught in snatches when an assemblage briefly crystallizes for our observation, then accommodations that can only be agreed-upon before a particular meeting of body-minds are destined to be limited.

Latour reassembles the social by introducing key uncertainties: he advocates viewing objects as agentic, understanding group formation as more important than the group itself, and foregrounding the risk of failure in writing up our accounts. We are here modeling a similar form of access that is much more commodious, if also precarious: understood not as an analytic set off from other features of a setting, but as the way body-minds relate to each other. We also appropriate Latour's insistence that failure is an important—*and not unwanted*—experience, both of doing social research and engaging in social action.

61. Bruno Latour, *Reassembling the Social: An Introduction to Actor-Network Theory* (New York: Oxford University Press, 2005).

In our own experiments with access configurations in various classes and presentations, the "excess-ability" we try out is only intermittently successful. Clare and Anne pull away from the crowd surrounding Christine Sun Kim's experiments in making sound textural and visible. Kevin and Clare bring varieties of "crip time" to Critical Feminist Studies. During our conference presentation, Jody wonders how 30-some different body-minds are taking in—or not—the words and presences of the four of us on video, in the flesh, in the clicking of our knitting needles. More extensively throughout the Identity Matters 360°, Anne's students resolve such trade-offs between competing needs for accommodations *through* failure, not in spite of it. Overlaps and mutual exclusions lead us, again and again, to reconfigure access, as im/possibilities repeatedly present themselves.

We are not framing this as an intervention into such debates, because—as Latour would tell us—reaching to these stark configurations as though radical intellectual breaks will save us is precisely the problem. Our attention here, as elsewhere throughout this book, is on the unlimited fecundity and diversity of the world—which, in the particular context of accommodation, means two things. One: acknowledging the limitlessness of diversity means recognizing its inevitable corollary, that there will always be particular limitations in access. Two: given this infinite capacity, we can also rely on that which we do not know, on the endless supply of the surprising, which lies hidden in the inexhaustible interconnections of the world, as well as in the complexities of others' unconscious, and in our own. What we may think of as "implacable" can shift—but we have to experiment and practice to make this happen.

Rosemarie Garland-Thomson's reflections on "how the particularities of embodiment interact with the environment in its broadest sense" have been helpful to us here: her focus "on the disjunctures that occur in the interactive dynamism of becoming," on "the relational and contingent quality of misfitting," bring to attention the endless range of "innovative perspectives and skills" that are available for "adapting to changing and challenging environments."[62]

Which brings, in turn, new risks, dangers…

This book as primer.

And crip ecology as the ever-moving ground on which it rests:

> our human future may depend on coming to grips with "crip ecology" in two senses. In one sense…life appears mutative, not as orderly as our gardenlike, bucolic picture of nature would have us imagine. In another sense…any number of us may live with what we today call disabilities. Climate change and epigenetic mutation…circulate through generations of human flesh. Ecology names an integrated network of humans-in-the-land… whatever we've attempted to throw 'away' come back through the bio-organic constitution of human flesh.[63]

And so, we here "bear witness" to such porosity, to what exceeds clear "identification": "alterity," "the remainder, the different, the heterogeneous."[64] Alterity is yet another formulation of what we worry about missing in a stable notion of "access." Riva invites students to imagine the "invisible body of desire," unbound by any restrictions. Hummingbird dreams that she is deaf. Anne slips, in a moment, from able to disabled. Her class slips, also momentarily, into hilarious, shared intersection and celebration:

> On Halloween, each of the students comes to my class dressed as another. When I walk in, to peals of laughter, they ask if I can identify their costumes. I realize that they've been paying much closer attention than I have to how each of them performs and presents self. What an appropriate ritual for a cluster of courses focused on "Identity Matters"! How comfortable they seem embodying each other:
>
> One making another feel seen, understood, and celebrated, yet another understanding the 'badass' self of a classmate, another saying that as a peer she could run and jump…and just so many ways in which they understand and respect one another.
>
> I feel as though I am filming moments of desire, like those Riva

---

62. Garland-Thompson, "Misfits," 594, 600, 604.

63. Miguel A. De la Torre, *Introducing Liberative Theologies* (Maryknoll: Orbis Books, 2015).

64. Levi R. Bryant, "Adorno, Representation, and Differential Ontology," *Larval Subjects*, June 13, 2011.

evoked in her first assignment: all the students are moving beyond their own skins, briefly occupying other selves, overcoming the boundaries that separate them, crossing what has kept them apart. It's a wonderful, joyful performance, one that's impossible to sustain. The concept and material of "identity" slip, the students' enactments of each other passing as they are happening. Limits reassert.

And yet.
There are multiple stories in that room.

> HUMMINGBIRD: I had such a different experience of this day—one of deep discomfort and fear…seeing myself reflected by another…was really disconcerting, and brought me back to quite a painful moment. In my senior year of high school, I had an English teacher who asked us…to respond to a question about our reading…as another member of the class. My peers almost unanimously spoke as one of two people in the class; [one was] me. I was passionate about my class and the topics, had come to a theory about the circularity of writing, shared it in different ways…I was easy to categorize, so I was easy to play in the classroom. The experience of seeing myself in this narrow way hurt. It was a moment of "Is that what they really think of me?" that I didn't have any understanding or view of before. Perhaps, also, it was disconcerting because as someone who has always been deeply self-reflective, my peers' analysis of me showed that I was missing a great deal of self-awareness. I learned that self-reflection is really not the same thing as self-awareness.
>
> So entering the 360° classroom and knowing someone would be "playing" me again was terrifying, because I imagined it would be like this…. I underestimated the closeness of the way we interacted with each other. But…I was also very aware that I'd actively separated myself from most of my 360° classmates…I needed distance from that environment, so I didn't have close social relationships with most of my peers, and I knew that meant their understanding of me would be confined to how I interact in the classroom and on Serendip…my (and most people's) classroom identity is not a whole understanding of my self, and I've spent my entire life working to keep it that way (consciously and unconsciously)…[65]

65. Hummingbird, E-mail message to author, June 8, 2016.

Negotiating this continual tension, between what is wanted and what is possible, between self and imagined other, between self-as-known to oneself, and self-as-seen-by others...

> HUMMINGBIRD: My fear is in that seemingly un-bridgeable gully between how I see myself and how others see me. But perhaps even more deeply, my fear is that the how-others-see-me perspective is the real version of me, and so, somehow, what is outside of my self is creating my self—and I've lost control.[66]

66. Hummingbird, E-mail.

To see space as relational, co-created among humans, the material configurations in which we find ourselves, and the multiple accommodations we use to navigate that world, is to imagine these sites always in motion. The intersecting locations we here interrogate—Clare's clothing, Jody's dreams, Kevin's butterfly bandage, the classroom and on-line arrangements that make Anne's students feel that they cannot speak and are not heard—are always unstable. And creative.

This matters for how we teach and learn, for how the multiplicity of differences bound together in any given point creates both abundance and constraint, for how participants are always desiring, accommodating, redrawing our and others' understandings and boundaries.

The concept of a stable self poses a real problem in the context of education, where forced content, testing regimes, and tightly scripted classrooms assume a transparency, and an equivalence, between output and uptake. We have come to understand this as a matter of access. Designing the "perfect" course, one that tries to accord with the principles of universal design, fails to acknowledge that each self is unstable, evolving, always exceeding its description. Acknowledging that none of us knows entirely what we need, as we gather for classes and conferences that are themselves contingent and porous, reminds us that there will always be remainders, those for whom even universal design fails to provide access. How better to shape these spaces, which we now understand as part of larger ecosystems characterized by an unlimited fecundity and diversity, which do not submit to the limitations of injunction, testing, command, or control?

In these circumstances, pedagogy becomes a capacious term that invites simultaneous authority and surrender. As teachers and facilitators, we bring to bear our particular kinds of knowledge while recognizing its incompleteness, the inevitability of multiple other perspectives, values, constraints, and desires in the room. We teach out of a vital responsiveness to a continually evolving environment in which competing needs fall into place, lose, gain, juxtapose.

EPILOGUE
UNEXPECTED RULES

A bird sanctuary,
guerilla cell,
resistance group.

An ecotone,
on the border,
high density,
high diversity.

A testing ground:
random discoveries,
edge effects.

A wildscape, ruin,
liminal space,
boxed in-but-not enclosable,
ripe for breaking through.

In restraint,
bursting out,
faithless.

Neither this nor that but
piercing,
intense,
unpredictable.

BIBLIOGRAPHY

a paper that does not have references is like a child without an escort walking in the night in a big city he does not know: isolated, lost, anything may happen to it.

—Bruno Latour

"$1 Million Grant Awarded from Andrew W. Mellon Foundation for New Justice-in-Education Initiative." The Heyman Center for the Humanities at Columbia University. May 12, 2015. http://heymancenter.org/public-humanities-initiative/phi-news/1-million-grant-awarded-from-andrew-w-mellon-foundation-for-new-justice-in/.

"360° Course Clusters." Bryn Mawr College. 2016. https://www.brynmawr.edu/academics/special-academic-programs/360.

"A Brief History of Bryn Mawr College." 2016. https://www.brynmawr.edu/about/history.

———. "Villager Portrait," December 14, 2014 (11:25 p.m.). https://serendipstudio.org/oneworld/identity-matters-being-belonging-becoming/villager-portrait-dd.

———. "Drawing," December 14, 2014 (11:26 p.m.). https://serendipstudio.org/oneworld/identity-matters-being-belonging-becoming/dds-drawing.

abradycole. "Zine Page," December 18, 2014 (10:23 p.m.). https://serendipstudio.org/oneworld/identity-matters-being-belonging-becoming/zine-page-camphill-village

"Accomplice." On-Line Etymological Dictionary. http://www.etymonline.com/index.php?term=accomplice.

"Accomplices Not Allies: Abolishing the Ally Industrial Complex." Indigenous Action Media. May 4, 2014. http://www.indigenousaction.org/accomplices-not-allies-abolishing-the-ally-industrial-complex/.

"Active Minds: Changing the Conversation about Mental Health." http://www.activeminds.org/.

Ackerman, Diane. "Chapter One." *Deep Play.* New York: Random House, 1999. http://www.nytimes.com/books/first/a/ackerman-play.html.

Adorno, Theodor. *Negative Dialectics.* Second Edition. London: Bloomsbury Academic, 1981.

Agatha Basia. "Decided. Dreams Collection." December 17, 2013 (8:57 p.m.). http://serendipstudio.org/exchange/eval/decided-dreams-collection.

———. "Spectacle." September 16, 2013 (12:13 a.m.). http://serendipstudio.org/exchange/play-city-2013/agatha-basia/spectacle.

Ahmed, Sara. *On Being Included: Racism and Diversity in Institutional Life.* Durham: Duke University Press, 2012.

Alaimo, Stacy. *Bodily Natures: Science, Environment, and the Material Self.* Bloomington: Indiana University Press, 2010.

alesnick. "play/ground." May 6, 2013 (5:56 a.m.). http://serendipstudio.org/exchange/courses/esem/playcity/f13/planning#comment-141467.

———. "Who Is the We?" May 10, 2013 (10:50 a.m.). http://serendipstudio.org/exchange/courses/esem/playcity/f13/planning#comment-141501.

Allen, Paula Gunn. "Kochinnenako in Academe: Three Approaches to Interpreting a Keres Indian Tale." In *The Sacred Hoop: Recovering the Feminine in American Indian Traditions*, 222–44. Boston: Beacon Press, 1986.

"Allover Painting." Museum of Modern Art. https://www.moma.org/cef/abex/html/know_more9.html.

Anderson, Benedict. *Imagined Communities: Reflections on the Origin and Spread of Nationalism*, Revised Edition. Brooklyn: Verso, 2006.

Anderson, Nick. "Feds Announce New Experiment: Pell Grants for Prisoners." *Washington Post.* July 31, 2015. http://www.washingtonpost.com/news/grade-point/wp/2015/07/31/feds-announce-new-experiment-pell-grants-for-prisoners/.

anneliese, "The Slippery Brain Sodality." June 25, 2009–November 8, 2011. http://serendipstudio.org/exchange/node/4493.

Anyon, Jean. "Social Class and the Hidden Curriculum of Work."

Journal of Education 162, no. 1 (Fall 1980): 67–92. doi: 10.1177/002205748016200106

Arao, Brian and Kristi Clemens. "From Safe Spaces to Brave Spaces: A New Way to Frame Dialogue Around Diversity and Social Justice." In *The Art of Effective Facilitation: Reflections from Social Justice Educators*. Edited by Lisa M. Landreman. Sterling, VA: Stylus Publishing, 2013. https://sty.presswarehouse.com/sites/stylus/resrcs/chapters/1579229743_otherchap.pdf.

Armstrong, Paul B. "The Politics of Play: The Social Implications of Iser's Aesthetic Theory." *New Literary History* 31 (2000): 211–23. http://www.jstor.org/stable/20057594.

"Arts of Resistance." 360° Cluster, Bryn Mawr College, Fall 2015. https://serendipstudio.org/oneworld/arts-resistance/arts-resistance-cluster.

"Aryan Nations." Southern Poverty Law Center. 2015. http://www.splcenter.org/get-informed/intelligence-files/groups/aryan.

Asturias, Miguel Angel. *The Mirror of Lida Sal: Tales Based on Mayan Myths and Guatemalan Legends*. Chicago: Latin American Literary Review Press, 1997.

"Assessing Assessment." (2011–2012). http://serendipstudio.org/exchange/assessment/.

Back, Les. "Haunted Futures: A Response to Avery Gordon." *Borderlands* 10, no. 2 (2011): 1–9.

Baldwin, James. "A Talk to Teachers." 1963. Reprinted in *The Price of the Ticket, Collected Non-Fiction 1948–1985*, 325-32. New York: Saint Martin's Press, 1985. http://richgibson.com/talktoteachers.htm.

Bannan, Pete. "All Black Lives Matter 'Die In' Held in Bryn Mawr During Evening Rush Hour." *Main Line Media News* (December 8, 2014). http://media.mainlinemedianews.com/2014/12/08/photos-all-black-lives-matter-die-in-held-in-bryn-mawr-during-evening-rush-hour/#1.

Barad, Karen. *Meeting the Universe Halfway: Quantum Physics and the Entanglement of Matter and Meaning*. Durham: Duke University Press, 2007. doi: 10.1215/9780822388128

The Barnes Foundation. "Yinka Shonibare MBE: Magic Ladders."

January 24 through April 21, 2014. http://www.barnesfoundation.org/about/press/media-info/shonibare-release.

Bartholomae, David. "The Tidy House: Basic Writing in the American Curriculum." *Journal of Basic Writing* 12, no. 1 (1993): 4–21.

Beard, Linda-Susan. "The Other Bryn Mawr History: The M. Carey Thomas Legacy." Talk. The Community Day of Learning: Race and Ethnicity at Bryn Mawr and Beyond. March 18, 2014. https://serendipstudio.org/oneworld/system/files/books/TheOtherBrynMawr%20.docx.

Berger, Peter. *Invitation to Sociology: A Humanistic Perspective.* New York: Bantam Doubleday Dell, 1963. http://www.soc.iastate.edu/sapp/Berger.html.

Berkman, Natalie. "The Silence of the Interlocutor in Camus' *The Fall*." Paper presented at the annual conference of the French Italian Graduate Society, University of Pennsylvania, Philadelphia, PA, March 2013.

Berlak, Ann. "Challenging the Hegemony of Whiteness by Addressing the Adaptive Unconscious." In *Undoing Whiteness in the Classroom.* New York: Peter Lang, 2008. 47–66.

——— and Sekani Moyenda. *Taking It Personally: Racism in the Classroom from Kindergarten to College.* Philadelphia: Temple University Press, 2001. doi: 10.1086/448884

Berlant, Lauren. "Claudia Rankine." Interview. BOMB: *Artists in Conversation,* 129 (Fall 2014). http://bombmagazine.org/article/10096/claudia-rankine.

——— and Michael Warner. "Sex in Public." *Critical Inquiry* 24, no. 2 (Winter 1998): 547–66. http://985queer.queergeektheory.org/wp-content/uploads/2013/04/Berlant-and-Warner-Sex-in-Public.pdf.

Berry, Thomas. "A New Story." In *The Dream of the Earth.* San Francisco: Sierra Club Books, 1988. 123–37.

Bersani, Leo. *Homos.* Cambridge: Harvard University Press, 1996.

Bettie, Julie. *Women without Class: Girls, Race, and Identity.* 2003. Revised, Oakland: University of California Press, 2014.

Bonner, Chris. "Staging a Dictatorship: Silence, Surveillance, and

Theatricality in Marie Chauvet's *Colere*." Paper presented at the annual conference of the French Italian Graduate Society, University of Pennsylvania, Philadelphia, PA, March 2013.

Borderdwelling. "The Ph.D. and Normative Time." Brooke's Blog. July 4, 2012. https://borderdwelling.wordpress.com/2012/07/04/the-phd-and-normative-time/.

Brin, Joseph. "Borders And Boundaries, Invisible To Most." *Hidden City Philadelphia*. October 23, 2013. http://hiddencityphila.org/2013/10/borders-and-boundaries-invisible-to-most.

Bromberg, Lisa and Andrew Korn. Call for Papers. Silence…Silenzio: Annual Conference of the French Italian Graduate Society, University of Pennsylvania, Philadelphia, PA, November 2012.

Brown, Stuart. "Play, Spirit, and Character." *On Being with Krista Tippett*. June 19, 2014. http://www.onbeing.org/program/play-spirit-and-character/143/audio?embed=1.

Brown, Wendy. "Feminism Unbound: Revolution, Mourning, Politics." In *Edgework: Critical Essays on Knowledge and Politics*. Princeton, New Jersey: Princeton University Press, 2005. 98–115.

———. "Freedom's Silences." In *Edgework: Critical Essays on Knowledge and Politics*. Princeton: Princeton University Press, 2005. 83–97.

Bryant, Levi R. "Adorno, Representation, and Differential Ontology." *Larval Subjects*. June 13, 2011. https://larvalsubjects.wordpress.com/2011/06/13/adorno-representation-and-differential-ontology/.

———. "Stacy Alaimo: Porous Bodies and Trans-Corporeality." *Larval Subjects*. May 24, 2012. https://larvalsubjects.wordpress.com/2012/05/24/stacy-alaimo-porous-bodies-and-trans-corporeality/.

"Bryn Mawr Bigotry." February 1, 2015 (1:52 p.m.). https://serendipstudio.org/oneworld/multicultural-education-2015/bryn-mawr-bigotry.

Bryn Mawr College. "Mission." 1998. https://www.brynmawr.edu/about/mission.

Buras, Kristen. "Race, Charter Schools, and Conscious Capitalism: On the Spatial Politics of Whiteness as Property (and the Unconscionable Assault on Black New Orleans)." *Harvard*

Educational Review 81, no. 2 (Summer 2011): 296–330. doi: 10.17763/haer.81.2.6l42343qqw360j03

Butler, Judith. *Notes Towards a Performative Theory of Assembly.* Cambridge: Harvard University Press, 2015. https://books.google.com/books?isbn=067449556X.

———. "Toward an Ethics of Cohabitation." The Mary Flexner Lectures: Bodies in Alliance. Bryn Mawr College. November 21, 2011. Notes by Anne Dalke. http://serendipstudio.org/exchange/node/11377.

———. *Precarious Life: The Powers of Mourning and Violence.* Brooklyn: Verso, 2006.

——— and Sunaura Taylor, "Examined Life," YouTube video, 14:23. October 6, 2010. https://www.youtube.com/watch?v=koнzaPkF6qE.

Callahan, Raymond. *Education and the Cult of Efficiency: A Study of the Social Forces that have Shaped the Administration of the Public Schools.* Chicago: The University of Chicago Press, 1962.

Cambone, Joseph. "Time for Teachers in School Restructuring." *Teachers College Record* 96, no. 3 (Spring 1995): 512–43.

"Campus Comes Together for Community Day of Learning." Bryn Mawr News. March 20, 2015 (1:06 p.m.) http://news.brynmawr.edu/2015/03/20/campus-comes-together-for-community-day-of-learning/.

Camus, Albert. "Create Dangerously." Lecture at the University of Uppsala, Sweden. December 14, 1957. http://www.nathanielturner.com/createdangerouslycamus.htm.

Carson, Rachel. "A Fable for Tomorrow." In *Silent Spring.* 1962. Reprint, Boston: Houghton Mifflin, 2002.

———. "The Marginal World." In *The Edge of the Sea.* 1955. Posted on-line 2016. http://bookanista.com/marginal-world/.

Carter, Angela. "Teaching with Trauma: Trigger Warnings, Feminism, and Disability Pedagogy." DSQ: *Disability Studies Quarterly* 35, no. 2 (2015). http://dsq-sds.org/article/view/4652/3935. doi: 10.18061/DSQ.V35I2.4652

Catanese, Elizabeth. "Some Thoughts on Teaching." February 3, 2006.

http://serendipstudio.org/local/scisoc/brownbag/brownbag0506/advice.html.

"Challenging Women: Investing in the Future of Bryn Mawr." *Alumnae Bulletin,* Bryn Mawr College. Spring 2003. http://www.brynmawr.edu/alumnae/bulletin/launch.htm.

Chandler, Elizabeth. "Cripping Community: New Meanings." *No More Pot Lucks.* September 5, 2013. nomorepotlucks.org/site/cripping-community-new-meanings-of-disability-ad-community.

Chandrea. "Different Forms of Expression?" December 3, 2011 (4:56 p.m.). http://serendipstudio.org/exchange/node/11433.

———. "Talking in a (High School/College) Class." September 16, 2012 (10:28 a.m.). http://serendipstudio.org/exchange/talking-high-schoolcollege-class.

———. "If I told you I was poor, would you see me differently?" December 9, 2011 (5:34 p.m.). http://serendipstudio.org/exchange/node/11512.

———. "In Response to Sarah Goode," October 21, 2011 (5:27 p.m.). http://serendipstudio.org/exchange/DiaBlog1#comment-131484.

Chang, David. "Protesters for Mike Brown, Eric Garner March Through Main Line." *NBC10.com.* December 8, 2014. http://www.nbcphiladelphia.com/news/local/Protesters-for-Mike-Brown-Eric-Garner-March-Through-Main-Line-285145371.html.

"Changing Our Story." Emily Balch Seminar. Bryn Mawr College. Fall 2015. https://serendipstudio.org/oneworld/changing-our-story-2015/sylla-ship-changing-our-story-fall-2015.

Chen, Mel. *Animacies: Biopolitics, Racial Mattering, and Queer Affect.* Durham: Duke University Press, 2012. doi: 10.1215/9780822395447

Chittister, Sister Joan. "Seeking the Interior Life." November 7, 2004. http://thirtygoodminutes.net/index.php/archives/reflections/23-member-archives/734-joan-chittister-program-4806.

Christian, Barbara. "The Race for Theory." *Cultural Critique: The Nature and Context of Minority Discourse* 6 (1987): 51–63. doi: 10.2307/1354255

Cisneros, Sandra. "From a Writer's Notebook." *The Americas Review* 15 (1987): 69–79.

Clare, Eli. "Meditations on Disabled Bodies, Natural Worlds, and a Politics of Cure." 1–25. http://disabilitystudies.wisc.edu/wp-content/uploads/2012/09/Eli-Clare-Meditations-UW-Madison.pdf.

Clarke, Edward. *Sex in Education; or, A Fair Chance for the Girls*. 1873. Reprint, New York: Arno, 1972.

"Class Observation/Notes." April 24, 2015 (12:53 a.m.). https://serendipstudio.org/oneworld/ecological-imaginings-2015/class-observation-notes.

Coates, Ta-Nehisi. *Between the World and Me*. New York: Spiegel & Grau, 2015.

———. "How I Met Your Mother." *The Atlantic*. In Paris: Dispatch #12. August 19, 2013. http://www.theatlantic.com/international/archive/2013/08/how-i-met-your-mother/278724/.

———. "The Case for Reparations." *The Atlantic*. June 2014. http://www.theatlantic.com/features/archive/2014/05/the-case-for-reparations/361631/.

Cohen, Jody. "Restructuring Instruction in an Urban High School: An Inquiry into Texts, Identities, and Power." Unpublished dissertation. University of Pennsylvania. 1993.

———, Anne Dalke, Kevin Gotkin, and Clare Mullaney. "Intervening in the Accessible: Reassembling the Social in Disability Studies." Panel at the Society of Disability Studies, Minneapolis, MN, June 2014. https://serendipstudio.org/oneworld/content/intervening-accessible-reassembling-social-disability-studies.

Cole, Teju. "The White Savior Industrial Complex." *The Atlantic*. March 21, 2012. http://www.theatlantic.com/international/archive/2012/03/the-white-savior-industrial-complex/254843/.

Comments. "Classism v. Feminism and Why a Discussion about MTV Can Get Very Complicated Very Fast." December 10, 2011 (2:39 a.m.)–February 2, 2012 (7:36 p.m.). http://serendipstudio.org/exchange/node/11513#comment.

Conn, Steven. "Callous or Callow: Waving the Confederate Flag at Bryn Mawr College." *The Huffington Post.* October 7, 2014. http://www.huffingtonpost.com/steven-conn/callous-or-callow-waving_b_5944478.html.

Cook-Sather, Alison, Catherine Bovill, and Peter Felten. *Engaging Students as Partners in Learning and Teaching: A Guide for Faculty.* San Francisco: Jossey-Bass, 2014.

Cornette, Carla. "Silence as Remedy: The Psychological Defense Mechanism of Silence in 'Mio Marito' by Natalia Ginzburg." Paper presented at the annual conference of the French Italian Graduate Society, University of Pennsylvania, Philadelphia, PA, March 2013.

Coscarelli, Joe. "Artist Who Inspired Kanye West's 'Famous' video: 'I Was Really Speechless.'" *The New York Times.* June 26, 2016. http://www.nytimes.com/2016/06/29/arts/music/kanye-west-vincent-desiderio-famous-sleep.html?emc=eta1&_r=1.

Costa, Arthur and Bena Kallick. "Through the Lens of a Critical Friend." *Educational Leadership* 51, no. 2 (October 1993): 49–51. http://www.ascd.org/publications/educational-leadership/oct93/vol51/num02/Through-the-Lens-of-a-Critical-Friend.aspx.

couldntthinkofanoriginalname. "Not Knowing Sucks, But Is Exclusion Necessary Sometimes?" September 20, 2012 (10:09 a.m.). http://serendipstudio.org/exchange/not-knowing-sucks-exclusion-necessary-sometimes.

———. "Reading Delpit's Words through a Third Lens: Silence." September 16, 2012 (11:57 a.m.). http://serendipstudio.org/exchange/reading-delpits-words-through-third-lens-silence.

———. "Reflections on Eva's Man." November 18, 2012 (3:33p.m.). http://serendipstudio.org/exchange/reflections-evas-man.

———. "Wow…" December 9, 2012 (1:37 p.m.). http://serendipstudio.org/exchange/thursdays-silence-class#comment-139791.

Crane, Mary Thomas. *Shakespeare's Brain: Reading with Cognitive Theory.* Princeton: Princeton University Press, 2000.

"Crip Time." *Dictionary of American Slang.* http://www.diclib.com/crip%20time/show/en/amslang/C/849/720/12/13/2159#.VzsuJwY8rIE.

Critical Feminist Studies. Bryn Mawr College. Fall 2013. http://serendipstudio.org/exchange/critical-feminist-studies-2013/.

"Critical Friend Toolkit." *Principal Class Performance and Development; Support Materials.* Queensland Government Education. http://education.qld.gov.au/staff/development/performance/resources/readings/critical-friend-toolkit.pdf.

"Critical Friend." *The Glossary of Educational Reform* (November 28, 2013). http://edglossary.org/critical-friend/.

"Critical Friend." *Wikipedia.* https://en.wikipedia.org/wiki/Critical_friend.

"Critical Friends: A Process Built on Reflection." *Community Campus Partnerships for Health.* https://depts.washington.edu/ccph/pdf_files/CriticalFriends.pdf https://depts.washington.edu/ccph/pdf_files/CriticalFriends.pdf.

Dalke, Anne. "Notes Towards Day 13." October 11, 2012 (10:50 p.m.). http://serendipstudio.org/exchange/notes-towards-day-12-tues-oct.

———. "Now Live! Our Costumes of Identity." October 30, 2014 (10:53 p.m.). https://serendipstudio.org/oneworld/identity-matters-being-belonging-becoming/now-live-our-costumes-identity.

———. "September 11, 2006." *Stranger in a Strange Land: Grokking in the Americas.* September 12, 2006. https://serendipstudio.org/oneworld/blog/september-11-2006.

———. "Silence is so Windowful: Class as Antechamber." In *Teaching to Learn/Learning to Teach: Meditations on the Classroom.* New York: Peter Lang, 2002. 95–114.

———. "'On Behalf of the Standard of Silence': The American Female Modernists and the Powers of Restraint." *Soundings: An Interdisciplinary Journal* 78, nos. 3–4 (Fall–Winter 1995): 501–19.

———. "structure!" February 10, 2012 (9:30 a.m.). http://serendipstudio.org/exchange/assessment#comment-133934.

——— and Alice Lesnick. "Teaching Intersection, Not Assessment: Celebrating the Surprise of Gift Giving and Gift Getting in the Cultural Commons." *Journal of Curriculum and Pedagogy* 8 (2011): 75–96. doi: 10.1080/15505170.2011.571176

——— and Jody Cohen. "Crafting Sustainable Teaching Practices." Workshop presented at the annual conference of Friends Association of Higher Education. Wilmington, OH, June 2012. http://serendipstudio.org/exchange/FAHE/12.

——— and Paul Grobstein. "Story-telling In (At Least) Three Dimensions: An Exploration of Teaching Reading, Writing, and Beyond." *Journal of Teaching Writing* 23, no. 1 (2007): 91–114.

———, Sophia Abbot, Sara Gladwin & Esteniolla Maitre. "The Pedagogy of Silence." Roundtable presented at the annual conference of the French Italian Graduate Society, University of Pennsylvania, Philadelphia, PA, March 2013.

Dalke, Marian (Paia). "For what(ever) It'$ Worth: Reflections, thoughts, and suggestions on Class Privilege, Inheritance, and Inequity from a young white woman of wealth." Self published. January 2009.

Dan, "Listening and Silence," September 9, 2012 (4:47 p.m.). http://serendipstudio.org/exchange/listening-and-silence.

———. "Silence, Air and Paradoxes," September 23, 2012 (1:19 p.m.). http://serendipstudio.org/exchange/silence-air-and-paradoxes.

Danticat, Edwidge. *Create Dangerously: The Immigrant Artist at Work.* New York: Vintage, 2010.

Davis, Angela. *Are Prisons Obsolete?* New York: Seven Stories Press, 2003.

Davis, Lennard. "The End of Identity Politics and the Beginning of Dismodernism: On Disability as an Unstable Category." In *The Disability Studies Reader,* edited by Lennard J. Davis. Second Edition. New York: Routledge, 2006. 231–42.

de la Cruz, Juana Inez. *La Respuesta/The Response* (1690). Translated and Edited by Electra Arenal and Amanda Powell. New York: Feminist Press, 1994.

De la Torre, Miguel. *Introducing Liberative Theologies.* Maryknoll, NY: Orbis Books, 2015.

Delpit, Lisa. *Other People's Children: Cultural Conflict in the Classroom.* 1995. Reprint, New York: The New Press, 2006. doi: 10.2307/358724

———. "The Silenced Dialogue: Power and Pedagogy in Educating

Other People's Children." *Harvard Educational Review* 58, no. 3 (1988): 280–98. doi: 10.17763/HAER.58.3.C43481778R528QW4

Delton, Jennifer. "Escaping Whiteness." HuffPost Media. July 12, 2015 (10:28 p.m.). http://www.huffingtonpost.com/jennifer-delton/escaping-whiteness_b_7781914.html.

"Democratizing Knowledge Project: Developing Literacies, Building Communities, Seeding Change." The College of Arts and Sciences. Syracuse University. http://democratizingknowledge.syr.edu/.

Dewey, John. "The Live Creature." *Art as Experience*. 1934. Reprint, New York: Perigee, 1980. 3–34.

"Disability Disclosure in/and Higher Education." Conference at the University of Delaware. October 2013. http://www1.udel.edu/csd/conference/.

"Diversity Leadership Group Selects Six 'Class Dismissed' Projects for Funding." May 12, 2011. http://news.blogs.brynmawr.edu/2011/05/12/diversity-leadership-group-selects-six-class-dismissed-projects-for-funding/.

Dolmage, Jay. "Universal Design: Places to Start." *DSQ: Disability Studies Quarterly* 35, no. 2 (2015). doi: 10.18061/dsq.v35i2.4632.

Donaldson, Elizabeth. "Revisiting the Corpus of the Madwoman: Further Notes toward a Feminist Disability Studies Theory of Mental Illness." In *Feminist Disability Studies*, edited by Kim Q. Hall. Bloomington: Indiana University Press, 2011. 91–113.

Dunbar, Eve. "Who Really Burns: Quitting a Deans' Job in the Age of Mike Brown." *Jezebel*. December 2, 2014 (12:10 p.m.). http://jezebel.com/who-really-burns-quitting-a-deans-job-in-the-age-of-mi-1665631269/all.

Duncan-Andrade, Jeffrey. "Note to Educators: Hope Required When Growing Roses in Concrete." *Harvard Educational Review* 79, no. 2 (Summer 2009): 181–94. doi: 10.17763/HAER.79.2.NU3436017730384W

E. T. D. "The Crime." *Fortnightly Philistine* 7 (February 1, 1901): 2–4. Internet Archive: Bryn Mawr College Library, Special Collections. https://archive.org/stream/fortnightlyphili07stud#page/n111/mode/2up.

"Earthquake Aftermath," April 17, 2015 (8:05 p.m.). https://serendipstudio.org/oneworld/ecological-imaginings-2015/earthquake-aftermath.

"Ecological Imaginings." English 313. Bryn Mawr College. Fall 2012. http://serendipstudio.org/exchange/courses/ecolit/f12.

"Ecological Imaginings." English 218. Bryn Mawr College. Spring 2015. https://serendipstudio.org/oneworld/ecological-imaginings-2015/sylla-ship-ecological-imaginings-spring-2015.

Edensor, Tim, Bethan Evans, Julian Holloway, Steve Millington, and Jon Binnie. "Playing in Industrial Ruins: Interrogating Teleological Understandings of Play in Spaces of Material Alterity and Low Surveillance." In *Urban Wildscapes*, edited by Anna Jorgensen and Richard Keenan. New York: Routledge, 2011. 65–79.

Elbow, Peter. "Silence: A Collage." In *Everyone Can Write: Essays Toward a Hopeful Theory of Writing and Teaching.* New York: Oxford University Press, 2000. 173–83.

Ellsworth, Elizabeth. *Places of Learning: Media, Architecture, Pedagogy.* New York: Routledge Taylor and Francis, 2005. doi: 10.4324/9780203020920

———. *Teaching Positions: Difference, Pedagogy, and the Power of Address.* New York: Teachers College Press, 1997.

Elstad, Emily. "Slipping into Something More Comfortable." Paper written for English 207: Big Books of American Literature. Bryn Mawr College. Spring 2003.

Emanuel, Gabrielle. "Pell Grants For Prisoners: An Old Argument Revisited." *NPREd.* July 30, 2015 (4:36 a.m.). http://www.npr.org/sections/ed/2015/07/30/427450422/pell-grants-for-prisoners-an-old-argument-revisited.

Erin. "Silence and Talking." September 16, 2012 (5:20 p.m.). http://serendipstudio.org/exchange/silence-and-talking.

Everglade. "Open to Serendipity." September 16, 2013 (12:01p.m.). http://serendipstudio.org/exchange/play-city-2013/evelynz/open-serendipity.

Fasching-Varner, Kenneth J., Roland W. Mitchell, Lori L. Martin, and Karen P. Bennett-Haron. "Beyond School-to-Prison Pipeline and Toward an Educational and Penal Realism." In *Excellence in Education* 47, no. 4 (2014): 410–29. doi: 10.1080/10665684.2014.959285.

FatCatRex. "Anonymity, Authenticity and Healing: Secrets of Truth-Telling Revealed." October 29, 2010 (4:59 p.m.). http://serendipstudio.org/exchange/node/8344.

Faulkner, William. *Light in August.* New York: Vintage, 1932. http://www.kkoworld.com/kitablar/william-faulkner-light-in-august_eng.pdf.

"Fear the Fear." February 8, 2015 (1:49 p.m.). https://serendipstudio.org/oneworld/multicultural-education-2015/fear-fear.

Felsenthal, Julia. "The Curious History of 'Tribal' Prints: How the Dutch Peddle Indonesian-Inspired Design to West Africa." *Slate.* March 1, 2012. http://www.slate.com/articles/arts/design/2012/03/african_fabric_where_do_tribal_prints_really_come_from_.html.

Ferreday, Debra and Kuntsman, Adi. "Haunted Futurities." *Borderlands* 10, no. 2 (2011): 1–14.

Final Booklet. December 9, 2015. https://serendipstudio.org/oneworld/system/files/FINAL%20BOOKLET.pdf.

Finch, Justin. "College Students Join Together for 'Die-In' Demonstration on the Main Line." *CBS Philly.* December 8, 2014. http://philadelphia.cbslocal.com/2014/12/08/college-students-join-together-for-die-in-demonstration-on-the-main-line/.

Fine, Michelle and Jessica Ruglis. "Circuits and Consequences of Dispossession: The Racialized Realignment of the Public Sphere for U.S. Youth." *Transforming Anthropology* 17, no. 1 (2009): 20–33. doi: 10.1111/j.1548-7466.2009.01037.x.

———, María Elena Torre, Kathy Boudin, Iris Bowen, Judith Clark, Donna Hylton, Migdalia Martinez, "Missy," Melissa Rivera, Rosemarie A. Roberts, Pamela Smart, and Debra Upegui. "Participatory Action Research: From Within and Beyond Prison Bars." In *Working Method: Research and Social Justice.* Edited by Lois Weis and Michelle Fine. New York: Routledge, 2004. 95–119.

Fisher-Wirth, Ann. "Extractive & Underground Poetics: Readings and Conversation." Plenary session at the biennial conference of the Association for the Study of Literature and the Environment. Moscow, ID, June 2015.

———. "Out of Silence, They Emerge." Paper presented at the biennial conference of the Association for the Study of Literature and the Environment. Moscow, ID, June 2015.

——— and Maude Schuyler Clay. "Mississippi: A Collaborative Project." *About Place Journal* 3, no. 2 (November 2014). http://aboutplacejournal.org/voices/s3-iii-ii/ann-fisher-wirth-iii-ii/.

——— and ———. "Mississippi: An Excerpt." *Bloom* (March 23, 2015). http://bloom-site.com/2015/03/23/ann-fisher-wirth/.

Flanagan, Mary. *Critical Play: Radical Game Design.* Cambridge: MIT Press, 2009. 1–15. doi: 10.7551/MITPRESS/7678.001.0001

Fraden, Rena. *Imagining Medea: Rhodessa Jones and Theater for Incarcerated Women.* Chapel Hill: The University of North Carolina, 2001.

"Freedom Forgotten: Works of Silence and Resistance (Some Photos and Commentary)." December 13, 2015 (7:51 a.m.). https://serendipstudio.org/oneworld/arts-resistance/freedom-forgotten-works-silence-and-resistance-some-photos-and-commentary.

Freeman, Elizabeth, Brian Herrera, Nat Hurley, Homay King, Dana Luciano, Dana Seitler, and Patricia White. "Trigger Warnings Are Flawed." *Inside Higher Ed.* May 29, 2014. https://www.insidehighered.com/views/2014/05/29/essay-faculty-members-about-why-they-will-not-use-trigger-warnings.

Freeman, Jo. "The Tyranny of Structurelessness." Talk presented at the Southern Female Rights Union. Beulah, MS. May 1970. http://www.jofreeman.com/joreen/tyranny.htm.

Freire, Paulo. *Pedagogy of the Oppressed.* Translated by Myra Bergman Ramos. New York: Continuum, 1990.

Fulwood, Sam III. "Race and Beyond: Income Differences Divide the College Campus in America." Center for American Progress, March 13, 2012. https://www.americanprogress.org/issues/race/news/2012/03/13/11357/race-and-beyond-income-differences-divide-the-college-campus-in-america/.

Gallop, Jane, and Carolyn Burke. "Psychoanalysis and Feminism in France."

In *The Future of Difference*. Edited by Hester Eisenstein and Alice Jardine. New Brunswick: Rutgers University Press, 1984. 106–21.

Garland-Thomson, Rosemarie. "Integrating Disability, Transforming Feminist Theory." In *Feminist Disability Studies*, edited by Kim Q. Hall. Bloomington: Indiana University Press, 2011. 13–47.

———. "Misfits: A Feminist Materialist Disability Concept." *Hypatia: A Journal of Feminist Philosophy* 26, no. 3 (Summer 2011): 591–609. doi: 10.1111/j.1527-2001.2011.01206.x.

Garrard, Greg, Ed. *Teaching Ecocriticism and Green Cultural Studies*. New York: Palgrave Macmillan, 2012. doi: 10.1057/9780230358393

Gaskew, Tony. "Developing a Prison Education Pedagogy." In *Bringing College Education into Prisons*, edited by Rob Scott. San Francisco: Jossey-Bass, 2015. 67–78. doi: 10.1002/CC.20145

Gaztambide-Fernández, Rubén A. "Decolonization and the Pedagogy of Solidarity." *Decolonization: Indigeneity, Education & Society* 1, no. 1 (2012): 41–67. http://decolonization.org/index.php/des/article/download/18633/15557.

Geertz, Clifford. "Deep Play: Notes on the Balinese Cockfight." In *The Interpretation of Cultures*, 412-53. New York: Basic Books, 1973. http://webhome.idirect.com/~boweevil/BaliCockGeertz.html.

George Washington Carver. "Do you need college to be successful in life?" October 20, 2011 (12:04 p.m.). http://serendipstudio.org/exchange/DiaBlog1#comment-131425.

Giananni, Claudia. "Yearlong 'Class Dismissed?' Aims to Spark Discussion of Socioeconomic Class on Campus." *Inside Bryn Mawr*. May 3, 2011. http://inside.blogs.brynmawr.edu/2011/03/03/class-dismissed/accessed.

Gladwin, Sara. E-mail message to author. May 19, 2014.

Goffman, Alice. "How We're Priming Some Kids for College—and Others for Prison." TED Talk. March 2015. https://www.ted.com/talks/alice_goffman_college_or_prison_two_destinies_one_blatant_injustice/transcript?language=en.

González, Jill. "Silence and Memory in Guadalupe Santa Cruz's *Cita capital*." Paper presented at the annual conference of the French

Italian Graduate Society, University of Pennsylvania, Philadelphia, PA, March 2013.

Gordon, Avery. *Ghostly Matters: Haunting and the Sociological Imagination.* Minneapolis: University of Minnesota Press, 1997.

———. "Some Thoughts on Haunting and Futurity." *Borderlands* 10 (2011): 1–21.

Gorski, Paul. "Working Definition." *Critical Multicultural Pavilion.* April 2010. http://www.edchange.org/multicultural/initial.html.

Gotkin, Kevin. "The Norm and the Pathological." *DSQ: Disability Studies Quarterly* 36, no. 1 (2016). http://dsq-sds.org/article/view/4281/4206. doi: 10.18061/DSQ.V36I1.4281

———. "The Rupture Sometimes." YouTube video. 27:44. September 19, 2012. https://www.youtube.com/watch?v=3YkWsk1tXLw.

GrayandGrey. "Some Other Shapes." March 27, 2009. http://grayandgrey.blogspot.com/2009/03/some-other-shapes.html.

Greene, Maxine. "Coda: The Slow Fuse of Change: Obama, the Schools, Imagination, and Convergence." *Harvard Educational Review* 79, no. 2 (Summer 2009): 396–8. doi: 10.17763/HAER.79.2.N43005263015V775

Grim, Ryan, Matt Sledge and Mariah Stewart. "From Daniel Pantaleo To Darren Wilson, Police Are Almost Never Indicted." *Huffington Post.* December 3, 2014 (5:15 p.m.). http://www.huffingtonpost.com/2014/12/03/police-indictments_n_6264132.html.

Grubb, Barbara Ward and Emily Houghton. "Building Muscles While Building Minds: Athletics and the Early Years of Women's Education." September–December 2005. http://www.brynmawr.edu/library/exhibits/buildingmuscles/.

Halberstam, Jack. "The Wild Beyond: With and For the Undercommons." In Stefano Harney and Fred Moten. *The Undercommons: Fugitive Planning and Black Study*, 5–12. Brooklyn, New York: Autonomedia, 2013. http://www.minorcompositions.info/wp-content/uploads/2013/04/undercommons-web.pdf.

Halberstam, Judith. *In a Queer Time and Place: Transgender Bodies, Subcultural Lives.* New York: New York University Press, 2005.

———. *The Queer Art of Failure.* Durham: Duke University Press, 2011.

Hall, Kim Q. "Reimagining Disability and Gender through Feminist Disability Studies: An Introduction." In *Feminist Disability Studies*, edited by Kim Q. Hall. Bloomington: Indiana University Press, 2011. 1–10.

Hall, Ruth and Michelle Fine. "The Stories We Tell: The Lives and Friendship of Two Older Black Lesbians." *Psychology of Women Quarterly* 29, no. 2 (June 2005): 177–87. doi: 10.1111/j.1471-6402.2005.00180.x.

Hall, Stuart. *The Multicultural Question*. Milton Keynes, United Kingdom: Pavis Centre for Social and Cultural Research, The Open University, 2001.

———. "The Question of Cultural Identity." In *Modernity: An Introduction to Modern Studies*. Edited by Stuart Hall, David Held, Don Hubert and Kenneth Thompson. Indianapolis: Wiley-Blackwell, 1996. 596–631.

Haraway, Donna. "When Species Meet: Staying with the Trouble." *Environment and Planning D: Society and Space* 28, no. 1 (2010): 53–55. http://www.envplan.com/fulltext_temp/0/d2706wsh.pdf. doi: 10.1068/D2706WSH

Harney, Stefano and Fred Moten. *The Undercommons: Fugitive Planning and Black Study*. Brooklyn: Autonomedia, 2013. http://www.minorcompositions.info/wp-content/uploads/2013/04/undercommons-web.pdf.

Harper, Douglas. "Crime." *Online Etymology Dictionary*. http://www.etymonline.com/index.php?allowed_in_frame=0&search=%22crime%22.

HCRL. "Final Field Paper." May 9, 2015 (2: 58 p.m.). https://serendipstudio.org/oneworld/multicultural-education-2015/final-field-paper-0.

Hempton, Gordon. "The Last Quiet Places." Radio show/Podcast. May 10, 2012. http://www.onbeing.org/program/last-quiet-places/4557.

Henig, Robin. "Taking Play Seriously." *New York Times*. February 17, 2008. http://www.nytimes.com/2008/02/17/magazine/17play.html.

Holling, C.S. "Surprise for Science, Resilience for Ecosystems, and

Incentives for People." *Ecological Applications* 6, no. 3 (1996): 733–5. doi: 10.2307/2269475

——— and Gary K. Meffe. "Command and Control and the Pathology of Natural Resource Management." *Conservation Biology* 10, no. 2 (April 1996): 328–37. doi: 10.1046/J.1523-1739.1996.10020328.X

hooks, bell. "Confronting Class in the Classroom." In *Teaching to Transgress: Education as the Practice of Freedom*. New York: Routledge, 1994. 177–90.

Horowitz, Helen. "Women and Higher Education: A Look in Two Directions." Heritage and Hope: Women's Education in a Global Context. Lecture at Bryn Mawr College. September 23, 2010.

HSBurke. "After last class.," November 9, 2013 (2:32 p.m.). http://serendipstudio.org/exchange/walled-women/hsburke/after-last-class.

———. "After walking around campus." November 20, 2011 (3:07 p.m.). http://serendipstudio.org/exchange/node/11327#comment-132225.

———. "Hi Chandrea!," December 9, 2012 (11:44 a.m.). http://serendipstudio.org/exchange/thursdays-silence-class#comment-139790.

———. "Web Event #2: Silenced by a Lack of Silence." September 23, 2012 (9:53 a.m.). http://serendipstudio.org/exchange/silenced-lack-silence.

Huber, Dave. "Confederate Flag at Bryn Mawr College Dorm Causes Uproar." *The College Fix*. October 5, 2014.

Hummingbird. "Classism v. Feminism and Why a Discussion about MTV Can Get Very Complicated Very Fast." December 9, 2011 (6:46 p.m.). http://serendipstudio.org/exchange/node/11513.

———. "Communication?: a Self-Reflection." December 18, 2014 (8:54 p.m.). https://serendipstudio.org/oneworld/identity-matters-being-belonging-becoming/communication-self-reflection.

———. E-mail message to author, June 8, 2016.

———. "Frustrated." October 23, 2012 (3:37pm). http://serendipstudio.org/exchange/frustratedhttp://serendipstudio.org/exchange/frustrated.

———. "Gender, Body Images, and (m)tv," December 16, 2011 (12:25 p.m.). http://serendipstudio.org/exchange/node/11601.

———."A Plea for Space." October 2, 2014 (5:27 p.m.). https://serendipstudio.org/oneworld/identity-matters-being-belonging-becoming/plea-space.

Hunt, Sarah and Cindy Holmes. "Everyday Decolonization: Living a Decolonizing Queer Politics." *Journal of Lesbian Studies*, 19, no. 2 (March 2015): 154–72. doi: 10.1080/10894160.2015.970975.

Hutcheon, Emily and Gregor Wolbring. "'Cripping' Resilience: Contributions from Disability Studies to Resilience Theory." *M/C Journal* 16, no. 5 (2013). http://journal.mediaculture.org.au/index.php/mcjournal/article/view697.

"The Icarus Project." http://theicarusproject.net/.

"Identity Matters: Being, Belonging, Becoming." A 360° cluster. Bryn Mawr College. Fall 2014. http://serendipstudio.org/oneworld/identity-matters-being-belonging-becoming/indentity-matters-2014.

"In Class/OutClassed: On the Uses of a Liberal Education." Emily Balch Seminar. Bryn Mawr College. Fall 2011. http://serendipstudio.org/exchange/courses/esem/f11.

Ingram, A.M., I. Marshall, D.J. Philippon, and A.W. Sweeting, eds. *Coming into Contact: Explorations in Ecocritical Theory and Practice*. Athens: The University of Georgia Press, 2007.

"The Inside-Out Prison Exchange Program." Temple University. 2016. http://www.insideoutcenter.org/.

Inzlicht, Michael, and Toni Schmader. *Stereotype Threat: Theory, Process, and Application*. New York: Oxford University Press, 2011. doi: 10.1093/ACPROF:OSO/9780199732449.001.0001

ishin. "Anxiety and Practiced Silence." December 9, 2012 (6:30 p.m.). http://serendipstudio.org/exchange/private/anxiety-and-practiced-silence.

———. "Oct12012S5: Universal Writing." October 2, 2012 (3:06 a.m.). http://serendipstudio.org/exchange/private/oct12012s5-universal-writing.

Izarrary, Jason G., and John Raible. "'A Hidden Part of Me': Latino/a

Students, Silencing, and the Epidermalization of Inferiority." *Equity & Excellence in Education* 47, no. 4 (2014): 430–44. doi:10.1080/10665 684.2014.958970.

j.nahig. "Consider the majority of," October 21, 2011 (5:37 p.m.). http://serendipstudio.org/exchange/DiaBlog1#comment-131485.

Jagose, Annamarie. *Queer Theory: An Introduction.* New York University, 1996. http://courses.missouristate.edu/RalphSmith/GEPfall2k/excerpts/gep397_jagose_excerpt.htm.

jHarmon. "Being Perfect." December 2, 2011 (2:56 a.m.). http://serendipstudio.org/exchange/node/11422.

jhunter. "Notes Towards Day 23." November 27, 2012 (11:37 p.m.). http://serendipstudio.org/exchange/notes-towards-day-22-thurs-nov-29-reclaiming-tacit-dimension.

Johnson, Barbara. *The Feminist Difference: Literature, Psychoanalysis, Race and Gender.* Cambridge: Harvard University Press, 1998.

Joie Rose. "The Last One (Prison Reflection)." December 15, 2015 (7:45 p.m.). https://serendipstudio.org/oneworld/arts-resistance/last-one-prison-reflection.

Jordan, June. "Nobody Mean More to Me Than You and the Future Life of Willie Jordan." *Harvard Educational Review* 58, no. 3 (September 1988): 363–75. doi: 10.17763/haer.58.3.d171833kp7v732j1.

Jost, Alison. "Mad Pride and the Medical Model." *Hastings Center Report* 39, no. 4 (July-August 2009). https://muse.jhu.edu/article/270597. doi: 10.1353/HCR.0.0159

Kafer, Alison. *Feminist, Queer, Crip.* Bloomington: Indiana University Press, 2013.

Kalamaras, George. *Reclaiming the Tacit Dimension: Symbolic Form in the Rhetoric of Silence.* Albany: State University of New York Press, 1994. doi: 10.2307/358442

Kane, Pat. "Protean Activism: The Constitutive Politics of Play." *The Play Ethic.* July 12, 2009. http://www.theplayethic.com/2009/07/proteanactivism.html.

Kearney, Timothy. "The Transforming Power of Vulnerability."

Irish Theological Quarterly 78, no. 3 (August 2013): 244–54. doi: 10.1177/0021140013484429.

Kerschbaum, Stephanie and Margaret Price. "Perils and Prospects of Disclosing Disability Identity in Higher Education." March 3, 2014. http://sites.udel.edu/csd/2014/03/03/perils-and-prospects-of-disclosing-disability-identity-in-higher-education/.

khinchey. "On Still Not Having All the Answers." December 18, 2014 (11:23 p.m.). https://serendipstudio.org/oneworld/identity-matters-being-belonging-becoming/still-not-having-all-answers.

Kim, Christine Sun. "Is Unlearning Sound Etiquette" and "Partial Thesis Statement." http://christinesunkim.com/.

Kingston, Mark. "Subversive Friendships: Foucault on Homosexuality and Social Experimentation." *Foucault Studies* 7 (September 2009): 7–17. doi: 10.22439/FS.V0I7.2634

Klein, Naomi. *This Changes Everything: Capitalism vs. The Climate.* New York: Simon and Schuster, 2014.

Koh, Adeline. "The Political Power of Play." *Digital Pedagogy Lab.* April 3, 2014. http://www.digitalpedagogylab.com/hybridped/political-power-of-play/.

Kohn, Eduardo. *How Forests Think: Toward an Anthropology Beyond the Human.* Berkeley: University of California Press, 2013. doi: 10.1525/CALIFORNIA/9780520276109.001.0001

Kosniowski, Jenny. "Textual Silences and the Amnesty for Torture Committed during the Algerian War: Maïssa Bey's *Entendez-vous dans les montagnes...*" Paper presented at the annual conference of the French Italian Graduate Society, University of Pennsylvania, Philadelphia, PA, March 2013.

Kudlick, Catherine. "A History Profession for Every Body." *Journal of Women's History* 18, no. 1 (Spring 2006): 163–67. doi: 10.1353/JOWH.2006.0018

Kumashiro, Kevin. *Against Common Sense: Teaching and Learning Toward Social Justice.* New York: RoutledgeFalmer, 2004.

Lacan, Jacques. "The Direction of the Treatment and the Principle of Its

Power." In *Ecrits: A Selection*, translated by Bruce Fink. New York: W.W. Norton & Company, 2002. 215–70.

"Language: A Conversation." Center for Science in Society, Bryn Mawr College. November 26, 2001-March 24, 2004. http://serendipstudio.org/local/scisoc/language/index04.html.

Lather, Patti. *Getting Smart: Feminist Research and Pedagogy With/In the Postmodern*. New York: Routledge, 1991. doi: 10.4324/9780203451311

Latour, Bruno. *Politics of Nature: How to Bring the Sciences into Democracy*, translated by Catherine Porter. Cambridge: Harvard University Press, 2004.

———. *Reassembling the Social: An Introduction to Actor-Network Theory*. New York: Oxford University Press, 2005.

———. "Why Has Critique Run Out of Steam? From Matters of Fact to Matters of Concern." Critical Inquiry 30, no. 2 (Winter 2004): 225–48. http://www.bruno-latour.fr/sites/default/files/89-critical-inquiry-gb.pdf. doi: 10.1086/421123

Laymon, Kiese. "My Vassar College Faculty ID Makes Everything OK." November 29, 2014 (1:56 p.m.). http://gawker.com/my-vassar-college-faculty-id-makes-everything-ok-1664133077.

lechatdargent (Simon Stafford-Townsend). "Gestalt Essentials: Contact, the Contact Boundary, and Awareness." *Le Chat D'Argent*. December 27, 2011. https://lechatdargent.wordpress.com/2011/12/27/gestalt-essentials-contact-the-contact-boundary-and-awareness/.

LeGuin, Ursula K. "Vaster than Empires and More Slow." In *The Wind's Twelve Quarters*. New York: Harper and Row, 1975: 148–78.

Lehrer, Jonah. "Urban Friction." In *Imagine: How Creativity Works*. Boston: Houghton Mifflin, 2012. 175–212.

Lehrer, Riva. "At 54." Acrylic and collage on paper. 2013. http://www.rivalehrerart.com/#!at-54/cmrb.

———. "Consent to Be Seen." Proposal for a panel on "The Ethics of Representation: How Context Matters," Society of Disability Studies, Atlanta, GA, June 2015.

———. "Jarred: Self Portrait in Formaldehyde." Talk presented at the

Chicago Humanities Festival. November 11, 2014. https://www.youtube.com/watch?v=obJaZtu3Ams.

Leichter, Hope Jensen. "A Note on Time and Education." *Teachers College Record* 81, no. 3 (Spring 1980): 360–70.

Lesnick, Alice. "Teaching and Learning in Community: Staff-Student Learning Partnerships As Part of a College Education." *Journal of Community Engagement and Scholarship* 3, no. 1 (June 19, 2012). http://jces.ua.edu/teaching-and-learning-in-community-staff-student-learning-partnerships-as-part-of-a-college-education/.

———. E-mail message to author. March 23, 2016.

———. E-mail messages to authors. May 22, 2015. August 8, 2015. August 25, 2015.

——— and Alison Cook-Sather. "Building Civic Capacity On Campus Through a Radically Inclusive Teaching and Learning Initiative," *Innovative Higher Education* 35, no. 1 (2010): 3–17. doi: 10.1007/s10755-009-9122-3

——— and Paul Grobstein. Comments. "The Evolving Systems Project." July 31, 2009. http://serendipstudio.org/exchange/evolsys/7july09#comment-109435.

Lindgren, Kristin. "The (S)paces of Academic Work: Disability, Access, and Higher Education." In *Transforming the Academy: Faculty Perspectives on Diversity & Pedagogy.* Edited by Sarah Willie-LeBreton. New Brunswick, NJ: Rutgers University Press, 2016: 113–24.

Lindquist, Julie. "Class Affects, Classroom Affectations: Working through the Paradoxes of Strategic Empathy." *College English* 67, no. 2 (November 2004): 187–209. doi: 10.2307/4140717

Linton, Simi, Susan Mello, and John O'Neill. "Disability Studies: Expanding the Parameters of Diversity." *Radical Teacher* 47 (Fall 1995): 4–10.

lissiem. "Workshop," November 13, 2011 (10:47 p.m.). http://serendipstudio.org/exchange/node/11312.

"Locks Don't Cure; They Strangle—Prison Tour Reflection." November 14, 2015 (5:39 p.m.). https://serendipstudio.org/oneworld/arts-resistance/locks-dont-cure-they-strangle-prison-tour-reflection.

Lopez, Nicole, et. al. "Petitioning Bryn Mawr College: Take the Necessary Actions as Requested by Current Students to Confront Issues of Institutional Racism on Campus, and to Create an Environment Safe for All Students." October 8, 2014. http://www.change.org/p/bryn-mawr-college-take-the-necessary-actions-as-requested-by-current-students-to-confront-issues-of-institutional-racism-on-campus-and-to-create-an-environment-safe-for-all-students.

Louse Armstrong (guest). "Is college needed to be successful." October 20, 2011 (11:56 a.m.). http://serendipstudio.org/exchange/DiaBlog1#comment-131419.

Lugones, Maria. "Playfulness, 'World'-Traveling and Loving Perception." *Hypatia* 2, no. 2 (Summer 1987): 3–19. http://www.jstor.org/stable/3810013. doi: 10.1111/J.1527-2001.1987.TB01062.X

Luttrell, Wendy. *Schoolsmart and Motherwise: Working-Class Women's Identity and Schooling.* New York: Routledge, 1997.

MacLeod, George. "'The Victim of His Victims': Silencing Survivors of the Genocide of the Tutsi in Rwanda in Immaculée Ilibagiza's *Left to Tell*." Paper presented at the annual conference of the French Italian Graduate Society, University of Pennsylvania, Philadelphia, PA, March 16, 2013.

Macy, Joanna. *World as Lover, World as Self: Courage for Global Justice and Ecological Renewal.* Berkeley, California: Parallax Press, 2007.

"Mad Pride—since when?" *Toronto Mad Pride.* http://www.torontomadpride.com/history/.

Maher, Jane. "Teaching Academic Writing in a Maximum Security Women's Prison." *New Directions for Community Colleges* 170 (Summer 2015): 79–88. doi: 10.1002/cc.20146.

"Manifesto for Environmental Studies." May 13, 2015 (6:45 p.m.). https://serendipstudio.org/oneworld/ecological-imaginings-2015/manifesto-environmental-studies-d1.

Martin L King Jr. (guest). "I learned how to interact." November 18, 2011 (12:33 p.m.). http://serendipstudio.org/exchange/node/11327#comment-132224.

Martin, Rachel. *Listening Up: Reinventing Ourselves as Teachers and*

Students. Portsmouth, New Hampshire: Heinemann Boynton/Cook, 2001.

Marx, Karl, and Freidrich Engels. *The Communist Manifesto*. 1848. Reprint in *The People's Cube*. February 26, 2009. http://thepeoplescube.com/peoples-tools/the-communist-manifesto-original-text-t3022.html.

Maxwell, James Clerk. *Theory of Heat*. 1871. Reprint, New York: Dover, 2001.

Maya Angelou. "Something that i taught." November 18, 2011 (12:45 p.m.). http://serendipstudio.org/exchange/node/11327#comment-132232.

McCarthy, Cameron, Goli M. Rezai-Rashti, and Cathryn Teasley. "Race, Diversity, and Curriculum in the Era of Globalization." *Curriculum Inquiry* 39, no. 1 (January 2009): 75–96. doi: 10.1111/j.1467-873X.2008.01438.x.

McDermott, Ray, and Hervé Varenne. "Culture as Disability." *Anthropology and Education Quarterly* 26 (1995): 323–48. doi: 10.1525/aeq.1995.26.3.05x0936z

McDonald, Anne. "Crip Time." Anne McDonald Centre. http://www.annemcdonaldcentre.org.au/crip-time.

McDonald, Joseph P. "Uncommon Common Principles: A CES Big Idea." *Coalition of Essential Schools*. 2016. http://essentialschools.org/uncommon-common-principles/.

McIntosh, Peggy. "Coming to See Privilege Systems: The Surprising Journey." Presentation at Bryn Mawr College, November 18, 2008.

McRuer, Robert. *Crip Theory: Cultural Signs of Queerness and Disability*. New York: New York University Press, 2006.

———. "Cripping Queer Politics, or the Dangers of Neoliberalism." *The Scholar & Feminist Online* 10 nos. 1–2 (Fall 2011/Spring 2012). http://sfonline.barnard.edu/a-new-queer-agenda/cripping-queer-politics-or-the-dangers-of-neoliberalism/.

Mentz, Steve. "Tongues in the Storm: Shakespeare, Ecological Crisis, and the Resources of Genre." In *Ecocritical Shakespeare*, edited by Lynne Bruckner and Dan Brayton. Farnham, Surrey: Ashgate, 2001. 155–72.

Mercado, Monica. "A (Short, Incomplete, and Often Invisible) History of Race and Higher Education." Paper presented at the Bryn Mawr Teach-In on Race, Higher Education, Rights and Responsibilities, Bryn Mawr College, November 2014. https://greenfield.blogs.brynmawr.edu/2014/11/17/teach-in/.

Michaela. "I have felt similarly—I." December 3, 2011 (2:51 p.m.). http://serendipstudio.org/exchange/node/11422.

Miller, Nancy. "Reviewing Eve." In *Regarding Sedgwick: Essays on Queer Culture and Critical Theory,* edited by Stephen Barber and David Clark. New York: Routledge, 2002. 217–25.

Millett, Kate. *The Looney-Bin Trip.* Champaign: University of Illinois, 2000.

Mills, C. Wright. *The Sociological Imagination.* London: Oxford University Press, 1959.

Mindell, Arnold. *The Leader as Martial Artist: Techniques and Strategies for Revealing Conflict and Creating Community.* 2nd Ed. Portland, OR: Lao Tse Press, 2000.

Minow, Martha. *Making All the Difference: Inclusion, Exclusion, and American Law.* Ithaca, New York: Cornell University Press, 1990.

mlord, "not changing mine," May 8, 2013 (6:19 a.m.). http://serendipstudio.org/exchange/courses/esem/playcity/f13/planning#comment-141483.

———. "poor b.b. (plus)." May 6, 2013 (11:21 a.m.). http://serendipstudio.org/exchange/courses/esem/playcity/f13/planning#comment-141468.

Mock, Janet. *Redefining Realness: My Path to Womanhood, Identity, Love & So Much More.* New York: Atria Books, 2014.

Mohanty, Chandra, Amina Mama, Margo Okazawa-Rey, Hayley Marama Cavino, Linda Carty, Susy J. Zepeda, and Carol Fadda-Conrey. "Transnational Challenges to Global Empire: Cultivating Ethical Feminist Praxis." Panel presented at the annual conference of the National Women's Studies Association, San Juan, PR, November 2014.

Morton, Timothy. *The Ecological Thought.* Cambridge: Harvard University Press, 2010.

———. *Ecology Without Nature: Re-thinking Environmental Aesthetics.* Cambridge, MA: Harvard University Press, 2007.

———. "The Mesh." In *Environmental Criticism for the Twenty-First Century*, edited by Stephanie LeMenager, Teresa Shewry, and Ken Hiltner. New York: Routledge, 2011. 19–30.

———. "Practising Deconstruction in the Age of Ecological Emergency." In *Teaching Ecocriticism and Green Cultural Studies*, edited by Greg Garrard. New York: Palgrave Macmillan, 2012. 156–65. doi: 10.1057/9780230358393_13

Moton, Kenneth. "Die-In Protest Reaches the Main Line." *ABC Action News*. December 9, 2015. http://6abc.com/news/college-students-stage-die-in-in-bryn-mawr/427678/.

Mulhere, Kaitlin. "A Flag and Race at Bryn Mawr." *Inside Higher Ed*. October 6, 2014. https://www.insidehighered.com/news/2014/10/06/confederate-flag-causes-controversy-bryn-mawr.

Mullaney, Clare. "Brandy Snaps and Battlefields." *The Breaking Project: Creative Disruptions in Thinking, Writing and Creating*. http://serendipstudio.org/exchange/breaking/mullaney.

Mumford, Lewis. "What Is a City?" *Architectural Record*. 1937. http://www.contemporaryurbananthropology.co/pdfs/Mumford,%20What%20is%20a%20City_.pdf.

Murphy, Patrick. *Ecocritical Explorations in Literary and Cultural Studies: Fences, Boundaries and Fields*. Lanham, MD: Lexington Books, 2009.

Myer, Sarah. "Into Great Silence? A Lacanian Reading of Samuel Beckett's *The Unnamable*." Paper presented at the annual conference of the French Italian Graduate Society, University of Pennsylvania, Philadelphia, PA, March 2013.

Natarajan, Samyuktha. E-mail message to author. February 26, 2016.

nbnguyen. "This is the thing I really want to learn." November 19, 2011 (2:38 p.m.). http://serendipstudio.org/exchange/node/11327#comment-132232.

Nelson, Maggie. *The Argonauts*. Minneapolis: Greywolf Press, 2015.

Neruda, Pablo. "The Word." *Full Woman, Fleshly Apple, Hot Moon: Selected Poems*. Translated by Stephen Mitchell. New York: Harper Perennial, 2009. http://www.colorado.edu/engineering/sites/default/files/Herbst-PoetrySeminar-Week2-0415-E.pdf.

New York Times. *Class Matters*. New York: Times Books, 2005.

"The Nez Perce Reservation and its Location." http://www.nezperce.org/rezinfo/npreservation.htm.

Noguera, Pedro. *City Schools and the American Dream: Reclaiming the Promise of Public Education.* New York: Teachers College Press, 2003.

Nolet, Victor. "Preparing Sustainability-Literate Teachers." *Teachers College Record* 111, no. 2 (February 2009): 409–42.

"Notes Towards Day 13: Cripping and Excessability." Critical Feminist Studies. Bryn Mawr College. Fall 2013. October 22, 2013. http://serendipstudio.org/exchange/critical-feminist-studies-2013/notes-towards-day-13-cripping-and-excessability.

O'Reilley, Mary Rose. *The Garden at Night: Burnout and Breakdown in the Teaching Life.* Portsmouth, New Hampshire: Heinneman, 2005.

Oakes, Jeannie, Martin Lipton, Lauren Anderson, and Jamy Stillman. "Schooling: Wrestling with History and Tradition." In *Teaching to Change the World*. 2nd Ed. Columbus, OH: McGraw-Hill Higher Education, 2006. 2–39.

Oaks, David. "Let's Stop Saying 'Mental Illness.'" *MindFreedom International.* April 26, 2012. http://www.mindfreedom.org/kb/mental-health-abuse/psychiatric-labels/not-mentally-ill.

Odum, Eugene and Gary Barrett. *Fundamentals of Ecology.* 5th Ed. Belmont, CA: Brooks and Cole, 2004.

Office of Institutional Diversity. "2009 Diversity Survey Highlights." Bryn Mawr College. 2010, 1–2. http://www.brynmawr.edu/diversitycouncil/cca/media.html#.

Orr, David. *Earth in Mind: On Education, Environment, and the Human Prospect.* Washington, DC: Earth Island Press, 2004.

Overholser, Geneva. "Rape and Anonymity: A Fateful Pairing." December 11, 2014. http://genevaoverholser.com/2014/12/11/rape-and-anonymity-a-fateful-pairing/.

Owens, Eric. "Tolerance and Diversity Cause FREAKOUT Over Confederate Flag at Fancypants Women's College." *The Daily Caller.* October 6, 2014. http://dailycaller.com/2014/10/06/freakout-over-confederate-flag-at-fancypants-womens-college/.

Owl, "I couldn't agree with you," November 19, 2012 (1:08 p.m.). http://serendipstudio.org/exchange/reflections-evas-man#comment-139494.

———. "Keepers of Silence." October 7, 2012 (5:20 p.m.) http://serendipstudio.org/exchange/keepers-silence.

Oxford English Dictionary, s.v., "be-*prefix*." http://www.oed.com.

———. "befriend." http://www.oed.com.

Painter, Nell Irvin. "What Is Whiteness?" *The New York Times.* June 20, 2015. http://www.nytimes.com/2015/06/21/opinion/sunday/what-is-whiteness.html.

Palmer, Daniel. "On the Organism-Environment Distinction in Psychology." *Behavior and Philosophy* 32, no. 2 (2004): 317–47. http://www.jstor.org/stable/27759490.

"Parade Night." February 1, 2015 (5:37 p.m.). https://serendipstudio.org/oneworld/multicultural-education-2015/parade-night.

pbernal. "Art Museums: Do they enlighten or isolate people?" December 10, 2013 (2:48 a.m.). http://serendipstudio.org/exchange/play-city-2013/jessica-bernal/art-museums-do-they-enlighten-or-isolate-individuals.

———. "Garden of Eden." November 25, 2013 (12:19 a.m.). http://serendipstudio.org/exchange/play-city-2013/jessica-bernal/garden-eden.

———. "Learning to Write Without Filters." December 18, 2013 (3:20p.m.). http://serendipstudio.org/exchange/eval/learning-write-without-filters-1.

Percy, Walker. "The Loss of the Creature." In *The Message in the Bottle: How Queer Man Is, How Queer Language Is, and What One Has to Do with the Other.* New York: Farrar, Straus and Giroux, 1975. 46–63.

Phillips, Thaddeus. *17 Border Crossings*. FringeArts. November 13–17, 2013.

Phoenix. "A Mosaic with Pomegranate." September 22, 2013 (10:47 p.m.). http://serendipstudio.org/exchange/play-city-2013/phoenix/mosaic-pomegranate-0.

"Planning to Play." Bryn Mawr College. May-August, 2013. http://serendipstudio.org/exchange/courses/esem/playcity/f13/planning.

"Play in the City." Emily Balch Seminar. Bryn Mawr College. Fall 2013. http://serendipstudio.org/exchange/courses/playcity/2013/homepage.

Plemons, Anna. "Tattooing Scar Tissue: Making Meaning in the Prison Classroom," Talk at Washington State University. March 27, 2015. http://annaplemons.com/?page_id=239.

Potter, Claire. "The Unfinished Agenda: Women's Education in the 21st Century." *Tenured Radical*. March 15, 2016. http://clairepotter.com/2016/03/15/the-unfinished-agenda-womens-education-in-the-21st-century/).

Pratt, Mary Louise. "Arts of the Contact Zone." *Profession* (1991): 33–40.

Price, Margaret. "Killer Dichotomies: Ir/rational, Crazy/Sane, Dangerous/Not." University of Michigan Press Blog. February 14, 2012. http://blog.press.umich.edu/2011/02/mad-at-school-author-responds-to-debate-over-mental-illness-on-campus/.

———. "Ways to Move: Mental Disability and the Kairotic Space of the Classroom." Lecture at Haverford College. February 9, 2012.

———. *Mad at School: Rhetorics of Mental Disability and Academic Life*. Ann Arbor: University of Michigan Press, 2011.

Prochnik, George. *In Pursuit of Silence: Listening for Meaning in a World of Noise*. New York: Doubleday, 2010.

Purple Finch. "Teach in Thoughts." April 17, 2015 (12:52 a.m.). https://serendipstudio.org/oneworld/ecological-imaginings-2015/teach-thoughts.

"Prison Reflection," December 17, 2015 (6:14 p.m.).

Pusey, Grace. "'Unghosting' African American Women's Labor History at Bryn Mawr College, 1880–1940." Unpublished manuscript. December 5, 2015.

———. "Response to 'Slippage' Essays from Grace Pusey." January 1, 2016 (4:42 p.m.). https://serendipstudio.org/oneworld/changing-our-story-2015/response-slippage-essays-grace-pusey.

"The Quiet Volume." FringeArts. August 2, 2013. http://fringearts.com/tag/the-quiet-volume/.

Rae Hamilton. "Hope for PHS students." November 27, 2011 (1:40 p.m.). http://serendipstudio.org/exchange/node/11327.

———. "The Workshop." November 15, 2011 (3:52 a.m.). http://serendipstudio.org/exchange/node/11318.

Raimy, Eric. "Meeting Notes." Language: A Conversation. February 4, 2002. http://serendipstudio.org/local/scisoc/language/mtgnotes2.html.

Rak, Julie. "Do Witness: *Don't: A Woman's Word* and Trauma as Pedagogy." *Topia* 10 (Fall 2003): 53–71. http://topia.journals.yorku.ca/index.php/topia/article/view/382. doi: 10.3138/topia.10.53

Raley, Rita. *Tactical Media*. Minneapolis: University of Minnesota Press, 2009.

Ralon, Laureano. *Figure/Ground: An Open-Source, Para-Academic, Inter-disciplinary Collaboration*. http://figureground.org/.

Rankine, Claudia. *Citizen: An American Lyric*. Minneapolis: Greywolf Press, 2014.

Ravitch, Diane. *The Death and Life of the Great American School System: How Testing and Choice are Undermining Education*. New York: Basic Books, 2010.

rebeccamec. "Fall Break Photos." December 2, 2014 (19:19 p.m.). https://serendipstudio.org/oneworld/identity-matters-being-belonging-becoming/fall-break-camphill-photos.

Rigoglioso, Marguerite. "Unconscious Racial Stereotypes Can Be Reversible." *Insights by Stanford Business* (January 1, 2008). https://www.gsb.stanford.edu/insights/unconscious-racial-stereotypes-can-be-reversible.

Roberts, Jennifer. "The Power of Patience." *Harvard Magazine* (November-December 2013). http://harvardmagazine.com/2013/11/the-power-of-patience.

Rodriguez, Richard. "The Achievement of Desire." In *Hunger of Memory: The Education of Richard Rodriguez*. New York: Bantam, 1982. 43–73.

Romaine, Claire. "Stubborn Writer." December 19, 2013 (9:24p.m.). http://serendipstudio.org/exchange/eval/stubborn-writer.

Rönnbäck, Fredrik. "The Sacred Word of Blanchot and Leiris." Paper presented at the annual conference of the French Italian Graduate Society, University of Pennsylvania, Philadelphia, PA, March 2013.

Rose, Deborah Bird, Stuart Cooke and Thom Van Dooren. "Ravens at Play." *Cultural Studies Review* 17, no. 2 (September 2011): 326–43. http://epress.lib.uts.edu.au/journals/index.php/csrj/article/view/2224.

Roughgarden, Joan. *Evolution's Rainbow: Diversity, Gender, and Sexuality in Nature and People*. Berkeley: University of California Press, 2004.

S. Yaeger. "Some Thoughts on Our Workshop." November 13, 2011 (3:55 p.m.). http://serendipstudio.org/exchange/node/11299.

Saenz, Arlette. "Confederate Flag Wavers Greeted President Obama in Oklahoma." *Good Morning America*. July 16, 2015. https://gma.yahoo.com/confederate-flag-wavers-greet-president-obama-oklahoma-114509650--abc-news-topstories.html.

Samudzi, Zoé. "We Need A Decolonized, Not A 'Diverse', Education," March 11, 2016. http://harlot.media/articles/1058/we-need-a-decolonized-not-a-diverse-education.

samuel.terry. "Matter." May 11, 2014 (3:08 a.m.). https://serendipstudio.org/oneworld/content/matter.

Samuels, Ellen. "Cripping Anti-Futurity, or, If You Love Queer Theory So Much, Why Don't You Marry It?" Paper presented at the Society for Disability Studies Conference, San Jose, CA, 2011.

Sandoval, Chela. *Methodology of the Oppressed*. Minneapolis: University of Minnesota Press, 2000.

Sapphire. *Push: A Novel*. New York; Vintage, 1997.

sara. gladwin. "Colonizing the Museum Exhibit." Paper written for 360° cluster. Bryn Mawr College. February 17, 2014.

——. "Divergent Thinking," December 2, 2012 (5:24 p.m.). http://serendipstudio.org/exchange/divergent-thinking.

—— "more on the subject of the barometer." February 25, 2014 (6:11 p.m.). http://serendipstudio.org/exchange/book/standing-wall/classroom-ideas-riverside#comment-145161.

——. "What's at the top of a Magic Ladder?" Paper written for the 360° cluster. Bryn Mawr College. March 17, 2014.

Sarah Goode. "I noticed that most Bryn Mawr." October 20,

2011 (12:08 p.m.). http://serendipstudio.org/exchange/DiaBlog1#comment-131429.

Sarah. "AGREE AGREE AGREE!" October 23, 2012 (4:23pm.). http://serendipstudio.org/exchange/frustrated#comment-138627.

Sasha De La Cruz. "Paper 2." September 23, 2012 (2:29 p.m.). http://serendipstudio.org/exchange/paper-2.

Schlosser, Joel. "A Poetics of American Citizenship: Race, Injury, and Claudia Rankine's *Citizen*." Paper presented at the Western Political Science Association Annual Meeting. San Diego, CA. March 2016.

———. E-mail message to authors. March 2, 2016.

———. E-mail message to authors. June 6, 2016.

Scott, Rob. "Distinguishing Radical Teaching from Merely Having Intense Experiences While Teaching in Prison." *Radical Teacher* 95 (Spring 2013): 22–32. doi: 10.5406/radicalteacher.95.0022

sdane. "I really liked that quote." December 10, 2012 (12:55 a.m.). http://serendipstudio.org/exchange/linda-susan-beards-visit-0#comment-139808.

Sedgwick, Eve. "Pedagogy of Buddhism." In *Touching Feeling: Affect, Pedagogy, Performativity*. Durham: Duke University Press, 2003. 153–82. doi: 10.1215/9780822384786-006

Serendip Studio. 1994–2016. https://serendipstudio.org/oneworld/.

Sharaai. "Linda-Susan Beard's Visit." December 9, 2012 (8:59 p.m.). http://serendipstudio.org/exchange/linda-susan-beards-visit-0.

"Sharon Zukin, The Cultures of Cities (1995)." urbanculturalstudies. May 21, 2012. https://urbanculturalstudies.wordpress.com/2012/05/21/sharon-zukin-the-cultures-of-cities-1995/.

Siebers, Tobin. "Disability and the Theory of Complex Embodiment." In *Disability Theory*, 272–91. Ann Arbor: University of Michigan Press, 2008. doi: 10.3998/mpub.309723

———. "Returning the Social to the Social Model." Paper presented at the annual conference of the Society of Disability Studies, Minneapolis, MN, June 2014.

Simmel, George. "The Metropolis and Mental Life." 1950. http://www.

blackwellpublishing.com/content/BPL_Images/Content_store/Sample_chapter/0631225137/Bridge.pdf.

Simon, Roger I., and Claudia Eppert. "Remembering Obligation: Pedagogy and the Witnessing of Testimony of Historical Trauma." *Canadian Journal of Education / Revue canadienne de l'éducation* 22, no. 2 (Spring 1997): 175–91. doi: 10.2307/1585906

Slobada, Agatha. "Julia of Eyes." https://soundcloud.com/fenceless/julia-of-eyes.

Smith, Anna Deavere. *Fires in the Mirror.* New York: Anchor, 1993.

———. *The Pipeline Project, a Work-In-Progress.* Directed by Anna Deveare Smith. Penn Museum, University of Pennsylvania, Philadelphia, PA, May 5, 2015.

snatarajan. "This is the thing I really want to learn." November 19, 2011 (2:38 p.m.). http://serendipstudio.org/exchange/node/11327.

Snyder, Sharon, and David Mitchell. *Cultural Locations of Disability.* Chicago: The University of Chicago Press, 2005.

Snyder, Susan. "Confederate Flag in Dorm Roils Bryn Mawr Campus." *Philadelphia Inquirer.* October 6, 2014. http://articles.philly.com/2014-10-06/news/54657530_1_confederate-flag-dorm-two-students.

Sommer, Doris. "Advertencia/Warning." In *Proceed with Caution, When Engaged by Minority Writing in the Americas.* Cambridge: Harvard University Press, 1999. ix-xv.

Sontag, Susan. "Against Interpretation." In *Against Interpretation and Other Essays.* New York: Farrar, Strauss & Giroux, 1966. 4–14.

Spade, Dean. Talk at Barnard College. April 2014. http://bcrw.barnard.edu/blog/dean-spade-on-trans-women-at-womens-colleges/.

Spear, Rachel. "'Let Me Tell You a Story': On Teaching Trauma Narratives, Writing, and Healing." *Pedagogy* 14, no. 1 (Winter 2014): 53–79. doi: 10.1215/15314200-2348911

Spivak, Gayatri. *Outside in the Teaching Machine.* New York: Routledge, 2008.

Stella, Christina. "the mawr you know: alice lesnick!" February 4, 2016. https://vimeo.com/153654955.

Stephen, Caroline. "Selections from *Quaker Strongholds* (1890)." In *Quaker Spirituality: Selected Writings*. Edited by Douglas Steere. New York: Paulist Press, 1984. 239–58.

Sterling, Stephen. "An Analysis of Sustainability Education Internationally: Evolution, Interpretation, and Transformative Potential." In *The Sustainability Curriculum: The Challenge for Higher Education*. Edited by John Blewitt and Cedric Cullingford. London: Earthscan, 2004. 43–62.

Stevens, Bethany. "Interrogating Transability: A Catalyst to View Disability as Body Art." *Disability Studies Quarterly* 31, no. 4 (2011). doi: 10.18061/dsq.v31i4.1705

Stewart, Kathleen. *Ordinary Affects*. Durham: Duke University Press, 2007. doi: 10.1215/9780822390404

Stickley, Keith. "Confederate Flag: Heritage or Hate? Old South Symbol Gains Popularity Here." *The Free Press*. July 30, 2015. http://shenandoahfreepress.com/article.php?ID=7045.

"Students Rally After Confederate Flag Display." NBC 10. Philadelphia, PA. September 19, 2014. http://www.nbcphiladelphia.com/news/local/Students-Rally-After-Confederate-Flag-Display_Philadelphia-275858081.html.

Sullivan, Patricia A. "Composing Culture: A Place for the Personal." *College English* 66 (2003): 41–55. doi: 10.2307/3594233

"Sunday Post." November 15, 2015 (11:58 a.m.). https://serendipstudio.org/oneworld/arts-resistance/sunday-post-16.

"Sunday Post." November 15, 2015 (5:14 p.m.). https://serendipstudio.org/oneworld/arts-resistance/sunday-post-17.

"Sunday Post, 11/5 (A little early)." November 14, 2015 (1:49 p.m.). https://serendipstudio.org/oneworld/arts-resistance/sunday-post-1115-little-early.

Suzuki, Shunryu. *Zen Mind, Beginner's Mind*. Boulder, CO: Shambhala, 2011.

Sweeney, Megan. *Reading Is My Window: Books and The Art of Reading in Women's Prisons*. Durham: University of North Carolina Press, 2010. doi: 10.5149/9780807898352_sweeney

"Tarots Marseille de Jean Noblet." 1650. Refreshed by Jean-Claude Flornoy, 2001. http://www.aeclectic.net/tarot/cards/noblet-marseilles/.

Taibbi, Matt. "Apocalyse, New Jersey: A Dispatch from America's Most Desperate Town." *Rolling Stone*. December 22, 2013.

"Teaching and Learning Institute at Bryn Mawr and Haverford Colleges." 2017. http://www.brynmawr.edu/tli/.

"This Is a Palimpsest (calicult)." *analepsis*. http://analepsis.org/2008/04/24/this-is-a-palimpsest/.

Thomas, M. Carey. "Present Tendencies in Women's College and University Education." *Educational Review* 35 (January 1908): 64–85.

Thomason, Andy. "Confederate Flag Raises Controversy at Bryn Mawr College." *The Chronicle of Higher Education*. October 6, 2014. http://chronicle.com/blogs/ticker/confederate-flag-raises-controversy-at-bryn-mawr/87491.

Thompson, Matt. "Five Reasons People Code Switch." *Code Switch*. National Public Radio. April 13, 2013 (12:26 p.m.). http://www.npr.org/sections/codeswitch/2013/04/13/177126294/five-reasons-why-people-code-switch.

"Thoughts about our talk and invisible diablities." October 8, 2014 (1:35 a.m.). https://serendipstudio.org/oneworld/identity-matters-being-belonging-becoming/thoughts-about-our-talk-and-invisible-diablities.

Tidmarsh, Karen. "The Highly Practical Liberal Arts." *Bryn Mawr Now* XXVI (Spring/Summer 1997): 1–7.

Tocqueville, Alexis de. *Democracy in America*. Translated by Henry Reeve. 1831. Reprint, Gutenburg EBook, 2013. https://www.gutenberg.org/files/815/815-h/815-h.htm.

Toews, Barb. "Toward a Restorative Justice Pedagogy: Reflections on Teaching Restorative Justice in Correctional Facilities." *Contemporary Justice Review: Issues in Criminal, Social, and Restorative Justice* 16, no. 2 (2013): 6–27. doi: 10.1080/10282580.2013.769308.

tomahawk. "The Barnes Foundation and Intellectual Property."

December 1, 2013 (10:33 p.m). http://serendipstudio.org/exchange/play-city-2013/tomahawk/barnes-foundation-and-intellectual-property.

———. "Ruminations on the Class." December 20, 2013 (2:38 a.m.). http://serendipstudio.org/exchange/play-city-2013/tomahawk/ruminations-class.

Tompkins, Jane. *A Life in School: What the Teacher Learned.* New York: Perseus Books, 1996.

Toshalis, Eric. "The Identity-Perception Gap: Teachers Confronting the Difference Between Who They (Think They) Are and How They Are Perceived by Students." In *Culture, Curriculum, and Identity in Education.* Edited by H. Richard Milner. New York: Macmillan, 2010. 15–36. doi: 10.1057/9780230105669_2

Tough, Paul. "The Poverty Clinic: Can a Stressful Childhood Make You a Sick Adult?" *The New Yorker.* March 21, 2011. http://www.newyorker.com/magazine/2011/03/21/the-poverty-clinic.

Tratner, Michael. E-mail message to authors. June 4, 2010.

"Trust Me, I Can Tell." February 1, 2015 (3:16 p.m.). https://serendipstudio.org/oneworld/multicultural-education-2015/trust-me-i-can-tell.

Tuck, Eve. "Suspending Damage: A Letter to Communities." *Harvard Educational Review* 79, no. 3 (Fall 2009): 409–27. http://jakeyspdfs.pbworks.com/f/Eve+Tuck_HEdPress.pdf. doi: 10.17763/haer.79.3.n0016675661t3n15

——— and C. Rhee. "Exemplar Chapter 33: A Glossary of Haunting." In *Handbook of Autoethnography*, edited by Stacey Holman Jones, Tony E. Adams, and Carolyn Ellis. Walnut Creek, CA: Left Coast Press, 2013. 639–58. http://static1.squarespace.com/static/557744ffe4b013bae3b7af63/t/557f2d6ce4b029eb4288a2f8/1434398060958/Tuck+%26+Ree%2C+A+Glossary+of+Haunting.pdf.

Utitofon. "Polarized Access to Education." September 13, 2011 (2:32 p.m.). http://serendipstudio.org/exchange/node/10797#comment-130778.

Verhey, Melissa. "Noisy Silence: Wordlessly Reclaiming Voice in Victor Hugo's *The Last Day of a Condemned Man.*" Paper presented at the annual conference of the French Italian Graduate Society, University of Pennsylvania, Philadelphia, PA, March 2013.

Villegas, Isaac, and Jason Rust. "Fugitive Democracy: Sheldon Wolin and Contemplating the Local." April 25, 2006. http://www.rustyparts.com/wp/2006/04/25/fugitive-democracy-sheldon-wolin-and-contemplating-the-local/.

Vocabulary.com, s.v. "befriend." https://www.vocabulary.com/dictionary/befriend.

Walker, Brian, David Salt, and Walter Reid. *Resilience Thinking*: *Sustaining People and Ecosystems in a Changing World.* Washington, DC: Island Press, 2006.

Walkerdine, Valerie. "Using the Work of Felix Guattari to Understand Space, Place, Social Justice, and Education." *Qualitative Inquiry* 19, no. 10 (2013): 756–64. doi: 10.1177/1077800413502934

Wallace-Wells, Benjamin, "The Hard Truths of Ta-Nehisi Coates." *New York Magazine.* July 12, 2015 (9:00 p.m.). http://nymag.com/daily/intelligencer/2015/07/ta-nehisi-coates-between-the-world-and-me.html.

Wallace, Mark. "The Introductory Environmental Studies Course." Panel discussion at the Tri-College Environmental Studies Workshop. Swarthmore College. May 16, 2012.

Wampole, Christy. "Quiet Impositions: On Involuntary Silence." Keynote Address at the annual conference of the French Italian Graduate Society, University of Pennsylvania, Philadelphia, PA, March 2013.

Waxler, Joie. Email message to author. April 16, 2016.

Weis, Lois. *Class Warfare: Class, Race, and College Admissions in Top-Tier Secondary Schools.* Chicago: The University of Chicago Press, 2014. doi: 10.7208/chicago/9780226135083.001.0001

——— and Michelle Fine. "Critical Bifocality and Circuits of Privilege: Expanding Critical Ethnographic Theory and Design." *Harvard Educational Review* 82, no. 2 (June 2012): 173–201. doi: 10.17763/haer.82.2.v1jx34n441532242.

Welch, Sharon. *A Feminist Ethic of Risk.* 1990. Revised Edition, Minneapolis: Fortress Press, 2000.

"Welcome to Crip Ecologies!" Composing Disability Conference. March 2016. http://www.composingdisability.blogspot.com/.

Wells, Emily and Emily Schalk. "2016 Community Day of Learning Examines Issues of Class." February 25, 2016 (2:38 p.m.). https://www.brynmawr.edu/news/2016-communty-day-learning-examines-issues-class.

Wendell, Susan. "Toward a Feminist Ethics of Disability." 1989. Reprinted in *The Disability Studies Reader*. Edited by Lennard J. Davis. Second Edition. New York: Routledge, 2006. 243–56.

"What Can a Body Do?" Exhibit curated by Amanda Cachia. Cantor Fitzgerald Gallery. Haverford College. October 26-December 16, 2012. http://exhibits.haverford.edu/whatcanabodydo/.

Wideman, John Edgar. *Brothers and Keepers*. New York: Vintage, 1995.

———. "In Praise of Silence." *Callaloo* 22, no. 3 (Summer 1999): 547–49. http://www.jstor.org/stable/3300543. doi: 10.1353/cal.1999.0131

Wilks, Jennifer. "Lessons of a Flag Flap." *Philadelphia Inquirer*. October 12, 2014. http://www.utexas.edu/cola/centers/caaas/news/8486.

Williams, Terry Tempest. *Refuge: An Unnatural History of Family and Place*. New York: Vintage, 1992.

———. *Finding Beauty in a Broken World*. New York: Vintage, 2009.

———. *An Unspoken Hunger: Stories from the Field*. New York: Vintage, 1994.

Wills, David. "Full Dorsal: Derrida's Politics of Friendship." 2005. http://pmc.iath.virginia.edu/text-only/issue.505/15.3wills.tx. doi: 10.1353/PMC.2005.0032

Winnicott, D.W. *The Family and Individual Development*. London: Tavistock, 1965.

———. *Maturational Processes and the Facilitating Environment: Studies in the Theory of Emotional Development*. *1957–1963*. Reprint, London: Karnac Books, 1996. http://gestaltnyc.org/uploads/WINNICOTT_-_Reading_Development-Studies-in-the-Theory-of-Emotional-Development-1965.pdf.

Winterson, Jeanette. *Why Be Happy When You Can Be Normal?* New York: Grove Press, 2012.

Wolin, Sheldon S. "Norm and Form: The Constitutionalizing of Democracy." *Athenian Political Thought and the Reconstruction of American Democracy.* Edited by Peter Euben, John R. Wallach and Josiah Ober. Ithaca, NY: Cornell University Press, 1994. 29–58. doi: 10.7591/9781501723995-002

Woolf, Virginia. *On Being Ill.* 1926. Reprint, Ashfield: Paris, 2002.

Yancy. "Deep Play." November 18, 2013 (12:04 a.m.). http://serendipstudio.org/exchange/play-city-2013/yancy/deep-play.

Zhou, Cathy. "Personal Reflections." September 11, 2013 (1:20 p.m.). http://serendipstudio.org/exchange/play-city-2013/cathy-zhou/personal-reflections.

Zora Neale Hurston. "Something I learned is that." November 19, 2011 (12:34 p.m.). http://serendipstudio.org/exchange/node/11327#comment-1322

www.ingramcontent.com/pod-product-compliance
Lightning Source LLC
Chambersburg PA
CBHW080405230426
43662CB00016B/2325